Well-Being and the Quality of Working Lives

Well-Being and the Quality of Working Lives

Daniel Wheatley

Reader in Business and Labour Economics, Birmingham Business School, University of Birmingham, UK

Cheltenham, UK • Northampton, MA, USA

© Daniel Wheatley 2022

Cover Image: Charlie Egan on Unsplash.

All rights reserved. No part of this publication may be reproduced, stored in a retrieval system or transmitted in any form or by any means, electronic, mechanical or photocopying, recording, or otherwise without the prior permission of the publisher.

Published by
Edward Elgar Publishing Limited
The Lypiatts
15 Lansdown Road
Cheltenham
Glos GL50 2JA
UK

Edward Elgar Publishing, Inc.
William Pratt House
9 Dewey Court
Northampton
Massachusetts 01060
USA

A catalogue record for this book
is available from the British Library

Library of Congress Control Number: 2022931126

This book is available electronically in the **Elgar**online
Business subject collection
http://dx.doi.org/10.4337/9781839108785

Printed on elemental chlorine free (ECF)
recycled paper containing 30% Post-Consumer Waste

ISBN 978 1 83910 877 8 (cased)
ISBN 978 1 83910 878 5 (eBook)

Printed and bound in the USA

Contents

List of figures	ix
List of tables	xi
List of boxes	xii

1	***Well-Being and the Quality of Working Lives*: an introduction**	1
	Introduction	1
	Well-being and work	3
	Work in context: flexibility and uncertainty in the labour market	5
	The dimensions of well-being at work	7
	A note on the measurement of well-being at work	13
	Contribution of the book	14
	Outline of the book	15

PART I DEVELOPING A FRAMEWORK FOR
WORKPLACE WELL-BEING

2	**Understanding well-being**	20
	Introduction	20
	What is well-being?	20
	Approaches to understanding well-being	22
	Measurement of well-being	34
	Chapter summary	40
3	**Well-being and work**	42
	Introduction	42
	Well-being at work	42
	Models of well-being at work	44
	Job quality and the quality of working lives	56
	A framework for workplace well-being	63
	Chapter summary	69

Well-being and the quality of working lives

PART II   THE DIMENSIONS OF WORKPLACE WELL-BEING

4   Job properties — 71

Introduction — 71
Intrinsic versus extrinsic characteristics of work — 71
Autonomy and control — 73
Workload, intensity and role overload — 82
Job resources — 87
Variety and complexity — 91
Meaning, purpose and environmental clarity — 94
Chapter summary: job properties and worker well-being — 97

5   Flexibility — 100

Introduction — 100
Balancing work and life — 100
Achieving balance — 103
Flexibilization of work — 107
Work-time and overwork — 108
Work recovery and breaks — 110
Flexible working arrangements — 111
Flexibility around the arrangement of time — 114
Reduced hours arrangements — 115
Remote working — 116
Agile working — 120
Working flexibly in other locations — 122
Case study: flexibility and work in the gig economy — 124
Chapter summary: the role of flexibility in workplace well-being — 128

6   Rewarding careers — 130

Introduction — 130
Intrinsic and extrinsic work motivation — 131
Pay and benefits — 134
Job security and contracts — 139
Training, skills and education match — 142
Career development and progression — 145
Achieving success in a career — 149
Case study: the changing role of travel in career success — 150

Contents vii

Effort–reward (im)balance 153
Chapter summary: towards a rewarding career 157

7 **Relationships** 159
Introduction 159
Social capital, social connectedness and social exchange theory 160
Relationships at work 168
Conflict at work 170
Conflict and diverse and inclusive workplaces 174
Leadership and trust within organizations 175
Worker relations and employee voice 181
Fun and playfulness in the workplace 183
Chapter summary: building and maintaining high-quality
relationships at work 184

8 **Giving** 187
Introduction 187
Motivations to give: self-interest, altruism and reciprocity 188
Giving in the workplace 191
Volunteering 192
Charitable giving 198
Social support at work 200
Workplace helping 203
Mentoring 205
Case study: experiences of balancing social enterprise with
work in academia 211
Chapter summary: giving well at work 215

9 **Physical space and activity** 217
Introduction 217
Workplace in context 218
Meaning and identity in workplace 220
Workspace territoriality 222
Workplace layout and design 223
Physical characteristics of the workplace 226
The homeworking environment 232
The office concepts framework 233

Physical wellness and work	235
Increasing physical activity at work	237
Active commuting	241
Case study: the Cardiff University Lifestyle Leadership approach	242
Chapter summary: a healthy and active work environment	246

PART III   ENHANCING THE QUALITY OF WORKING LIVES

10	**Conclusions: ways to working well**	249
	Introduction	249
	Linking the dimensions of workplace well-being	250
	Understanding the outcomes of workplace well-being	257
	Linking the dimensions and outcomes of workplace well-being	272
	Building and maintaining a thriving workplace	273
	Additional mechanisms for managing and supporting worker well-being	275
	The future of well-being at work	278

References	280
Index	328

Figures

2.1	The capabilities approach	23
2.2	The dimensions of psychological well-being	29
2.3	The Dynamic Model of Well-being	32
2.4	Five Ways to Well-being	33
3.1	The ASSET Model of Workplace Well-being	47
3.2	Factors influencing SWB at work	49
3.3	CIPD Five Domains of Well-being	51
3.4	Three Aspects of Wellness at Work	52
3.5	NHS Workforce Health and Wellbeing Framework	54
3.6	Workplace well-being themes and constituent concepts	55
3.7	CIPD Model of Job Quality	61
3.8	Strategic elements of the workplace well-being framework	64
3.9	The framework for workplace well-being	65
3.10	Mapping well-being models to the dimensions of the framework for workplace well-being	67
3.11	Sub-dimensions of the workplace well-being framework	68
4.1	Allowed to decide how daily work is organized	80
4.2	Allowed to choose/change pace of work	81
4.3	My job requires that I work very hard	86
4.4	Adequacy of job resources (%)	90
4.5	There is a lot of variety in my work	93
4.6	My job requires that I keep learning new things	94

4.7	Meaning and worthwhileness of work (%)	96
4.8	Designing jobs for workplace well-being	98
5.1	Availability and use of flexible working arrangements	114
5.2	Home-based work potential	118
5.3	Employing an agile working approach for workplace well-being	122
6.1	Employee non-pension benefits (%)	135
6.2	Subjective measures of pay	139
6.3	Effort–reward imbalance (ERI) model	153
6.4	Methods for addressing ERI using the framework for workplace well-being	157
7.1	Main causes of stress at work	173
7.2	Relationship quality at work (%)	179
7.3	Senior leadership relationships at work (%)	180
7.4	Realizing positive relationships at work for workplace well-being	185
8.1	Barriers to volunteering	197
8.2	Giving well at work using the framework for workplace well-being	215
9.1	DARE noise distraction guidance	230
9.2	Conceptual model linking office concepts via demands and resources to short- and long-term reactions	234
9.3	Workspace layouts before and after the Lifestyle Leadership Approach	245
9.4	Power posing on a lunchtime Lifestyle Leadership session	245
9.5	Creating a healthy and active work environment for workplace well-being	247
10.1	The framework for workplace well-being	251
10.2	Dimensions and outcomes of workplace well-being	272

Tables

2.1	Personal well-being measures	38
2.2	Personal and social well-being measures in the European Social Survey	39
3.1	Selected job quality models	59
5.1	Work–life balance options	112
6.1	Predicted outcomes of the ERI model	154
6.2	Effort–reward imbalance questionnaire	156
7.1	Employee voice mechanisms	183
8.1	A typology of mentoring forms	210
10.1	Shortened version of the General Health Questionnaire (GHQ-12)	271

Boxes

2.1	Positive illusions and unrealistic self-assessment of well-being	27
4.1	Measurement of autonomy and control	74
4.2	Organizational commitment	76
4.3	Patterns of autonomy and control	79
4.4	Empirical measurement of the intensity of work	85
4.5	Measurement of job resources	88
4.6	Empirical patterns of variety and complexity	92
4.7	Measurement of meaningful work	95
5.1	Empirical measurement of balance	102
5.2	Selected work–life balance policies	104
5.3	Measurement of working hours and overwork	109
5.4	Measurement of flexibility in work	113
5.5	Rapid expansion of remote working in the Covid-19 pandemic	117
6.1	Employee non-pay benefits	134
6.2	Objective and subjective measures of pay	138
6.3	Measurement of job security	141
6.4	Gender, careers and reward	147
7.1	Measurement of social connectedness	165
7.2	Evidence on conflict at work	172
7.3	Measurement of leadership	178

8.1	Patterns of volunteering: evidence from the community life survey	196
8.2	Measuring social support at work	201
8.3	Measurement of mentoring using the mentor role instrument	206
9.1	Measuring the impact of the physical characteristics of the workplace	229
9.2	Methods for capturing physical activity levels at work	236

1. *Well-Being and the Quality of Working Lives*: an introduction

INTRODUCTION

Work is central to the health of individuals, organizations and society (Kalleberg, 2011; Knox et al., 2011). It forms an integral part of most of our lives that accounts for substantial direct (i.e. working hours) and indirect (e.g. the commute) time-use, acts as a source of income that influences our standards of living, can provide us with a sense of identity, meaning and fulfilment, and helps us to build and maintain relationships with others. As such, work has an important, and interdependent, relationship with our physical and mental well-being. It should be acknowledged at the outset of this book that not all work is paid; indeed housework, the provision of care and volunteering are important forms of work that are unpaid (Drinkwater, 2015; Hardill, 2012). The focus of this book is on expanding our understanding of how paid work influences the well-being of workers, the organizations for which they complete tasks of employment, and the societies in which we live.

While well-being is a frequently used term and one that most of us are comfortable with in its common meaning, it is a multifaceted concept which has no single agreed definition (Dodge et al., 2012). As a concept, well-being is closely linked with definitions of 'happiness' and 'quality of life', and incorporates both physical well-being associated with the condition of our body and factors that influence it, and psychological well-being which is concerned with our mental health and happiness. It is linked to the ability of an individual to manage their life in a productive and meaningful manner (Tennant et al., 2007). It is a concept that is multi-disciplinary and global in its literature base. Origins of understanding around this concept can be traced back to Ancient Greece and the development of two distinct schools of thought, hedonism and eudaimonia. Hedonism views happiness as derived from the pursuit of pleasure reflected in the presence of positive and/or absence of negative 'affects', where 'affects' are a pleasure–pain component of well-being (Bradburn, 1969, 9; Stutzer and Frey, 2010, 683). Eudaimonia, meanwhile, views true happiness as achieved through leading a virtuous life with well-being derived from fulfilment through accomplishing meaningful and worthwhile goals, and positive psychological functioning, that is, acceptance of our true selves and personal growth (Dodge et al., 2012).

A number of approaches to well-being have been developed, some of which focus on hedonic and others on eudaimonic traditions, and indeed many that incorporate elements of both. While well-being remains a much-debated concept, it is becoming more generally accepted that it is a multi-dimensional construct. As not only the elements of, but also how we measure, well-being are central in developing our understanding, well-being can also usefully be understood in terms of objective and subjective approaches (Galloway et al., 2006, 19–22). Objective understanding of well-being centres on the idea that well-being is influenced by the achievement, or otherwise, of certain worthwhile pursuits, which can be measured objectively, including, for example, levels of achieved education; relationships, including getting married or having children; and career success (Parfit, 1984; Schueller and Seligman, 2010). Subjective well-being, in contrast, is a self-reported well-being indicator which consists of emotional responses and experienced feelings that can be positive and negative. It can act as an overall assessment of well-being reflected in measures of satisfaction with life and can also offer insight into well-being in specific domains or areas of life, for example satisfaction with leisure, health or income (Pavot and Diener, 2013).

Measuring quality of life and well-being have long been acknowledged as central to societal progress. Academics, governments and international bodies have highlighted the importance to the economy and society of well-being (Diener and Tay, 2015; Eurofound, 2012, 2013a, 2013b; Stevenson and Farmer, 2017; Taylor et al., 2017). Public debates regarding the role of gross domestic product (GDP), and its profile in policymaking, have prompted governments and international organizations including the EU and OECD to explore alternative and complementary measures of well-being (see Stiglitz et al., 2009) including the OECD's (2013) Better Life Index. Measuring quality of life has been identified as fundamental in assessing the relative progress of societies and as having relevance for monitoring and policymaking purposes (OECD, 2013). In the UK context, the Office for National Statistics (ONS, 2014) developed a Happiness Index to complement standard measures of societal improvement such as GDP, and in 2011 introduced well-being indicators in a range of social surveys (ONS, 2014). Questions attempting to capture well-being have been added to a range of social surveys such as the European Social Survey (ESS), European Working Conditions Survey (EWCS) and European Quality of Life Survey (EQLS), in the UK context the Integrated Household Survey and Understanding Society, and in surveys developed by independent organizations such as the Chartered Institute of Personnel and Development's (CIPD) UK Working Lives Survey. In these surveys as well as various questions which explore aspects of an individual's life and job, respondents are asked questions of the following type: how satisfied are you with your life nowadays? How happy did you feel yesterday? How anxious did you feel yesterday? To what extent do you feel the things you do in your life are worthwhile?

WELL-BEING AND WORK

The relationship between well-being and work has long been recognized, including, for example, in the work of Karasek and Theorell (1990). They argued that work could be designed and organized in a way that would allow it to be undertaken without having a negative impact on employee well-being and potentially could promote or enhance employee well-being. Recognition of the importance of the relationship between well-being and work has prompted the development of a multitude of models attempting to capture it under different monikers such as 'employee well-being', 'worker well-being', 'well-being at work', 'workplace well-being' and 'wellness at work', including those developed by Hackman and Oldham (1976), Karasek (1979), Bakker and Demerouti (2007), Robertson and Cooper (2011), the CIPD (Suff and Miller, 2016), and the Global Wellness Institute (Yeung and Johnston, 2016). Within this book both workplace well-being and well-being at work are used relatively interchangeably to refer to the relationship between work and well-being. In both cases the focus is expansive with the terms used in a broad sense, encapsulating the relationship at multiple levels from the individual through to the organization and beyond, and without reflecting any specific definitional differences that may be present in other existing contributions to the field.

Well-being at work has risen significantly in profile, being explored in reference to ideas of 'decent' (ILO, 2013; United Nations, 2015), 'meaningful' (de Bustillo et al., 2011) and 'good' work (Taylor et al., 2017), which are increasingly acknowledged in both policy and organizational spheres as being centrally important to our understanding of paid work and its impacts on our lives (Findlay et al., 2017, 4–5). A range of high-profile reports have been commissioned by governments, for example in the UK the *Thriving at Work: The Stevenson/Farmer Review of Mental Health and Employers* (Stevenson and Farmer, 2017), and published by independent bodies such as the Global Wellness Institute and the CIPD, with the former producing a raft of reports on a frequent basis and the latter similarly considering aspects of well-being at work in a number of projects and publications including annually since 2018 in the *UK Working Lives Survey Report* (see Gifford, 2018; Wheatley and Gifford, 2019).

At the organizational level, themes of 'good' and 'decent' work, and indicators of job quality and well-being, have similarly captured increased standing. Job search websites and top employer lists give growing significance to factors such as work–life balance (e.g. Glassdoor; see *HR Magazine*, 2017) and a work environment that promotes well-being (e.g. *Fortune*'s 'Best Companies to Work For') (Combs and Milosevic, 2016), in addition to more traditional measures of the quality of jobs including pay and other benefits. Where well-being has not been given adequate consideration by employers this has been linked to negative outcomes for organizations, including damage to reputation. High-profile examples include treatment of employees at Amazon (*Guardian*, 2019), Foxconn (Morrison, 2011; *The Economist*, 2010), Sports Direct (Unite Union, 2015; Wallop, 2015) and Walmart (*Financial Times*, 2011). Meanwhile, examples of good practice can act as a significant benefit to organizations through enhancing recruitment and retention of high-quality workers. In response to these trends, employers are taking greater notice of the importance of well-being at work and recognizing the potential benefits to reputation and the health of the organization from investment in well-being strategies and initiatives and improvements in job quality.

Our well-being at work is closely linked to the quality of work that we encounter. Job quality is, as such, a useful lens through which to consider the constituents of well-being at work. It can be defined as the extent to which a job exhibits characteristics which generate benefits for the employee, including to both physical and psychological well-being (Green, 2006). However, within the existing literature base we find that across disciplines a range of definitions and terms are applied including the quality of work(ing) lives, quality of work, quality of employment, and extending to the aforementioned concepts of 'meaningful', 'decent' and 'good' work (Coats and Lekhi, 2008; Eurofound, 2012, 2013a, 2013b; Green, 2006; ILO, 2013; Kalleberg, 2012; Martel and Dupuis, 2006). These themes have received increased attention in the policy sphere in recent years, including, for example, in the UK in *Good Work: The Taylor Review of Modern Working Practices* (Taylor et al., 2017), which identified a number of key concerns relating to experienced job quality. Although existing definitions and contributions to our understanding of job quality differ, consistent among them is the importance of the conditions of work that we encounter and their influence, and impact, on our well-being (Felstead et al., 2019; Green, 2009).

The factors influencing relative job quality have been much debated. Job quality has been categorized and structured in many different forms in existing contributions including consideration of types of jobs and their characteristics along with identifying differences between good and bad jobs or those that involve high or low demand or commitment, with contributions from Karasek and Theorell (1990), Holman (2013) and Vidal (2013), among others. Meanwhile, a significant amount of research has been conducted into the individual dimensions that influence job quality. The existing literature base offers us a range of different categorizations of the dimensions of job quality, although most include a common distinction between extrinsic dimensions such as pay and other benefits, which are also sometimes referred to as hygiene factors (Herzberg et al., 1959), and intrinsic dimensions which refer to characteristics of the job itself such as skill/complexity, variety and levels of control and autonomy. A number of contributions have extended this basic distinction, including those offered by Connell and Burgess (2016) and the CIPD (see Warhurst et al., 2017), as well as in the ILO indicators of 'decent' work (ILO, 2013) and the Work Foundation's conceptualization of 'good' work (Coats and Lekhi, 2008). While there is no clear consensus on the exact structure of job quality, and its dimensions, there is increasing agreement over the majority of the components of work that influence the quality of our working lives.

The impact of job quality on our working lives has been highlighted in existing research which has shown that good jobs generate a number of benefits (Hoque et al., 2017), including, importantly, job satisfaction and broader well-being (Green, 2008, 2009; Wheatley, 2017a, 2017b). Work in good jobs has been shown in research to be associated with better mental health among workers and lower levels of stress (Wood, 2008). Meanwhile, as well as acting as a constituent of job quality, improvements in the balance between work and life have also been shown to be an outcome of better job quality. Low job quality, in contrast, can have considerable detrimental effects. Some evidence has even suggested that low-quality work could actually be worse for our well-being than unemployment (Chandola and Zhang, 2018). Many of the existing definitions of job quality also recognize the benefits that can be realized by employers from the provision of good work, including more productive employees, increased work effort, reduced levels of absenteeism, reductions in workplace conflicts and enhanced retention of their existing workforce (Green, 2009; Hoque et al., 2017; Preenen et al., 2017). At an aggregate level, higher job quality can also potentially act to facilitate transitions between employment, unemployment and labour market inactivity through promoting increased levels of labour market participation (Smith et al., 2008, 588), and reducing rates of exit from the labour market (Siegrist et al., 2006, 64).

WORK IN CONTEXT: FLEXIBILITY AND UNCERTAINTY IN THE LABOUR MARKET

This book explores the relationship between work and well-being, recognizing the changes to paid work that have occurred since the 2007–09 global economic crisis. This period has witnessed a movement towards more flexible labour market organization, in part as employers attempt to increase their adaptability to uncertain external environments and find alternative ways to reduce the costs of labour (Raess and Burgoon, 2015, 95–6). Evidence has pointed to managerial choice as having an important role in these changes, as employers can choose to adopt a strategy which takes the 'high road' of good job quality or the 'low road' focusing centrally on cutting costs (Vidal, 2013). During this period, much of the policy from governments has targeted job creation and reductions in unemployment, rather than actively seeking to enhance experiences of paid work. The changes have created opportunities for some workers, in particular in highly skilled occupations (Green, 2011), to work in more flexible ways (e.g. using information and communication technology (ICT) to work in remote locations including at home). Where this has been realized, workers have been able increase their control over the timing and location of work, facilitating balance between work and the rest of their lives. However, these changes may have impacted negatively on encountered job quality in other increasingly flexibilized forms of employment (Fenwick, 2012, 597; Kalleberg, 2012; Raess and Burgoon, 2015, 95–6). A more flexible labour market has resulted in a growing tension between, on the one hand, efforts to enhance job quality and workplace well-being and, on the other hand, highly flexible employment and own-account self-employment (e.g. gig work), which is imposed by firms on workers (Friedman, 2014). These changes have prompted an intensification of work, higher levels of insecurity and uncertainty, and reductions in autonomy and control (Houlihan, 2002, 69; see also Choi et al., 2008), aspects of work which undoubtedly have implications for the quality of our working lives.

The Covid-19 global pandemic has had further significant impacts on economic activity since 2020. Government-imposed lockdowns and social distancing measures across many nations, requiring work from home wherever possible on grounds of public health, resulted in a rapid expansion of home-based remote work. At peak around two-in-five workers shifted to working at home across many developed economies such as the EU-27, USA, UK and Brazil (ILO, 2020). At the same time, other workers were subject to furlough or redundancy where jobs could not be converted to homeworking (e.g. certain jobs in hospitality and retail). Other workers still, including many classed as self-employed, were faced with either loss of income or continuing to journey to a workplace during the pandemic and the associated risks to their health. The longer-term impacts of the changes witnessed remain uncertain although the expansion of homeworking, while temporary in principle, has prompted significant debate regarding the future landscape of work. Despite the enforced nature of the expansion of remote working, reflecting a less than flexible arrangement in many respects, evidence has indicated that many workers show a preference to continue to work at home at least some of the time (Eurofound, 2020). The changes created by the pandemic could have considerable impacts on future routines and experiences of paid work. While this book does not focus centrally on the impacts of the pandemic on the quality

An introduction 7

of our working lives, recognition is given throughout the book where relevant to areas where considerable change has occurred, such as in the application of flexible forms of work.

THE DIMENSIONS OF WELL-BEING AT WORK

This book contributes to our understanding of well-being at work through consideration of existing models and evidence approached through the lens of job quality. The book explores the ways in which work interacts with our well-being to develop a new framework for workplace well-being which offers a comprehensive account of the influences and impacts of paid work on the quality of our working lives. The dimensions developed and outlined incorporate existing understanding but extend the focus beyond these approaches to fully capture the dimensions of workplace well-being. The framework is formed around three strategic elements, namely the culture of the organization and its workers, the structures that govern their activities, and the physical and psychological environment. Underpinning these strategic elements are six core dimensions of workplace well-being: (1) job properties; (2) flexibility; (3) rewarding careers; (4) relationships; (5) giving; and (6) physical space and activity.

Job Properties

The job properties dimension captures the nature of work, referring to the range of aspects of the job we do which collectively make up the job. It refers to the intrinsic factors which form a job from the levels of complexity and variety of tasks, to control and autonomy, and the meaning we derive from our work. Evidence on the nature of work suggests it has a number of important relationships with well-being at work. Complexity, which captures the types and variety of activities involved in a job (Holman, 2013), as well as the skills we use in order to complete tasks is highly relevant to the nature of work. More complex and varied tasks help to keep a job interesting and can act to motivate us at work (Holman, 2013). As well as documented concerns over the length of work-time, the intensity of work, which refers to how hard someone works in their job to complete tasks in a given time period, has been argued as being highly relevant to job quality and the impact of work on well-being (Green, 2006; Kalleberg, 2012). A lack of time to complete tasks, reflecting a lack of resources, and task overload, as well as lack of clarity over tasks associated with intense work routines, can act as significant sources of work-related stress and burnout among workers (Greenhaus et al., 2012).

Levels of autonomy are an important intrinsic component of work. They reflect the level of control workers have over the decisions and activities which make up their job (Wheatley, 2017b). Autonomy takes the form of both levels of control over tasks and work conduct, termed job control, and schedule control which refers to levels of discretion over the timing and location of work (Glavin and Schieman, 2012). It is an important component of our well-being and the relative quality of a job, as evidenced in many existing models and taxonomies. In particular, autonomy offers employees a method of coping with greater work demands, impacting both the well-being of employees and the health of their employers (Choi et al., 2008). The meaning an individual assigns to their work is a further characteristic of the nature of work with wider relevance to worker well-being, as we can derive a deep sense of meaning from our job which can act as a source of achievement and fulfilment (Spencer, 2009). Equally, where work is disconnected from the individual or perceived as an 'alien' activity, it may only reflect a more negative experience and be viewed in terms of toil or a laborious activity (Edgell, 2012; Spencer, 2009).

Flexibility

Levels of flexibility in paid work have undoubtedly increased in recent decades, aided by ICT and mobile technologies. Work has continued to evolve and change, with the pace and intensity of work having increased, and work moving out of traditional workplaces and spaces (Felstead and Henseke, 2017; Green, 2017). The observed expansion in the flexibility of work has both positive and negative implications and is driven by a range of factors. Key to much of this change is that it has resulted in a blurring of work and life. Achieving a desirable balance between work and the rest of our lives can be challenging, prompting governments to promote flexibility through agendas focusing on work–life balance, parental care, and the provision of flexible working arrangements.

The flexibility dimension considers ways that flexibility in work is realized and its implications for our working lives. This dimension highlights the importance of balancing work and life, considering, on the one hand, the impacts of working hours and overwork and, on the other, work recovery and breaks from work. It incorporates the impacts of the availability and use of flexible working arrangements (FWAs) which offer potential work–life balance and quality of life benefits (Gregory and Connolly, 2008), acting as a mechanism for flexing the timing and/or location of paid work (Wheatley, 2017a). FWAs can be broadly split into arrangements that focus on the reduction of work-time including reduced hours, job sharing and term-time working, those which focus on the arrangement of work-time, including flexi-time (sometimes called flextime) and compressed hours (Atkinson and Hall, 2009), and those focused on flexibility in work location including working from home. While flexibility can offer a range of benefits, evidence suggests lower job quality and

An introduction 9

potentially negative impacts on job satisfaction and other well-being measures among those using reduced hours arrangements (Wheatley, 2017a). Flexibility in work extends beyond these formal flexible working arrangements to include more informal or ad hoc arrangements (e.g. working at home one afternoon per week, as well as adoption of more comprehensive agile approaches to work). Further, this dimension acknowledges the well-being implications of changes in the structures of paid work that have resulted in a growth in flexible forms of work which can offer benefits to workers and organizations through enhancing control over work, but can also create a range of challenges associated with precarious work arrangements.

Rewarding Careers

The third dimension of well-being at work collects together the extrinsic factors which facilitate, or create barriers to, achieving a healthy and rewarding career from training and career development opportunities to job security and the pay and other benefits we receive from work. Pay and other rewards have an important impact on the well-being of workers influencing our ability to afford the necessities of life as well as enjoy luxuries. High pay by itself does not necessarily equate to good job quality, however, as some highly paid jobs exhibit characteristics associated with low job quality and negative well-being impacts including high workloads and intense work routines (Kalleberg, 2012; Wheatley, 2021). Pay is nevertheless relevant to our understanding of well-being at work as are the wider benefits received from paid work including pensions and other job perks (e.g. company cars), not least as levels of pay influence standards of living. The contractual nature of employment and level of security offered by a job have an important role in our well-being at work. Greater job security provides stability and enables longer-term planning. This is relevant given the growth in highly flexible forms of work, many of which involve precarious fixed-term or non-guaranteed contracts (Fenwick, 2012, 597; Kalleberg, 2012; Raess and Burgoon, 2015, 95–6). Where jobs are insecure, this may have negative impacts on intentions to leave, performance levels, and employee well-being (Sverke et al., 2002).

Career development opportunities are undoubtedly relevant to the quality of our working lives. Careers, though, have become increasingly diverse in structure with movement away from more traditional hierarchical 'career ladder' structures to encompass a range of models which are flatter and are characterized by flexibility and change (Dickmann and Baruch, 2011). Evidence suggests some movement towards a focus among workers on achieving work–life balance and/or greater levels of happiness and job satisfaction rather than only hierarchical career progression (Dickmann and Baruch, 2011; Hall, 2004). Equally, the extent to which there is a 'match' between a job and the skills of an individual employed to do it is also relevant to experienced job quality. Where we find workers are, or perceive themselves to be, over-qualified or over-skilled this can result in a number of negative impacts to experiences of a job including to job satisfaction resulting from incidence of boredom and lower levels of engagement, and can lead to negative impacts on earnings and career stagnation. Lack of skills (i.e. being under-skilled) is a key cause of underperformance and work-related stress (Piper, 2015). These concerns also have potential wider macroeconomic implications as skill mismatch and underuse of skills limits workforce productivity and, as such, is a waste of human capital, something which has formed a significant area of political and economic debate (Lawton, 2015; OECD, 2015). Provision of suitable training and career development opportunities, therefore, has important consequences at the individual, organizational and societal level.

Relationships

Most of us spend a good number of hours each week with colleagues and clients at work, either physically or virtually. In some cases, we may actually spend more time with these individuals than we do with family and friends in the non-work sphere. Relationships with others at work are, therefore, highly important to our well-being both in and out of work. In the work sphere, relationships with colleagues and clients have an important role in creating and maintaining social connectedness, which refers to the quantity and quality of social relationships in our lives (Lancee and Radl, 2012; Toepoel, 2013, 357). Occupational networks, in addition, act as a central source of social capital (McDonald and Mair, 2010), a term used to describe the social resources that are available through social interactions (Bourdieu, 1984) such as access to information, opportunities and support that might be otherwise unavailable (Putnam, 2000, 2001).

This dimension considers the nature of the interactions we have with others and the range of impacts they have on our working lives. Relationships with those within our workplace, including managers and colleagues (referred to as insiders) and those with outsiders (i.e. clients and customers) have implications for our experienced job quality (Deery et al., 2011). Interactions which are more positive in nature can engender a more positive atmosphere within the workplace, increasing levels of commitment and motivation (Chiaburu and Harrison, 2008), and offering associated benefits to worker well-being. Where conflict is present at work it can result in incidence of burnout and increase the likelihood of us wishing to leave our jobs (Deery et al., 2011). Workers also wish to be heard and involvement in decision-making and opportunities for employees to voice their opinions, either formally through trade unions and other employee groups, or informally through interactions with senior

An introduction 11

colleagues, has considerable impact on the conditions of work we encounter (Connell and Burgess, 2016; Wilkinson et al., 2014).

Giving

Giving is something that most of us engage in every day but is perhaps not something we consciously consider in the work sphere, nor do we necessarily link this activity to our well-being. In the work context, giving can be defined as involving employees and organizations engaging in philanthropic contributions of time, skills and expertise, support and/or money (i.e. through pay and employer-matching donation schemes, fund-raising and employer grants) (Rimes et al., 2019, 828). Debates have long existed over the motivations for giving, with some scholars arguing that giving behaviours can be devolved to self-interest, while others argue that giving reflects altruistic behaviour (André et al., 2017). Reciprocity, that is, engagement in activities with some expectation of benefit in kind, offers a third possible explanation for giving (André et al., 2017; Blau, 1964). Giving can be engaged with both formally and informally, with the former involving acts such as volunteering through an organization, and the latter including a wide range of activities such as time giving (Woolvin and Hardill, 2013) and offering support to colleagues. As such, giving can take many forms from simply taking time to listen to others and providing social support, to, for example, distributing workload which under more formal arrangements can take the form of work sharing usually involving a workforce distributing workload to avoid job loss and redundancy (Crimman et al., 2010). Other methods of giving at work captured in this dimension include coaching and different forms of mentoring.

Giving offers a range of potential rewards to both the individual giving and to the recipient, including to well-being. Individuals may enhance their own well-being through caring about the recipients' well-being, gaining enjoyment from the act of giving to others, and from seeing the well-being of others increase. In addition, giving can act as a source of human and social capital. This is important to consider with regard to giving in the workplace. Engaging in this activity offers the opportunity to enhance skills and networks (Folbre, 2012; Meier and Stutzer, 2008) which can have broader benefits to the working lives of the individual engaged in the act of giving and to the working lives of those around them.

Physical Space and Activity

The physical space in which we work incorporates the physical structures, fixtures and fittings, and equipment we have available to us (Elsbach and Pratt, 2007). As such, this dimension of workplace well-being is closely linked with health and safety; however, it goes beyond the objective impacts of the work environment as also relevant is our subjective response to it. A range of physical characteristics impact our experiences of the work environment including comfortable and ergonomic furnishings (Haynes, 2008), thermal comfort (Lamb and Kwok, 2016), lighting and air quality (Elsbach and Pratt, 2007), noise levels (Ryherd et al., 2008), and the provision of green space (Lee et al., 2015). The physical layout also has a significant influence over the level to which employees feel connected to one another (Sander et al., 2019). As with other dimensions of workplace well-being, the nature of the physical work environment is altering with broader changes in the landscape of paid work. Employers are trading-off different workplace designs, such as open plan and private office space (Lee and Brand, 2005; Kim et al., 2016), while also giving due consideration to cost implications and alternative workplace arrangements such as homeworking and working in other remote locations. Many employers are looking to more agile working environments which offer workers higher levels of flexibility, including opportunities to work at home, with space within the workplace focused more around collaboration and flexible space utilization rather than personalized space. The future of the workplace is quite uncertain. Debates continue regarding the relative benefits of centralized (i.e. workers being brought together in a single co-located workplace) versus decentralized and highly flexible workplace arrangements (Shearmur, 2018), a debate which has gathered significant pace following the experiences of workers and organizations in 2020.

Our interaction with the physical work environment also has implications for our levels of physical activity at work. There is an expanding evidence base which shows the benefits of being active to both physical and mental well-being (Kavetsos, 2011; Taylor et al., 2015). Opportunities for physical activity at work vary significantly depending on the nature and content of a job. Some forms of work are inherently physically demanding, or in some cases even involve relatively high levels of physical health risks and implications. The increasing proportion of employment in services and growth in use of ICT, though, has led to a considerable increase in sedentary routines of work which have potentially negative implications for our physical health and wider well-being (Brierley et al., 2019; Kazi et al., 2014; Maes et al., 2020; Renaud et al., 2020; Zhu et al., 2020). Creating opportunities to be active is essential to a healthy workplace and this dimension outlines mechanisms through which this can be achieved from the design of the physical work environment to promotion of active ways of working and commuting. Being physically active at work not only offers benefits to workers, but also to the organization through enhanced worker performance and reduced absence (Knight and Baer, 2014; Oppezzo and Schwartz, 2014).

A NOTE ON THE MEASUREMENT OF WELL-BEING AT WORK

Throughout the book we will consider how perspectives differ on the measurement of well-being at work. Some approaches adopt objective methods (i.e. factual representation such as data on productivity or sickness absence) and others subjective methods (i.e. based on reported feelings, opinions or perspectives such as preferences over working hours or levels of job satisfaction) in assessing the factors influencing, and outcomes for, well-being at work. The evidence base provides useful advice regarding the appropriateness and/ or effectiveness of different methods and within each chapter relevant discussion of best practice and guidance is included. Both objective and subjective methods of measurement have their strengths and weaknesses and, in many research exercises, it can be useful to employ a mix of these approaches to best capture understanding of well-being. Certain dimensions and sub-dimensions are more subjective in nature and in turn lend themselves more to subjective measures, such as some of the sub-dimensions of the job properties dimension (see Chapter 4). Others can be more accurately understood using objective methods, including sub-dimensions of the physical space and activity dimension (see Chapter 9). Measures can take the form of single-item and multi-item or composite indicators and can comprise individual elements of the quality of work through to overall measures of well-being. Some multi-item scales are designed to be compiled into a single measure, in some cases using a simple average and in other cases through the application of weightings to components. This can be desirable to help understand overall patterns; however, it can also result in differences between components being missed due to the averaging out of overall results (e.g. a low figure and a high figure suggesting a middling result overall). Composite or overall measures, as such, need to be carefully employed in researching well-being at work.

As well as the debate over the relative effectiveness of objective and subjective measures of well-being, the benefits of quantitative versus qualitative methods of capturing worker well-being are important to consider. Many of the example measures included throughout this book are quantitative in nature, often utilizing scale measurement to understand different factors influencing well-being. These measures are widely used and have been shown to be reliable indicators. However, as with all quantitative data, they can suffer from concerns around validity associated with how questions are interpreted by respondents, whether questions are leading (i.e. elicit a certain response), the choice of measures included and excluded (in both multi-item measures and overall survey instruments), and the ability of the data to explain relationships and causality (i.e. what factors drive what outcomes). Qualitative methods can offer rich data delving deep into the drivers and impacts of well-being at work. Understanding of this nature can be captured through focus groups, formal and informal conversations between workers and line managers both individually and in teams, and employee voice channels including online forums or chat rooms and through worker representatives. These methods can be used effectively alongside quantitative methods or as a sole form of data collection. They may be particularly suitable where the aim is to capture the voices of certain groups of workers that may be underrepresented or responses to specific aspects of work that may be difficult to capture using staff surveys and other mechanisms. In larger research exercises and/or organizations, the resource requirements of qualitative methods do need to be considered and this may prompt use of a mixed methods approach incorporating, for example, staff surveys with qualitative methods.

An often-cited criticism of well-being programmes, and indeed research, is that it can be difficult to measure outcomes and impact with any degree of accuracy, something that is reflected upon in Chapter 10. It does have to be acknowledged that difficulties are faced in extracting the direct influence of specific dimensions/sub-dimensions and programmes and interventions targeting well-being at work. Throughout the book we note the multifaceted nature of well-being at work, and how it leaks into all aspects of our working lives and is subject to a wide array of influences, both work and non-work related. When engaging in measurement exercises using the measures outlined in this book, researchers and organizations should consider the benefits of collecting and analysing longitudinal data (i.e. data which is collected at more than one point in time). This can be quantitative or qualitative in form. Collecting data at multiple time-points enables us to monitor and assess the impact of change, something that can be most insightful in research exercises and for organizations wishing to understand the effectiveness and impact of well-being programmes. An associated consideration is the use of benchmarking exercises. This provides an opportunity to capture a starting point (i.e. pre-intervention) to provide a baseline understanding of the well-being of workers that can be used to assess change and impact. In all cases it is important to ensure that prior to undertaking data collection and analysis exercises there is thorough understanding of the dimensions and sub-dimensions of workplace well-being which are to be explored, as well as the purpose of the exercise so that appropriate methods are employed.

CONTRIBUTION OF THE BOOK

This book contributes to understanding of the relationship between well-being and work, exploring its complex and interdependent nature to develop a new framework for workplace well-being. As themes of good work, job quality and worker well-being have risen in profile in recent years, academics and practitioners have sought to offer contributions which aid our understanding and/or collect together existing evidence bases. However, many of the existing contributions tend to be either discipline focused (e.g. human resource management (HRM), psychology), or offer a simpler collection of literature with lesser synthesis of overall observations and implications. In addition, a number of current contributions in this field focus entirely on employers and offer more organizational policy-focused approaches. This book is written for the researcher and practitioner, for the worker, organization and policymaker, as well as offering interest to general audiences. It presents academically rigorous discussion and analysis of the wide array of factors affecting well-being at work, and the book also incorporates case studies and practical insights including detailed discussion of methods for measuring dimensions of well-being at work, which can be used in research and to enhance well-being at individual and organizational levels. The dimensions and sub-dimensions of workplace well-being in the framework developed in this book can be used to guide research exercises and, equally, can be applied in practice by organizations to inform well-being strategy and programmes. In addition to its academic audience and being used by organizational policymakers, line managers and workers, the book acts as a useful resource for more advanced teaching and learning activities for a range of disciplines including in the social sciences (e.g. HRM, labour economics, social policy, and other fields). This book draws together the expansive international and interdisciplinary evidence bases on well-being and work, using the lens of job quality. By doing so the book contributes to, and extends, our understanding of the complex and dynamic relationship between well-being and the quality of our working lives.

OUTLINE OF THE BOOK

Following this introduction, Chapter 2 turns our focus to developing our understanding of well-being. It begins with a conceptual discussion of well-being definitions including the debates which exist around well-being as a concept. It then explores a number of approaches to well-being to provide a foundation of understanding which is applied in subsequent chapters. This book considers several contributions but is by no means exhaustive in its coverage. Contributions considered include Sen's capabilities approach (Parfit, 1984; Sen, 1987), desire-satisfaction (Parfit, 1984), subjective well-being (Diener et al., 1999; Pavot and Diener, 2013), psychological well-being (Ryff, 1982, 1989) and the PERMA model (Seligman, 2011). The exploration of different approaches also includes more practically focused contributions such as the UK government-funded New Economics Foundation (NEF) Dynamic Model of Well-being and Five Ways to Well-being (Aked et al., 2008; Thompson and

Marks, 2008). The chapter finally moves to outline differing methods of measuring well-being, including reference to a number of existing applications and extends the debate around the relative effectiveness of objective and subjective measurement briefly considered in this introduction.

Chapter 3 builds on the broader understanding of well-being developed in Chapter 2 to develop a new framework for workplace well-being. The chapter begins with a discussion of the relationship between work and well-being including reference to the impacts of work on well-being at the individual, organizational and societal level. The chapter then presents a range of existing models and frameworks for approaching well-being at work, incorporating into this discussion a specific consideration of the contribution of the literature on job quality. The chapter includes contributions by Hackman and Oldham (1976), Karasek (1979), Bakker and Demerouti (2007), Robertson and Cooper (2011), the UK National Health Service (NHS), CIPD (Suff and Miller, 2016), the Global Wellness Institute (Yeung and Johnston, 2016), and US National Institute for Occupational Safety and Health (NIOSH), amongst others. The chapter synthesizes these contributions to develop a new framework for workplace well-being which also guides the structure of the remainder of the book.

Chapter 4 presents the first of the six dimensions of workplace well-being, the job properties dimension. The chapter and dimension evidence the central relevance of the content of work to the quality of our working lives. It initially explores the distinction between intrinsic and extrinsic characteristics of work to provide context for the discussion which follows exploring the range of intrinsic aspects of work that influence workplace well-being. The chapter reflects on the role of autonomy and control over work, the growing debate around workloads and the intensity of work, including links with stress, and the role of job resources, which in this book refers to the time and space, equipment and tools, materials, facilities and support services required to complete job tasks successfully. The chapter further considers the variety and complexity of work, and the meaningfulness and purpose of work.

Chapter 5 of the book explores the second dimension, flexibility, highlighting the impacts of our ability to combine work with the rest of our lives. The chapter begins with a discussion of work–life balance in the context of contemporary work. It also reflects on the relationship between work-time and overwork, and the need for recovery and breaks from work. It explores both formal flexible working arrangements and informal methods of flexibility. It also reflects on flexibility over the location of work, including remote and homeworking, terms of employment (i.e. contracts) and agile approaches to work organization. The chapter includes discussion of recent developments in work including gig working and the impact of technology on how we work, as well as the impacts of the global pandemic on work location.

Chapter 6 draws on elements of the discussion from the preceding chapters, but with a specific focus on how we can achieve a healthy and rewarding balance between work and the rest of our lives in the pursuit of a career. The chapter explores notions of reward at work and the influence of extrinsic factors such as pay and other benefits on well-being at work. It gives specific consideration to the role of learning in our well-being, including reflecting on the impacts of skills match and over-/under-qualification. It extends content from Chapters 4 and 5 to consider the impacts of the changing nature of work, including the growth in flexibility, on career progression and job security. The chapter also demonstrates the importance of the balance between effort and reward.

Chapter 7 highlights the essential role of relationships in influencing our well-being at work. It considers the range of different ways in which relationships with others impact our well-being at work. It begins with a conceptual discussion of social connections in the workplace, drawing on the literature on social connectedness, social capital and social exchange theory. The chapter then moves to consider the range of ways in which relationships influence the quality of our working lives, including relationships between managers and employees, and challenges around conflicts faced at work. The role of leadership and trust in relationships is highlighted, as is the importance of providing mechanisms for employee voice. The chapter also includes consideration of the role of fun in the workplace.

Chapter 8 emphasizes the relevance of giving our time and resource to others to well-being at work. The chapter begins with a conceptual discussion of the reasons for, and benefits generated from, giving. This discussion centres around the debate over self-interest, altruism and reciprocity as motives of giving behaviours. The chapter then turns to a discussion of different mechanisms for giving during our working lives, including volunteering at work or through an employer, charitable giving (i.e. monetary donations), and the provision of social support, including drawing on the literature on perceived organizational support (POS). The chapter extends the latter discussion to also consider notions of workplace helping and forms of mentoring.

Chapter 9 turns the attention to the physical environment in which we work and our levels of physical activity at work. It begins with a discussion of the changing nature of workplace, extending some of the themes explored in Chapter 5. It moves to explore the layout and design of the physical work environment, incorporating key debates over open plan versus personalized workspaces, and activity-based flexible workplace design. It considers the physical characteristics of the workplace including lighting, temperature, air quality, noise and connections to nature (e.g. views, plants). The chapter then moves to physical wellness, including exploring what it means to be active at work, and reflecting on the existing evidence base on the range of ways in which work can be made more active. The chapter considers the links between keeping active and social connections, including the mutual benefits of group-based activities which involve social interaction and physical activity. The chapter underlines how the physical work environment and levels of physical activity impact both our physical and mental health.

The final chapter of the book draws together the dimensions of well-being at work. Its main purpose is in linking the six dimensions together and evidencing the importance of taking a holistic approach when considering the influences, and impacts, of work on well-being. The chapter outlines objective and subjective methods of measuring well-being outcomes and impacts. This includes a mix of indicators such as productivity and performance, turnover intention and actual turnover rates, levels of work engagement, organizational commitment, occupational health data, job satisfaction and associated subjective well-being indicators. The chapter offers guidance and recommendations for building and maintaining a healthy workplace, including linking to concepts of resilience and mindfulness. The chapter and book then end with a brief discussion of the future of well-being at work, reflecting on potential influences, including changes in work routines and technology.

PART I

Developing a framework for workplace well-being

2. Understanding well-being

INTRODUCTION

This chapter explores our understanding of well-being. It begins with a discussion of well-being definitions including reviewing the ongoing debates around well-being as a concept and reflecting on the interaction between physical and mental well-being. Different approaches to well-being are explored, beginning with objective well-being including Sen's capabilities approach (Parfit, 1984; Sen, 1987), before turning to desire–satisfaction (Parfit, 1984), subjective well-being (Diener et al., 1999; Pavot and Diener, 2013), psychological well-being (Ryff, 1982, 1989) and positive psychology through the PERMA model (Seligman, 2011). The discussion is extended to more practical approaches to well-being including the UK government-commissioned New Economics Foundation (NEF) Dynamic Model of Well-being and Five Ways to Well-being (Aked et al., 2008; Thompson and Marks, 2008). The chapter then moves to outline methods of measuring well-being, focusing on the distinction between objective and subjective methods of measurement. This discussion includes reference to examples of approaches employed by the UK government in measuring personal and national well-being, and that adopted in the European Social Survey (ESS). The chapter is not exhaustive in its conceptualization and coverage of well-being. Instead, the chapter presents a number of prominent and relevant approaches and methods of measurement to inform the focus of this book on well-being at work, including acknowledging areas of agreement and continued enquiry and debate.

WHAT IS WELL-BEING?

Definitions of well-being are closely linked to definitions of both 'happiness' and 'quality of life', and incorporate physical well-being which reflects the condition of our body and factors which influence it, and psychological well-being which is concerned with our mental health and happiness. Well-being is a multi-dimensional construct (Dodge et al., 2012), definitions of which have throughout history been much debated. Origins of these debates can be traced back to Ancient Greece where two distinct schools of thought emerged, hedonism and eudaimonia. Advocates of hedonism included Epicurus, who argued that well-being and experiences of a good life centred on happiness which is derived from the presence of positive and/or absence of negative 'affects', where 'affects' are a pleasure–pain component of well-being (Bradburn, 1969, 9). In contrast, the alternative eudaimonic school of thought proposed by Aristotle argued that true happiness is achieved through leading a virtuous life. In this approach, well-being is not simply a function of feeling good, but rather being good and achieving something worthwhile. The eudaimonic school, as such, is linked to the concept of flourishing which involves well-being derived from fulfilment through accomplishing meaningful and worthwhile goals, and positive psychological functioning (i.e. acceptance of our true selves and personal growth) (Seligman, 2011).

Since then, definitions have evolved somewhat but retain the core elements of these different schools of thought. A range of approaches to well-being have been developed, many of which draw from both hedonic and eudaimonic traditions. Debates continue over the definition of well-being with acknowledgement that well-being as a concept is 'intangible, difficult to define and even harder to measure' (Thomas, 2009, 11, cited in Dodge et al., 2012). Increasingly, it is acknowledged, for example in the work of Ed Diener (e.g. Diener, 2013; Diener et al., 1999), that the role of positive and negative affect is central to well-being, and alongside life satisfaction these components form the concept of subjective well-being, a self-reported or self-assessed measure of well-being (Diener et al., 1999) that is outlined later in the chapter. Well-being may reflect the presence of positive affects, including, for example, positive mood and the presence of social support, or simply an absence of negative affects, reflected in low levels of stress, low depression and anxiety, and the absence of feelings of loneliness.

Other contributions, though, focus more on well-being as the ability of an individual to manage their life in a productive and meaningful manner (Tennant et al., 2007), or as the ability to fulfil goals (Aked et al., 2008). Meanwhile, connections have been drawn between well-being and the concept of quality of life. For example, Shin and Johnson (1978, 478) argued that well-being is a 'global assessment of a person's quality of life according to his own chosen criteria'. The World Health Organization (WHO) definition of quality of life also incorporates the idea of goal fulfilment:

> An individual's perception of their position in life in the context of the culture and value systems in which they live and in relation to their goals, expectations, standards and concerns. It is a broad ranging concept affected in a complex way by the person's physical health, psychological state, level of independence, social relationships, personal beliefs, and their relationship to salient features of their environment. (World Health Organization, 1997, 1)

Well-being has, equally, been argued as a state of positive mental health (Huppert, 2009). Mental health in this sense has been defined by a range of government and international bodies including the National Health Service (NHS) in the UK (see UK Department of Health, 2011) and the WHO. Common among definitions is that positive mental health refers to a state of mind and body, in which individuals are able to cope, feel safe, work productively and feel a sense of connection to others, their community and the wider environment.

While there are clear synergies within each of these definitions of well-being, and at the same time a growing consensus on a number of the factors which influence well-being, the use of mixed terminology and definitional distinctions continues to leave well-being as a concept over which there is not comprehensive agreement. There is certainly a degree of overlap in the concepts and approaches presented, and an increasingly common understanding of the broad meaning of well-being. At the most basic distinction, hedonic well-being has been evidenced as being positively correlated with eudemonic well-being (European Social Survey, 2015, 7). Many models of well-being equally draw on elements of both hedonic and eudaimonic understanding. And while there may be distinctions in definition, there is consensus that well-being is central to the health of individuals, organizations and society.

APPROACHES TO UNDERSTANDING WELL-BEING

A wide range of approaches to understanding well-being have been developed. A useful taxonomy conducted by Dolan et al. (2006) summarized these into five broad categories of models: (1) objective-list; (2) desire/preference satisfaction; (3) hedonic; (4) evaluative; and (5) eudaimonic (flourishing). Within this broad categorization are approaches which employ quite distinct understandings of well-being. We nevertheless find a level of consistency in several of the components and relationships present in the models. Discussion of a number of the most prominent existing approaches is provided in this section.

Objective (List) Well-being and Sen's Capabilities Approach

Objective approaches define well-being in terms of quality of life. Central to these approaches is that well-being, including relative levels, can be measured objectively (Parfit, 1984; Schueller and Seligman, 2010). These models usually focus on the objective understanding of whether our basic needs are being met and/or whether we reach certain milestones or achievements. These approaches are, as such, referred to as 'objective-list' or 'basic needs' with the list or need element reflecting a range of objectively measured indicators which offer insight into well-being. Objective indicators of well-being include material resources, for example food, income levels and housing, and social attributes which include education levels, health, political voice, social relationships and networks (Western and Tomaszewski, 2016).

The capabilities approach, developed by Nobel Prize winner Amartya Sen (see Sen, 1987), offers an extension of the objective-list style approach to well-being. It focuses on the idea that well-being is influenced by the achievement, or otherwise, of certain worthwhile pursuits. Sen argues that the impact of economic, social and personal 'objective' factors, including milestones such as getting married, having children and having a successful career, enable people to choose their lives and thus contribute to human welfare (Pugno, 2015). These pursuits can thus be used as indicators of well-being where evaluation of well-being comprises both actual achievements referred to as 'functionings', and effective levels of freedom or choice over functionings which forms the 'capability' component from which the approach is named. The model is summarized in Figure 2.1. The concept rests on the ability of an individual to turn resources (e.g. a laptop) into capability sets which are sets of potential functionings (e.g. working on the laptop) which the individual has access to and which can positively influence well-being. The capability set represents the set of options available to the individual not all of which will be chosen. We may be able to work on a laptop, work with paper and pen, or think to complete a task. The achieved functioning is the option from these that we select. The ability of an individual to turn resources into capability sets, and in turn achieved functionings, is dependent on personal characteristics, sometimes referred to as 'conversion factors', including personal physiology (such as health) and skills, social norms, and the physical environment. Important to note is that subjective well-being is viewed as both an outcome of achieved functioning and also a functioning itself, represented in Figure 2.1 by the double-ended arrow.

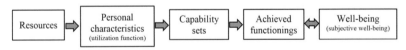

Source: Adapted from Sen, 1987.

Figure 2.1   The capabilities approach

A key aspect of Sen's approach is that it recognizes the need for a level of objective observation of individual circumstances as a result of the impact of 'adaptive preferences' which he argues are a key limitation of subjective approaches to well-being. Adaptive preferences refers to situations where an individual experiencing quite difficult circumstances (e.g. ill health), may still consider themselves to be in a good situation, in this case good health, and offer a subjective response consistent with an individual in good health. The neutral observation present in the capabilities approach recognizes this difference and is applied to correct any subjective error. It should be noted, however, that Sen is not in opposition to the inclusion of happiness in understanding or measuring well-being, considering it as being of 'intrinsic value' and reflecting 'a momentous achievement in itself'. Sen, though, does reject the sole use of happiness to measure well-being, arguing its limitations associated with the impact of adaptive preferences and other factors (Sen, 2008).

Although celebrated by many, Sen's approach has been criticized in a number of areas. The external valuation of what a good life looks like is one such criticism levelled at the capabilities approach. This criticism from liberalists including Pogge (2002, cited in Robeyns, 2016) argues that individuals should be free to pursue whatever they perceive to be a good life rather than this being determined externally by others. A further criticism centres on the individualist nature of the approach, as it gives lesser consideration to the influence of collective decision-making and ignores the inherent need in certain circumstances for freedom of choice to be limited (e.g. when this freedom could result in harm to others) (Nussbaum, 2003). Finally, practical difficulties in empirical measurement due to gaps in availability of information pertaining to some components of capability sets limits on the effective application of this approach.

Desire–Satisfaction

Desire or preference satisfaction models centre on whether we get what we want (i.e. our preferences are realized) (Parfit, 1984). In principle, our well-being could be influenced by items or experiences that do not actually make us better off, as long as our desires are met, for example where we lack information or understanding of the items/experiences available to us. More recent contributions to this approach to well-being argue that preferences must be informed, meaning that our desires reflect a more considered and informed outcome of the options available, and that even when informed, 'anti-social' desires (i.e. those that could negatively impact others) should be excluded (Harsanyi, 1996). The desire–satisfaction approach is closely linked to that employed within the mainstream economics discipline where there is a focus on 'revealed' preferences, which are evident in our willingness to pay for goods or services (Dolan et al., 2006, 15). Importantly, under this type of well-being approach, an increase in income would be expected to increase levels of satisfaction, as higher income enables consumption of more goods and services. This can be considered a substantial limitation, however, given the more complex relationship between income and happiness which has been evidenced in the existing literature, which suggests that income increases do not always deliver increases in well-being (see e.g. the work of Easterlin, 1974, 2001; Kahneman et al., 2006).

Hedonism

As already noted, hedonistic approaches to well-being focus on well-being as happiness that is derived from pleasure, which itself involves the balancing of positive (pleasure) and negative (pain) affects. The focus in the hedonistic approach is on pleasure for the individual that enjoys it. In this sense, what is a good life is determined by what an individual considers to be pleasurable or otherwise. This aspect of hedonism has generated some debate regarding its value as a measure of well-being. Specifically, difficulties in operationalizing the idea of feeling is problematic, as it is challenging for us to actually 'feel' many of our experiences. Defences of hedonism have argued that through considering hedonistic pleasure as an attitude rather than a feeling, this addresses many of the criticisms levelled at the approach. This idea, termed attitudinal pleasure, focuses on our awareness of a state of affairs, for example our understanding of what we enjoy about a particular activity such as playing a game where we may derive pleasure from the hope and anticipation of winning (Feldman, 2002, 605–7). A second major criticism centres on the value of pleasure derived from something which is generally considered to be bad or evil. More recent contributions have argued that the value of this type of pleasure is necessarily lesser due to its inherent properties (Feldman, 2002, 619). At an empirical level, exploring hedonism usually involves attempting to capture positive and negative feelings and emotions, including their relative frequency and intensity over time (Dolan et al., 2006). The hedonistic account of well-being forms an important component of subjective well-being, which has become one of the more dominant approaches in both the research and practitioner sphere.

Subjective Well-being

Subjective well-being (SWB) is an approach which is centred on experienced feelings which can be both positive and negative, and includes both a 'cognition' (i.e. evaluative/judgmental) and an 'affect' (i.e. pleasure/pain) component (Stutzer and Frey, 2010, 683). SWB is a 'stated preference' measure of well-being, in contrast to the 'revealed preference' approaches which have traditionally been preferred in disciplines such as economics. The affect component of subjective well-being is perhaps most appropriately considered as a hedonic balance which is determined by the overall positive affect (PA) and negative affect (NA) and the difference between these two states (Bradburn,

1969, cited in Kafka and Kozma, 2002). SWB, therefore, has three separate but linked components: PA (affect), NA (affect) and cognition reflected in an overall evaluative judgement of life usually termed 'life satisfaction' (Diener, 2013, 663; Diener et al., 1999; Pavot and Diener, 2013, 135). Higher levels of SWB can, as such, represent both the presence of positive influences and an absence of negative influences.

Given the subjective nature of this approach, there remains a significant level of debate regarding the potential impact of 'adaptive' preferences as noted with regard to the work of Sen earlier in the chapter, and unrealistic preferences which are discussed in more detail in Box 2.1. In addition, there has been considerable debate regarding whether individual well-being reflects a variable or stable state (Headey, 2008). As a variable state, referred to as a 'bottom-up' theory, SWB is argued as a composite outcome of our engagement in a variety of external events and activities undertaken throughout our lives. In contrast, if SWB is viewed as an internally determined stable state of personality, referred to as a 'top-down' theory of SWB, this implies some form of underlying process which results in greater or lesser levels of happiness being reported by an individual throughout their entire lives (Diener, 2013, 663; Pavot and Diener, 2013, 136). While these perspectives are contrasting ones, within the 'bottom-up' approach it is accepted that, while reflecting a variable state, the SWB of an individual will necessarily return to happiness levels or 'set-points' (Headey, 2008). At different times in our lives we may, therefore, exhibit different happiness set-points which both influence our participation in particular events and activities and the amount of pleasure we derive from them. The existing evidence base is indicative of SWB as both a product of 'top-down' personality traits and 'bottom-up' life experiences (Pavot and Diener, 2013, 137).

While SWB represents a global assessment of well-being, this approach also offers the opportunity to assess different aspects of our lives, referred to as 'domain satisfaction' (van Praag et al., 2003, 30). Adopting this approach enables a more nuanced perspective on the individual components of our lives that impact our experienced feelings and determine levels of SWB. It has been argued that this is particularly relevant when exploring the interaction between different aspects of our lives, for example work, leisure and health (Pavot and Diener, 2013, 135), and how these influence our overall self-assessment of well-being (Schimmack, 2008).

BOX 2.1 POSITIVE ILLUSIONS AND UNREALISTIC SELF-ASSESSMENT OF WELL-BEING

The positive illusion and unrealistic self-assessment hypothesis focuses on the idea that individuals may have a systematic tendency towards forming an overly positive outlook, even where this may be badly supported or rendered false by the evidence available (Jefferson et al., 2017). The hypothesis can be explained with reference to three related concepts. First, the 'better than average effect' in which it is argued that we often tend to overestimate our desirable attributes, for example believing the quality of the work we produce to be better than it would objectively be considered. Second, the illusion of control which centres on the propensity of an individual to believe they are in control of a situation or their life even where the evidence does not support this being the case. This is linked to the final concept, which is that of unrealistic optimism which refers to the tendency for us to exhibit an unrealistically optimistic outlook, for example with regard to the future health risks we face as we get older. The presence of biases in both the better than average effect and unrealistic optimism is argued as being symptomatic of motivated reasoning and epistemic irrationality (Jefferson et al., 2017). It is acknowledged, though, that these perspectives are not fixed as our outlooks are constantly reconstructed through our experiences.

The evidence base supporting the unrealistic optimism hypothesis has grown (e.g. through research in the neurobiology discipline; see e.g. Simmons and Massey, 2012). It is contended that the presence of positive illusion and unrealistic self-assessment can in certain circumstances actually be beneficial. Notably, given the focus of this book, well-being and health are identified as areas where a more positive outlook may in fact be beneficial. It has been argued that this perspective can increase well-being, contribute to mental and physical health, and can stimulate higher levels of productivity and motivation (Bortolotti and Antrobus, 2015). However, the presence of positive illusion, especially where wildly optimistic, can have harmful effects including through reducing our ability to learn from feedback (self-protection) which can result in a skewed perspective where our own self-perception is in stark contrast to that of objective reality, high levels of complacency (e.g. not taking precautions with our health), and high risk behaviours (e.g. gambling). There remains, though, a limited evidence base on the impacts of positive illusions and unrealistic optimism (Shepperd et al., 2017).

Psychological Well-being

Psychological well-being (PWB) develops the eudaimonic school of thought on well-being and was proposed in the work of Carol Ryff (1982, 1989). Ryff's approach draws on the work of scholars, including Neugarten (1968), Maslow (1968), Jung (1933) and Erikson (1959). The PWB approach integrates a range of perspectives into six core dimensions summarized in Figure 2.2: self-acceptance; positive relationships; personal growth; purpose in life; environmental mastery; and autonomy. Within the approach, self-acceptance refers to a longer-term self-evaluation in which awareness and acceptance of both strengths and weaknesses is emphasized (Ryff and Singer, 2008, 21). Positive relationships highlight the importance to our well-being of love, empathy and affection obtained from relationships with others. Personal growth is the dimension of PWB which most closely matches with Aristotle's eudaimonia, emphasizing self-realization and personal development. The need for a purpose in life also forms an important dimension of PWB, evidencing the impact of meaning and the relevance of having goals to our experiences of life. Control over, and active participation in, the environments we inhabit is also argued as essential to our well-being. Finally, the sixth dimension of PWB is autonomy, a feature common in many models of well-being. Present in the work of Maslow, Jung and others, autonomy in the form of determining our own actions, independence in thought, and resistance to conventions and norms, is identified as a central component of well-being.

Together, it is argued that the six primary dimensions are joined together by a single higher order factor which Ryff defines as well-being (Ryff and Keyes, 1995). Within this approach it is also noted that there is a need for balance if we are to live well, for example between the needs and expectations of others reflected in the dimension of positive relationships and our own needs and preferences which enhance well-being in the dimension of autonomy (Ryff and Singer, 2008).

Measurement of PWB is performed through the Ryff Scales of Psychological Well-being (SPWB). Within the SPWB, each of the six dimensions of PWB is explored using 20 items, ten of which are positive and ten negative. Each of these items is scored on a 6-point scale which ranges from 'strongly agree' to 'strongly disagree'. PWB is also measured in the context of work, for example, through the five-factor Index of Psychological Well-Being at Work developed by Dagenais-Desmarais and Savoie (2012). This measure of eudaimonic well-being at work collects responses on five dimensions: interpersonal fit, thriving, feeling of competency, desire for involvement and perceived recognition. Each of these dimensions is measured by five items (25 items in total) which use a 6-point scale from 'disagree' to 'completely agree'.

Source: Ryff and Singer, 2008.

Figure 2.2   The dimensions of psychological well-being

Empirical evidence has suggested that the Ryff SPWB contains both a SWB and positive psychological functioning component. As such, SPWB is related, but not identical to SWB. SWB not only reflects psychological functioning but also the influence of a range of domain satisfactions, environmental factors and personality traits (Kafka and Kozma, 2002). The eudaimonic well-being component of PWB, comprised of positive relationships, personal growth and other dimensions, is generally considered to be relatively stable over time. For example, research has shown a strong positive correlation (.75 test-retest) over a six-month period (Dagenais-Desmarais et al., 2018). Life satisfaction can similarly be argued as reflecting a more stable state, as per the arguments relating to happiness set-points already outlined from the SWB literature (Headey, 2008; Pavot and Diener, 2013). Positive and negative affects, however, can be considered as more variable states, changing on a regular and even daily basis.

Positive Psychology and PERMA

The PERMA model was developed by positive psychologist Martin Seligman and gained significant exposure through his book *Flourish: A Visionary New Understanding of Happiness and Well-being* (Seligman, 2011). Positive psychology focuses on the study of the factors and processes which determine positive psychological functioning and flourishing of individuals, groups and institutions (Gable and Haidt, 2005, 104), where flourishing is achieved through fulfilment derived from accomplishing tasks and goals, connecting with others and our ability to grow as a person through both good and bad experiences.

The PERMA model distinguishes between five dimensions that constitute the elements of well-being: (1) positive emotion, (2) engagement, (3) relationships, (4) meaning, and (5) accomplishment (Seligman, 2011, 2018). Positive emotion, as defined in the model, centres on our feelings of hope and thankfulness. Engagement refers to our ability to be in the moment, and focus on our strengths to help us overcome challenges to our well-being. Relationships with family, friends and work colleagues form an important dimension of well-being. Meaning reflects the well-being we derive from contributing, and feeling part of, something that is worthwhile and has a purpose. Finally, accomplishment refers to the completion of rewarding tasks (Seligman, 2011).

The PERMA model has been quite widely promoted and applied by organizations and management consultants, with a focus on using this framework as a method of designing strategies and activities to enhance well-being (Bailey and French, 2018), as well as development of measurement tools including surveys (Butler and Kern, 2016). Examples of initiatives which may have a positive impact on positive emotion in the context of work include the introduction of training and activity programmes including those focused on resilience and mindfulness (see Chapter 10 for discussion). Workplace-focused interventions that could impact engagement include identification of, and reductions in, non-valued work and streamlining policies and processes as well as work–life balance policies. In the work sphere, measures which may enhance relationships at work include use of mentoring and the introduction of inter- and intra-departmental professional networking and social activities. Use of reflective activities and promotion of values and vision of the organization can help to motivate meaningfulness in the workplace. Well-being at work associated with the accomplishment dimension could be enhanced through the adoption of a culture which focuses on autonomy and minimization of micromanagement, and adequately rewards and recognizes success.

Existing research supports the relevance of each of the dimensions of PERMA in influencing our well-being. For example, it has been argued that higher levels of each of the PERMA dimensions can help to protect against negative emotions, reduce stress and depression, improve resilience and life satisfaction, and reduce incidence of physical illness (see Iasiello et al., 2017). Evidence has shown PERMA to be highly correlated (0.98) with subjective well-being (Goodman et al., 2018; Seligman, 2011). This is indicative of a very close relationship between these two approaches to understanding well-being. There has been a level of debate in the literature over the relative contribution of PERMA in this respect. Questions have been raised over whether its close correlation with SWB means it does not offer much insight beyond the already widely embedded concept of subjective well-being, thus rendering it somewhat redundant (Goodman et al., 2018). Seligman (2018), however, defends the approach by arguing that PERMA does not offer a new kind of well-being, but instead has its value in recognizing and bringing together the elements that constitute well-being.

The Dynamic Model of Well-being

The Dynamic Model of Well-being was proposed in 2008 by the NEF as part of a UK government project exploring mental capital and mental well-being (Thompson and Marks, 2008). The approach argues that the five broad categories of well-being models grouped by Dolan et al. (2006) as introduced at the beginning of the chapter, instead of representing contrasting or conflicting approaches to well-being, actually describe different elements of a dynamic process which together explain well-being. The dynamic model, summarized in Figure 2.3, argues that external conditions surrounding work, home, family and physical health drive the relative opportunities, challenges, norms and cultures we face. Together with psychological resources including optimism, self-esteem and resilience, these external conditions determine whether our needs are satisfied and we function well (i.e. our eudaimonic well-being). In turn, our functioning feeds back into the external conditions we experience and at the same time determines our feelings and evaluative judgements of life (i.e. happiness, satisfaction etc.), with the latter feeding back into our psychological resources. This model is useful as it draws together a number of the core components of each of the different approaches to well-being considered within this chapter and offers a coherent method of understanding the links between them.

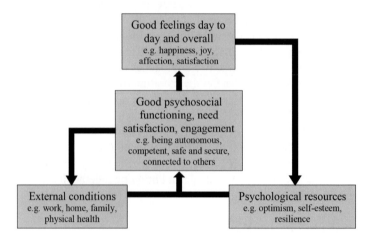

Source: Adapted from Thompson and Marks, 2008.

Figure 2.3 The Dynamic Model of Well-being

The Five Ways to Well-being

A more practical approach to well-being, focused around five evidence-based actions which can be used to enhance personal well-being (Aked et al., 2008), was developed by the NEF, who were commissioned by the UK government in 2008 to develop the Five Ways to Well-being. This involved a process of exploring the existing evidence base, drawing on both UK and international data sources, to develop an initial long-list of actions and subsequently to narrow to a short-list of key actions for enhancing well-being through good functioning. The actions 'connect', 'be active', 'take notice', 'keep learning' and 'give' were identified from this research. These actions and their relationship with mental capital and well-being are represented in Figure 2.4.

The *connect* action is identified in response to the evidence which highlights the importance of social relationships in both promoting well-being and also acting to guard against mental health problems. It involves consideration of how we interact with others, including friends, family, and colleagues at work. Building broader, and maintaining stronger, social connectedness contributes to functioning well (Topoel, 2013, 357). Physical activity has been shown to have not only benefits to physical health, but also to psychological well-being through enhancing feelings of well-being and reducing anxiety and depression (Biddle and Ekkekakis, 2005). *Be active* is an action which aims to promote

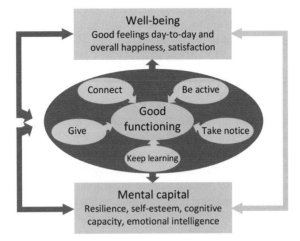

Source: Aked et al., 2008, 17.

Figure 2.4 Five Ways to Well-being

the benefits of physical activity for both physical and psychological well-being for those of all physical abilities (Kavetsos, 2011; Taylor et al., 2015). It acknowledges that this activity does not need to be intense to have some positive impact with activities such as walking and gardening providing benefits to well-being.

The *take notice* action builds on research into both resilience and mindfulness (CIPD, 2011; Windle, 2002). It centres on how we can increase our awareness of the world around us and our present state. It focuses on using this information effectively to reflect on the things we experience including what enhances our well-being, helping us to make decisions which align better with our values and motivations. The benefits of lifelong learning are at the core of the *keep learning* action. It is derived from evidence which has shown the links between engaging in learning and the development and maintenance of self-efficacy and social connections. It draws from the idea that the fulfilment of goals enhances well-being (Aked et al., 2008), and is consistent with the personal growth dimension of the psychological well-being model considered earlier in this chapter (Ryff and Singer, 2008). Finally, *give* is an action which focuses on the benefits of giving our time and effort to others. This action is informed by the argument that well-being is enhanced when we feel a sense of purpose in society and contribute to our community (Aked et al., 2008). The Five Ways to Well-being is a valuable practically focused approach which is informed by existing research and conceptual models of well-being. It offers

34 *Well-being and the quality of working lives*

understanding of some of the key factors which influence our well-being in the broader context. It can be used at the individual level as a framework for managing and enhancing well-being. While application to the work sphere or at an organizational level is not the primary focus of the approach, all of the identified five actions can be applied to workplace well-being.

MEASUREMENT OF WELL-BEING

The conceptual models explored in this chapter have evidenced the wide range of approaches to understanding well-being. A number of these models incorporate methods for measuring levels of, and changes in, well-being including Ryff's SPWB and various methods of measuring subjective well-being. Measuring quality of life and well-being have long been acknowledged as central to societal progress as a result of the considerable limitations of traditional measures of economic growth such as gross national product (GNP). As Robert F. Kennedy famously stated in his speech at the University of Kansas in 1968:

> Gross National Product counts air pollution and cigarette advertising, and ambulances to clear our highways of carnage. It counts special locks for our doors and the jails for the people who break them. It counts the destruction of the redwood and the loss of our natural wonder in chaotic sprawl. It counts napalm and counts nuclear warheads and armored cars for the police to fight the riots in our cities. It counts Whitman's rifle and Speck's knife, and the television programs which glorify violence in order to sell toys to our children. Yet the gross national product does not allow for the health of our children, the quality of their education or the joy of their play. It does not include the beauty of our poetry or the strength of our marriages, the intelligence of our public debate or the integrity of our public officials. It measures neither our wit nor our courage, neither our wisdom nor our learning, neither our compassion nor our devotion to our country, it measures everything in short, except that which makes life worthwhile. (18 March)

Measurement of well-being can be broadly divided into two main methods; objective and subjective (see Galloway et al., 2006, 19–22). Objective measurement of well-being is a revealed preference measure of well-being which is usually comprised of a basket of indicators or composite index with examples including the Measure of Domestic Progress (Cobb and Daly, 1989). These measures, as per objective approaches to well-being, aim to capture the material conditions that influence well-being. Many of these methods of measurement involve the adjustment of GNP to better capture non-market activities. This could include the subtracting of costs related to crime. Consideration is also given to the resources available to us that influence well-being; for example, access to housing and water. Sen's capabilities approach extends basic objective methods with its focus on functioning, acknowledging that resources alone do not result in achieved functioning as personal characteristics influence our ability to utilize resources. While resources can be used to some extent as a proxy for functionings, measurement needs to better capture the extent to which a level of choice accompanies a realized achievement (Sen, 2008). Measures also need to reflect inequalities across individuals, groups and generations, and should account for the cumulative effects of multiple disadvantages (e.g. being in ill health *and* low paid). Although accounting for these additional factors enables objective measurement of well-being to be more effective, they do, however, render this form of measurement empirically challenging. Objective measures are also problematic as a result of the presence of bounded rationality, which refers to decision-making based on limited information or understanding, which can result in choices being made which do not reflect our 'true' preferences (Kahneman and Krueger, 2006, 3).

Measures of subjective well-being, as a stated preference measure of well-being, put emphasis on capturing the ways in which individuals experience the quality of their lives through self-reporting. SWB measures integrate emotional responses (reflecting positive and negative affects) and cognitive (evaluative) judgements. Studies that measure SWB usually employ a method in which self-assessed well-being is considered to reflect a reporting function (r) of 'true' subjective well-being (h) (see Dolan et al., 2008, 95):

$$SWB_{report} = r(h)$$

'True' subjective well-being within these approaches is determined by social, economic, and environmental factors (Xs). The relationship is expressed as an additive function of the following form:

$$SWB_{it} = \alpha + \beta_1 X_{1it} + \beta_2 X_{2it} + \beta_3 X_{3it} + \ldots + \varepsilon_{it}$$

Subjective well-being measures themselves fall into two broad categories, 'single-item scale' and 'multi-item measures' (Downward and Rasciute, 2011, 333; MacKerron, 2012, 709). A note should also be made regarding the difference between measures of 'momentary' and 'reflexive' well-being. Momentary well-being is measured while respondents are participating in an activity, capturing feelings experienced during the activity. Reflexive measures, meanwhile, consider experiences in the present/recent past (e.g. 'these days' or 'nowadays') and are the more common form of measure of SWB (see Bryson and MacKerron, 2016). As per the title, single-item scales involve measurement of SWB using a single item or question. The most commonly applied single-item scales to measure SWB are 'happiness with life' and 'satisfaction with life' (Dolan et al., 2008). Responses are provided by individuals on a scale which can be divided into either five, seven, ten or eleven categories, with these categories comprising differing terminology, but usually ranging from 'completely dissatisfied/happy' to 'completely satisfied/happy' (Hicks et al., 2013, 78; see also Helliwell et al., 2015, 2019). The UK Understanding Society survey, for example, includes a single-item measure of overall life satisfaction as follows:

Q. On a scale of 1 to 7 where 1 means 'Completely dissatisfied' and 7 means 'Completely satisfied', how dissatisfied or satisfied are you with your life overall?						
7	6	5	4	3	2	1
Completely satisfied	Mostly satisfied	Somewhat satisfied	Neither satisfied or dissatisfied	Somewhat dissatisfied	Mostly dissatisfied	Completely dissatisfied

Both happiness and life satisfaction single-item scales have been shown empirically to generate largely consistent responses (Smith and Exton, 2013). In addition to capturing understanding of how we feel about our lives on 'aggregate' or 'overall', SWB measures can also focus on specific domains of life as outlined earlier in the chapter, for example, levels of satisfaction with job, health or leisure (van Praag et al., 2003, 30).

Multi-item scales involve multiple lines of questioning with well-being a product of the composite of responses to these questions. Examples of these types of well-being measures include the Life Satisfaction Index (LSI) (Neugarten et al., 1961); the Positive and Negative Affective Scale (PANAS); Ryff's (1982, 1989) SPWB; the Satisfaction with Life Scale (SWLS) (Diener et al., 1985); and the General Health Questionnaire (GHQ). The SWLS, as one of the most popular multi-item methods of measuring SWB is comprised of five items scored on a 7-point scale which together provide an assessment of satisfaction with life overall (Diener et al., 1985). The GHQ, meanwhile, involves many more individual questions, but is often included in social surveys in a shortened form (e.g. GHQ12) focused on the measurement of subjective well-being (Dolan et al., 2008, 95). (See Chapter 10 for an example of the GHQ.) Further examples are included in the subsequent sections which outline the UK method for measuring personal and national well-being and the method employed in the ESS.

When applying measures of subjective well-being in empirical research, the treatment of the scales can be handled in two potential ways – cardinal or ordinal. If we apply a cardinal treatment to the variables, this assumes that responses are provided on a scale, similar to what we may find for a question on the number of hours worked per week. However, the data on well-being is usually collected using scale answer sets. Considering subjective well-being measures as cardinal in analysis is difficult to accept in most cases (see Fielding, 1999, for an extended discussion). This data is ordinal in form (i.e. possible responses are discretely ranked), alternatively referred to as ordered choice categories (e.g. very dissatisfied, dissatisfied, neither satisfied nor dissatisfied, satisfied, very satisfied). The ordinal nature of the data is more suited to analysis using certain statistical techniques such as ordered logit or probit regression (Stutzer and Frey, 2010, 688), where an assumption is present in the model that the same response by different individuals represents a similar level of satisfaction (van Praag et al., 2003, 34).

Capturing well-being using SWB methods has been the subject of significant debate, including its potential use as a substitute, or complement, to objective and income-based welfare measures within economics (Kesebir and Diener, 2008). Ordered response scale measures of well-being raise concerns around measurement validity associated with potential problems associated with happiness set-points (Headey, 2008) and the adaptive preferences referred to by Sen (2008) which create uncertainty around assumptions of consistency in responses. Radical perspectives within the economics discipline are also critical of the acceptance of measures of happiness and life satisfaction. They argue that interpretations of self-reported well-being need to acknowledge the structural drivers that influence relative satisfaction, as well as the role of norms and expectations in determining relative satisfaction levels (Spencer, 2009, 130). Debate is also present over the validity of smaller-scale primary data collection exercises against large-scale data which enable the inclusion in analyses of a greater range of control factors (Brown et al., 2012, 1009; Dolan et al., 2008, 96). Despite these argued limitations, an ever-expanding evidence base supports the validity and comparability of subjective measures of well-being (see Stutzer and Frey, 2010, 684–7).

UK Personal and National Well-being Measures

The approach to measurement adopted by the Office for National Statistics (ONS) in the UK includes both measurement of personal well-being, captured through responses to a set of four questions summarized in Table 2.1 which are collected using a 10-point scale, and broader data capturing national well-being. The personal well-being measures used by the ONS are fairly standard in form, with the items on life satisfaction and whether things done in life are worthwhile adopting more reflexive formats focusing on a broader timescale, and measures of feelings regarding anxiety and happiness in the more immediate past (Day and Clements, 2019).

Table 2.1   Personal well-being measures

Sub-dimension of personal well-being	Measure
Life satisfaction	Overall, how satisfied are you with your life nowadays?
Worthwhile	Overall, to what extent do you feel that the things you do in your life are worthwhile?
Happiness	Overall, how happy did you feel yesterday?
Anxiety	Overall, how anxious did you feel yesterday?

Source: Day and Clements, 2019.

The national well-being data incorporates the personal well-being measures alongside a mix of individual and macro-level indicators in nine other dimensions. These measures comprise: (1) our relationships (e.g. unhappy relationships, loneliness); (2) health (e.g. life expectancy, disability); (3) what we do (e.g. job satisfaction, leisure satisfaction, arts, culture and sport participation); (4) where we live (e.g. feelings of safety, access to services, satisfaction with accommodation); (5) personal finance (e.g. household income, subjective feelings over financial status); (6) economy (e.g. public sector debt, inflation); (7) education and skills (e.g. human capital, population with no qualifications); (8) governance (e.g. voter turnout, trust in government); and (9) environment (e.g. greenhouse gas emissions, recycling).

European Social Survey Measures

The European Social Survey employs the Dynamic Model of Well-being, outlined earlier in this chapter, to inform the design of the survey module on well-being. Measures of well-being are included in the core questionnaire of the ESS, comprising a single-item measure of satisfaction with life and a measure of happiness. Additional depth of understanding on well-being is captured through the 'Personal and Social Well-being' module in periodic rounds of the collection of the ESS (e.g. data collected in round three (ESS, 2006) and round six (ESS, 2012)), the questions from which are summarized in Table 2.2. The ESS uses a six-dimension approach consisting of evaluative well-being (life satisfaction and happiness), emotional well-being (e.g. feelings around sadness, anxiety, enjoyment and happiness), functioning (e.g. feelings of worth, enthusiasm, optimism, failure), vitality (e.g. effort, energy), community well-being (e.g. feelings of community including trust and helping one another), and supportive relationships (e.g. closeness, loneliness and support from others). The six dimensions facilitate a more nuanced understanding of the different aspects of well-being and have generated useful insight into differences in well-being across Europe (European Social Survey, 2015, 9).

Understanding well-being 39

Table 2.2   Personal and social well-being measures in the European Social Survey

Well-being dimension	ESS Survey Measure
Evaluative well-being	How satisfied are you with life as a whole?
	How happy are you?
Emotional well-being	How much of the time during the past week you …
	felt sad?
	felt depressed?
	enjoyed life?
	felt happy?
	felt anxious?
	felt calm and peaceful?
Functioning	I feel I am free to decide for myself how to live my life.
	In my daily life I get very little chance to show how capable I am.
	Most days I feel a sense of accomplishment from what I do.
	How interested you would generally say you are in what you are doing.
	How absorbed you would generally say you are in what you are doing.
	How enthusiastic you would generally say you are about what you are doing.
	I generally feel that what I do in my life is valuable and worthwhile.
	To what extent do you feel that you have a sense of direction in your life?
	I'm always optimistic about my future.
	There are lots of things I feel I am good at.
	In general I feel very positive about myself.
	At times I feel as if I am a failure.
	When things go wrong in my life, it generally takes me a long time to get back to normal.
	How difficult or easy do you find it to deal with important problems that come up in your life?
Vitality	How much of the time during the past week you …
	felt that everything you did was an effort?
	sleep was restless?
	could not get going?
	had a lot of energy?

Well-being dimension	ESS Survey Measure
Community well-being	Would you say that most people can be trusted, or that you can't be too careful in dealing with people?
	Do you think that most people would try to take advantage of you if they got the chance, or would they try to be fair?
	Would you say that most of the time people try to be helpful or that they are mostly looking out for themselves?
	To what extent people in your local area help one another?
	I feel close to the people in my local area.
Supportive relationships	How many people, if any, are there with whom you can discuss intimate and personal matters?
	Do you feel appreciated by the people you are close to?
	Do you receive help and support from people you are close to when you need it?
	How much of the time during the past week you felt lonely?

Source: ESS, 2012.

CHAPTER SUMMARY

This chapter has considered current understanding of well-being. Exploring a range of different approaches to well-being, the chapter has reflected on how each of these approaches adds to our understanding, as well as offering insight into debates and conflict which exist around this concept. The chapter began by defining well-being and recognizing the distinct schools of thought, hedonism and eudaimonia, as a basis for conceptualizing well-being. A range of approaches to well-being were then outlined beginning with objective-list approaches and Sen's capabilities approach (Parfit, 1984; Sen, 1987), before considering desire–satisfaction (Parfit, 1984), subjective well-being (Diener et al., 1999; Pavot and Diener, 2013), psychological well-being (Ryff, 1982, 1989), the PERMA model (Seligman, 2011), the NEF Dynamic Model of Well-being and the more practically focused Five Ways to Well-being (Aked et al., 2008; Thompson and Marks, 2008).

The approaches explored throughout the chapter have emphasized a number of important components of well-being as well as factors which act to influence it. While all of the approaches explored are well-regarded and widely applied, SWB is perhaps the most prevalent of the approaches considered in this chapter. It views well-being as being comprised of an evaluative 'cognition' and a pleasure/pain 'affect' component with the latter incorporating both positive and negative experienced feelings (Stutzer and Frey, 2010). Beyond this understanding of the core composition of well-being, it is evident from the chapter that there are a number of common features to well-being.

Taking meaning from our lives, having a sense of purpose and achievement of goals and/or tasks are all components of well-being identified in a number of the approaches considered. Individual-level personal characteristics and personality traits are also identified as important factors, incorporating our physical and mental state including psychological resources such as levels of resilience and self-efficacy. The presence of autonomy over decision-making and other aspects of our lives is also identified, for example in psychological well-being and the Dynamic Model of Well-being. Meanwhile, the importance of positive relationships and social functioning is also highlighted by many of the approaches including psychological well-being and PERMA. Many of the approaches also explicitly acknowledge the role of external influences such as work, family and the wider societal environment.

Consistent with the breadth of conceptual approaches, we find that empirical measurement of well-being has been developed in a range of different forms. Many involve elements of SWB, but measures do follow the differing schools of thought and as such attempt to capture understanding of, and evidence for, different components of well-being as well as overall indicators. The measures explored in this chapter involve lines of questioning which capture overall satisfaction with life, through to feelings around meaning and worthwhileness of life, community and relationships. The understanding of conceptual approaches and measurement of well-being developed in this chapter is employed in the next chapter to inform the exploration of different models of well-being at work.

3.   Well-being and work

INTRODUCTION

This chapter focuses on developing our understanding of the interaction between well-being and work, building on the broader understanding of well-being developed in Chapter 2. The chapter begins with a discussion of the relationship between work and well-being, including reference to the impacts of work on well-being at the individual, organizational and societal level. The chapter then presents a range of existing models and frameworks for approaching well-being at work, including those developed by Hackman and Oldham (1976), Karasek (1979), Bakker and Demerouti (2007), Robertson and Cooper (2011), the UK National Health Service (NHS), the Chartered Institute of Personnel and Development (CIPD) (Suff and Miller, 2016), the Global Wellness Institute (Yeung and Johnston, 2016), US National Institute for Occupational Safety and Health (NIOSH), and What Works Well (2018) methodology for well-being at work. Particular attention is given to the concept of job quality (Felstead et al., 2019; Kalleberg, 2011) and how this intersects with understanding of well-being in the context of work. As per the previous chapter, the discussion is not exhaustive. Instead, the chapter draws upon a number of the most recognized as well as newer models and frameworks of well-being at work and job quality. The chapter ends by outlining the development of a new model for workplace well-being which builds on the conceptual understanding developed in Chapter 2 and the models and frameworks for well-being at work and job quality presented in this chapter.

WELL-BEING AT WORK

Well-being at work can be defined as the quality of life associated with the experiences and conditions of work we encounter in our jobs. It is synonymous with a range of other expressions including workplace well-being, worker well-being and wellness at work. It involves all individuals having 'the right to work in a manner that is healthy, motivating, and edifying' (Yeung and Johnston, 2016, 29). It is influenced by a range of work-related environmental, organizational, and psychosocial factors (Chari et al., 2018). Multiple different frameworks of well-being at work have been developed and implemented by governments, think tanks, professional associations, and scholars in recent years in an attempt to comprehensively capture the factors that influence our well-being at work and their impacts. Each of these frameworks offers a distinct approach, although there is clear overlap between the components that comprise workplace well-being identified in each approach. The distinctions present in the approaches considered centre on how different dimensions of well-being at work are conceptualized and also in the consideration of differing structures for grouping the elements which together impact our working lives.

One of the main divisions in how organizations approach well-being at work is whether they are proactive, that is, developing strategies and policies focused on enhancing worker well-being, or reactive in which the focus is primarily on taking action when worker well-being has already been compromised (e.g. sickness absence). Evidence has suggested that a considerable proportion of organizations, perhaps as many as three in five, are more reactive in their approach to well-being, and around half report that operational demands take precedence over employee well-being and that well-being is not seen as a priority by senior leaders (Suff and Miller, 2016, 17). However, reactive approaches and/or lesser support for workplace well-being ignore the substantial benefits that can be realized through embedding worker well-being throughout the organization. Evidence has shown benefits in the form of reduced sickness absence, associated cost savings, increased levels of job performance, enhanced recruitment and retention associated with reputation in the prior case and working conditions in the latter, and even potentially increased customer satisfaction (Kalleberg, 2011; Knox et al., 2011; Suff and Miller, 2016, 18; Wright and Huang, 2012).

It has been estimated that only around 9 per cent of the global workforce enjoys the benefits of some form of access to wellness or well-being programmes at work (Yeung and Johnston, 2016, 9). Poor-quality staff health and well-being has a significant cost implication for organizations, linked to sickness absence and lowered performance. For example, in the UK context, absence caused by sickness and injury in 2018 equated to around 141.4 million working days, representing around 4.4 days lost per worker. A significant portion of absences related to minor illnesses such as cold and flu (27 per cent of total absences). However, also prominent are absences associated with musculoskeletal problems (20 per cent), while approximately 12 per cent of working days lost, around 17.5 million working days, were the result of stress, anxiety or depression (Leaker and Nigg, 2019). The costs associated with poor-quality health and well-being have been estimated by the Centre for Mental Health at £34.9 billion in 2017, equating to approximately £1,300 for every employee in the UK economy (Parsonage and Saini, 2017). Costs have been similarly estimated to be significant to other economies. For example, the cost to the US economy has been estimated at around $2.2 trillion per year, equivalent to 12 per cent of GDP. This estimate comprises the costs of chronic disease ($1,100 billion), work-related injuries and illnesses ($250 billion), work-related stress ($300 billion), and employee disengagement ($550 billion) (Yeung and Johnston, 2016, 5). These reported costs associated with low-quality health and well-being to organizations and the economy more broadly highlight the potential value, not only in cost savings, but also in improved individual-level health and well-being, of giving adequate consideration and resource to enhancing workplace well-being.

MODELS OF WELL-BEING AT WORK

As noted at the beginning of the chapter, there exists an expansive range of models which attempt to capture the dimensions of well-being at work. Within this section a number of the most prominent models are considered from seminal contributions such as the Job Characteristics Model developed by Hackman and Oldham (1975, 1976) and the job demand-control model developed by Karasek (1979), to recent additions to the field such as the CIPD's Model of Job Quality.

The Job Characteristics Model

An early contribution to the literature on well-being at work, Hackman and Oldham's (1975, 1976) Job Characteristics Model is considered a seminal study. It identifies five core job characteristics which make work satisfying: (1) skill variety, which reflects the level to which a job requires the use of a range of skills; (2) task significance, which focuses on the impact the job has on others, both within and outside of the organization, and links to ideas of meaning and purpose in work; (3) task identity, which deals with how identifiable specific outcomes are from the job; (4) autonomy, referring to the level of choice and discretion available to an individual in their job; and (5) feedback from job, covering the extent to which a job provides a worker with information on their relative performance, although worthy of note here is that this characteristic refers to feedback from the completion of the job itself rather than from colleagues, managers or others.

The model argues that these five dimensions impact three psychological states of an individual, in turn influencing their motivation, performance and satisfaction with work, as well as absenteeism and turnover intention. The psychological states which form the causal core of the model are: (1) the knowledge of the results of the work; (2) experienced meaningfulness of the work; and (3) the experienced responsibility associated with the outcomes of the work (Hackman and Oldham, 1976, 255). The causal structure implies, as

Hackman and Oldham (1976, 55–6) state, 'that an individual experiences positive affect to the extent that he *learns* (knowledge results) that he personally (experienced responsibility) has performed well on a task that he cares about (experienced meaningfulness)'. The contribution from Hackman and Oldham is significant as it recognizes the centrality of the feelings, motivation and satisfaction of workers when designing jobs (Robertson and Cooper, 2011). It triggered a considerable shift in emphasis away from organizations focusing solely on performance and efficiency, and generated debates around the importance of well-being at work which have motivated significant progress in this field.

The Job Demand-Control Model

The job demand-control model (JD-C) was developed by Karasek (1979). Referred to as a 'stress-management' or 'balance' model of employee well-being (Bakker and Demerouti, 2007; Karasek, 1979), at the simplest level it proposes that job demands are balanced against levels of job control. Job demands are requirements of work that act as stressors including levels of effort, availability and time pressure, and level of difficulty. High job demands, in particular the presence of work overload and intense work routines, and low levels of job control, create job strain and in more extreme cases burnout. The impacts of job strain include incidence of job-related anxiety, health problems including cardiovascular illness, exhaustion and dissatisfaction with work. Discretion over the demands faced in a job is argued as enabling workers to cope with, or even avoid, experiencing job strain (Karasek, 1979, 287). The model further identifies job types which have different combinations of job demands and job control, with jobs exhibiting high levels of both termed 'active' and jobs with low levels of both termed 'passive', with the latter likely to result in greater dissatisfaction with work (Karasek, 1979, 288). This notation has been employed widely in the literature on job quality which is considered later in the chapter. Much existing research has supported the JD-C, with evidence clear on the presence of job strain as an outcome of job demands and the negative impacts this can have on worker well-being. Evidence on the buffering effect of job control is conflicting in some respects, though, and suggests that job control may only be able to offset the impacts of high job demands to a certain degree (see Bakker and Demerouti, 2007, for a discussion).

The Job Demands-Resources Model

A more recent contribution, the job demands-resources (JD-R) model, was developed by Bakker and Demerouti (2007). This model expands on the JD-C as it suggests that the work environment can be divided into two categories, job demands (JD) and job resources (JR). Job resources is broader in concept than the job control component of the JD-C. It refers to physical, psychological, social and organizational elements of a job that are functional to the achievement of work goals, reduce job demands and associated psychological and physiological costs, and/or stimulate personal growth, learning and development (Bakker and Demerouti, 2007, 312). Job resources incorporate job control as well as various other aspects, such as pay, career development opportunities, job security, positive relationships, skill, variety, task identity and significance, role clarity and feedback on performance. The model supposes two processes which impact worker well-being. The first is that poor job design and high job demands deplete the physical and mental resources of a worker. Meanwhile, the second process is motivational, as it is argued that job resources act to engender positive outcomes in the form of high work engagement (i.e. the worker finds work meaningful and invests effort in their job; Kahn, 1990), low cynicism, and good performance. These outcomes of workplace well-being are considered in more detail in Chapter 10. In contrast, where workers are subject to high levels of job demands and lower job resources it is likely to be reflected in negative well-being impacts which can act to limit the ability of a worker to achieve their goals. Similar to the job control component of the JD-C, it is argued that the presence of job resources, as well as certain personality resources, can have a mediating effect on the negative well-being impacts of job demands (Bakker and Demerouti, 2007).

The ASSET Model of Workplace Well-being

The ASSET Model of Workplace Well-being was developed by Sir Cary Cooper and colleagues (see Robertson and Cooper, 2011; Faragher et al., 2004). This model develops the original ASSET model (which stands for 'a shortened stress evaluation tool') with a specific focus on measuring stress and psychological well-being (PWB) at work. It is founded on the principle of well-being having three main components: (1) physical well-being, linked to exercise, sleeping and eating habits; (2) social well-being, which reflects the need for a positive and supportive social network; and (3) PWB (Robertson and Cooper, 2011, 3–4). Focusing on the PWB component primarily, the model shown in Figure 3.1 identifies six key workplace factors that influence workplace well-being.

The resources and communication factor identifies the role of access to resources and equipment needed to perform the required tasks of a job, and the effectiveness of communication within the organization to workplace well-being. Consistent with broader models of well-being, the model incorporates the presence of control and autonomy as an important factor in workplace well-being. The third factor acknowledges the role of workload and

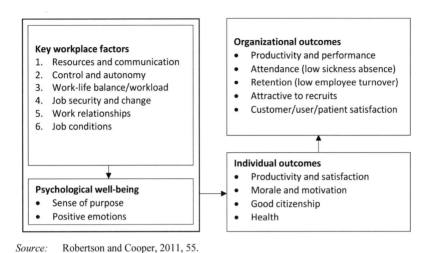

Source: Robertson and Cooper, 2011, 55.

Figure 3.1   The ASSET Model of Workplace Well-being

the ability to balance work with the rest of our lives, while the fourth centres on job security and change. Work relationships emphasizes the need for good working relationships with colleagues, leaders and other stakeholders. The final factor, job conditions, reflects the conditions of work encountered by an individual. Robertson and Cooper (2011, 79) also acknowledge the role of pay and benefits as an important driver of an individual engaging in paid work; however, it is not explicitly included in the model as it is argued that once a certain threshold is passed pay becomes largely unrelated to happiness at work (Robertson and Cooper, 2011, 79). This argument is supported by a wide array of existing evidence which has offered insight into the relevance, often, of relative levels of pay rather than overall pay (i.e. how much you earn in comparison to colleagues or those doing a different job) (Easterlin, 1974, 2001; Kahneman et al., 2006). Even then, the other workplace factors outlined in the model have a much greater relevance to PWB at work, as pay is not viewed as an integral aspect of a job (Robertson and Cooper, 2011, 79). The representation of the model usefully incorporates a set of both individual and organizational outcomes associated with positive PWB at work, evidencing the potential win–win that can be realized for workers and employers from giving well-being at work due consideration.

The focus on PWB in the model is defended through reference to the body of evidence on the positive links between PWB and job performance, including career success and physical health (Robertson and Cooper, 2011, 4–6). In addition, the model differentiates PWB from other concepts such as job satisfaction and motivation. It is argued that while these concepts may be linked, they are distinct. Job satisfaction, for example, may be high for an employee who is happy with their job; however, they may have poor relationships with colleagues that negatively impact the resources and communication factor of workplace well-being. Similarly, a worker may feel a high level of motivation to complete a task but is overloaded in their work which negatively impacts their work–life balance.

Practically, the ASSET is employed as an instrument to capture data indicating stress at work through responses to a number of statements divided into four questionnaires. Three questionnaires are used to 'assess perceptions of the sources of pressure and the outcomes of work stress' (Johnson and Cooper, 2003, 182), under the headings, 'Perceptions of your job', 'Attitudes toward your organization', and 'Your health'. The fourth questionnaire is used to capture biographical information. The perceptions of your job questionnaire includes a number of items on work relationships (e.g. my relationships with colleagues are poor), work–life balance (e.g. I work unsociable hours), overload (e.g. I do not have enough time to do my job as well as I would like), job security (e.g. my job skills may become redundant in the near future), control (e.g. I am not involved in decisions affecting my job), resources and communication (e.g. I do not have the proposed equipment and resources to do my job), pay and benefits (e.g. my pay and benefits are not as good as other people doing the same or similar work) and the job itself (e.g. my physical working conditions are unpleasant). Attitudes towards your organization focuses on commitment and includes items on perceived commitment of the employee to the organization (e.g. I am proud of this organization), and perceived commitment of the organization to the employee (e.g. I feel valued and trusted by the organization). These items use a 6-point scale from 'strongly disagree' to 'strongly agree'. The 'Your health' scale focuses on the occurrence of poor health symptoms. It is divided into psychological well-being (e.g. panic or anxiety attacks) and physical well-being (e.g. lack of appetite or over-eating) and uses a 4-point scale from 'not at all' to 'much more than usual'.

Subjective Well-being at Work Framework

With a focus on understanding the impacts of worker well-being on job performance, Bryson et al. (2014) developed a conceptual framework, shown in Figure 3.2, of the factors influencing subjective well-being at work. The model centres on a division between individual-level characteristics and characteristics of the job and workplace. The inclusion of personal characteristics is useful for contextualization of the wider environment which can influence our well-being. The framework gives direct reference to job characteristics including demands, levels of control, role clarity, security, pay and equity. In addition, it recognizes the role of relationships with co-workers, the structures in place within the organization in the form of HR practices, and the workplace environment in influencing well-being at work. The model proposes that due to personal characteristics being more rigid and difficult to change, at least in the short term, it is through alterations to job design and HR practices that we can achieve considerable benefits to the well-being of workers.

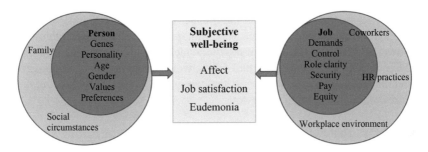

Source: Bryson et al., 2014.

Figure 3.2 Factors influencing SWB at work

New Economics Foundation Well-being at Work

Adopting the Dynamic Model of Well-being developed by the New Economics Foundation (NEF) (Thompson and Marks, 2008) outlined in Chapter 2, the well-being at work approach presented by the Centre for Well-being at NEF (see Jeffrey et al., 2014) is structured in four dimensions: (1) personal resources; (2) organizational system; (3) functioning at work; and (4) experience of work. Each of these broad dimensions includes several sub-dimensions. Personal resources includes health and vitality which reflect aspects of physical and mental health, including physical activity at work. This dimension also contains work–life balance including hours of work and flexible working. The organizational system dimension incorporates elements referred to as job design which include: fair pay; job security; environmental clarity, which relates to the sharing of information as well as well-defined career development processes; management systems, which include the provision and quality of feedback from leaders as well as the quality of organizational management; work environment, which reflects health and safety; and social value, which links to meaning derived from work and the wider social value associated with a job. Functioning at work includes skills and qualification match and opportunities for development, which is referred to as 'use of strengths and feeling a sense of progress', degree of autonomy, and work relationships, which include both social and professional aspects of relationships at work. Finally, experience of work is an outcome-focused dimension involving the presence of positive and negative feelings at work.

The well-being at work approach presented by Jeffrey et al. (2014) is a useful contribution which includes explicit reference to a number of different sub-dimensions that influence well-being at work. This approach explicitly acknowledges the links between the broader drivers and individual constituents that influence well-being at work, although there is a considerable level of overlap across some of the dimensions including, for example, aspects of career development and health and safety, which could render operationalization and monitoring of well-being strategy and synthesis of well-being data more complex under this framework.

CIPD Five Domains of Well-being

The CIPD developed a model for workplace health and well-being outlined in the report *Growing the Health and Well-Being Agenda: From First Steps to Full Potential*, published in 2016 (see Suff and Miller, 2016). With a focus on developing HR strategies and policies, this approach presents a model that separates well-being into five domains summarized in Figure 3.3: (1) health, (2) work, (3) values and principles, (4) collective/social, and (5) personal growth.

In the model, the health domain comprises both physical health and safety and mental health. The work domain includes a range of aspects of work which comprise both those focused on the nature of the job including autonomy and work demands (e.g. workload, working hours), as well as line management, change management and the work environment both in its physical form (i.e. workspace) and in terms of the promotion of an inclusive culture. Finally, this domain also includes aspects of pay and reward, focusing on fairness and transparency. Values and principles focuses on leadership, which includes the clarity of the mission and values provided by leaders of the organization, ethical standards such as corporate social responsibility and volunteering, and equality, diversity and inclusion. The collective/social domain includes employee voice and positive relationships both within teams and with management. Personal growth incorporates aspects of career development and lifelong learning, as well as emotional growth including resilience, and creativity which is focused on developing innovation.

Importantly, the model acknowledges the presence of overlap between domains and the sub-domains; for example, the quality of line management or culture within the organization. The CIPD argues that if we are to achieve a healthy workplace a fully integrated approach to workplace well-being in

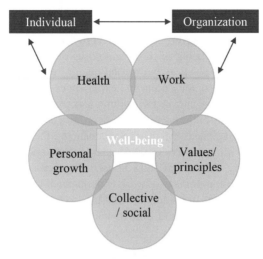

Source: Suff and Miller, 2016.

Figure 3.3   CIPD Five Domains of Well-being

which culture, leadership and people management are effectively addressed is essential. The model also emphasizes the interaction between the individual worker and the organization. The effectiveness of well-being policies and initiatives is dependent on the co-existence of these two parties. The primary limitation of this model is the breadth of the work dimension which includes a wide range of sub-dimensions that could have quite distinct impacts on experiences of work and render exploration and evaluation of this dimension complex.

Global Wellness Institute's Three Aspects of Wellness at Work

The Global Wellness Institute, based in Miami, Florida in the United States, developed a framework for wellness at work (Figure 3.4) founded on three key aspects: physical environmental aspects, personal aspects, and social & community aspects (see Yeung and Johnston, 2016, 29–35). The physical environment incorporates the physical spaces and places in which we work, whether that is an office, factory, on the move or at home, as well as the physical demands of our jobs from working with heavy machinery to working on visual displays. Enabling and enhancing wellness in this aspect of work includes health and safety considerations as well as environmental conditions of work including, for example, lighting, temperature and access to outdoor spaces. In addition, this aspect of work includes elements of workspace design including personal and private spaces, layout and equipment (e.g. standing or sitting desks), food options and on-site fitness facilities.

Personal aspects of work focus on the interdependence between our own well-being and our job performance. It acknowledges the impacts on our well-being and the well-being of those around us of the interaction between our wellness to work – physical and mental health, relationships with family and friends and our personality traits and experiences – and the working conditions we encounter – organizational culture, leadership styles, pay and other benefits. Improvements in this aspect of work require acknowledgement of the diversity of workforce needs. Methods for enhancing the personal aspects of work include addressing sources of work-related stress and work–life conflict including unhealthy cultures of long hours and intense working routines, aligning the intrinsic components of work with personal values and motivation through, for example, greater autonomy and involvement in decision-making, and supporting healthy eating and workers taking breaks and exercise.

Source: Yeung and Johnston, 2016.

Figure 3.4   Three Aspects of Wellness at Work

The final aspect of work – social & community – acknowledges the role of relationships with others to the quality of our working lives. It highlights the importance of positive relationships and friendships at work and beyond. It further emphasizes the role of leadership in creating a culture in which well-being of workers is given adequate status in regard to its role in the success of the organization, and where the organization is governed in a way that is fair and responsible, and can deliver some form of social benefit. This aspect of work also incorporates the notion of workers making a positive impact through their work including through voluntary activity at, and outside of, the workplace. The focus on physical and mental wellness is a particular strength of this model, as is the acknowledgement of the role of the physical work environment and our interaction with it, and of the impacts of our relationships with others.

NHS Workforce Health and Wellbeing Framework

The National Health Service in the UK developed its Workforce Health and Wellbeing Framework in 2018 (NHS, 2018). The framework, summarized in Figure 3.5, is structured so that enablers to well-being are prioritized, with preventative measures and self-management second, and finally targeted interventions (e.g. physiotherapy). Enablers at the organization level include leadership and structural and cultural building blocks which can enhance worker well-being. It is argued that in order to be successful it is important that health and well-being is embedded throughout the organization, from the vision and strategy of leadership to engagement with individual departments and workers. Also central is that leadership is accountable, clear reporting is in place and adequate resources are provided. Structures, in the form of policies and management processes act as key enablers, as do positive cultures around workload (e.g. taking breaks) and disclosure of health conditions.

The role of a healthy working environment is also explicitly identified in relation to both the physical infrastructure and facilities provided, and the enabling of healthy lifestyles through physical activity and diet. The framework is built on the premise that approaches to well-being should be evidence-based (data driven), and incorporate use of a diagnostic tool which can be used to benchmark and monitor progress of well-being strategies within organizations. Beyond the enablers and more preventative actions, the second tier of the model emphasizes health interventions (mental health, musculoskeletal and healthy lifestyles) which have a more reactive focus on reducing sickness absence and its associated costs.

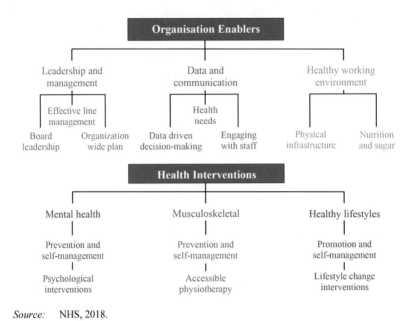

Source: NHS, 2018.

Figure 3.5   NHS Workforce Health and Wellbeing Framework

US NIOSH Framework for Worker Well-Being

The Framework for Worker Well-being was developed by Chari et al. (2018) on behalf of the National Institute for Occupational Safety and Health (NIOSH) in the USA through an extensive review of existing literature alongside consultation with an expert panel. The framework has five domains: (1) workplace physical environment and safety climate, which includes health and safety and the physical features of the workplace; (2) workplace policies and culture; (3) health status, which focuses on the physical and mental health of the individual; (4) work evaluation and experience which reflects on experienced quality of working lives; and (5) home, community and society, which acknowledge the external influences outside of work on our working lives (Chari et al., 2018).

Central to the approach adopted by Chari et al. (2018) is that the framework gives due consideration to both work and non-work aspects of life, as well as both subjective and objective domains of well-being. With respect to the former consideration, in this framework focus is given to workers rather than employees. This term was chosen in acknowledgement of the growing flexibility in the nature of paid work, and better captures the complex, and often blurred, boundaries between work and non-work aspects of our lives. In terms of the latter consideration, the framework provides a strong argument that it is essential to capture both subjective feelings regarding experiences of work, which are mainly incorporated into the work evaluation and experience domain of the framework, as well as more objective understanding of the extent to which basic living or working conditions are fulfilled which are captured across the remaining four dimensions.

What Works Centre for Wellbeing Workplace Well-being Themes

Drawing on a number of existing frameworks of well-being and well-being at work including PERMA, job quality and the functioning and flourishing of the Dynamic Model of Well-being employed by the European Social Survey, the What Works Centre for Wellbeing (2018) approach divides workplace well-being into five themes: (1) health; (2) security; (3) environment; (4) relationships; and (5) purpose. Within each of the themes, which are summarized in Figure 3.6, there are at least two sub-themes and from these sub-themes individual components that impact our well-being at work. As per the NEF structure (Jeffrey et al., 2014), this framework is useful in that it provides explicit reference to the wide range of sub-themes that influence well-being at work. It also gives weight to the content and quality of jobs, and the impact of relationships at work (under the security and relationships themes).

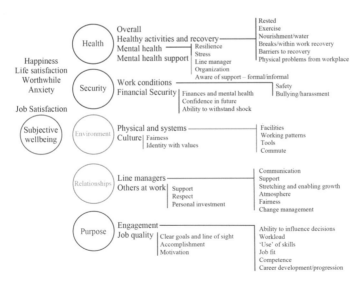

Source: What Works Well, 2018.

Figure 3.6   *Workplace well-being themes and constituent concepts*

The Effective Workplace Index

The Effective Workplace Index, developed by the Families and Work Institute (FWI) in the USA, offers a seven-dimension model for understanding what makes an effective workplace (see Pal et al., 2020). It draws on data from the National Study of the Changing Workforce (NSCW). The seven dimensions in the model and examples of items used in constructing the index are as follows: (1) job challenge and learning opportunities (e.g. *I get to do a number of different things in my job*); (2) supervisor support for job success (e.g. *My supervisor provides me with feedback that helps me to improve my performance*); (3) autonomy (e.g. *I have the freedom to decide what I do in my job*); (4) culture of respect, trust and belonging (e.g. *I can openly share my ideas and opinions with any level of management*); (5) work–life fit (e.g. *I have the schedule flexibility I need at work to manage my personal and family responsibilities*); (6) satisfaction with wages, benefits and opportunities to advance (e.g. *I am satisfied with how much I earn in my job*); and (7) co-worker support for job success (e.g. *I have the support from co-workers that I need to do a good job*). Each of the items within each dimension is measured using Likert-style scales. Notably, as with a number of other existing models, the dimensions used in constructing the Effective Workplace Index identify the importance of the intrinsic components of work including autonomy and challenge (1 and 3), extrinsic factors such as pay and benefits (6), flexibility and balance between work and the rest of our lives (5), and relationships with others (2, 4 and 7).

JOB QUALITY AND THE QUALITY OF WORKING LIVES

The literature on job quality differs to a degree in its focus to that of workplace well-being, although there is clear overlap and blurring between conceptualisations and models of well-being at work and job quality, rendering job quality a useful lens through which to understand the wide array of influences that work has on our well-being. As outlined in Chapter 1, across different disciplines we find differing definitions and conceptualizations of job quality, with alternative terminology including the quality of work(ing) lives, quality of work, quality of employment, and extending to concepts of 'meaningful', 'decent' and 'good' work (Coats and Lekhi, 2008; Eurofound, 2012, 2013a, 2013b; Green, 2006; ILO, 2013; Kalleberg, 2012; Martel and Dupuis, 2006). A useful concept to begin with that is broad in scope is that of the quality of work life proposed by Seashore (1975). The quality of work life comprises three separate dimensions: (1) employer; (2) employee; and (3) community. This concept suggests that the employer dimension is focused on the performance of the firm/organization which is measured relative to levels of productivity, production costs and quality of products/services. The employee dimension comprises income, health and safety, and the inherent satisfaction which is gained from engaging in paid work. Finally, community reflects on whether job roles are effective in their application; for example, if talent is underused this results in a loss to society. This definition of the quality of working life, however, is itself subject to continued debate with definitions varying within the existing academic literature (see Martel and Dupuis, 2006). The concept of job quality is somewhat distinct and can be defined as the extent to which a job exhibits characteristics which generate benefits for the employee, including both physical and psychological well-being (Green, 2006). Consistent in the understanding developed by these different approaches is that the quality of our working lives is influenced by the conditions of work we encounter and the impacts felt to our well-being (Felstead et al., 2019; Green, 2009).

Taxonomies of Job Quality by Job Types

A number of contributions to the job quality literature have provided useful insight into the types of jobs we encounter, and the factors which characterize them. For example, Holman (2013, 477–8) offered a fairly simple broad split between types of jobs: (1) low-quality 'low-commitment', and (2) high-quality 'high-commitment'. Under this structure low-quality jobs have a number of common characteristics including low levels of autonomy and control, lower skill/complexity, lack of employee-focused flexibility (i.e. flexibility that enables better work–life balance), low or uncertain pay and wider insecurity, and a lack of, or limited, opportunities for training and development. At the opposite end of the spectrum, high-quality jobs offer higher levels of autonomy, variety and skill/complexity, opportunities for flexible working, better pay and security, and good career prospects.

More detailed taxonomies of job types identify different components or dimensions that influence the quality of work we encounter and structure jobs into different groups. Karasek and Theorell (1990) identified four types of job which are determined by relative control over tasks and level of demands put onto the worker. Their taxonomy splits jobs into: (1) active jobs, (2) high-strain jobs, (3) passive jobs, and (4) low-strain jobs. Karasek and Theorell (1990) argue that active jobs, which are characterized by higher levels of autonomy, but also higher demands on workers, generate well-being benefits for employees associated with greater levels of control even in the incidence of demanding work roles and routines. Lesser presence of autonomy in demanding jobs, found in high-strain jobs, can result in significant occurrence of work stress. Job types (3) and (4) are more likely to generate low to moderate impacts on well-being at work as passive jobs offer low levels of autonomy,

58 *Well-being and the quality of working lives*

and place fewer demands on workers, and low-strain jobs provide higher levels of autonomy but similarly low demands.

Research by Holman (2013) extended the taxonomy of Karasek and Theorell (1990) using cluster analysis to group jobs into six types: (1) active jobs which are characterized by high levels of autonomy, social support, high complexity, high security, moderate pay and moderate workloads; (2) saturated jobs which are highly demanding, involve long hours and high pay; (3) team-based jobs which are high autonomy and high demand, have higher levels of job security, and involve frequent team-working; (4) passive-independent jobs which are less demanding, have lower levels of autonomy, and infrequent team-working; (5) insecure jobs which are characterized by being temporary, low demand and low pay; and (6) high-strain jobs which have low autonomy, but are very demanding. An alternative taxonomy of job quality, offered by Vidal (2013, 600), structures jobs into 18 types and three job quality groups, 'good jobs', 'decent jobs' and 'bad jobs'. In this case, good jobs are those which offer us at least some autonomy, relatively high wages and are secure, or may have lower levels of autonomy but afford relatively high wages, security and career enhancement opportunities including training and promotion (Vidal, 2013, 600). Relevant to our discussion in this chapter is that common among these taxonomies as indicators of higher quality work are autonomy, variety, flexibility, security and career development opportunities. Among these taxonomies of types of jobs, it is also worth acknowledging that even jobs which are higher quality overall can still contain negative characteristics such as highly demanding and intense working routines and work–family conflict (Kalleberg, 2012, 433).

Models of Job Quality

A number of different taxonomies and frameworks for organizing the dimensions of job quality have been developed, summarized in Table 3.1. Muñoz de Bustillo et al. (2011), for example, separate job quality into five dimensions within two broad categories, pay and amenities. Based around mainstream economic understanding of paid work acting as a source of disutility (i.e. an adverse or negative experience), this model gives pay a special function in job quality determination as it acts as the primary source of compensation. Amenities incorporates the other four dimensions comprising the intrinsic characteristics of work (skills, autonomy, powerfulness, meaningfulness, social support, self-fulfilment), terms of employment (contracts, development opportunities), health and safety (physical and mental), and work–life balance (work-time and intensity).

Many other structures include, or develop, core dimensions outlined within the Eurofound (2012, 2013a, 2013b) framework, namely (1) earnings, (2) job

Well-being and work 59

Table 3.1   Selected job quality models

Job quality dimensions	Source
1. Pay and fringe benefits (including flexible work time options and whether a job provides opportunities for increasing earnings over time) 2. Job security (terms of employment) 3. Control over tasks 4. Intrinsic rewards 5. Time at work	Kalleberg, 2011
1. Pay and benefits 2. Amenities, comprising: 2a. Intrinsic characteristics of work 2b. Terms of employment 2c. Health and safety 2d. Work–life balance	Muñoz de Bustillo et al., 2011
1. Earnings 2. Job prospects 3. Intrinsic dimensions 4. Quality of working time	Eurofound, 2012, 2013a, 2013b
1. Job prospects 2. Extrinsic dimensions 3. Intrinsic dimensions 4. Quality of working time	Connell and Burgess, 2016
1. Health and safety features of work 2. Ergonomic and ambient features of work 3. Accident rates 4. Employment contract 5. Job security 6. Autonomy 7. Working hours 8. Work intensity 9. Adequate and fair remuneration	Piasna et al., 2017

Job quality dimensions	Source
1. Pay and benefits	CIPD (see Warhurst et al., 2017; Wright et al., 2018)
2. Contracts	
3. Job design and the nature of work	
4. Work–life balance	
5. Relationships at work	
6. Voice and representation	
7. Health and well-being	
Job demands (JD) and job resources (JR):	Felstead et al., 2019
1. Work intensity (JD)	
2. Task discretion (JR)	
3. Worker voice (JR)	
4. Working time autonomy (JR)	
5. Work–life balance (JR)	
6. Managerial support (JR)	
7. Required learning (JD)	
8. Promotion prospects (JR)	
9. Job security (JD)	
10. Pay (JR)	

prospects, (3) intrinsic job quality, and (4) working time quality. Job prospect dimensions include levels of job security, opportunities for training and career development, and recognition received in our jobs (e.g. receiving praise for good work). Intrinsic characteristics are those that are determined by the nature of our work, including the skill/complexity involved in a job, levels of control and autonomy, variety, work intensity, and involvement in decision-making. Also included in this dimension are features of jobs related to working conditions including the physical work environment and health and safety. Working time quality includes the length of the working day/week and availability of flexible working arrangements. Connell and Burgess (2016) develop the Eurofound framework and structure job quality into four dimensions and separate explicitly the extrinsic and intrinsic components of job quality, with the former incorporating income as well as other factors such as work environment. Their dimensions comprise (1) job prospects, (2) extrinsic job quality, (3) intrinsic job quality, and (4) working time quality.

Other taxonomies have opted to extend the frameworks offered by Eurofound, Muñoz de Bustillo et al. (2011) and others, including the CIPD Model of Job Quality which divides job quality into six dimensions. This model is represented in Figure 3.7 and was developed through an extensive literature review of existing conceptualizations and approaches to job quality. It recognizes that individual experiences of work are shaped by worker demographic and socio-economic characteristics, and acknowledges the individual, organizational and societal factors that influence, and are outcomes of, job quality. The CIPD model was subsequently developed into the CIPD Job Quality Index which extends this taxonomy even further into seven dimensions with relationships at work separated out into the seventh dimension (see Warhurst et al., 2017; Figure 3.7). A more recent contribution from Felstead et al. (2019) is structured around the JD-R model outlined earlier in the chapter and divides ten dimensions of job quality into two broad groupings, job demands (three dimensions) and job resources (seven dimensions). Dimensions reflecting job demands are those which relate to pressures encountered in paid work, including the intensity of work and job security. Job resources dimensions are those which enable the achievement of work goals, mediate job demands (and associated well-being costs) and/or promote personal growth, learning and development, including levels of task discretion, work–life balance and promotion prospects.

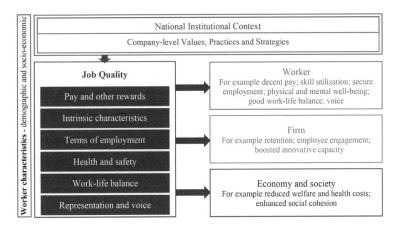

Source: Warhurst et al., 2017, 29.

Figure 3.7   CIPD Model of Job Quality

A further example is the International Labour Organization (ILO) indicators of decent work. This incorporates measures which account for economic context and structural factors which could result in income inequality or lower labour productivity, similar to the macro/national institutional context present in the Eurofound and CIPD models (ILO, 2013). The ILO defines decent work as that which adequately incorporates fundamental rights at work and international labour standards; job and income opportunities; policies and processes which reduce poverty and vulnerability (social protection) and social security; and social dialogue and tripartism (i.e. cooperation between employers, employee representatives such as trade unions and government). Meanwhile, the concept of 'good work' developed by The Work Foundation (see Coats and Lekhi, 2008) concentrates on the aspects of jobs which create a positive work experience. It notes the importance of status and income, as well as seven other aspects of work: (1) job security; (2) variety in work (i.e. non-repetitive/monotonous); (3) levels of control and autonomy; (4) balance between worker effort and rewards (pay and other benefits, recognition); (5) worker skill level relative to job demands; (6) fairness in processes and structures used to resolve disputes and allocate resources (procedural justice); and (7) positive relationships at work which create and maintain social capital. It is argued that these features have benefits for both employees, through health and well-being benefits, and for employers through enhanced productivity.

Debates remain present, however, over the effectiveness of certain measures of job quality. Consistent with broader measurement of well-being at work (as noted in Chapter 1), there is disagreement over the use of objective (e.g. pay) versus subjective (e.g. satisfaction with job) indicators of job quality. For example, Felstead et al. (2019) have argued that subjective measures are limited as they can be affected by the amount of available information and individual-level differences in preferences and aspirations. Difficulties in objectively capturing some aspects of jobs such as levels of autonomy or work intensity, however, render purely objective methods challenging to realize (Wright et al., 2018). When used in combination with objective indicators, subjective measures have been shown to enable considerable insight into the perceptions of workers regarding the quality of their job. Subjective measures have been widely employed in research including Gifford (2018), Green (2009), and Connell and Burgess (2016). In addition, measures of overall job satisfaction have been recommended by the UK government (see HM Government, 2018, 22).

Some attempts have also been made to provide an overall score for job quality (see Piasna, 2017 and, for a discussion, Felstead et al., 2019). However, developing an effective overall measure of job quality using a composite indicator is difficult, as decisions over specific weightings given to individual component elements could result in these components having too great or little an influence on an overall job quality measure. In addition, there is a risk of misleading averaging out occurring where differences in high or low component elements are hidden by wider averages presented in the scoring of broader dimensions. For example, an individual could have a job which offers high levels of autonomy and variety but is low paid and insecure. A single overall measure would not show these subtleties and while perhaps correctly presenting the job as one of middling overall quality, this would limit our understanding of the good and bad dimensions of the job. These problems, therefore, act to limit the usefulness of overall score measures of job quality, and it is increasingly acknowledged that a more granular approach is more effective in understanding and monitoring job quality.

While overall measures of job quality are problematic, the strength of the understanding developed by contributions to the job quality literature, and that of other related concepts, is in structuring in detail the distinct, but interconnected, components of jobs which together influence our overall experiences of paid work. The models and frameworks developed complement and enhance the workplace well-being frameworks outlined in this chapter and have been used to inform the development of a new framework for workplace well-being.

A FRAMEWORK FOR WORKPLACE WELL-BEING

This section outlines a new framework for well-being at work that puts well-being firmly at the centre of a successful workplace. The framework captures the interdependencies between the dimensions of work that comprise workplace well-being. It synthesizes the strengths and common components of the existing approaches explored in this chapter, to provide an innovative and comprehensive framework which captures the dimensions of workplace well-being. The framework is formed around three strategic elements – structure, culture and environment – that guide understanding of well-being at work. Six dimensions of workplace well-being form the key operational framework and within each of the six well-being dimensions there are constituent sub-dimensions.

The strategic elements of the framework are presented in Figure 3.8. The structure element involves the development of policies, guidance and legal frameworks, including those relating to career development, job security (including contracts), work routines and work–life balance, and extends to policies around occupational health and safety. The structure element is, by its nature, closely linked with leadership and human resource management within organizations. It is informed by the 'leadership and management' and 'data and communication' organization enablers of the NHS model (NHS, 2018), and the HR practices outlined in the framework by Bryson et al. (2014). It is also informed by the job quality literature including, for example, terms of employment and more formal mechanisms for work–life balance including policies around flexible working arrangements, as outlined in the CIPD model (Warhurst et al., 2017).

The culture element refers to the norms, values and behaviours of individuals, including leaders, and the organization. It influences our experiences of work including a number of the identified constituents of job quality such as workloads, discretion over tasks, meaning derived from work, and our relation-

Figure 3.8   Strategic elements of the workplace well-being framework

ships with others including experiences of conflict. This element of workplace well-being is identified in a number of existing models and frameworks but does not always take the central role it should as one of the major influences on our experiences of work. It is present in the values/principles dimension of the CIPD model (Suff and Miller, 2016) and forms an underlying element of the NHS Workforce Health and Wellbeing Framework (NHS, 2018). In other models it is combined with policies (e.g. in the US NIOSH model; Chari et al., 2018), or is included within the environment dimension (e.g. in the well-being themes presented by the What Works Centre for Wellbeing (What Works Well, 2018) and in the model by Bryson et al. (2014).

Finally, evident in the existing contributions to workplace well-being is that the environment we create and experience is fundamental to well-being at work. The environment element is incorporated into all of the models which have been considered in this chapter in some form, in reference, for example, to the workplace physical environment (Chari et al., 2018) or healthy working environment (NHS, 2018), and is included in the CIPD 'Work' dimension (Suff and Miller, 2016). It refers to both the physical and psychological work environment. The physical environment comprises the workspaces and places in which we work, as well as how we interact, and are active, within them. It includes health and safety, facilities and infrastructure, and aspects of physical comfort and activity. The psychological environment, meanwhile, is closely linked to the other strategic elements through the cultures that influence how we work and the structures that govern our working routines.

Figure 3.9 presents the full framework with the inclusion of the six dimensions of workplace well-being: (1) job properties, (2) flexibility, (3) rewarding careers, (4) relationships, (5) giving, and (6) physical space and activity. Each of the strategic elements is more closely related to certain dimensions; however, clear intersection is present between the strategic elements and dimensions, and the representation of the model acknowledges that each of the strategic elements has some reach into every dimension of workplace well-being. It should also be noted that equality, diversity and inclusion (ED&I) falls across all six dimensions. In this context, diversity can be seen as recognizing and effectively valuing individual, social and cultural difference within the workplace, while inclusion refers to provision of an environment in which we feel valued and included, and which enables participation. ED&I is not represented by its own dimension or as a sub-dimension within one of the six dimensions of workplace well-being but is instead an underlying component of all dimensions within the model.

Figure 3.9   *The framework for workplace well-being*

The process of synthesizing existing models and interconnections between the themes of the existing models and the six well-being dimensions is visualised in Figure 3.10. The job properties dimension of the framework reflects the nature and design of jobs and is informed heavily by Hackman and Oldham's (1976) Job Characteristics Model, the JD-C, JD-R, and existing models of job quality, incorporating the different intrinsic constituents which make up our jobs and how we engage with them, including autonomy, variety and meaning. Flexibility and work–life balance are incorporated into many models of workplace well-being including amongst others the ASSET Model of Workplace Well-being (Robertson and Cooper, 2011), the Well-being at Work approach presented by the Centre for Well-being at NEF (Jeffrey et al., 2014), and are present in much of the literature on job quality. The flexibility dimension is focused around the flexibility present in work including flexible working (either formal or formal), the hours we work and how and when we take breaks from our work tasks. It also acknowledges the role of mobility in work including the commute and other work-related travel (e.g. business travel). Rewarding careers captures the extrinsic characteristics of our jobs, sometimes referred to as hygiene factors (see Chapter 4 for a discussion of intrinsic and extrinsic job characteristics). These include the contracts governing our jobs and job security, the pay and other benefits we receive from our work, opportunities for training and career development, the match between the skills and qualifications we have and use in our jobs, and recognition received both qualitatively (i.e. praise for good work) and through enhanced pay and opportunities. Elements of this dimension are present in the JD-R, ASSET, CIPD Five Domains of Well-being and other frameworks considered in this chapter as well as the job quality literature. All three of the dimensions outlined so far are heavily focused on the job itself and are a product, in particular, of the culture and structure strategic elements.

Relationships reflects the role of effective leadership within the organization, professional relationships and experiences of conflict at work, and extends to social relationships encountered in our working lives. The dimension has been informed by the broader well-being models explored in Chapter 2, as well as the CIPD's Five Domains of Well-being (Suff and Miller, 2016) and the Global Wellness Institute's model amongst others. Giving is arguably given lesser significance in many existing models, and is informed in particular by the Five Ways to Well-being (Aked et al, 2008) outlined in Chapter 2, as well as the CIPD Five Domains of Well-being, Global Wellness Institute's Three Aspects of Wellness at Work, and the Effective Workplace Index. It centres on the different ways in which we can give in our jobs and the mechanisms which enable this, including through formal and informal volunteering, social support, and mentoring. Finally, the physical space and activity we engage in during our working lives, which are most heavily influenced by the

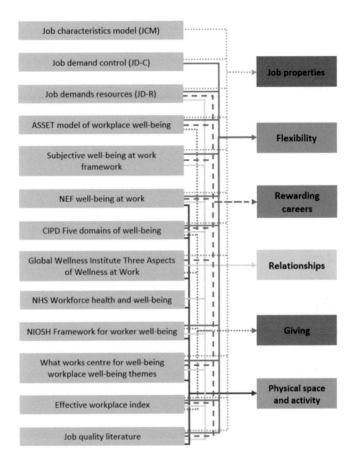

Figure 3.10   Mapping well-being models to the dimensions of the framework for workplace well-being

environment in which we work, forms the final dimension of the framework for workplace well-being. Physical space includes the facilities and equipment we use in our work, as well as the health and safety factors involved in their use, while the physical activity component focuses on our activity levels at work and its impacts on our lifestyles. This final dimension is informed by, amongst others, the NHS (2018), NIOSH Framework for Worker Well-being (Chari et al., 2018), and the Five Ways to Well-being.

Within each of the dimensions of workplace well-being we can usefully identify sub-dimensions which are presented in Figure 3.11. The presentation of the sub-dimensions in this manner has been informed by the What Works

Centre for Wellbeing (What Works Well, 2018) approach, in order to provide an explicit reference point to the wide range of constituents of workplace well-being in a more visual format. The additional detail in the lower level representation of the framework is particularly useful for guiding the implementation of well-being strategy and policy within organizations, and attaching the benchmarking and measurement of outcomes using action plans or toolkits against each of the well-being dimensions including, for example, the development of key performance indicators (KPIs). This is returned to in Chapter 10 in reference to linking the dimensions and outcomes of workplace well-being.

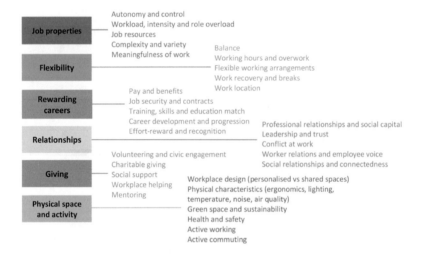

Figure 3.11   Sub-dimensions of the workplace well-being framework

The workplace well-being framework provides a comprehensive framework for well-being at work. It provides a structure for researching well-being at work and for the development of strategy, measurement and monitoring of well-being in the work sphere. The strategic elements of the framework inform the strategic approach to well-being within organizations, while the six dimensions of workplace well-being guide the design and operationalization of wellness programmes, and the sub-dimensions further facilitate implementation, benchmarking and monitoring of workplace well-being. The framework provides a conceptual foundation for understanding workplace well-being and enables effective management of well-being at the organizational level, offering the potential to enhance worker well-being for the benefit of individuals, organizations and society.

CHAPTER SUMMARY

This chapter has considered the expansive range of frameworks and models of well-being at work and job quality, using these to inform the development of a new framework for workplace well-being. The chapter has reflected on models of well-being at work put forward by academics, government, independent research institutes and professional associations including the New Economics Foundation, UK National Health Service, Global Wellness Institute, CIPD, US NIOSH and others. It has also drawn on the job quality literature as a lens through which to develop the new framework. The strengths and common components of existing approaches and contributions have been synthesized to develop an innovative and comprehensive framework that captures the dimensions of workplace well-being. The framework proposes that well-being should be firmly placed at the centre of a successful workplace. It is founded on three strategic elements: (1) a culture that promotes well-being, (2) structures which enable well-being, and (3) an environment which supports well-being. The strategic elements guide the full framework which is structured into six dimensions: (1) job properties, (2) flexibility, (3) rewarding careers, (4) giving, (5) relationships, and (6) physical space and activity. Each of these dimensions, in turn, contains a series of sub-dimensions which together provide a basis for more complete understanding and application of the framework. In the subsequent chapters of the book, each of the six dimensions outlined in the framework for workplace well-being are explored in detail including deeper conceptualisation, evidence, and methods of measuring each dimension and its constituent sub-dimensions.

PART II

The dimensions of workplace well-being

4. Job properties

INTRODUCTION

This first chapter exploring the dimensions of workplace well-being focuses on job properties. The job properties dimension is developed from existing models of well-being at work and job quality and considers the nature and content of work that we undertake. The nature of work refers to the different components which collectively make up a job (Hertzberg et al., 1959; Kalleberg, 2011). As such, the discussion in this chapter has particular relevance to job design. The components considered comprise many of the intrinsic factors which together form a job, from the levels of complexity and variety of tasks involved in a job (Holman, 2013; Leach et al., 2010), to levels of control and autonomy (Wheatley, 2017b), the meaning and sense of purpose we derive from our work (Robertson and Cooper, 2011), the intensity at which we work (Green, 2001, 2006), and finally the resources we have available to us where we draw on the approach adopted by Rousseau and Aubé (2010). The existing evidence base is indicative of the properties of a job having a number of important relationships with well-being at work (Edgell, 2012; Green, 2006; Greenhaus et al., 2012; Holman, 2013; Kalleberg, 2012; Wheatley, 2017b). This chapter draws on the existing international evidence base as well as presenting data from the UK Working Lives Survey and the European Social Survey, to explore these relationships. It begins with a discussion of the distinction between intrinsic and extrinsic characteristics of work before exploring the range of intrinsic components of jobs. The chapter reflects on the interconnectedness of different job properties and their impacts, evidencing the relevance of the content of work, and in turn design of jobs, to workplace well-being.

INTRINSIC VERSUS EXTRINSIC CHARACTERISTICS OF WORK

A key distinction often employed in categorizing and analysing the characteristics of work is between the intrinsic and the extrinsic. This duality was developed by Herzberg et al. (1959) in the Two Factor Theory model which focuses on work motivation. Within this approach, intrinsic characteristics (termed 'motivators') are the inherent qualities contained within a job and associated with the nature of work. They include levels of control and autonomy, skill and complexity, variety and workloads. Extrinsic characteristics, meanwhile, refer to elements of jobs which operate outside of the job itself (Herzberg et al., 1959, cited in Morgan et al., 2013, 804). Extrinsic characteristics are also referred to as 'the external work environment' or 'hygiene factors', and include pay and other benefits, job security and opportunities for progression and development. Kalleberg summarizes this distinction succinctly:

> Intrinsic rewards are benefits and utilities that people obtain *from* task performance, as opposed to extrinsic rewards such as money or fringe benefits, which people obtain *for* performing their work. (Kalleberg, 2011, 7)

Other contributions have offered differing terminology for this duality, although all evidence a consistent understanding. For example, Handel (2005) refers to material (extrinsic) and non-material (intrinsic) dimensions of work. In work commissioned by the Chartered Institute of Personnel and Development (CIPD), although considering a slightly different division relating to the quality of work, reference is made to the difference between 'objective' (extrinsic) and 'subjective' (intrinsic) characteristics of work (Warhurst et al., 2017, 19). A further way of conceptualizing this duality is that it distinguishes between aspects of work which generate meaning, and those which represent forms of compensation (Morgan et al., 2013).

The intrinsic–extrinsic division is useful for understanding our motivation to work, as per Herzberg et al.'s (1959) terminology, and the relationship between motivation and reward from work is discussed in detail in Chapter 6. Reflecting on the usefulness of the intrinsic–extrinsic duality for our broader understanding of the quality of working lives, it has been argued that intrinsic characteristics of work may have a more important role in generating satisfaction with work and maintaining employee well-being (Connell and Burgess, 2016; Herzberg, 1959). Indeed, despite rhetoric in some spheres suggesting workers have become more instrumental towards work, focusing on pay and other benefits, evidence continues to show that the intrinsic components of a job remain highly valued by workers (Gallie et al., 2012, 811). In contrast, the presence of 'good' extrinsic characteristics does not necessarily enhance satisfaction, but rather is argued as driving an absence of dissatisfaction with work, consistent with original terminology applied to these characteristics as hygiene factors (Herzberg, 1959). The evidence base does not unfailingly support this argument, though, as both extrinsic and intrinsic factors have been shown in existing research to be important determinants of job satisfaction (Morgan et al., 2013). In the workplace well-being framework outlined in this book, intrinsic characteristics are predominantly contained in the job properties dimension explored in this chapter, whereas extrinsic characteristics

Job properties 73

predominantly form elements of the rewarding careers dimension discussed in Chapter 6.

AUTONOMY AND CONTROL

Autonomy is undoubtedly an important component of well-being. It is identified in many of the models of well-being considered in Chapter 2, including in Ryff's psychological well-being (Ryff, 1982, 1989) and the Dynamic Model of Well-being (Thompson and Marks, 2008). Existing models of well-being at work similarly identify autonomy as a significant intrinsic component of job quality and well-being, as outlined in Chapter 3. As such, autonomy is included as a central factor in the job properties dimension of workplace well-being. Autonomy in the context of work refers to the freedom, control and independence workers have over decisions within a job (Fielding, 1990; Hackman and Oldham, 1976). It is alternatively referred to as discretion or control. It involves both the role of workers in determining the tasks they perform in their job, the level of control over how these tasks are completed, and the order in which they are completed (Braverman, 1974; Thompson and Smith, 2010). Within the existing literature, autonomy has been broadly categorized into two forms: 'job control' and 'schedule control'. In this dichotomy, job control reflects levels of autonomy over tasks and work conduct (Karasek, 1979, 289). Schedule control, in contrast, is the control we have over the timing and location of paid work, and may have particular relevance to flexibility experienced in work and work–life balance (Glavin and Schieman, 2012, 75; Jang et al., 2011, 136), which are the focus of the flexibility dimension of workplace well-being covered in Chapter 5. Returning to job control, it can, in turn, be considered as comprising two elements: (1) skill discretion which refers to decision-making over the use of specific skills in work and (2) decision-making authority which refers to the ability of an employee to make work-related decisions including over method and timing of work (Häusser et al., 2010).

Job control can usefully be understood with reference to the concept of job crafting. Job crafting considers 'the actions employees take to shape, mould, and redefine their jobs' (Wrzesniewski and Dutton, 2001, 180). It focuses on the notion that workers will take the opportunity and be motivated to craft their jobs to create work with which they are more satisfied (Brewster and Holland, 2021). It is often conceptualised as a worker response to poor working conditions, as a method of mediating low quality aspects of their work (although it need not be only applied or seen in this light). Workers engage in job crafting in order that they can apply some level of control over their job to avoid work feeling like an alien activity, help to engender a positive self-image, and to fulfil a basic human need for belonging and social connectedness (see Chapter

7). Job crafting enables workers to change job task boundaries (i.e. the type and number of job tasks); cognitive task boundaries (i.e. viewing the job as a whole or as discrete tasks); and relational boundaries of work (i.e. altering those we interact with and the nature of interactions with others at work) (Wrzesniewski and Dutton, 2001, 185) (Box 4.1). This, it should be acknowledged, occurs within limits set by employers related to performance and output. Existing evidence, nevertheless, indicates that job crafting is associated with higher levels of work engagement (Petrou et al., 2012; Van Wingerden et al., 2017, cited in Brewster and Holland, 2021) and improved job performance (Leana et al., 2009). This is consistent with workers deriving greater satisfaction from their work when they are allowed input in the design of their jobs (Bakker and Demerouti, 2007).

BOX 4.1 MEASUREMENT OF AUTONOMY AND CONTROL

Levels of autonomy are often captured empirically through subjective measurement of control over tasks and conduct in work (Jeffrey et al., 2014). Questions tend to focus on the levels of autonomy we experience 'usually' or 'in the last three months'. Many social surveys include fairly consistent lines of questioning on levels of autonomous experience, with the UK Understanding Society longitudinal survey and CIPD's UK Working Lives Survey, for example, both including lines of questioning taking the following form (exact question wording taken from Understanding Society):

In your current job, how much influence do you have over ...
What tasks you do in your job?
The pace at which you work?
The order in which you carry out tasks?
The time you start or finish your working day?

Answer options are given as follows:

1	2	3	4
A lot	Some	A little	None

An alternative approach to capturing autonomy was developed by Breagh (1999). It disaggregates autonomy into three forms, method autonomy which is consistent with the aforementioned job control, scheduling autonomy (i.e. schedule control), and a third component criteria autonomy which reflects the level of input into how job performance is evaluated. These forms of autonomy are captured using nine items as follows:

Method Autonomy
1. I am allowed to decide how to go about getting my job done (the methods to use).
2. I am able to choose the way to go about my job (the procedures to utilize).
3. I am free to choose the method(s) to use in carrying out my work.

Scheduling Autonomy
1. I have control over the scheduling of my work.
2. I have some control over the sequencing of my work activities (when I do what).
3. My job is such that I can decide when to do particular work activities.

Criteria Autonomy
1. My job allows me to modify the normal way we are evaluated so that I can emphasize some aspects of my job and play down others.
2. I am able to modify what my job objectives are (what I am supposed to accomplish).
3. I have some control over what I am supposed to accomplish (what my supervisor sees as my job objectives).

The quality of our working lives is influenced considerably by the control we have over our work. It enables us to be creative and develop skills (Gallie, 2007, 212) and evidence how capable we are at our jobs (Jeffrey et al., 2014). Existing evidence identifies autonomy as reducing levels of work-related stress and work–family conflict (Grönlund, 2007; Kalleberg et al., 2009) through enabling greater levels of control over the content, timing and location of work. A large body of research supports these observations. Undertaking a systematic literature review of 259 research articles, Humphrey et al. (2007) identified that greater levels of perceived job control generate improved job satisfaction, organizational commitment (Box 4.2), intrinsic motivation and job performance among employees. The classic study of workers in the USA by Hackman and Oldham (1976) found moderate to strong positive relationships between autonomy and general satisfaction levels. Other US research by Ducharme and Martin (2000, 234), analysing the US National Employee Survey, reported that the strongest predictor of lower job satisfaction is lower levels of job control. Batt and Valcour (2003, 212), also drawing on US data from service sector workers, found that job design which affords higher degrees of job control increases employee perceptions of control and their ability to negotiate work–family conflict. Consistent with this latter finding, evidence from the US National Study of the Changing Workforce revealed greater perceived job control to be associated with higher reported job, family and life satisfaction (Thompson and Prottas, 2006, 107). Osnowitz and Henson

(2016, 348) identify benefits of non-standard employment for levels of autonomy, using data for workers in the USA. Fixed-term contract employment may provide greater schedule control, including enabling workers to avoid unpaid overtime and long hours of work.

BOX 4.2   ORGANIZATIONAL COMMITMENT

Organizational commitment refers to the relative level of psychological attachment a worker has to their organization, reflecting the strength of identification with, and involvement in, the organization (Mowday et al., 1979). It results in workers having a strong belief in the goals and values of the organization; a willingness to put considerable effort into their work; and a desire to remain part of the organization thus reducing the likelihood of them leaving. Organizational commitment takes multiple forms. The three-component model (TCM) developed by Meyer and Allen (see Meyer and Allen, 1991, 1997) recognizes affective commitment (AC) (i.e. emotional attachment and desire to stay with the organization); normative commitment (NC) (i.e. the sense of obligation to stay with the organization) and continuance commitment (CC) (i.e. awareness of the costs involved in leaving the organization). While AC is identified as having the greatest impact on relative levels of performance, it has been argued that the three components of the TCM should be viewed as components in a commitment profile which can all be experienced by workers to varying degrees (Meyer et al., 2012). Profiles can exhibit a dominance in different components; for example, an AC-dominant profile is likely to result in the highest levels of retention and job performance, whereas workers with a CC-dominant profile will be more likely to stay with their organization than uncommitted employees, but may not perform to any greater level. Organizational commitment is influenced by a wide range of factors that can be broadly grouped into personal characteristics: demographic (e.g. age, gender) and personality (e.g. work values, expectations) factors, and organizational characteristics which reflect experiences of work. With regard to the latter, the intrinsic rewards derived from work that are the focus of this chapter have long been argued as generating greater levels of organizational commitment than extrinsic rewards (Mottaz, 1988).

Evidence from other countries offers a number of consistent findings, as well as additional insights. Research by Boxall and Macky (2014), using survey data from New Zealand, found that working practices which enable greater job control, referred to as high-involvement work practices, generate a range of benefits including higher levels of job satisfaction and reductions in fatigue, work-related stress and negative work/non-work spillover. Cheng et al. (2014) use longitudinal data from Finland for three years (2008, 2009 and 2010) to explore employee well-being at work measured with reference to job satisfaction and work vigour (i.e. high energy levels and mental resilience). They show that job control can offset the effects of job insecurity and promote work vigour even over extended periods of time. Evidence from employees in South Korea, reported in Jang et al. (2011), provides further support to the suggested benefits to job satisfaction of schedule control in reducing work–life conflict. Lyness et al. (2012, 19–20), analysing data from 21 countries, found benefits to both job satisfaction and organizational commitment from greater levels of schedule control. Benefits were found to be particularly strong for women in reducing work–family conflict. They also found that while women more often use schedule control, access to it may be more common among men due to occupation-level differences in availability (Lyness et al., 2012). Van Miero et al. (2006, 295), meanwhile, show that benefits go beyond the individual. Reporting on the results of a survey of individual and team autonomy (i.e. autonomy at the level of a team) in healthcare teams in the Netherlands, they found evidence that greater team job control can provide individual-level benefits to well-being through improved task design. Finally, using a sample of over 400 medical professionals in Italy, Galletta et al. (2011, 13) investigated the relationship between job control, motivation and organizational commitment. Greater levels of job control were found to create positive feelings and attitudes among employees, while generating benefits for employers through enhanced employee retention.

Although considerable potential and realized benefits are outlined in the existing evidence base, autonomy and control over paid work does not always equate to good job quality and higher levels of well-being at work. While not directly a negative consequence of greater levels of autonomy, in some cases autonomy may be traded-off with other characteristics in jobs. In addition, although evidence remains conflicting, some indication has been found of potential negative impacts being felt where too much autonomy is present in a job. An 'asymmetric curvilinear relationship' has been suggested which refers to the idea that low levels of job control generate dissatisfaction, while well-being is derived from higher levels of autonomy and control, but that there is a diminishing benefit and even potentially detrimental effects felt at the highest levels (Robertson and Cooper, 2011; Warr, 2007). Jobs with higher degrees of autonomy can contain characteristics of lower job quality including long hours and/or intense working patterns and lower levels of job security (Gallie et al., 2014, 216; Kalleberg, 2012, 433; Wheatley, 2021). Indeed, some developments in paid work that have increased flexibility and autonomy, including technological change enabling 24/7 work routines from any location, do have potential adverse effects through increasing blurring of the separation between work life and home life, and potential for overwork and associated incidence of work-related stress, potentially offsetting well-being benefits (Boxall and Macky, 2014). Further, research into working routines among self-employed internet-based workers reported incidence of low job satisfaction even where job and schedule control is high. Non-standard routines of work can create conflict with social norms around work-time and location, reflecting the influence on job satisfaction of social expectations around work (Lee and Lin, 2011, 464).

Notwithstanding the potential of a curvilinear relationship rendering less than positive outcomes at the highest levels of autonomy, the primary problem associated with autonomy remains the reduction of autonomy by employers, which has been widely shown to have negative impacts. A trend has been observed of employers providing an appearance of control to employees, but at the same time imposing more rigid monitoring and sub-division of tasks (Brannen, 2005). The degree of control over the nature and timing of tasks may have actually declined for many employees (Eustace, 2012; Green, 2006). Evidence from call centre employees in Scotland offers an example. Findings from research which considered the impact of speech appropriation of workers, reported in Eustace (2012), evidences that measures aimed at reducing discretion offered few benefits to customer interactions, but caused indirect discrimination against workers whose accent or dialect left them feeling insecure or subordinate. Also exploring the impacts of discretion measures in call centres, Sallaz (2015), drawing on evidence collected from a call centre in the USA, found that measures employed can offer relatively high degrees of job control in some respects, but these are ineffective where they are within structures which subject employees to rigid targets such as average call handling times, steep learning curves, and limited real incentives. Turning to professional occupations, Ogbonna and Harris (2004, 1198), investigating a sample of workers within UK Higher Education, reported greater work-related stress, reduced interactions between colleagues, and an intensification of work as a product of the introduction of performance-related remuneration systems. US research, reported in Glavin (2013), similarly showed that loss of control, whether actual or perceived, can act as a chronic work-stressor, and that this may be particularly prominent in older workers. While changes in labour market occupational structures may have increased levels of control and autonomy, this varies considerably between organizations and sectors and may be traded-off against intense working routines that impact relative well-being at work (Messenger, 2011, 302; see also Green, 2006).

Autonomy and control, although more often found to higher degrees in managerial and professional occupations (Wheatley, 2017b), can be offered to some degree at all levels of an organization and in all types of jobs (Box

Job properties 79

4.3). The nature and volume of the potential autonomy and control that can be offered differs of course, but it is nevertheless possible and highly beneficial to both worker and employer. Empowering workers in this way can offer a range of benefits to motivation, providing an enhanced feeling of meaning and worthwhileness from our work. While the provision of greater levels of control may appear more straightforward in highly skilled roles or those involving higher degrees of cognitive function, employers can implement measures to enhance levels of control in the majority of jobs. Employers may fear shifting control to the worker, and the loss of direct control over labour that this necessitates. However, the risks can be more than offset by the evidenced benefits to productivity and performance from enhanced satisfaction and motivation.

BOX 4.3   PATTERNS OF AUTONOMY AND CONTROL

A number of social surveys include items on autonomy and control that provide useful insight into relative levels of autonomy and its relationship with well-being. For example, the European Social Survey (ESS) has included in several waves a series of items which offer useful subjective insight into a number of job property sub-dimensions (ESS, 2010, 2018). The ESS either annually or periodically (dependent on question) includes questions on control and autonomy, the intensity of work, job resources, variety and complexity, as well as a question that offers some insight into meaning and purpose to experiences of paid work.

Using an 11-point scale ranging from 'I have no influence' to 'I have complete control', two indicators in the ESS ask respondents about the level of control they have over (1) how their work is organized, included in each survey wave, and (2) whether they can choose/change the pace of work, included in waves 2 and 5 of the ESS. The evidence from the ESS suggests levels of autonomy vary considerably across Europe. Almost two thirds (63.1%) of workers in Norway and three-in-five (60.1%) in Sweden, for example, report high levels of autonomy (a response of 8 or above on the scale) over how their work is organized (Figure 4.1). In comparison, only two-in-five (19.1%) workers in Bulgaria report high levels of autonomy. In some nations there is a notable split, as around one third of workers in Italy and Serbia report high levels of control over the organization of work, while one quarter and one third, respectively, report no influence at all. In these cases, differences are likely to be the product of industrial structures in these countries and greater prevalence of self-employment.

80   *Well-being and the quality of working lives*

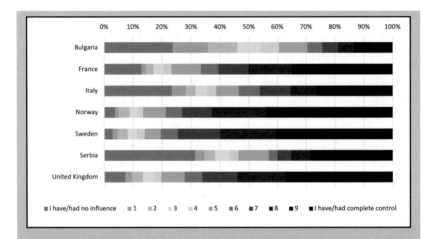

Source: European Social Survey, Wave 9 (ESS, 2018).

Figure 4.1   Allowed to decide how daily work is organized

Consistent with the first measure of autonomy, the measure of control over the pace of work also indicates higher degrees of control among workers in Nordic countries including Denmark and Sweden. Well over half of workers (59.2% and 53.6%, respectively) in both of these European economies report high levels of autonomy over the pace of work, with similar patterns also present in Germany (Figure 4.2). France and the UK both follow relatively closely the average for all of the European countries included in the ESS, while autonomy levels over the pace of work are notably lower in some countries including Lithuania and Ukraine.

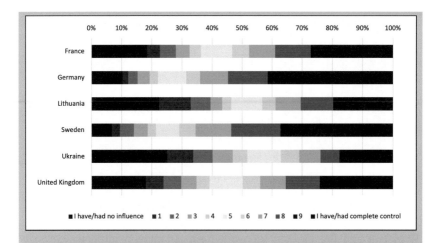

Source: European Social Survey, Wave 5 (ESS, 2010).

Figure 4.2   Allowed to choose/change pace of work

Data for the UK from wave 2 (2010–11) and 4 (2012–13) of the Understanding Society survey, reported in Wheatley (2017b), also provide useful insights into relative levels of autonomy at occupation level. Autonomy levels are found to differ considerably as around 90% of managers report having 'some' or 'a lot' of autonomy over all aspects of job control (see Box 4.1 for measures used in the survey). Managers report lesser schedule control, with fewer than half reporting 'a lot' of control over working hours. Professionals report relatively high levels of job control, but these are less than those enjoyed by managers. Some workers in skilled trades report high levels of job and schedule control. However, the picture is quite inconsistent, particularly for working hours, which is possibly indicative of differences between contractors and individuals working for large construction firms. The lowest levels of job control are found in lower skilled jobs, including sales and customer service, with almost one quarter reporting no autonomy.

The research also considers the relationship between different forms of autonomy and subjective well-being, in terms of reported satisfaction with job, leisure time, and life overall. Autonomy was found to have positive effects on well-being, especially where 'a lot' of autonomy is reported. Differentiated effects on well-being (and by gender) are observed, though, between job control and schedule control. Control over job tasks appears

> strongly related to job satisfaction; for both men and women even 'a little' or 'some' autonomy in this aspect of work has positive effects. Greater control over the intensity or pace of work has positive effects on job satisfaction for both men and women. The order of task completion, meanwhile, does not have statistically significant effects, and the manner of work appears to have significant effects on life satisfaction for women only. Schedule control has positive effects on job, leisure and overall life satisfaction. Overall, these findings are consistent with greater levels of autonomy and control having positive, but differentiated, effects on worker well-being.

WORKLOAD, INTENSITY AND ROLE OVERLOAD

Workload and the intensity of work form an integral intrinsic dimension of work, and one that presents us with a number of challenges in both concept and measurement. As a concept, the intensity of work is somewhat under-developed. It has been conceptualized in relation to how hard we work, which itself is argued as having both a time (i.e. length of hours worked) and an intensity component (i.e. how much pace and effort we put in during the time worked) (Burke et al., 2010). It can also be understood in terms of the literature on job demands, introduced in Chapter 3. The demands present in a job, such as time pressure, effort required and level of difficulty, directly influence the level of intensity required to fulfil work tasks (see Bakker and Demerouti, 2007; Karasek, 1979). The intensity of work has, in turn, been conceptualized in reference to 'work effort'; for example, in the work of Green (see Green, 2001, 56), where it has been defined as the 'rate of physical and/or mental input to work tasks'.

The intensity of work has risen in prominence in terms of its importance to experiences of paid work, in part as a growing body of evidence has identified an increase in the intensity of work encountered by many during their working lives (Green, 2006, 2017; Kalleberg, 2012). The observed increase has been driven by changes in the structure of work in recent decades. The adoption of Taylorist low-discretion work organization (so called after Frederick Taylor, whose work is covered briefly later in the chapter) and certain 'high-performance' and 'high-commitment' management practices has occurred alongside technological change which has increased connectivity and productive potential (Perrons et al., 2005), while at the same time creating a range of additional tasks (e.g. expectations around frequent reporting). It is also argued that declining union representation and greater job insecurity can act as sources of work intensification, although this may differ by sector and other factors including relative level of individual bargaining power (Green, 2004).

Where intense routines of work are present, there is often a potential for incidence of overwork (see Chapter 5) and 'workaholism' (Mazzetti et al., 2014). Initially defined in the work of Oates (1971), workaholism is a psychological condition which results in an obsession with work driving excessive levels of work effort (Schaufeli et al., 2008). Workaholism has two potential drivers, personality drivers and forced drivers, with the latter reflecting organizational work arrangements including excessive workloads. Personality drivers comprise two components, working excessively and working compulsively. Working excessively is a behavioural component reflecting the tendency to expend excessive amounts of time and energy to work, beyond that needed to meet organizational or financial requirements. Working compulsively is a cognitive dimension reflecting an obsession with work and tendency to think about work all of the time, including outside of work-time (Schaufeli et al., 2008, cited in Mazzetti et al., 2014). Workaholism results in workers allocating an excessive, and potential unsustainable, amount of time and energy to work as they cannot resist the compulsion to do so (Bakker and Schaufeli, 2008). The incidence of workaholism has been argued as being particularly prominent where there exists a work environment characterized by an overwork climate. However, personality traits play an important role, as workaholism is more likely among workers who exhibit a greater degree of achievement motivation and perfectionism (Mazzetti et al., 2014, 243). Perfectionism has long been considered a key driver of workaholism, reflected in a need for orderliness and control, and unwillingness to delegate tasks to others due to expectations around high standards. It refers to our own and external pressures resulting in us becoming obsessive about being the best and feeling disappointed or worse if and/or when this is not realized (Flett and Hewitt, 2002). Perfectionism has been linked to a number of negative influences on our psychological well-being, including stress, anxiety, depression and burnout. It is also associated with negative behaviours including risk taking, and as a risk to our physical health through, for example, eating disorders (Egan et al., 2011).

Greater intensity of work is often present in more senior jobs (Burke et al., 2010). While problematic in itself due to the impacts it may have on these workers, this also reflects a wider concern given the considerable influence that managers and leaders have over the work culture experienced throughout the organization (McCarthy et al., 2010). Managers who are unsupportive of, enforce, or simply allow intensive and/or extensive work cultures to be present create an environment in which workers may be subject to work-stressors, that is, experiences which generate stress (Greenhaus et al., 2012). It has been shown, for example, that work intensity may be greater among those reporting flexible and non-standard working patterns (e.g. zero hours, part-time) where the control over flexibility is employer-led (Piasna, 2018).

The impacts of intense work routines are considerable. Evidence has found lower work-related well-being to be associated with more intensive work routines (Green, 2008; Green et al., 2016a). Meanwhile, greater job demands have been shown to reduce happiness in a number of areas of working life (Warr, 2007). The intensification of work, alongside reductions in task autonomy, has also been argued as reducing job satisfaction among workers (Green, 2004, 622). A particular problem arising from intense working routines is incidence of role overload. Role overload refers to a situation where the job demands faced by a worker exceed, or at least are perceived to exceed, the resources, time available, and/or capabilities of the worker (Beehr et al., 1976, cited in Alfes et al., 2018). The job demands–resources model (Bakker and Demerouti, 2007), outlined in Chapter 3, is useful in understanding the relevance of role overload, as role overload can be considered to be a hindrance job demand (Alfes et al., 2018). Role overload can act as a barrier to work engagement (Crawford et al., 2010). Workers encountering role overload have to invest their existing resources (e.g. time, energy) heavily in response to overload. However, this effectively uses all resources available, leaving them with a lack of resources (Montania and Dagenais-Desmarais, 2018, 758). As such, the presence of role overload, alongside other hindrance demands including task ambiguity, create stress and a loss of resources, and can lead to burnout and/or increased turnover intention (Alfes et al., 2018; Burke et al., 2010; Greenhaus et al., 2012).

Moeller et al. (2017), for example, surveyed a representative sample of US workers to explore the relationship between engagement and burnout using the job demands-resources (JD-R) model. They found overall that burnout tends to be lower among workers who exhibit higher levels of engagement. However, they did find that almost 20 per cent of workers reported both high engagement and burnout, and that this mix resulted in strong mixed (positive and negative) emotions and turnover intention. In another study, of UK Higher Education, Ogbonna and Harris (2004, 1198) explored work intensification in the context of witnessed reductions in autonomy. They reported that performance-related remuneration systems had increased work intensity and competition between workers, resulting in higher levels of stress and reduced cooperation between workers. The presence of high-performance and high-commitment management practices can act to create additional pressure on the lives of workers which act as a source of work–life conflict (Brown, 2012; White et al., 2003).

The nature of the intensity of work also presents a measurement challenge. Work intensity is composed of a combination of physical, mental and emotional demands at work, which all present difficulties to measurement (Felstead and Green, 2017). It is problematic to measure the relative intensity of work in

Job properties 85

an objective form as this would require controlled experiments to be reliable. This is partly a product of effort levels being uneven throughout a period of work (a working day or week) including periods of paid time on-the-job which are inactive but used for work recovery (i.e. to rest), and in turn enable more productive periods afterwards (Felstead and Green, 2017, 190). In practice, this often results in more subjective self-reporting exercises being employed, which can involve smaller-scale primary data collection (Burke et al., 2010). However, these approaches are themselves subject to limitations given the potential for differing subjective understanding of what it means to work hard, as well as potential gaps between what a worker and their employer may consider to equate to an acceptable or intense workload (Box 4.4).

BOX 4.4   EMPIRICAL MEASUREMENT OF THE INTENSITY OF WORK

Empirical measurement of the intensity of work is challenging due to difficulties in measuring how hard someone is working. For this reason, subjective measurement is often employed, as already noted. A practical difficulty for researchers exploring patterns and trends using secondary data from social surveys is that these measures are in some cases periodic in their inclusion, for example in the ESS, where the most recent measure of work intensity to date is in wave 5 (2010) of the survey. Figure 4.3 summarizes the findings from this single measure from the ESS. Across Europe, around two thirds of workers report having to work hard in their job, with a small increase recorded between wave 2 and 5 of the survey. In the more recent data collected in 2010, workers in the UK (87%) and Ukraine (85%) report the most intense working routines, with a marginally higher proportion of workers in the Ukraine strongly agreeing that their job requires them to work very hard. In contrast, workers in Denmark, Sweden and France report relatively less intense patterns of work, with a little over half of workers in both Denmark and France agreeing that they have to work hard in their jobs.

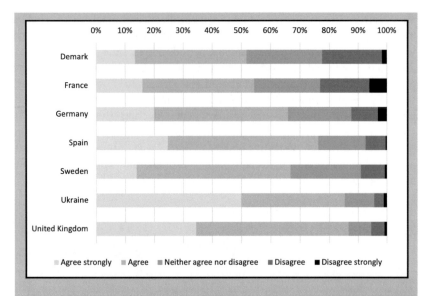

Source: European Social Survey, Wave 5 (ESS, 2010).

Figure 4.3   My job requires that I work very hard

The nature of questions attempting to capture the intensity of work varies. Some social surveys have more of a focus on the volume of work. For example, in the ESS interviewees are asked to respond to the statement 'my job requires that I work very hard' using a 5-point scale with responses from agree to disagree. Questioning can equally focus more on the pace at which we work. The European Working Conditions Survey (EWCS) includes a question on the frequency of working at high speed, as well as a question on whether workers have to complete tasks to tight deadlines.

In the UK, both the Skills and Employment Survey (SES) and CIPD's UK Working Lives Survey (UKWLS) include measurement of work intensity, with the prior including questioning around whether the job requires hard work. In the UKWLS, measurement is performed using a single-item scale, which asks respondents 'In a normal week, is the workload in your job … ?' with responses given on a 5-point scale from 'far too little' to 'far too much'. Data from the 2019 UKWLS survey suggested around one third of workers face workloads that are intense, and that approximately one-in-twenty feel completely overloaded by their jobs (see Wheatley and Gifford, 2019, 26). Permanent employees are those that reported the greatest incidence of

Job properties 87

> intense working routines and this is especially the case among mid-level managerial and professional workers, reflecting both a concern for these workers, but also for the working culture that is created for others by those with leadership responsibilities, as already noted.

JOB RESOURCES

The concept of job resources has been subject to different treatments within the existing literature base. In the JD-R model outlined in Chapter 3, Bakker and Demerouti (2007, 312) adopt an expansive definition as they summarize job resources as encompassing the physical, psychological, social and organizational aspects of a job that (1) are functional in the achievement of work goals; (2) moderate job demands and any associated mental and physical costs; and (3) act to stimulate personal growth, learning and development. This broad definition incorporates a wide array of sub-dimensions of workplace well-being including a number covered elsewhere in this, and other, chapters of this book. These can be categorized into (1) organizational-level resources (e.g. pay, opportunities for career development, job security); (2) professional and social relationship resources (e.g. supervisor and co-worker support, team climate); (3) work organization resources (e.g. environmental clarity, participation in decision-making): and (4) task-level resources (e.g. skill variety, task identity, task significance, autonomy, performance feedback). In contrast to Bakker and Demerouti's approach, job resources has been defined in other research in a narrower context as reflecting a set of situational factors which reflect the means we have at our disposal in our current work situation that enable us to effectively accomplish work-related goals given our ability and motivation (Rousseau and Aubé, 2010, 324). The concept of job resources in this case is more centred on the resources we require to perform tasks which include time and space, equipment and tools, materials, facilities, and support services (Box 4.5). It is important as well to note here that these resources tend to be outside of the control of employees; at any one time we have to work with the resources available to us (Rousseau and Aubé, 2010).

Consistent with the approach adopted in Rousseau and Aubé (2010), in the workplace well-being framework developed in this book, job resources are used to refer to the narrower set of situational factors which enable us to operate effectively in our jobs. While it is acknowledged that the approach of Bakker and Demerouti (2007) captures a comprehensive range of resources, the 'situational job resources' approach is adopted in this book in order to enable consideration of other sub-dimensions of workplace well-being separately, including pay and benefits, career development, relationships, autonomy, variety. Job resources, as defined in this book, are a sub-dimension of the intrinsic quality of work most closely associated with the environment element of the framework for workplace well-being (Bakker and Demerouti, 2007). Job resources include the availability of time and space, as well as any equipment and tools, materials, facilities and support services required to get the job done.

Time acts as an important resource for workers, and is an aspect of workplace well-being that is captured in a number of dimensions (e.g. job properties, flexibility) and sub-dimensions. In the context of its role as a resource, we must consider that in order for us to perform in our job while maintaining a healthy work–life balance, we need adequate time to complete the tasks in our job. Where there is a lack of time available this is likely to result in highly intense patterns of work, as per the discussion in the previous section, which in turn could lead to work overload and incidence of work–life conflict and burnout (Burke et al., 2010; Greenhaus et al., 2012). The relevance of time as a resource also extends to the time during the working day or week which we spend in non-work. This time is used for work recovery, which helps to build resources that can then be used when working to complete tasks (Robertson and Cooper, 2011, 76). Space is a further component of resources, and one that is closely linked with the physical space and activity dimension of well-being at work (see Chapter 9). In order to perform in our role we need access to working space which is suitable for our activities, both in terms of function and health and safety. While there are multiple considerations present in building an effective work space, which are considered in detail in Chapter 9, it is the overall access and availability of space which is suitable for work that acts as a form of situational resource in our jobs.

BOX 4.5   MEASUREMENT OF JOB RESOURCES

Job resources can be usefully understood through empirical measurement by asking workers about the provision of a number of resources in their jobs. A set of common measures are often employed in existing research. For example, Rousseau and Aubé (2010) develop a six-item scale informed by the work of Tesluk and Mathieu (1999) and Peters and O'Connor (1980). The scale focuses on responses to six statements regarding the basic resources provided for completing tasks and uses a 5-point scale, as follows:

I have adequate materials and supplies to do my job
I have adequate tools and equipment to accomplish my work
I can get adequate training to do my job
I have access to technical support when needed
I have the space needed to execute my tasks
I have the time needed to complete the assigned work

1	2	3	4	5
Strongly disagree	Disagree	Neither agree nor disagree	Agree	Strongly agree

As a second example, in the CIPD's UK Working Lives Survey a three-item question is included which explores the resources available to workers. Again, using a scale format, the questions are as follows (note the opposite numbering for responses compared to the previous example):

To what extent do you agree or disagree with the following statements?

I usually have enough time to get my work done within my allocated hours
I have the right equipment to do my job effectively
I have a suitable space to do my job effectively (e.g. office space or workshop)

1	2	3	4	5
Strongly agree	Agree	Neither agree nor disagree	Disagree	Strongly disagree

A summary of the responses to these measures from the 2019 UKWLS is provided in Figure 4.4. The data indicates that the majority of workers have access to adequate resources in their jobs. Approximately three quarters report access to suitable equipment and workspace. It should, though, be acknowledged that time is a more limited resource; one fifth of UKWLS workers reported that they lack enough time to get their work done within allocated hours. This latter finding highlights both the challenges faced in managing workloads and also the close links between the job resources and workload and intensity intrinsic components of work.

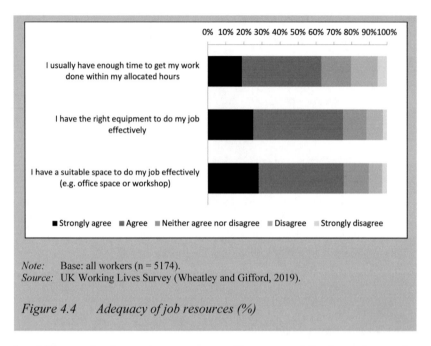

Note: Base: all workers (n = 5174).
Source: UK Working Lives Survey (Wheatley and Gifford, 2019).

Figure 4.4   Adequacy of job resources (%)

In addition to the time and space aspects of resources, it is also necessary for us to have access to the correct equipment. This includes both physical tools and technology as well as suitable software and other materials. Access to the correct equipment can provide significant productivity benefits, for example a faster personal computer providing quicker processing time for complex calculations. One can look to some of the observations of Frederick Taylor (1967) in his book *The Principles of Scientific Management* to illustrate this point. Through time and motion experiments, Taylor emphasized the benefits of the adoption of standardized tools and time-saving devices. One such experiment performed in a factory environment focused on workers shovelling. Through an iterative process he identified a design which enabled significantly more efficient performance in the job. However, while Taylor correctly identified the performance benefits, much of his work ignored the role of worker well-being and its relationship with motivation, and instead focused on the imposition of low-discretion work routines. It is therefore important to not only consider the performance benefits, but also the wider implications for worker well-being when designing jobs and determining and allocating resources. A lack of suitable equipment, space and time is likely to negatively impact not only our productivity, but also our well-being at work. Working in an unsuitable environment creates problems associated with physical discomfort, alongside time wasted due to inefficiency and incompatibility problems (Martínez-Tur

Job properties 91

et al., 2005). Obviously the benefits have to be traded-off against the costs of the provision of such resources; however, the potential dual benefits to productivity and worker well-being which can be attained from job resources act as a significant rationale for this investment.

VARIETY AND COMPLEXITY

Job complexity, which is also referred to in terms of the level of challenge present in a job, is undoubtedly relevant to our understanding of the intrinsic characteristics of work. It is often considered alongside task variety which encompasses the types and range of activities involved in a job (Hackman and Oldham, 1975; Holman, 2013). Several contributions to the job quality literature explicitly identify task variety (Barling et al., 2003), challenge (Kalleberg, 2011), and complexity and difficulty (Leach et al., 2010) as dimensions influencing the quality of our work. These intrinsic characteristics of work could also be argued as being an important aspect of what makes a job interesting, something that is identified in a number of models of job quality such as those offered by Handel (2005), Kalleberg (2011) and Stier (2015). These sub-dimensions are subjective in nature, reflecting that the assessment of one worker who may consider a job to be interesting or challenging may not be consistent with the view of another (Kalleberg, 2011, 144).

In research exploring job quality factors in 27 European countries, Holman (2013) refers to variety and complexity in the context of the degree of challenge present in a job, forming part of what is described as 'job challenge demands' which also incorporates workload. In his work, Holman differentiates these concepts, referring to variety in reference to the 'extent to which [an] employee completes different types of tasks'. In their research, Barling et al. (2003) measure variety using a single-item scale, '*I do lots of different tasks in my job*', with responses measured on a 3-point scale (1 = agree, 2 = neither agree nor disagree, 3 = disagree).

Complexity, meanwhile, is defined by Holman as the 'extent to which [a] job involves unforeseen problems, complex tasks and learning new things' (Holman, 2013, 483), with this latter definition emphasizing a self-development component to this intrinsic characteristic of work. In their research into job quality in Australia, Leach et al. (2010) measure aspects of complexity and challenge through responses to the following statements, '*My job is complex and difficult*', '*My job often requires me to learn new skills*' and '*I use many of my skills and abilities in my current job*', using a 7-point scale from 0 = strongly disagree to 6 = strongly agree. Note that the latter statement can also help to explain the relative skills match involved in a job, something that is considered in Chapter 6.

Task complexity is undoubtedly linked to both workload and the time component of job resources. More complex tasks could create real time pressures and challenging workloads which could in turn act as a work-stressor should tasks be felt to be too complex or difficult to complete in the time available (Warr, 2007). However, the presence of variety and challenge is generally acknowledged as a positive component of the quality of work which is linked to a number of aspects of worker well-being, including self-development, achievement and fulfilment (Bryson et al., 2014; Holman, 2013; Karesek and Theorell, 1990). These intrinsic characteristics also have a close relationship with levels of control and autonomy as the presence of both control and variety may have particularly beneficial effects for workers in terms of experienced job quality (Kalleberg, 2011). Control over the ordering and manner of completion of tasks also offers the worker the chance to create more variety in their job. Where a lack of variety is present in a job, this has been shown to be associated with lower levels of job satisfaction, and more broadly to be associated with lower levels of well-being among workers when considered in the wider context as an element of a job which also exhibits other characteristics of low-quality work (Holman, 2013; Warr, 2007). Lack of variety can also result in feelings of boredom and a lack of focus, which can lead to an increase in the likelihood of errors and unsafe working practices (Barling et al., 2003) (Box 4.6).

BOX 4.6 EMPIRICAL PATTERNS OF VARIETY AND COMPLEXITY

Returning to data from the ESS, understanding of the variety and complexity involved in a job are captured empirically through two measures. The first asks workers to respond to a statement surrounding the level of variety in their work. Overall, in both wave 2 and 5 of the survey around two thirds of respondents agreed (responding 'quite true' or 'very true') that their jobs involve a lot of variety. At the country level, however, a considerable amount of diversity is reported. Figure 4.5 summarizes the differences for a selection of countries for the more recent data from wave 5. A higher proportion of workers in Switzerland (85%) and Norway (83%) reported lots of variety in their work, while only a quarter reported this in Portugal. The UK, meanwhile, was much closer to the average of the European nations surveyed with respect to this sub-dimension of job properties.

Job properties 93

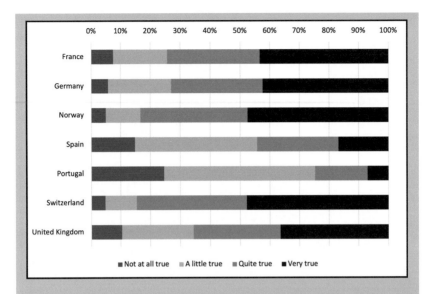

Source: European Social Survey, Wave 5 (ESS, 2010).

Figure 4.5   There is a lot of variety in my work

The second measure linked to this sub-dimension asks respondents whether they need to keep learning new things as part of their job, offering insight into both the variety and complexity present in their job, and the level of challenge. Across Europe, three-in-five workers report that their job requires them to learn new things (responding 'quite true' or 'very true'), although as per the other job properties sub-dimension measures explored, there is a quite stark variation by country (Figure 4.6). The requirement to keep learning is undoubtedly relevant to the quality of work we encounter and its presence is notably higher in Norway and Sweden, and to a slightly lesser degree in the UK and France. In contrast, this aspect of work is only reported by 28% of workers in Portugal, while it is reported by 40% in Bulgaria.

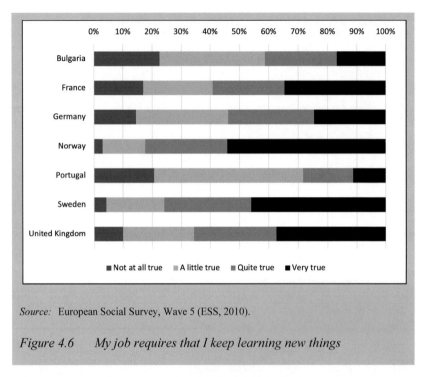

Source: European Social Survey, Wave 5 (ESS, 2010).

Figure 4.6   My job requires that I keep learning new things

MEANING, PURPOSE AND ENVIRONMENTAL CLARITY

In addition to the sub-dimensions already explored in this chapter, the job properties dimension of workplace well-being incorporates the extent to which we extract meaning and a sense of purpose from our job (Box 4.7). Together these form significant components of psychological well-being as outlined in the ASSET Model of Workplace Well-being (Robertson and Cooper, 2011) discussed in Chapter 3. The level of clarity we have over our responsibilities and position, and whether the job acts as a source of achievement and fulfilment form the final sub-dimensions outlines in this chapter.

Work can provide a deep sense of meaning, reflecting that we make an inner connection with the work we are doing and see it as worthwhile (Robertson and Cooper, 2011). This can, but does not need to, reflect that we engage in some form of altruistic behaviour. It could instead simply be that we take meaning or feel a sense of purpose from the opportunity to progress and improve our own situation. Meaning is influenced by a series of factors. These include satisfaction and interest in work, work centrality (i.e. whether work is

Job properties   95

engaged with purely for economic reasons or has deeper meaning), interpersonal relationships at work (see Chapter 7), entitlement norms (i.e. normative assumptions regarding expectations from work) and obligation norms (i.e. expectations regarding required contributions in a job) (Harpaz and Fu, 2002). If, in contrast, we feel a level of disconnect from our work or perceive it as an 'alien' activity, it can engender a perspective of work being a laborious activity or toil (Edgell, 2012; Spencer, 2009). This can occur in cases where low-discretion work organization is employed, and can result in lower productivity and performance, and lower levels of job satisfaction. A sense of meaning has been shown to have positive impacts on levels of enthusiasm with work (Jung and Yoon, 2016), and provide a sense of achievement and fulfilment (O'Toole and Lawler, 2006; Spencer, 2009). In turn, where work provides a sense of fulfilment, it follows that it can have positive impacts on our well-being, as outlined in Chapter 2. These well-being benefits are felt from workers gaining a sense of purpose and personal agency (Warhurst et al., 2017), further evidencing the interconnectedness of these subjective elements of the job properties dimension.

The sense of meaning and purpose we derive from work, however, is not limited to the organization. There is increasing acknowledgement of workers placing significant stock in the wider social value created by their organization (Warr, 2007). Where workers have a clear understanding of how their contribution to the organization feeds into the wider context, it can provide workers with a sense that the work they are engaged in is worthwhile and offers some form of societal, rather than solely financial, benefit. As such, this component of work is closely linked to the giving dimension of workplace well-being (see Chapter 8) and reflects some of the wider intrinsic rewards that can be obtained by an individual through their job.

BOX 4.7   MEASUREMENT OF MEANINGFUL WORK

Measures of meaning, purpose and sense of worthwhileness take many forms and are captured in a number of social surveys. For example, the UK Working Lives Survey includes questions exploring the sense of meaning and worthwhileness derived from work. This incorporates the level of meaning a worker takes from their contribution to their organization (or client in the case of the self-employed) as well as to society. It also includes responses to a statement reflecting on the motivation derived from the purpose of the organization/client. All are measured on a 5-point scale from strongly disagree to strongly agree. Example distributions among workers sampled in the 2019 UKWL are included in Figure 4.7. The data evidences that the majority of workers do take meaning from the work they complete; in the UKWL, approximately three quarters agreed with this statement. The wider impact of the contribution made through work is also evident, although to a lesser degree, with around half of workers reporting that they feel their work is useful for society. A similar proportion of workers also consider the purpose of the organization/client to act as a significant motivator.

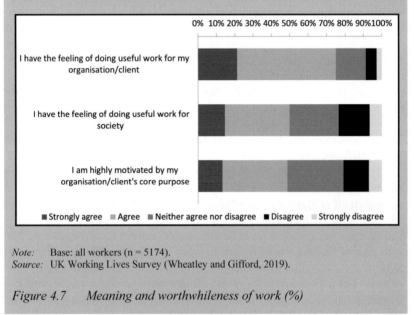

Note: Base: all workers (n = 5174).
Source: UK Working Lives Survey (Wheatley and Gifford, 2019).

Figure 4.7   Meaning and worthwhileness of work (%)

Having a clear sense of our responsibilities and position within an organizational structure, often referred to as environmental clarity, is a further component of the job properties which can impact on workplace well-being. Where there is a high degree of clarity over what is expected within a role (including clear task outcomes) and how this fits into the wider organizational context, this is associated with a higher level of experienced meaningfulness (Hackman and Oldham, 1976), clearer understanding of purpose, and enables workers to obtain a sense of achievement from their job (Hackman and Oldham, 1976; Warr, 2007). A lack of clarity and/or the presence of uncertainty regarding purpose and position within an organization can have considerable detrimental effects on worker well-being, creating anxiety and tension. As well as effective job design, good communication and information sharing practices, which represent key components of the relationships dimension of workplace well-being (see Chapter 7), have been cited as integral to environmental clarity, and in turn measures of both eudaimonic and evaluative well-being at work (Robertson and Cooper, 2011).

CHAPTER SUMMARY: JOB PROPERTIES AND WORKER WELL-BEING

This chapter has considered the wide array of intrinsic characteristics of work which together comprise the sub-dimensions of the job properties dimension of workplace well-being. Existing evidence is clear in identifying the nature and content of our jobs (i.e. the intrinsic characteristics of the work we complete) as having a central role in our experiences of paid work, influencing the quality of our working lives. These characteristics include levels of control and autonomy, the relative intensity of work, the resources we have at our disposal to complete the tasks in our job, the variety, complexity and challenge present in our work, and the level of meaning, purpose and environmental clarity. The existing evidence base supports the argument that these aspects of work, together, have a considerable influence on the quality of work encountered and on our well-being at work.

The intrinsic characteristics of work are highly interconnected which renders it important to consider each in the broader context of the job properties dimension. It is possible, and could be useful to differentiate and understand the intrinsic aspects of work in isolation, where there is a need for this level of granularity to be understood and fed into (e.g. design of workplace policy). It is also important to note here that the relative importance of each of the aspects of the nature of work considered in this chapter will differ between jobs and individuals, while some have been shown to have a generally greater significance to our experiences of work, such as autonomy. However, it is unwise to approach any exploration of the intrinsic properties of a job, either for research or practice purposes, without fully reflecting on the close connections between the multiple intrinsic components of work.

Many of the characteristics discussed in this chapter are more subjective in nature, or at least are more likely to require subjective measurement. For example, while one worker may take a considerable amount of meaning and fulfilment from completing a task they regard as offering a good degree of challenge, these subjective responses to work may not be present among all of their colleagues. This does act as a limitation of sorts which needs to be considered when designing jobs and developing policies and practices or monitoring worker well-being and offers evidence to support the importance of avoiding one-size-fits-all approaches to job design and workplace policies. Notwithstanding these challenges, consideration of these elements of paid work remains highly significant to our understanding of experiences of work and their relationship with well-being.

For organizations aiming to enhance this dimension of workplace well-being, action necessarily centres heavily on the consideration of job design. Ways to effectively approach job design for workplace well-being within the organization are summarized in Figure 4.8. Job (re)design could include fairly small and iterative change by, for example, increasing the level of control workers have over the order of task completion, or indeed enabling them to engage in some degree of job crafting. A more comprehensive approach, meanwhile, could include complete redesign of jobs from the ground up. An obvious area for change is in the historical focus on time in job design. Increasingly jobs are more appropriately based around task and outputs rather than time spent in activities. Many job contracts, and in turn the design of these jobs, remain too heavily centred on hours of work, in many cases hours worked per week. However, this measure does not correspond to work effort and associated levels of performance which are influenced by a diverse range of factors including skill and dexterity and motivation (discussed further in Chapter 6). This is even more relevant in light of the changes witnessed in paid work in response to the global pandemic in 2020. The move to home-based remote work among large portions of the working population and the indications from organizations that they intend to retain at least some of these working routines post-pandemic suggest an increased need to reflect on the design of jobs and refocus around task and output quality, rather than time. Reconsidering job design also offers the opportunity for organizations to reflect on ways they can embed in jobs many of the intrinsic components of work shown in this chapter to be highly relevant to workplace well-being.

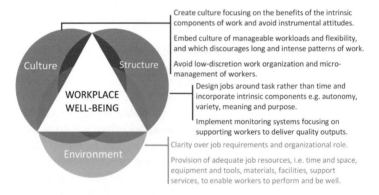

Figure 4.8   Designing jobs for workplace well-being

Alongside changes to the design of jobs it is necessary to consider new ways of monitoring and rewarding workers which better align with job design which is well-being enhancing. Again, historical norms of Taylorist low-discretion work organization including high levels of micromanagement is increasingly unsuitable and both ineffective and inefficient. The temptation to retain tried and tested methods or simply adapt these to different contexts such as the monitoring of remote working using technical control systems (see Chapter 5) will not deliver the potential dual benefits to worker well-being and the organization. Enacting these changes in practice does impose a cost on the organization; however, significant potential benefits can be realized through enhanced performance and motivation, and reduced employee turnover and absence.

5. Flexibility

INTRODUCTION

This second dimension of workplace well-being explores the role, and impact, of flexibility in work. It reflects on the benefits and challenges that different forms of flexibility present to our ability to combine work with the rest of our lives. The conceptualization of flexibility employed in the framework for workplace well-being, and explored in this chapter, is expansive. It considers centrally the role of balance between work and the rest of our lives in the context of contemporary work including the length of time spent in work, a sub-dimension of workplace well-being which links flexibility to job properties. We also consider the role of breaks and work recovery in supporting balance between work and life and providing well-being benefits (Sonnentag, 2001; Sonnentag and Fritz, 2007; Trougakis et al., 2014). The flexibility dimension incorporates more formal flexibility in work including use of flexible working arrangements, such as flexi-time and homeworking, and extending to flexibility over the terms of employment associated with, for example, gig working (Aloisi, 2016; Friedman, 2014) which itself links this dimension of workplace well-being to the rewarding careers dimension. The chapter also contemplates the importance of more informal methods of flexibility, often associated with higher degrees of control and autonomy in work (Wheatley, 2017a). Further, the flexibility dimension acknowledges how flexibility over workplace and space impacts on our well-being at work. Here we link the discussion in the chapter to the physical space and activity dimension of workplace well-being covered in Chapter 9 and consider the impacts of different modes of work including remote, mobile and agile working. The chapter ends with a case study focusing on flexibility and work in the gig economy, and finally a reflection on the role of flexibility in workplace well-being.

BALANCING WORK AND LIFE

Achieving a desirable balance between work and the rest of our lives is essential to our well-being, but is increasingly challenging for many of us as the pace and intensity of work require high levels of work effort, while developments in technology act to blur the boundaries between work and non-work (A. Green, 2017; F. Green, 2006; Kalleberg, 2012). While there is a common understanding of the term work–life balance given its use in academic, policy and wider social spheres for a number of decades, as a concept work–life balance has been defined and used in a variety of ways and contexts (Greenhaus et al., 2012). Work–life balance can be defined in reference to our ability to combine work and household or family responsibilities successfully or with minimum conflict (Clark, 2000, 751). It has been differentiated into a psychological and social perspective (Agosti et al., 2017), with the former viewing work–life balance as a feeling of satisfaction generated from achieving a successful balance between work and non-work life, and with work and family roles. Meanwhile, the social perspective focuses on the accomplishment of role-related expectations within an individual's work and family context. Work–life balance has been alternatively referred to as work–family balance (Clark, 2000), work–life integration (Atkinson and Hall, 2009, 652; Fagan et al., 2012), and also in several contributions as work–life conflict (i.e. an absence of work–life balance, which has a greater focus on the conflict aspect of balancing work with the rest of our lives) (Chang et al., 2010).

The concept of work–life balance aims to improve conditions for all workers by altering work practices (Atkinson and Hall, 2009, 652; Fagan et al., 2012). It has gathered increased relevance in recent decades as developments in ICT have amplified the blurring of the household–workplace interface (Bulger et al., 2007). Workers face increasing difficulties in separating work from the rest of their lives as they remain in contact with colleagues and clients through electronic devices including PCs and mobile phones. These changes create specific difficulties in achieving balance as workers encounter intense routines of work (Brown, 2012; Wheatley, 2012a). This is important to our understanding of the dimensions of workplace well-being as a lack of balance can have negative impacts on well-being and result in stress-related health problems (Zheng et al., 2015).

The close relationship between work and the rest of our lives results in the presence of spillover between these two spheres. Spillover refers to work or non-work influencing or impacting the other in either a positive or negative way (Guest, 2002, 258–9). Positive spillover from non-work to work has been argued as being a more common occurrence than work having a positive impact on the rest of our lives (Carlson et al., 2014). This has been conceptualized in the context of psychological well-being. For example, Greenhaus and Powell (2006) suggest that resources such as self-efficacy or interpersonal skills obtained in the family and social domain can have positive impacts on the work domain through positive affect which can be realized through improved work performance. In contrast, work is more often contended as having a negative spillover effect on family and leisure time, for example as a result of high-intensity working routines creating difficulties in achieving balance.

Work–life balance is influenced by a variety of work and non-work factors. It has been argued that 'choice' is central to the achievement of work–life balance, as Clutterbuck (2003) states it involves 'being aware of different demands on time and energy; having the ability to choose how to allocate time and energy; knowing what values to apply to choices, and making choices'. Consistent with this assertion, higher levels of schedule control (i.e. control over the timing and location of work) have been shown to aid in reducing work–family conflict. For example, research using the US Work, Stress and Health Survey identified the presence of high levels of schedule control to be related to lower incidence of work–family conflict (Glavin and Schieman, 2012, 86). Similarly, and also using US data from a case study organization, Kelly et al. (2011, 267) reported that the introduction of initiatives to increase schedule control reduced work–family conflict. They argue that schedule control can be used as a mechanism to generate considerable employee benefits through greater flexibility, and that more so than job control (discussed in reference to autonomy and control in Chapter 4) it can have positive effects both at, and outside of, work. This is not to say that job control doesn't generate benefits in relation to balance. Evidence has shown, for example, that job (autonomy over decision-making) and schedule control (use of flexible technologies) can help in successfully managing work and family (Batt and Valcour, 2003, 215). Acknowledging the choice component of work–life balance, it should be noted that achieving a desirable or successful balance is highly subjective and will differ from one individual to the next (Box 5.1). For some, balance may be achieved with a greater amount of time and effort spent in work, while for others the opposite may be found. Choice may also be limited by household and family responsibilities such as the provision of care. Evidence has indicated that, on average, women (especially mothers) may benefit more from additional control over the timing and location of work as this enables them to better manage work alongside household responsibilities (Dikkers et al., 2010; Fagan et al., 2012, 23–4; Lyness et al., 2012).

BOX 5.1   EMPIRICAL MEASUREMENT OF BALANCE

Balance is measured in a number of social surveys primarily through lines of subjective questioning about how work impacts and is managed alongside the rest of our lives. For example, the European Social Survey includes six items which focus on the relative frequency of problems encountered in balancing work and life, which are asked on a 5-point scale with responses from 'never' to 'always'.

How often do you ...
... keep worrying about work problems when you are not working?
... feel too tired after work to enjoy the things you would like to do at home?
... find that your job prevents you from giving the time you want to your partner or family?
... find that your partner or family gets fed up with the pressure of your job?
... find that your family responsibilities prevent you from giving the time you should to your job?
... find it difficult to concentrate on work because of your family responsibilities?

The UK Working Lives Survey also includes a set of questions which offer insight into balance between work and the rest of our lives. Using a 5-point scale format with responses from 'strongly disagree' to 'strongly agree', respondents are asked the extent to which they agree or disagree with a series of statements regarding the spillover they experience between work and non-work.

To what extent do you agree or disagree with the following statements?

- *I find it difficult to fulfil my commitments outside of work because of the amount of time I spend on my job.*
- *I find it difficult to do my job properly because of my commitments outside of work.*
- *I find it difficult to relax in my personal time because of my work.*

ACHIEVING BALANCE

At the practical level, work–life balance is facilitated through the enactment of formal legislation and organizational policy, as well as more informal guidance and support mechanisms. Across a number of nations, legislation has taken the form of regulations governing parental leave, the provision and use of flexible working arrangements and rights for those with caring responsibilities. Work–life balance policies enacted in a selection of countries are summarized in Box 5.2. In the UK, as an example, the approach which has been adopted has focused on awareness-raising alongside the enactment of a number of work–life balance or 'family-friendly' policies. Launched in

2000 under the banner of the Work–Life Balance Campaign (WLBC), the awareness-raising campaign focused on demonstrating to employers through a range of mechanisms – advice, case study research, partnerships with leading employers, modest financial support for consultancy services to develop policies and practices – the potential organizational benefits which can be realized through the introduction of policies and practices which enable workers to achieve a desirable balance between work and home life (Arrowsmith, 2001; Kodz et al., 2002).

BOX 5.2 SELECTED WORK–LIFE BALANCE POLICIES

Australia

The approach to work–life balance policy in Australia is fairly consistent with that of other nations including the UK and Canada. The right to request flexible working arrangements was introduced through the Fair Work Act 2009, providing employees the right to request a flexible working arrangement from their employer if (i) they are 55 years or older; (ii) disabled; (iii) have caring responsibilities; (iv) are experiencing violence from their family; or (v) providing care for family members experiencing violence. Employers can refuse requests on grounds of business need, but must provide reasons, including the imposition of excessive costs, a significant loss in efficiency and/or productivity, negative impact on customer service, and/or a lack of capacity to accommodate the request (Fair Work Act, 2009). A national scheme of paid parental leave was also introduced from 2011 (Baird, 2011). Beyond these legislative measures, the Australian government has actively encouraged work–life balance policies to be negotiated between employers and employees.

Germany

Germany has, since 2002, introduced a range of work–life balance policies, with a particular focus on increasing labour market participation and providing greater opportunity for parents. Historically, a combination of social security thresholds and social attitudes had acted to promote women exiting the labour market for extended periods following childbirth (O'Reilly and Bothfeld, 2002). The Elterngeld (parent's money) was introduced in 2007 in an effort to facilitate the return to work for parents, allowing paid leave of up to 14 months following childbirth (providing a variable-rate benefit equal to two thirds of previous earnings). Reform of parental leave in 2015, meanwhile, offered both parents the ability to take leave on a part-time basis with the provision of a partnership bonus where both parents work part-time hours of around 25–30 hours per week (Adema et al., 2017). Germany has also had in place for a long time a range of policies focused on flexibility in work including a law enabling full-time workers to request a move to part-time (since 2001) and a framework for flexi-time (Hunt, 2013).

Norway
Norway, consistent with other Scandinavian countries including Finland and Sweden, is considered a world leader with regard to the provision of progressive flexible working and family-friendly policies. The Working Environment Act introduced in 2006 enables workers to request a flexible working arrangement as long as it can be arranged without major inconvenience to the employer. Developed around the concept of a symmetrical family of two worker-carers (Kitterød and Rønsen, 2012), Norway has implemented significant paid parental leave entitlements for up to a year, much of which can be shared (Brandth and Kvande, 2009, 192–5). As such, Norway has developed some of the strongest parental leave entitlements for fathers, although evidence has suggested that trends in long hours limit take-up of these entitlements (Pascall, 2008). Flexible parental leave and long-term use of part-time work remains more common among women. This is driven by their need for flexibility to ease work–family conflict (Kjeldstad and Nymoen, 2012, 103–4).

UK
A range of policy has been enacted in the UK with a focus on increasing labour market participation (Lewis and Campbell, 2008, 535–6). Legislation has included support for informal carers including the Carers (Equal Opportunities) Act 2004 (see Carmichael et al., 2008, 6–7). Family leave policy has, since December 2014, had an increased focus on choice in the allocation of caring responsibilities. Shared Parental Leave and Shared Parental Pay were introduced through the Shared Parental Leave Regulations 2014. Parents of babies born after 5 April 2015 have since been able to share up to 50 weeks of leave, 37 weeks of which is paid, subject to meeting certain eligibility criteria (Gov.uk, 2015). Policy with a central focus on providing greater flexibility over paid work, acknowledging the impacts of unpaid work, was implemented in 2003 through the Flexible Working Regulations (see Deakin and Morris, 2012, 750–2). The Flexible Working Regulations have been expanded on several occasions, most recently in 2014, to cover all workers, following 26 weeks of service.
The Flexible Working (Procedural Requirements) Regulations, SI 2002/3207, and the Flexible Working (Eligibility, Complaints and Remedies) SI 2002/3236 are amendments to the Employment Act 2002,

s47, consolidated in the Employment Rights Act 1996, ss80F–80I. Initial implementation applied only to parents of disabled and young children. In 2007 the coverage was extended to carers of certain adults and parents of older children. From 2009 it was expanded to include employees with parental responsibility for children under 16.

USA
The USA remains characterized by its liberal and open labour market. It is the only nation in the OECD which to date does not have in place a national paid parental leave policy. Paid parental leave is provided in four states – California, Georgia, New Jersey and Rhode Island – but not at the federal level. The available (unpaid) parental leave, provided through the Family and Medical Leave Act of 1993, is relatively short at a maximum of 12 weeks and only covers employees in organizations of 50 or more workers (Block et al., 2013). Policies around flexible working have been primarily driven at the sector or organization level by the demand from workers, and in return the response from employers to ensure they are able to attract and retain high-quality workers. That said, policies are becoming more common at the state level, as some state governments have introduced 'flex-work' and 'right to request' policies for employees since the mid-2000s. The federal government also introduced The Telework Enhancement Act of 2010 which requires federal agencies to establish telework policies for their employees.

At the organizational level, work–life balance can form a key component of workplace well-being strategy. Work–life balance policies comprise a number of constituent elements, which can be summarized as flexible working arrangements; health and well-being programmes; childcare benefits or services; leave options (including maternity and paternity leave); and organizational understanding and support (Zheng et al., 2015, 358). In addition, it has been argued that it is important for there to be a supportive work–family culture embedded within the organization (Lyness and Kropf, 2005). This is particularly relevant to the effectiveness of work–life balance policy as it has significant impacts on the relative availability and usage of such policies, which evidence has shown continues to vary considerably (Wheatley, 2017a).

Beyond state and organization-level interventions, it has been argued that work–life balance can be successfully negotiated at the individual level through a combination of attitude and ability (Zheng et al., 2015, 357). Drawing on the work of Martin Seligman explored in Chapter 2 of this book, the positive psychology perspective argues that approaching situations with a positive attitude and an ability to remain positive even in difficult circumstances can help us to develop our ability to negotiate work–family conflict and realize improved health and well-being (Seligman and Czikszentmihalyi, 2000). Further abilities which facilitate successful balance have been usefully summarized in Zheng et al. (2015, 358–9) and include the ability to self-control situations (i.e. to minimize stressful situations); manage the work commitments of family members, especially a spouse/partner; coordinate caring responsibilities; and engage in non-work lifestyle (social, recreational and sporting), and community (volunteering and civic engagement) activities to fulfil non-work life goals.

FLEXIBILIZATION OF WORK

The work–life balance agenda has undoubtedly promoted a growth in non-standard employment contracts and an increased emphasis on flexible working (Lewis and Plomien, 2009). Despite efforts to provide a range of enabling policy and practice, however, there has been observed since the global economics crisis of 2007–09 a continued focus among some employers on employer-friendly flexibility, which has also been referred to as employer-driven flexibilization (McCrate, 2012). This involves the application of both functional (shift-work, overtime, varying work weeks using balancing-time accounts) and numerical (fixed-term, agency, mandated part-time work) flexibility (Raess and Burgoon, 2015, 95–6). It has motivated an expansion of 'precarious' or 'contingent' work including the use of casualized contracts (Kalleberg, 2009, 2). This includes zero-hours contracts (i.e. on-call non-guaranteed hours) (Mandl et al., 2015), fixed-term, temporary and seasonal contracts, on-call systems and forms of shift-work, and work as independent contractors (King, 2014, 152). Importantly, many of these contracts do not provide workers with holiday and sick pay and other rights present for full-time employees. Employers taking this path, it is argued, have been unwilling to offer their workers the same level of flexibility they expect them to demonstrate in performing their job. The result is that workers face difficulties in achieving work–life balance (Gregory and Milner, 2009, 123). In many countries, including the UK and Australia, employers are given the power to make 'allowance decisions' and have the legal right to reject requests for flexible working on the basis of business need (Poelmans and Beham, 2008). Decision-making is subject to a set of criteria; for example, there are three criteria in the UK Flexible Working Regulations: (1) cost of accommodating the request; (2) difficulty finding replacement cover; and (3) impacts on the quality/delivery of service, all of which are difficult to evaluate objectively (Deakin and Morris, 2012).

The significance of not only flexibility but also regularity – referring to whether working patterns are consistent and reliable or subject to short-term change – has also been emphasized. McCrate (2012, 65) argues that the work–

108   *Well-being and the quality of working lives*

life balance implications of regularity of working routines must be accounted for by employers. Workers on casualized or flexibilized contracts often have little guarantee of work or pay from week to week. Where workers face greater irregularity this can act as a source of work–life conflict impacting their ability to plan, and contribute to, activities such as childcare. This is highly relevant for workers in a range of flexibilized and casualized forms of employment. Organizations, therefore, need to reflect on the use of employer-driven flexibilization, given its potential negative consequences for workers.

WORK-TIME AND OVERWORK

Lengthy work-time is a potential source of conflict with balance. Despite policy being enacted across the globe with a focus on limiting maximum working hours in an effort to avoid the negative health and well-being consequences of extensive work-time, long hours persist for many workers (Messenger, 2011, 302; OECD, 2020; Philp and Wheatley, 2013). A long-standing problem affecting the lives of many workers, long hours have persisted in a number of sectors and occupations due to both individual and organizational drivers, with the former potentially reflecting financial drivers and/or workaholism (see Chapter 4) and the latter structures and cultures which view long hours as evidencing commitment or professional competence (Cha, 2010, 304). In Europe, a limit of 48 hours, averaged over a 17-week period, was introduced through the European Working Time Directive (Council Directive 94/103/EC) in 1993 (European Commission, 2005). The UK adopted the Directive incorporating a voluntary opt-out waiver for workers through the Working Time Regulations (WTR), implemented in 1998. Similar policies have been enacted in other countries, including for example in South Korea. A limit of 40 hours per week (on average) plus a maximum of 12 hours overtime to give a total of 52 hours per week, albeit with exemptions for small businesses, was introduced in 2018.

Overwork is a particular concern, although this term is subject to differing definition. Overwork has been defined in reference to long hours of work (50 or more hours per week) (Cha and Weedon, 2014). Hours-based definitions of this form are also offered which use alternative terminology including 'excessive hours' referring to working over 48 hours per week (Messenger, 2011). However, the concept of overwork has also been considered by the Chartered Institute of Personnel and Development (CIPD), for example, in relation to differences between reported hours of work and preferred hours of work taking into account the need to earn a living (Wheatley and Gifford, 2019, 8). In extreme cases, long hours and overwork can lead to significant negative social and health and well-being implications for workers (Kahneman et al., 2006; Philp et al., 2005). The potential for, and dangers of, overwork is well documented in the international context. In particular in Japan, where

Flexibility 109

the concepts of *Karoshi*, referring to death from overwork, and *Karo-jisatsu*, which denotes suicide associated with depression caused by overwork, have long been identified (Uehata, 1991; Yamauchi et al., 2017).

Evidence suggests a greater level of resistance to reductions in work-time among some of those in leadership and managerial roles (e.g. Bielenski et al., 2002, 13; Wheatley et al., 2011). Cultures of overwork may not only be damaging to worker well-being, but also actively disadvantage certain groups including carers and especially mothers as they may simply be unable to work lengthy hours or where they do this may have significant negative impacts on health and well-being (Cha, 2010). The presence of long hours cultures within organizations or teams including micromanagement and monitoring of workers and incidence of meetings cultures extend time spent working without, in many cases, providing a clear productive benefit (Box 5.3). Where there is good task clarity within teams, which should be the aim of leaders/managers, use of Taylorist control methods is particularly difficult to justify. These behaviours act as a barrier to the ability of employees to be flexible in their working routines, and can limit use of both formal and informal flexible working arrangements and autonomy over the timing and location of work.

BOX 5.3   MEASUREMENT OF WORKING HOURS AND OVERWORK

Methods for the measurement of working hours and overwork are often quite objective and simple in their nature. This includes measures of working hours, which can be split into measures of usual hours (i.e. the number of hours you would normally work), and actual hours (i.e. the number of hours worked in a specific week). Measures extend to paid and unpaid overtime, with the latter reflecting time spent working which is not rewarded directly. Measures of overwork can similarly take a simple form, such as measuring the difference between actual/usual and contracted hours, or the difference between actual/usual and preferred hours of work. The latter measure of preferences regarding working hours can take the form of a question asking for the number of hours that would be preferred, therefore enabling the comparison with contracted or actual/usual worked hours, or it can involve questioning around broader preferences for longer or shorter hours. Example questions from the UK Working Lives Survey and British Household Panel Survey, respectively, illustrate these two alternatives.

> **UK Working Lives Survey**
> Question: *While taking into account the need to earn your living, how many hours per week would you like to work if you could freely choose?*
> Answer: [open ended number allowing decimal place]
>
> **British Household Panel Survey**
> Question: *Thinking about the hours you work, assuming that you would be paid the same amount per hour, would you prefer to work fewer hours than you do now?*
> Answer options:
>   Work fewer hours than you do now.
>   Work more hours than you do now.
>   Or carry on working the same number of hours?
>   Don't know/can't say.

WORK RECOVERY AND BREAKS

Research into the concept of work recovery explores the ways in which different types of breaks from work, and the nature of the activities undertaken during these breaks, act to counteract work fatigue and replenish personal resources (Sonnentag, 2001; Sonnentag and Fritz, 2007). The existing literature on work recovery highlights a number of potential benefits to employee well-being, from the use of breaks in working routines, and in turn benefits for employers to levels of productivity and reduced employee absence. Using a sample of US workers, Trougakos et al. (2014) reported that taking lunch and/or coffee breaks, especially those that involve socializing and light exercise, is beneficial as it helps employees experience greater positive emotions. They also identify that having a greater level of choice over how to spend our time during breaks is highly important to the effectiveness of this recovery period (Trougakos et al., 2014, 416).

Systems have been designed to monitor breaks, such as the 'Break-Time Barometer', which aims to persuade workers to socialize by taking breaks in common spaces at the same time as one another (Kirkham et al., 2013, cited in Gallacher et al., 2015). The Break-Time Barometer utilizes a relatively simple system of displaying how many workers are in a staff common room within a workplace. This system is based on the assumption that workers will feel it is a good time to take a break when others are also doing so. Kirkham et al.'s (2013) research in the UK, however, indicated that a system of this nature in some cases can have the opposite effect as employees use it to gauge quieter times when fewer colleagues are taking breaks in order to take a break alone.

Flexibility

While perhaps not always creating the informal interactions and sociability initially desired, the system nevertheless can provide a method for workers to gauge when to take a break, be it when others are around or when break rooms are quieter.

Breaks which involve physical activity have also been shown to have positive effects on the well-being of employees (Taylor et al., 2016). Conducting qualitative research with 35 participants in the US, Taylor et al. (2013) reported several benefits from the use of short 'booster' breaks, including (1) reductions in stress and higher levels of enjoyment; (2) increased awareness of the health benefits of being more active and associated changes in behaviour; and (3) enhanced social interaction among employees. It was, however, identified that greater variety in activity undertaken during booster breaks is likely to be beneficial. US-based research which explored the use of 10-minute outdoor booster breaks, which provide employees with connection to the natural environment, suggested that these types of breaks reduced levels of stress for employees in the workplace (Largo-Wright et al., 2017). Even breaks which are short in duration (40 seconds) have been shown to have restorative benefits to employees where they involve viewing green spaces and the natural environment (Lee et al., 2015). Research has emphasized the potential organizational benefits of breaks including to worker performance. Using a daily diary study of over 100 employees over five work days, Kühnel et al. (2017) suggested positive effects of short breaks on work engagement.

FLEXIBLE WORKING ARRANGEMENTS

Flexible working arrangements can be broadly split into three forms; those that involve the arrangement of work-time, the reduction of work-time and the location of work. A summary of flexible working arrangements and other work–life balance options is provided in Table 5.1. Flexible work options focused on the arrangement of work-time include flexi-time (sometimes referred to as flex-time), compressed hours, and annualized hours (Atkinson and Hall, 2009, 651). Options which focus on the reduction of working hours include part-time, term-time and job share. Arrangements which enable greater flexibility over the location of work comprise forms of remote working including homeworking and teleworking. Finally, there are a range of flexible leave options which can be offered including those focused around parental leave, but also extending to holiday banking, volunteering leave and career breaks. Availability of these arrangements differs considerably by sector and organization, and relative application of different flexible working options varies between countries, dependent on legislation, organizational culture and social norms.

112 · Well-being and the quality of working lives

Table 5.1 · Work–life balance options

Working time arrangements	
Flexi-time	Flexible starting and finishing hours of work, often around a set of core hours (e.g. 10 a.m.–3 p.m.)
Compressed hours	Work fewer but lengthier working days (e.g. four 10-hour days per week)
Annualized hours	Employees undertake contracted number of hours per year, with allocation of hours determined either through agreement between employee and employer, or by the employer in response to 'business need'
Reduced hours arrangements	
Part-time	Reduced hours, often defined as working under 30 hours per week
Term-time	Working only during term-time and taking extended breaks, usually in line with school holidays
Job share	One full-time position is shared between two employees. The job is divided, equally or otherwise, between sharers. Salary, leave and other benefits are divided between each worker on a pro-rata basis
Work location arrangements	
Homeworking (including home-based teleworking)	Working at or from home. This increasingly involves use of mobile technologies, reflected in the term home-based teleworking
Teleworking	Distributed work: paid work outside of the normal place of work including at home, client sites, on the move, and communicating using ICT
Leave arrangements	
Parental leave	Including maternity, paternity and forms of shared and other parental leave (e.g. adoption/fostering leave)
Phased return	Return to work on a reduced schedule typically after sick or parental leave
Annual leave	Annual leave is not necessarily considered as a work–life balance option, but more often a legislated minimum condition of work. Levels of annual leave vary greatly between organizations, sectors and by country
Holiday banking	Buying and selling of holiday hours and/or the ability to build up holiday by working flexibly (flexi-days)
Volunteering leave	Leave given to spend time volunteering
Career breaks and sabbaticals	Leave granted, usually unpaid in the case of career breaks, for a break in employment

Source: Adapted from Wheatley, 2017c.

Flexibility 113

Use of flexible working arrangements and greater control over the timing and location of work, referred to as schedule control, may have particularly positive effects on balance, and has been reported to have strong positive effects on job satisfaction (Jang et al., 2011, 140). The provision of schedule control has been identified as forming a central factor in the successful use of flexible working arrangements such as telework (Clear and Dickson, 2005, 226). Beyond the formal arrangements available to employees at many organizations, the provision of informal flexibility may be preferred or offered in combination with formal arrangements (Box 5.4). It can take the form of varying the start and end times of the working day, or working at home or in other remote locations on an ad hoc basis. Informal flexibility of this nature has been identified in existing research as being highly valued by employees, as it provides a greater degree of schedule control (Hall and Atkinson, 2006, 383). The main limitation to these benefits being realized, however, is that informal flexibility is often limited in availability to certain groups of workers, including those in managerial and professional occupations (Golden, 2009, 46–7).

BOX 5.4   MEASUREMENT OF FLEXIBILITY IN WORK

Measurement of flexible working can include lines of questioning focusing on both formal and informal flexibility. For example, measures of the presence of informal flexibility over the timing of work, and availability and use of formal flexible working arrangements are captured in the Understanding Society survey. Availability of flexible working arrangements is captured through the question, 'If you personally needed any, which of the following arrangements are available at your workplace?' A follow-up question asks about use of flexible working arrangements, 'Do you currently work in any of these ways?' with answer options comprising part-time working; working term-time only; job sharing; flexi-time; working compressed hours; to work annualized hours; to work from home on a regular basis; zero-hours contract; on-call working; other flexible working arrangements, and none of these. Informal flexibility is captured through the question, 'Aside from any formal arrangements for flexible working you have, are you able to vary your working hours on an informal basis, for example by re-arranging your start or finish times if you need to?' with answers comprising yes, no, and sometimes. Example data from the Understanding Society survey, summarized in Figure 5.1, provides insight into availability and use of some of these flexible working arrangements evidencing gaps in provision and differences in use, including by gender, with flexi-time and part-time the most commonly applied. For a full discussion, see Wheatley (2017d).

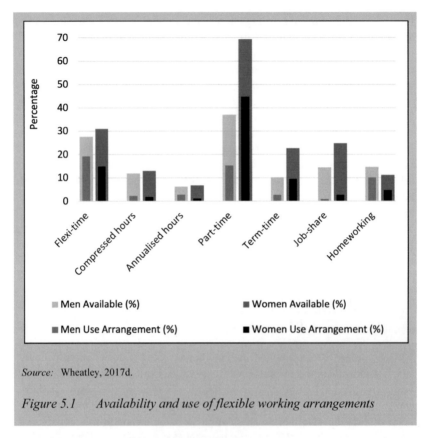

Source: Wheatley, 2017d.

Figure 5.1   Availability and use of flexible working arrangements

FLEXIBILITY AROUND THE ARRANGEMENT OF TIME

Flexible working arrangements focusing on the arrangement, rather than reduction, of work-time can often allow the retention of full-time equivalent hours (Stavrou, 2005, 931). These comprise flexi-time (or flex-time), compressed hours, and annualized hours (Atkinson and Hall, 2009, 651). Flexi-time focuses on the varying of starting and finishing hours of work. In some cases this can include a set of core hours (e.g. 10 a.m.–3 p.m.), or minimum requirements for the number of hours worked in a day or other period (Lee and DeVoe, 2012, 299). Evidence suggests that flexi-time can improve work–life balance through enhancing control over work-time and reducing work pressure (Russell et al., 2009, 89–91; Wheatley, 2017a). An employee-centred flexi-time strategy, rather than adoption of flexibility as part of a cost-reduction strategy can increase profitability of firms (Lee and

DeVoe, 2012, 311) through more effective deployment of workers and performance improvements from workers having greater control over the timing of work. However, use of this arrangement can create conflicts, for example with attendance at meetings or access to workplace car parking which may limit realized levels of flexibility (Wheatley, 2012a). Working fewer, but longer days (e.g. working a four-day week or nine-day fortnight) is referred to as a compressed hours flexible working arrangement. Annualized hours, meanwhile, focuses on the allocation of work-time on an annual basis, with either an agreement between employee and employer, or the employer determining the distribution of these hours in response to business needs (Stavrou, 2005, 931). While offering useful flexibility for workers and employers, the main difficulties faced with both compressed and annualized hours surround the potential for uneven workloads and difficulties surrounding the length of some work days/weeks which could limit work–life balance benefits.

REDUCED HOURS ARRANGEMENTS

Reduced hours arrangements focus on the reduction of work-time and include part-time, term-time and job share. Part-time work is a major form of employment in terms of numbers employed in this manner. Working part-time is often defined in reference to working less than 30 hours per week. This arrangement can provide improved work–life balance, including increased satisfaction with leisure time, although evidence is conflicting and impacts on life satisfaction are less clear (Gregory and Connolly, 2008, F2; Wheatley, 2017a). It is highly gendered as, for example, in the UK around two in five women work part-time compared to one in seven men (Wheatley, 2017a). It is also engaged with differently throughout our working lives. Women working part-time often do so during the middle part of their working life when childcare and other household responsibilities place particular demands on their time, whereas among men it is more common at either end of the working age spectrum (Lawton and Wheatley, 2018). Younger men often work part-time alongside study commitments and/or when entering the labour market, and older men move into part-time working as a form of partial retirement (Gregory and Connolly, 2008, F4). As per the name, term-time involves only working during term-time with breaks in work aligned with school holidays. More common among the professions, in some cases this arrangement can reflect an employer-driven approach used to contract employees only during term-times when demand is greater. Job share, meanwhile, is an arrangement in which a single full-time job is shared between two employees (often equally but not in all cases). Each worker can therefore benefit from improved work–life balance while retaining career opportunities and status. It has been argued that employers, in turn, could benefit from enhanced productivity, resilience, leadership, commitment, retention and knowledge sharing (Stavrou, 2005), although realizing all of these benefits may be quite challenging. Job sharers are responsible for the entire job which is divided by task/time/role or other criteria (Branine, 2004, 137). It is a less commonly used arrangement with most job sharers being mothers (Russell et al., 2009, 83), although in certain senior roles workload can act as a rationale for job share (Durbin and Tomlinson, 2010, 633).

Reduced hours arrangements present workers with a number of difficulties including work intensification (i.e. working fewer but more intense hours or not taking breaks where workloads are not commensurate with a reduced hours role) and pay reductions which can result in these arrangements having significant financial consequences (Hall and Atkinson, 2006, 380; Lewis and Humbert, 2010, 246). Constraints associated with the household division of labour, including care, can act as key drivers for the move into reduced hours arrangements (Fagan et al., 2012, 23; Lawton and Wheatley, 2018). Meanwhile, some employers may simply enact these arrangements to generate numerical flexibility. A problematic and common perception among workers (also held more broadly in society) is that reduced hours jobs are poor quality and/or temporary (Fagan et al., 2012). A number of other factors have to be considered in the adoption of reduced hours, by both the organization and worker, including the tendency for reduced responsibilities and associated reductions in opportunities for development and promotion, and poor workplace support for workers on reduced hours (Foster, 2007, 74; McDonald et al., 2009, 153–4). These factors require considerable reflection and should be fed into organizational strategy, especially given the observed differences in the use of reduced hours arrangements by gender which could act to perpetuate gender segregation and wage gaps (Plantenga and Remery, 2010), and have wider implications on workplace well-being.

REMOTE WORKING

Remote working has taken on increased significance since early 2020 due to the global Covid-19 pandemic. Rapid expansion occurred which, while in some cases temporary, has the potential to create a shift in patterns of work towards greater long-term use of remote working. Remote working is a fairly broad term. It is alternatively referred to as teleworking or telecommuting, and is often conflated with homeworking. A range of other terms have been used to capture this form of work including distributed work, virtual work, mobile work and distance work which are themselves distinct in the types of work they capture, and are discussed separately later in this chapter. While remote or teleworking typically involves paid work taking place at home, it can more completely be described as paid work which takes place outside of the normal or main workplace (Green, 2017; Pyöriä, 2011). It can occur in a range of loca-

Flexibility 117

tions including on the move, in hotels, airports, at client sites, in a co-working location, smart centre or digital work hub (Bentley et al., 2016, 207). Remote working has been defined as a 'flexible work arrangement that affords employees the ability to periodically, regularly, or exclusively perform work for their employers from home or another remote location that is equipped with the appropriate computer-based technology to transfer work to the central organization' (Caillier, 2012, 462). Remote work involves the use of ICT including broadband internet, cloud computing, wireless technology and smartphones (Bentley et al., 2016). Common among these technologies is the opportunity for virtual and location-independent working and 24/7 connectivity.

In the context of work taking place within the home, remote working can be used to refer to home-based teleworking. Although homeworking is also commonly used as an interchangeable term to describe this activity it should be acknowledged that this term describes two distinct forms of work taking place at home. These are (1) industrial homeworking (e.g. more traditional forms of homeworking including craft workers whose residence also acts as their workshop) and (2) home-based teleworking (i.e. homeworking facilitated by ICT which includes workers whose main workplace is in the business premises of an employer) (Mokhtarian et al., 2004; Wheatley, 2020). Homeworking statistics have been indicative of relatively low incidence among employees, although with steady growth recorded in recent decades. Levels of remote or home-based teleworking eclipsed these figures due to the lockdowns witnessed in many nations in 2020. Further discussion of this growth is remote working is provided in Box 5.5.

BOX 5.5   RAPID EXPANSION OF REMOTE WORKING IN THE COVID-19 PANDEMIC

The rapid expansion of homeworking across the globe in response to the Covid-19 pandemic has been unprecedented. Prior to the pandemic, estimates suggested a relatively slow growth in those working exclusively at home. For example, across the EU-27 countries, around 5.4 per cent of those employed reported usually working from home in 2019, and this figure had been relatively constant since 2009. Where growth has been present is in more flexible applications of homeworking where working at home is combined, for example, with time spent at the office or visiting clients; this was reported by 5.2 per cent of those employed in 2009 across the EU-27, and had risen to 9 per cent in 2019 (Milasi et al., 2020). Patterns had been relatively consistent elsewhere, including in the UK (Wheatley, 2021).

Statistics on the short-term impact of Covid-19 evidence a level of relative consistency across a number of countries in the temporary growth in remote working, with around two in five of those who continued working reporting homeworking at peak in the UK, EU-27, Brazil and USA (ILO, 2020; Milasi et al., 2020). These changes are, in principle, temporary and the rates of homeworking quickly diminished, with for example only 20 per cent of workers reporting exclusively homeworking in the UK by September 2020. However, the changes have prompted wider debates around the future of work and more permanent changes in working routines towards greater application of homeworking, on the basis that this could deliver benefits to workers (e.g. improving work–life balance), organizations (e.g. reducing the need for workspace) and society (e.g. lowering environmental impacts of economic activity by reducing levels of commuting).

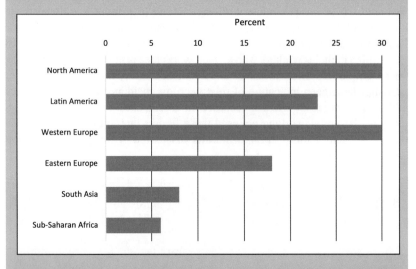

Source: ILO, 2020.

Figure 5.2   Home-based work potential

Nevertheless, there are limits to the application of remote working. Many jobs cannot be converted to homeworking in their current design, including jobs associated with mass production and highly divided labour (e.g. machine operatives, assembly workers). Other jobs, meanwhile, are reliant on workers continuing to travel to employment centres, those working in the hospitality sector for example. Based on the existing evidence, permanent exclusive homeworking would also likely have quite distinct impacts, both in relation to the careers and well-being of workers, compared with working remotely on a more hybrid basis (i.e. combining working at home and in the office), where more positive impacts have generally been reported (Wheatley, 2017a, 2021). Estimates suggest that currently around 18 per cent of workers globally could work from home (ILO, 2020). However, this is split highly unevenly, as outlined in Figure 5.2. In low- and middle-income countries, in particular, homeworking is not feasible for a much greater proportion of workers due to (1) the task-intensity of many jobs associated with the organization of production; (2) the size of the informal employment sector; and (3) the low level of technology adoption, which limits the practical potential of conducting work at home.

Remote working offers an array of potential benefits to workers including greater control over the timing of the working day and avoidance of the time and cost involved in the commute (Tietze et al., 2009; Wheatley, 2012b). The evidence base also supports the notion that remote working, and especially homeworking, can enhance job satisfaction (Felstead and Henseke, 2017; Morganson et al., 2010; Wheatley, 2012b, 2017a). However, it may be dependent to some degree on the personality of the individual as those who are more extroverted in particular may find distance from the workplace and colleagues more problematic (Virick et al., 2010). Outcomes for homeworkers also differ between groups of workers. Highly skilled homeworkers more often report good jobs and associated benefits to satisfaction levels, while part-time and self-employed homeworkers report lower-quality experiences in their jobs (Wheatley, 2020). A range of other benefits can be realized through the adoption of remote working routines. These include increased accessibility, including among those who may not be able to access a traditional workplace due to mental and/or physical health concerns, and for whom working remotely may offer a route into paid work (Green, 2017, 1646); reductions in absenteeism associated with, for example, the need to provide childcare; and reduced accommodation costs as office or other workspaces can be reorganized and rationalized (Bailey and Kurland, 2002; Moos and Skaburskis, 2008).

A number of common challenges are faced in the use of remote working including lack of face-to-face contact, difficulties in coordinating collaborative and team-working tasks, and potential negative impacts on career development as a result of reduced visibility within the organization and associated reduction in managerial support (Virick et al., 2010). Workers may also encounter negative well-being effects from the loss of professional and social networks, resulting in feelings of isolation (Bentley et al., 2016; Tietze et al., 2009). Remote workers face difficulties in dividing time and space, impacting work–life balance due to the blurring of work with the rest of their lives. Those working at home often encounter longer and more intense patterns of work which reduce leisure time (Nätti et al., 2011). Delanoeije et al. (2020) report evidence of blurring and both work-to-home (i.e. work interrupting home activities outside of work-time), and home-to-work (i.e. home activities interrupting work tasks) conflict among workers who combine working at home and working at a workplace.

Concerns around lack of control and misuse of company time have historically limited remote working. This has been reported in pre-pandemic research exploring use of teleworking in Japan where Sato (2019) reported that many organizations, even larger businesses, did not allow formal teleworking among the majority of their employees. However, despite this lack of availability of formal arrangements, many workers reported it necessary to take work home due to the high-intensity work culture in Japan. Remote working may also be less beneficial where it simply reflects a cost reduction exercise by employers, effectively shifting the costs of workspace onto the worker (Moos and Skaburskis, 2008, 336). Where employers do not fully embrace remote working and lack trust in their employees, they may engage in monitoring and micromanagement as they have concerns over malfeasance and misuse of company time (Wight and Raley, 2009). This can be enacted using technical control methods such as software which automatically records and monitors data on productivity and task completion (Callaghan and Thompson, 2001). These systems are used to monitor and evaluate workers and can be used effectively to promote task completion and work effort through targets and monitoring workers in most remote contexts. However, technical control systems suffer from limitations including potential exploitation by workers who could take advantage of monitoring systems by asking others to occasionally log activity when not working. Concerns of this nature, which can reflect a very real risk or a lack of trust dependent on the case in question, act to limit buy-in from some employers (Wight and Raley, 2009). Fear of this type of response to the provision of flexibility can prompt the application of Taylorist 'low discretion' work organization involving high levels of micromanagement and monitoring and surveillance systems (Choi et al., 2008). However, this creates a vicious cycle of distrust and inflexibility which perpetuates intense and demotivating working conditions. Adoption of remote working in this way also results in an invasion of privacy and increased work-related stress (Russell et al., 2009, 89), counteracting work–life balance benefits which can be realized from paid work taking place outside of the traditional workplace.

AGILE WORKING

Agile working, alternatively referred to as activity-based working (ABW), is an approach to working which involves maximizing levels of flexibility in order to empower workers to choose how, when and where to work so that

Flexibility 121

they are able to perform to their optimum (Hesselberg, 2018). It is sometimes used interchangeably with terms such as teleworking or remote working but is distinct in its meaning. As per teleworking and remote working, agile working incorporates working in different locations including the company office, co-working spaces, client premises, on the move, in cafes, hotels, airports, and at home (Bentley et al., 2016, 207). It extends to working across different time zones (in virtual geographically distributed teams), using different routines and methods including flexible working arrangements (e.g. flexi-time, part-time, job share, compressed hours), and the adoption of agile practices such as the 'Daily' in which workers meet and update each other on progress with their tasks, priorities for that day and any support they require.

Adopting an agile approach, however, goes beyond the activities of the individual worker and provision of flexible working arrangements. It is not just about the provision of flexible working hours and hot-desking in open-plan offices. It involves the implementation of an agile approach throughout the organization. The agile approach can be usefully understood using the strategic elements of the framework for workplace well-being (structure, culture, environment), as adopting an agile approach involves incorporating agile organizational structures (e.g. processes, policies), an agile organizational culture (e.g. leadership, behaviours) and an agile working environment (e.g. physical workspace). A range of potential benefits can be realized from being agile as it better places the organization to improve, innovate and adapt to change (Hesselberg, 2018). Many of the dimensions and sub-dimensions of workplace well-being are directly influenced by an approach to working which is agile. Core aspects of agile working include expanded levels of autonomy and control (a job properties sub-dimension), flexibility (itself a core dimension) and differences in the nature of the physical space in which we work (a further core dimension). Given the clear intersection between well-being and a number of the core components of agile working, including greater degrees of autonomy and flexibility, when adopted in an effective manner agile working has the potential to act as major tool for enhancing workplace well-being alongside the already identified benefits to worker and organizational performance. This requires 'buy-in' to agile working across the organization. Aspects of agile working to consider and monitor for effective implementation within the organization are summarized with respect to the framework for workplace well-being in Figure 5.3.

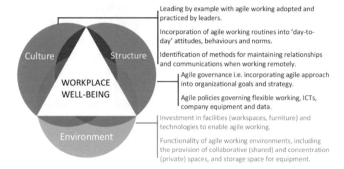

Figure 5.3   Employing an agile working approach for workplace well-being

WORKING FLEXIBLY IN OTHER LOCATIONS

Teleworking is a relatively expansive term which identifies that work can take place in a wide range of locations. Working outside of the traditional workplace may involve working at home; however, it can consist of working in multiple locations or in co-working spaces, or involve travelling. Working in multiple locations is often referred to as mobile working, multi-location working or mobile teleworking (Hislop and Axtell, 2009, 74). It is conducted on the move, at client sites, and in remote locations such as coffee shops, airports and public spaces. Mobile workers may have no main workplace, but equally may report at differing levels of frequency into a base at an employer premises. Mobile working offers greater flexibility and control to the worker, and potential job satisfaction benefits from interacting with different colleagues and clients in secondary workplaces (Vartiainen and Hyrkkänen, 2010, 133). Organizations also benefit from cost reduction as they are able to lessen capital investment in workspaces and can adopt agile working routines.

However, a number of difficulties are faced in the adoption of mobile working practices. These include productivity difficulties associated with suitability of certain tasks to working remotely or on the move; short-term impacts of technology failures; potential for property and data loss/theft when working in remote and public spaces; lack of a consistent professional/social network; and difficulties in continually adapting to different workplaces (Boell et al., 2016, 125–6; Hislop and Axtell, 2009, 73; Vartiainen and Hyrkkänen, 2010, 133). Work in which travel is a core function, such as taxi and delivery driving, has been altered dramatically in recent years by technological developments including app-driven and smartphone platforms (Srnicek, 2017). Demand for these services, for example Uber and Deliveroo, has grown exponentially. In

Flexibility 123

line with other highly flexible forms of work, including gig working which is discussed in the case study at the end of this chapter, workers in these jobs can benefit from the considerable level of flexibility (Howcroft and Bergvall-Kåreborn, 2019; Osnowitz and Henson, 2016, 348). However, these jobs have been recognized as often being of low quality, or at least having lower-quality characteristics, including irregular and uncertain (at least in the short term) patterns of work; extensive, intensive and unsociable working hours; associated work-related stress and health and safety concerns; and (relatively) low pay (De Stefano, 2016; Scholz, 2016; Srnicek, 2017).

Co-working and makers-spaces offer small firms, start-ups and freelancers (including gig workers) a location to centre their business activity. They operate on a pay-for-use basis offering a high degree of flexibility to micro and start-up businesses (Spinuzzi, 2012). Makers-spaces employ the same shared space concept as co-working spaces, but are specifically designed around the manufacture, maintenance and repair of goods by artisan craft makers, tinkerers and digital-era inventors (Dougherty, 2012). Both of these types of flexible workspace offer a location that encourages collaboration, creativity, idea sharing, networking, socializing, and generation of opportunities (Fuzi, 2015, 462). Fairly basic accommodation is often offered in smaller co-working spaces, while larger spaces offer conference/event space and areas to meet, socialize and relax (e.g. gardens and cafes) (Mariotti et al., 2017, 58). Considerable growth has been witnessed in these workspaces; estimates suggest around 2,000 spaces were being used by approximately half a million workers in 2013 (Johns and Gratton, 2013), and this had grown to half a million workers in 4,000 co-working spaces in the USA alone by 2017 (Emergent Research, 2018, cited by Small Business Labs, 2018). Co-working spaces are more common in urban centres, although examples are found in rural and less populated areas (Fuzi, 2015; Mariotti et al., 2017). The potential benefits of the use of co-working spaces are considerable, including agglomeration and networking benefits among micro-entrepreneurs and freelance workers (Bouncken and Reuschl, 2018; Fuzi, 2015). Co-working spaces also enable those who would otherwise work alone to avoid isolation (Fuzi, 2015, 467; King, 2017). Challenges faced in the use of co-working spaces include the cost of use, loss of privacy, knowledge leakage, competition between users limiting agglomeration benefits, and opportunistic behaviours including theft of both physical and intellectual property and misuse of knowledge or contacts (Bouncken and Reuschl, 2018, 331). For a fuller discussion of working in non-standard locations, see Wheatley (2020).

CASE STUDY: FLEXIBILITY AND WORK IN THE GIG ECONOMY

Adam Badger, Royal Holloway, University of London.

The gig economy has been heralded as the new free and flexible way to work; as workers undertake piecemeal tasks for piece-rate pay, as and when they are able to as an independent contractor or consultant (Aloisi, 2016; Friedman, 2014). This case study looks explicitly at freedom and flexibility in the gig economy and emerges from the broader academic, policy and corporate discussions that are currently playing out – in addition to findings from a nine-month-long covert ethnography working as a food-delivery cyclist in London. Gig working usually offers a high degree of temporal and spatial flexibility, although this is dependent on the type of work involved. Woodcock and Graham (2019) identify two forms of gig work: (1) cloud work that is highly flexible and can be performed anywhere using an internet connection (e.g. web design) and (2) geographically tethered work that offers less location flexibility (e.g. delivery driving). This case study focuses on geographically tethered gig work. While the platform I worked for cannot be named for legal and ethical reasons (for more, see Badger and Woodcock, 2019) it will be referred to throughout as 'The Platform'. The Platform is a current industry leader, valued at $7 billion. They operate in approximately 800 cities throughout Europe and Asia, with an unknown number of workers.

Along with other companies, The Platform has garnered significant attention with the British government who recognize their offering as a new and important work form that will become critical to the economy in the future (Taylor et al., 2017). This reflects the gig economy's promise to provide thousands of flexible jobs to the under- and unemployed in markets across the world. Gig work can enable workers to bargain specific working conditions, enhancing control over the timing and location of work (Osnowitz and Henson, 2016, 348); however, this may be the privilege of workers who are more employable (e.g. the highly skilled) (Green, 2011), and by definition in demand. Despite the glossy PR campaigns by platforms and the pledge to improve working lives through flexible scheduling, the reality is that workers are struggling to survive. In fact, gig economy workers have been going on strike across the world to protest the terms and conditions of their work, seeking greater job security, increased pay and a base level of benefits that would allow them to lead a less precarious existence and achieve greater well-being (Cant, 2019; Keith et al., 2019).

This case study outlines legal and contractual flexibility. It then discusses the benefits of flexibility in the gig economy, before ending with analysis of the 'faux' or false sense of flexibility workers feel that impacts their mental, physical and financial health. It is essential to remember throughout that this type of work is done by a varied group of people for various reasons. Often, workers are also facing other intersectional vulnerabilities, such as being migrants without recall to welfare and security; or are workers who also have informal caring responsibilities (such as children or ill family members). As such, those who are most reliant on the platforms are also the most precarious, and thus more susceptible to any negative impacts this highly flexible business model creates.

Contractual Flexibility

Workers at The Platform, like those in the rest of the gig economy are classified as 'self-employed independent contractors'. In my case, this meant signing a 'Supplier Agreement' rather than an 'Employment Contract' as with more traditional forms of work, which included clauses stating that my account could be 'terminated at any time with immediate effect'. In this regard, The Platform operationalizes flexibility to hire and fire staff at a moment's notice (a type of employer flexibility), while workers do not share the same powers. In more traditional self-employment relationships, workers are able to negotiate remuneration and terms for individual jobs; however, in the case of the gig economy, workers are unable to negotiate pay and the terms of the agreement. Their only 'flexibility' is in deciding whether to sign the contract and get work on The Platform's terms, or to not sign the contract and not receive the work and remuneration. This is complicated by the positionality of the worker who may experience diminished agency in this process if they are unable to find alternative work elsewhere. This became particularly poignant in 2020 during the Covid-19 pandemic, which left many people redundant and searching for income opportunities in the gig economy.

The contractual situation has led to Moore and Joyce (2020) and De Stefano and Aloisi (2019) to declare that gig economy workers are part of a 'bogus' self-employment relationship, whereby the contractual framing of the work does not reflect the realities of working life. As such, while platforms state that workers are in fact self-employed, the way in which their work is done through The Platform, and their contractual lack of negotiating power does not actually reflect a self-employment relationship. In this sense, workers are given some flexibility at work, but this is tokenistic in comparison to the flexibility and freedoms the organization enjoys. While this is a bleak picture, in my own and others' findings (Cant, 2019; Rosenblat, 2019; Woodcock and Graham, 2019), most gig workers do not want to be made into employees of a platform, as they perceive this would restrict the freedoms they need at work.

In a European and US context, this is difficult because there are only two employment statuses enshrined into employment law – either 'employed' or 'self-employed'. However, in the UK, there is a middle 'worker' status that reflects the position of workers who have the flexibility of someone self-employed, but lack the negotiating powers and broader autonomy self-employed workers have in practice (Employment Rights Act, 1996). In this classification, workers maintain flexibility with regard to scheduling and autonomy at work; however, they are also given some of the protections regular employees would expect. These include 'the national minimum wage; protection from unlawful deduction of wages; statutory minimum paid holiday; statutory minimum rest breaks; a maximum 48-hour working week unless agreed otherwise; protection against unlawful discrimination; protection from whistleblowing; the right to equal treatment if working part time' (RSA, n.d.). This provides a level of flexibility to workers that is beneficial, with a degree of security that would mitigate against broader precarity and therefore aid well-being both at work and beyond. Trade unions argue that this is the perfect classification type for workers in the gig economy. Reclassification as 'workers', rather than 'self-employed independent contractors' has been at the centre of high-profile legal disputes in the platform economy (UK Employment Tribunals, 2016).

Real Flexibility Benefits

Moving beyond the contract to focus on working life in the gig economy, it is undeniable that flexibility brings essential benefits to workers. For example, one interviewee recounted that they took the job because 'it's important that I have the flexibility to look after my Mum who is disabled. I also have intermittent health problems myself that mean I need to take time off at short notice now and again' (Interviewee 1). Here, the interviewee chose work in the gig economy because of the scheduling flexibility that allowed her to manage her caring responsibilities. This is distinctly different from the scheduling rigidity in other service sectors of the economy, where missing a shift at short notice – even for emergencies – can result in being fired or disciplined (Ehrenreich, 2001; Wood, 2020). This reinforces the analysis by Milkman et al. (2020) who found that for women especially, gig economy work allowed them to undertake paid work and unpaid care work for their own families. However, it is crucial to remember the gendered and classed elements of this analysis. Often it is women who carry out caring labour in the home and in the workplace, and it is often unremunerated and presents barriers to entry to formal employment. As a result, while people are liberated to carry out essential care work in the home, they also become reliant upon the platforms for any income in lieu of suitable welfare provision.

Beyond scheduling flexibility, workers also enjoy the job flexibility that gig work brings. While they are unable to negotiate payment for individual tasks, gig workers are able to deploy limited autonomy in rejecting certain jobs. In this sense, gig workers divine a sense of agency and meaning from their work through developing the relevant expertise to know when to deploy their flexibility to best effect; feeling further involved and in control of their own fate. However, in reality this is simply window-dressing on an otherwise exploitative labour relation (Gregory, 2020; van Doorn and Badger, 2020), as while there is limited flexibility available, this is set within very narrow constraints with the more existential realities of the work still being dictated by platforms. Schor et al. (2016, 66) term this a 'paradox of openness and distinction' that exists between the imagined freedom workers are promised and the lack of real freedom they experience.

Faux Flexibility: Scheduling Freedom?

When investigating the realities of scheduling flexibility, it is clear that what exists in theory (total freedom to schedule work whenever a worker likes) and reality (the need to work regularly at specific times) are different. This stems from the fact that in a piece-rate system, being available for work and being offered paying work are not the same thing. In the case of food delivery, workers are free to log into the app and make themselves available for work whenever they like; however, if there are no orders in the system, they won't be offered jobs and won't be able to earn any money. While some people order food at odd times of day, the reality of customers' circadian and dietary rhythms are that orders are made in a very specific temporal window; from 11 a.m. to 2 p.m., and from 6 p.m. to 9 p.m. In my time working for The Platform, I experimented with different scheduling arrangements, such as working from 2 p.m. to 5 p.m., for example, and regularly found that over the course of a three-hour window of being logged in and available for work, I would earn nothing as there would be no jobs for me to take. This was reiterated by all other workers I spoke to at interview, who said that through trial and error they had worked out the best times for them and now only worked those times. The nature of the food delivery market represents a landscape of feast and famine for workers who must work at peak times to make work worthwhile – the flexibility to log in becomes worthless if you are unable to earn. In short, while you have the flexibility to log in for work whenever you like, this isn't the same as having the flexibility to work and earn when you like, as there may be no work available.

With regard to worker well-being, this often means that gig workers end up working odd and unsociable hours that have deleterious impacts on their mental and familial health. Customers want food delivered at mealtimes and at the weekends; the times most valued by people to spend with family or friends. The price for not working these times is financial insecurity and, as

128   *Well-being and the quality of working lives*

such, many feel coerced into going to work even when they do not want to, despite the so-called freedoms the work offers. Compounding this reality with the very low rates of pay common in the gig economy means that many end up working 12-hour broken shift days, six days a week, just to be able to survive and support their families and financial dependants. Flexibility in practice becomes the flexibility to overwork, which can present significant challenges to mental and physical health.

In conclusion, it is clear that there are elements of flexibility bound up in gig work. However, as we begin to scratch beneath the surface it becomes evident that the advantages and disadvantages this flexibility may bring are distributed neither fairly nor equitably between workers and the organization. While there is an ultimate flexibility to make yourself available for work whenever suits, the reality of just-in-time gig work means that there may not be any tasks available for you to complete. Due to the lack of sufficient employment protections, this leaves workers exposed to – and reliant upon – the platform and food delivery marketplace to earn enough to survive. For many, the cost of flexibility without protection is a state of in-work poverty. In my own time working for The Platform, I'd even met other workers who were now homeless, despite working 60 hours a week. When understanding flexibility and well-being at work, it is crucial to remember that being flexible to make yourself available for work, and actually getting any work, are two very different things: that without protection, workers can be left in a precarious position, needing to work longer and longer hours to survive and, finally, that this precarity and flexibility is experienced differently by different people. For those just topping up their income, or earning a bit of 'beer money' the uncertainty of this ultimately flexible work isn't a massive concern. For those reliant on gig work to pay their bills and feed themselves and their families, this flexibility becomes rendered into extreme precarity, with significant impacts on their physical, mental and financial well-being.

CHAPTER SUMMARY: THE ROLE OF FLEXIBILITY IN WORKPLACE WELL-BEING

Flexibility is a core component of workplace well-being. It permeates throughout our jobs and its impact is felt in the rest of our lives. Used effectively, flexibility can enable the achievement of a desirable balance between work and life and associated positive outcomes for well-being. Embedding flexibility within organizations can take the form of effective management and monitoring of workloads, putting in place cultures which promote use of breaks, and availability and use of both formal and informal flexible working arrangements.

The positive response of workers and employers to the unprecedented rapid expansion of remote working due to the global Covid-19 pandemic reinforces the mutual benefits for workers and employers to performance, job satisfaction and work–life balance that can be realized from flexibility in work, in this case from working at home. Nevertheless, work does, and should, continue to occur outside of the home. Large-scale shifts in the way we work, such as the recent temporary growth in remote working, have highlighted the importance of individual choice regarding the timing and location of work, and continue to show the value, to worker well-being in particular, of physically connecting with others (colleagues and clients) in the workplace. Moving forward, use of hybrid models combining time spent at a co-located workplace with time spent working in other locations, including the home, could offer a particularly successful approach for both worker and organization. Success, though, requires organizational buy-in to flexible working including provision of adequate job resources such as ICT infrastructure.

Potential difficulties associated with flexibility include the potential for gaps between provision and use of flexible working arrangements, which requires effective communication and signposting of these opportunities and a culture which is enabling of flexibility. Equally, a focus on cost reduction and numerical flexibility (including application of flexible contracting such as gig working and zero-hours contracts) is not likely to result in mutual benefits arising, if employee-focused flexibility is not given adequate consideration, and any gains for the organization obtained from this course of action could well be limited to the short term. Where flexibility results in a lack of centralization of workplace and distance between workers and their employer, including forms of remote working considered in this chapter, this can reduce feelings of connectedness and coherency and can create problems with communications and the monitoring of job activity. A number of digital solutions are available to facilitate these activities, although the implementation of these must be managed carefully. The greatest benefits to both organizations and workers can be obtained from successfully embedding flexibility into working routines within an organizational strategy and culture that promotes and supports employee-led flexibility.

6.   Rewarding careers

INTRODUCTION

The rewarding careers dimension of workplace well-being comprises extrinsic factors which facilitate, or create barriers to, achieving a healthy and rewarding career from the pay and other benefits we receive from work, to relative levels of job security and opportunities for training, career development and progression. In this sense this dimension of workplace well-being acts in synergy with the job properties dimension which focuses predominately on the intrinsic factors influencing our well-being at work. This chapter begins with a discussion of work motivation (i.e. the factors which drive us to put in effort and work hard), including the distinction between intrinsic and extrinsic motivation drawing on the work of Hertzberg et al. (1959) and Deci and Ryan (2000) amongst others. This assists our understanding of workplace well-being by linking together the discussion of intrinsic characteristics of work from Chapter 4 with the extrinsic concepts explored in detail in this chapter. The chapter then moves on to consider the sub-dimensions of the rewarding careers dimension of workplace well-being, beginning with pay and benefits, before reflecting on the contracts governing work including the flexibilization of contracts and the impacts of job insecurity on worker well-being. Different models of career development and progression are explored, including the protean (Briscoe et al., 2006; Hall, 2004; Hall et al., 2012) and kaleidoscope career (Sullivan et al., 2009), with consideration given to the gendered nature of careers. This discussion is extended with the use of a case study that explores the role of travel-for-work in career development and reflects on this relationship in the context of debates over physical mobility in the post-pandemic future of work. The chapter then considers different conceptualisations of career success including those focused around balance and well-being, before reflecting on the implications for well-being at work of the relative balance between effort and reward drawing on the literature on effort-reward imbalance (Siegrist et al., 1986, 1999, 2004). The chapter ends by drawing together the exploration of the components of the rewarding careers dimension with respect to the framework for workplace well-being.

Rewarding careers

INTRINSIC AND EXTRINSIC WORK MOTIVATION

Key to discussion and debate around reward from work is the concept of motivation. Much like other components of workplace well-being, motivation has both intrinsic and extrinsic forms. The discussion here extends that introduced in Chapter 4 which considered the distinction between intrinsic and extrinsic characteristics of work including reference to the seminal work by Herzberg et al. (1959) which divides these characteristics into 'extrinsic hygiene factors' and 'intrinsic motivators'. Motivation in the context of work refers to the range of factors which act to drive an individual to work hard (Locke and Latham, 2004). It reflects a desire to perform which is influenced by both intrinsic factors (i.e. originating from the individual's own desires) and extrinsic factors (i.e. external demands) (Ryan and Deci, 2000). It should also be acknowledged that where there is an absence of these extrinsic and intrinsic sources of motivation, workers may suffer from amotivation (i.e. have no intention to do anything). From a conceptual standpoint, Deci and Ryan (2000) propose in their self-determination theory (SDT), which centres on how autonomy over our actions influences effort, happiness and subjective well-being, that intrinsic and extrinsic motivations exist within a continuum of self- and non-self-determined behaviours. SDT emphasizes that when individuals feel they have control over their lives this acts to motivate them, that is, the motivation to grow and change is realized through the fulfilment of three psychological needs: (1) competence (i.e. skills and mastery), (2) connection (i.e. relatedness/belonging), and (3) autonomy and control. Motivation is of particular interest from the organizational perspective as it has a close relationship with productivity and performance; motivated workers are likely to perform better and be more productive.

Motivation is driven by a number of the intrinsic dimensions of work considered in Chapter 4 including levels of control and autonomy (as per SDT), variety and challenge, and the importance or purpose of job tasks, all of which have been shown to have significant impacts on levels of performance and productivity and workplace well-being. Factors of particular relevance to intrinsic work motivation have been identified as job satisfaction, which is in some cases argued as reflecting more of an outcome than an intrinsic factor in its own right; organizational commitment, which reflects an alignment between the goals of the organization and those of the individual resulting in the worker having a higher degree of commitment to their job (see also Box 4.2 in Chapter 4); and job involvement, which refers to the relative importance and identity that an individual draws from their job (Caillier, 2012).

Extrinsic demands and rewards can also act as motivators for workers to perform, although the evidence base is more conflicting on their relative benefit (Kuvaas et al., 2017). Extrinsic demands are an integral part of paid work. This term refers to the tasks a worker is required to complete by the employer. These may be loosely or heavily prescribed dependent on the nature of the job and the approach of the employer or manager, and in this sense are linked to job properties discussed in Chapter 4. The most obvious extrinsic reward from paid work is pay (and associated benefits). Undoubtedly, pay is central to the engagement of a worker with their job, and indeed is a core component in driving workers to offer their labour to the market. However, while pay could be the only or primary driver for some workers, pay alone is commonly agreed to not act as a long-term motivator for most workers. Moreover, while pay may act as a key driver in our decisions over whether to work, it is one of many intrinsic and extrinsic factors that influence our decision over the type of work we do, which employer we work for, and other features of our working lives. Pay is more often cited as a component of motivation, where it is referred to in regard to the provision of a competitive base wage or salary that enables a desired standard of living or quality of life. Other extrinsic rewards include the recognition and praise we receive from leaders or peers, or indeed in some cases the absence of punishment, satisfaction obtained from feelings of completing a job to a good standard, and the potential for career development and progression (Benedetti et al., 2015).

The relative balance of intrinsic and extrinsic motivators will vary between workers, providing a rationale for some level of tailoring of job design at the individual level, but also because of the relative presence of factors within the job. For example, if a job offers high levels of variety and challenge and the completion of tasks is inherently satisfying, intrinsic motivation will likely dominate. In contrast, if a job is designed with more of a focus on performance and results which are directly rewarded (e.g. through bonuses), then extrinsic motivation will dominate (Kuvaas et al., 2017, 246). Evidence suggests that intrinsic motivation has a positive relationship with worker performance, commitment, and lower incidence of burnout and work–life conflict. It is acknowledged, though, that intrinsic factors may be less effective in motivating us to work when we suffer from fatigue, stress and/or resource depletion (Benedetti et al., 2015, 40).

Extrinsic motivation, meanwhile, has been found in some cases to have either a negative or little to no effect, suggesting these mechanisms could be less beneficial to workers and organizations (Benedetti et al., 2015; Kuvaas et al., 2017). This follows the argument that you cannot actively motivate someone, but rather that you have to create an environment that lets them motivate themselves. The literature on incentives is useful for understanding the limitations of extrinsic rewards. The evidence base highlights a range of potentially counterproductive outcomes including promoting a narrow focus on only directly rewarded tasks, fixed mind-sets, risk taking which can

Rewarding careers

generate work-related stress and impact on health and safety (dependent on the workplace context), and high employee turnover (Kuvaas et al., 2017, 245). Given these limitations, the use of incentives has been adapted in recent decades. Case study evidence from the UK manufacturing sector, for example, suggests that the use of individual-level incentive pay systems is increasingly uncommon as managers use aggregate bonus schemes and appraisals supported by key performance indicators (KPIs) to extract effort from employees (Arrowsmith and Marginson, 2010).

It is also worthy of note that there is continued debate as to whether intrinsic and extrinsic motivation are separate or linked dimensions (see Kuvaas et al., 2017, for a summary). Within some portions of the economics discipline, for example, extrinsic motivation is (implicitly) assumed, under the *separability assumption* (Bowles and Polanía-Reyes, 2012), to operate independently from intrinsic motivation. However, evidence is conflicting with some suggesting that intrinsic and extrinsic motivators operate in synergy (Stajkovic and Luthans, 2003), while others suggest there may be a trade-off between these forms of motivation, in that a greater degree of, or focus on, extrinsic motivation may act to limit intrinsic motivation, and vice versa (Kuvaas et al., 2017, 246–7). This is argued as being the product of forms of motivation having potentially divergent effects as centring a job heavily on performance-related pay, for example, could act to reduce the satisfaction gained from the job as the incentives could limit team-working and opportunities for innovative and creative thinking. Problematic outcomes of this nature, however, could well reflect the limitations of job and reward design rather than an inherent divergence of intrinsic and extrinsic motivators.

We should also acknowledge the potential danger to physical and mental well-being from 'excessive' levels of motivation where this leads to incidence of overwork and even workaholism (Schaufeli et al., 2008). The outcomes can be driven by both intrinsic and extrinsic motivators as workers can be driven to work excessively through both feelings of commitment and purpose and through poorly constructed incentives, although as already noted the evidence base suggests incidence of burnout, often an outcome of overwork, to be lesser where intrinsic motivators dominate. Organizational culture is central to embedding and promoting behaviours which enable workers to achieve a sustainable balance between work and the rest of their lives. Motivating workers to perform and be productive while avoiding incentivizing overwork is likely to be drive better outcomes for workers and organizations, evidencing the importance of understanding the interconnectedness of the job properties, flexibility and rewarding careers dimensions of workplace well-being. What balance looks like and how much weight and effort can be given to paid work will differ at the individual level and throughout the life course as a result of a range of influences including, for example, caring responsibilities.

134   *Well-being and the quality of working lives*

Motivation systems should, therefore, be multifaceted in order to extract the best from the individual while supporting their well-being.

PAY AND BENEFITS

Pay as well as other benefits received from paid work act as an important extrinsic motivator and an indicator of the relative quality of work. Pay or earnings refers to the amount of money we receive from engaging in paid work, be that via a wage or a salary. Income can be differentiated slightly from these terms as it is usually used as a broader measure which includes benefits we receive such as pensions, and other non-pension benefits which are discussed in Box 6.1. As already noted, pay is of particular interest given its complex relationship with the motivation to work and with our well-being both at work and, more broadly, given its influence over relative quality of life through the ability it provides for us to consume goods and services and afford both the necessities and luxuries of life.

BOX 6.1   EMPLOYEE NON-PAY BENEFITS

There are a wide range of non-pay benefits which are available to many employees. Employer-provided pensions act as a particularly important component of many non-pay benefits. Employers contribute to pension schemes which employees pay into and which provide workers with an income in addition to any statutory pension payments following retirement. Non-pension benefits include, but are not limited to, child support (e.g. childcare vouchers, on-site crèche facilities), on-site or discounted gym memberships, healthcare services, and transport benefits (travel season tickets, cycling vouchers). Notably some of these benefits reflect the provision or otherwise of job resources. Data on employee benefits is collected in a number of labour market and social surveys. In the UK Working Lives Survey, for example, respondents are asked about the availability of employee benefits at their organization. As well as details around pension schemes they are asked about career development, healthcare, enhanced leave and travel benefits, amongst others. Response options are 'have used this benefit', 'available to me but I do not use this benefit' and 'not available to me'. The question is shown below and a summary of responses taken from the 2019 survey are included in Figure 6.1.

In the last 12 months, have you made use of the following employee benefits, and if not, are they available to you?

- *Career development benefits (e.g. paid study leave, or professional subscriptions paid)*
- *Financial assistance benefits (e.g. relocation assistance, or homeworker allowance)*
- *Food benefits (e.g. subsidised restaurant or free tea and coffee)*
- *Health care and insurance benefits (e.g. death-in-service/life assurance, flu jabs, dental or health insurance)*
- *Well-being benefits (e.g. subsidised gym membership, massage or exercise classes)*
- *Enhanced leave benefits (e.g. paid bereavement leave, emergency eldercare support, or more than 20 days paid annual leave excluding bank holidays)*
- *Social benefits (e.g. Christmas or summer party)*
- *Technology benefits (e.g. mobile phone for personal use, or home computer)*
- *Transport benefits (e.g. free/subsidised on-site car parking, travel season ticket loan, company car).*

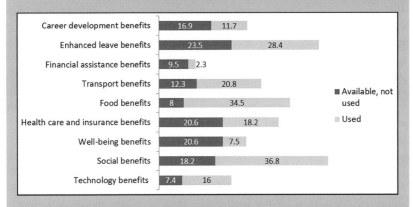

Note: Base: all employees (n = 4189).
Source: UK Working Lives Survey (Wheatley and Gifford, 2019).

Figure 6.1   Employee non-pension benefits (%)

Traditional approaches to pay, typified by mainstream economics, centre on its use as a source of compensation for the disutility (i.e. adverse or harmful effect) that is encountered when engaging in paid work. Work under this rather limited assumption is a source of dissatisfaction, an arduous task, for

136   *Well-being and the quality of working lives*

which we must be compensated (Spencer, 2009; Weiss and Kahn, 1960). Considering pay as a form of compensation it can potentially be used as a powerful incentive mechanism. Many organizations historically have focused on motivating workers using piece-rate or performance-related pay systems. These usually involve workers being given a base wage or salary, with additional pay received relative to performance. An extension of this approach is the application of tournaments. First introduced as a concept by Lazear and Rosen (1981), Tournament Theory is founded on the assumption that 'in a [simple] tournament, an agent is paid a lot if he produces more than his rival, and little otherwise' (Dye, 1992, 28). In this sense, tournaments are a simple form of a Relative Performance Evaluation (RPE) scheme which rewards the relative performance of workers (Dye, 1992, 27). For example, RPE contracts exist that reward executives for the performance of their firm relative to an average of a set of similar firms. A key limitation of performance-based and tournament systems is that they can promote risk taking behaviours, and a loss of team-working where rewards are focused on the individual (Dye, 1992; Lazear, 1989). In the case of tournaments, a 'sure loser' outcome is also created (Nalebuff and Stiglitz, 1983), which can potentially be damaging to the well-being of both the worker and organization, as 'weaker' employees take bigger risks in an attempt to 'win', lose motivation and/or engage in destructive working behaviours such as collusion or sabotaging others.

Evidence suggests that despite assumptions of income acting as a compensator and driving work effort, income from work does not have a simple linear relationship with the quality of work we encounter, or workplace and wider well-being; high levels of pay and other benefits do not always equate to good job quality and higher levels of well-being. Most studies which explore the relationship between income and well-being report a U-shaped relationship, in that reported well-being increases with levels of income, but to a diminishing extent (Clark et al., 2008; Mentzakis and Moro, 2009). The seminal work exploring the broader relationship between income levels and subjective well-being was produced by Richard Easterlin (Easterlin, 1974). In his work, Easterlin reported a surprising finding, coined the 'Easterlin paradox', which shows that while a positive correlation appears present between income and subjective well-being at the individual level, increases in national income do not appear to result in an identifiable increase in subjective well-being. Relative income has been argued as explaining these findings. Easterlin (2001) reported that his finding could reflect that relative income has a bigger influence over subjective well-being than absolute income (i.e. we may not feel happier to such a degree when we earn more if everyone else around us also earns more as we do not feel relatively better off).

Other research has extended our understanding of the links between relative income and well-being to include perceptions of wealth and financial status.

It highlights the relevance of subjective measures of financial status, that is, our feelings regarding whether we are able to live comfortably, just about manage or find it difficult to maintain current standards of living (Black et al., 2017; Mentzakis and Moro, 2009). In some of these studies it is posited that as we become wealthier our expectations of necessary income also increase, resulting in lesser increases in subjective well-being as our desired standard of living increases (Stutzer and Frey, 2010, 691). Pay or income at the individual level may not give a complete picture, however, as it has also been argued that consideration should be given to household income (Jorgensen et al., 2010, 621). While an individual themselves may not receive high pay from their job, if their household achieves a desirable income overall they are likely to report higher levels of subjective well-being. It may, therefore, be the pooling of incomes from members of a household which has a greater influence over well-being. This is not to disregard the importance of individual-level pay and benefits, though, to workplace well-being.

When we consider the specific case of workplace well-being as opposed to well-being in a more general context, we must acknowledge again that there is not simply a linear positive relationship between well-being at work and pay and benefits. A number of highly paid jobs exhibit characteristics which are generally considered to reflect lower quality, including high workloads and intense working routines (Kalleberg, 2012). These characteristics may negatively impact on worker well-being as a result of incidence of work–life conflict, as the amount of time for leisure is limited. Kahneman et al. (2006) suggested in their research that spending more and more time in activities linked to work which are associated with lower subjective well-being helps to explain the apparent diminishing returns found when we consider the reported well-being of those on higher incomes. Workers under these conditions encounter greater levels of work-related stress and tension. Higher pay is, in some cases, compensation for these negative characteristics; however, the extrinsic nature of pay means that while it can lessen the dissatisfaction present in paid work, it does not necessarily act as a source of satisfaction nor can it always offset the negative motivational and well-being impacts of low-quality characteristics present in many jobs.

Pay is employed differently in existing models of job quality and workplace well-being. A useful model to begin with in this regard is that proposed by Muñoz de Bustillo et al. (2011). As outlined in Chapter 3, in this model of job quality, pay is separated from other dimensions as it is argued that is has a special function in compensating workers, founded on the assumption that work itself is 'disagreeable'. The model has two main categories, 'pay and benefits' and 'amenities', with the latter including four dimensions (intrinsic characteristics of work, terms of employment, health and safety, and work–life balance). Other models include pay and benefits as its own dimension, but as one which is more evenly considered alongside other dimensions of well-being at work. Warhurst et al. (2017), for example, include pay and benefits as one of six dimensions. Within this conceptualization the pay and benefits dimension includes both objective measures of pay comprising wage/salary received, details on types of pay (e.g. fixed salary, performance pay) and non-pay benefits including employer-provided pensions schemes and non-pension benefits, as well as subjective measures including satisfaction with pay and subjective financial status. Given the limitations of pay as an extrinsic motivator and wider component of the quality of work, it is incorporated into the rewarding careers dimension of the model for workplace well-being alongside several other extrinsic factors. The framework promotes the inclusion of both objective and subjective measures of pay and benefits which are discussed further in Box 6.2. That is, we should not solely consider the objective levels of pay, pensions and other benefits given to workers, but must also incorporate subjective measures of pay reflecting whether workers feel justly rewarded and financially stable. Pay and benefits can be used most effectively as a way of incentivizing work effort alongside improvements to the intrinsic characteristics of work. Central is that, as a hygiene factor, workers will want to feel they are being paid fairly for their work and that their job gives them a desired standard of living.

BOX 6.2 OBJECTIVE AND SUBJECTIVE MEASURES OF PAY

Pay can be divided into two forms, objective pay (i.e. the amount we earn) and subjective pay (i.e. our feelings about the pay received for our work and its impact on our financial status) (Black et al., 2017). Objective measures of pay can be captured using data on earnings in absolute terms or can be considered relative to costs of living. Costs of living are an important consideration and one that is impacted by a range of factors such as local housing markets, presence of dependent children, and preferred or expected living standards (Black et al., 2017).

Rewarding careers 139

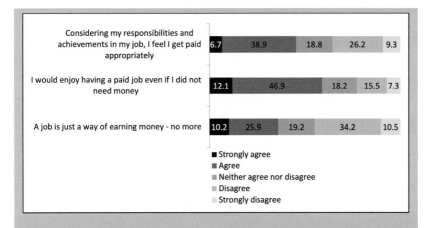

Note: Base: all employees (n = 5174).
Source: UK Working Lives Survey (Wheatley and Gifford, 2019).

Figure 6.2   Subjective measures of pay

Subjective measures of pay can take multiple forms, but often the focus is on whether workers feel they are paid fairly or appropriately for the work they perform. The UK Working Lives Survey includes lines of questioning in this regard. A summary of the results of three subjective pay-related questions from the 2019 survey is included in Figure 6.2. Alternatively, questions may focus on how workers feel about their current financial status. In the UK Understanding Society survey, respondents are asked, 'How well would you say you yourself are managing financially these days?' Available responses are on a 5-point scale: 'finding it very difficult', 'finding it quite difficult', 'just about getting by', 'doing alright' and 'living comfortably'. Subjective measures of pay can suffer from potential bias, for example where workers overestimate their own value (Lupton et al., 2015). However, they do offer a useful understanding of how workers feel about their pay relative to both individual and household costs of living.

JOB SECURITY AND CONTRACTS

The contracts governing our employment have an important role in workplace well-being. Contracts provide a level of certainty, or indeed uncertainty, over our working lives. The presence of a higher degree of job security enables longer-term planning and stability, influencing aspects of our lives from short-term working routines to the ability to gain financing for housing. Job insecurity, in contrast, can have negative impacts on intentions to leave a job, productivity levels and employee well-being (Sverke et al., 2002). The nature of contracts and job security has become increasingly relevant to workplace well-being in recent years given the observed growth in flexibilized forms of work (Fenwick, 2012, 597; Kalleberg, 2012; Raess and Burgoon, 2015, 95–6), as outlined in Chapter 5.

Across many economies there has been a polarization within the labour market between secure and often better paid jobs and low-paid and insecure work (Green et al., 2015; Kalleberg, 2011). This has been driven by neoliberal employment and labour market policies since the 1980s (Green et al., 2015; Lewis and Campbell, 2008), and in recent years in the aftermath of the global economic crisis of 2007–09 as employers have sought to minimize labour costs and retain higher degrees of numerical flexibility over their workforce (Raess and Burgoon, 2015; Smith, 2016). 'Precarious' or 'contingent' work, characterized by contract flexibility and/or insecurity has become more common and at certain points in recent years has dominated the growth areas of paid work. These include zero-hours, temporary, seasonal, fixed-term and part-time jobs (Kalleberg, 2009, 2; Mandl et al., 2015; Raess and Burgoon, 2015, 95–6). Attempts to redress the imbalance in job security associated with these flexible forms of employment have been made at the policy level including, for example, exclusivity clauses in zero-hours contracts (i.e. only being allowed to work for one employer), being outlawed in the UK in 2014 (Wheatley, 2021). Alongside the changes to contracts governing employees, there have been notable increases in rates of self-employment and freelancing including work as an independent contractor (King, 2014, 152). New modes of work have emerged as a result of enhancements in digital technology, such as crowdworking/e-lancing, which are captured by the term 'gig economy' as discussed in Chapter 5 (Friedman, 2014; Green, 2017, 1640–1; Howcroft and Bergvall-Kåreborn, 2019). The greater flexibility present in the labour market has also given rise to larger numbers of both employed and self-employed workers who report holding second jobs (Atherton et al., 2016; Friedman, 2014, 173). In some cases, contract flexibility of this nature remains desirable, but more often it is a product of financial necessity (Garthwaite, 2016).

Job security is an extrinsic 'hygiene' factor, defined by Herzberg et al. (1959) as an 'assurance for continued employment either within the same company or within the same type of profession or work'. Job insecurity, meanwhile, can be defined as 'the perceived powerlessness to maintain the desired continuity in a threatened job situation' (Greenhalgh and Rosenblatt, 1984, 438). Methods for measuring job security are outlined in Box 6.3.

Much like pay, job insecurity can be measured in both objective and subjective forms. Objective job insecurity considers the relative security provided by the contracts and terms of employment. The prevalence of precarious and con-

Rewarding careers 141

tingent employment means that objective insecurity is a very real concern for an increasing number of workers. Subjective job insecurity reflects the feelings a worker has about the risk or threat of job loss (Burchell, 2002, 62). Job loss is not the only factor to consider, though, when studying job insecurity. Also relevant is the potential loss of job features.

A useful approach to understanding this aspect of job insecurity is the distinction between 'quantitative' and 'qualitative' job insecurity offered by Hellgren et al. (1999). This approach argues that not only are the 'quantitative' threats of downsizing, redundancy and termination associated with job loss important to job insecurity and job quality, but also relevant is the loss of 'qualitative' job features such as career development and promotion opportunities, pay rises, autonomy and others. Workers may not only feel insecure due to the threat of job loss, but also as a result of the potential for loss of desired, or currently experienced, working conditions. Finally, the well-being implications of job insecurity require us to acknowledge the distinction between cognitive and affective job insecurity. Huang et al. (2012) argue that the job insecurity definition offered by Greenhalgh and Rosenblatt (1984) is focused on cognitive job insecurity, but does not account for affective responses of individuals. Cognitive job insecurity is the 'awareness of the possibility of job or benefit loss', whereas affective job insecurity is 'the emotional experience of being worried or emotionally distressed about these potential losses' (Huang et al., 2012, 752). Cognitive job insecurity involves the worker estimating the probability, timing and content of job loss and evaluating their ability to respond to the threat. Where this cognitive stage identifies a threat, this can then result in job insecurity acting as an affective stressor. The distinction is particularly relevant when we consider workplace well-being as it highlights that awareness and emotional experiences can differ both in their relative severity and longevity.

BOX 6.3   MEASUREMENT OF JOB SECURITY

Many social surveys capture both objective and subjective data on job security. Objective data is collected through questions focusing on, for example, contractual arrangements and length of time with employer. Subjective measures take a number of forms, but often include questions on risk of losing a job (i.e. quantitative insecurity), as well as on loss of features (i.e. qualitative insecurity). Questions can take the form of 'the probability of losing their job in the next year' or 'the probability of becoming unemployed in the near future'. In the UK Understanding Society survey respondents are asked, 'Thinking about losing your job by being sacked, laid-off, made redundant or not having your contract renewed, how likely do you think it is that you will lose your job during the next 12 months?' with a 4-point response scale of 'very likely', 'likely', 'unlikely' and 'very unlikely'. A range of more expansive measures have been developed, including those by Hellgren et al. (1999) and Huang et al. (2012) outlined below (for a fuller discussion, see Karapinar et al., 2019).

Hellgren et al. (1999) present a two-dimensional scale which measures quantitative and qualitative job insecurity. Quantitative job insecurity uses three items which focus on the potential loss of the job, comprising: 'I am worried about having to leave my job before I would like to', 'There is a risk that I will have to leave my present job in the year to come' and 'I feel uneasy about losing my job in the near future'. Qualitative job insecurity is measured through four items which instead focus on the potential for loss of job features, comprising: 'My future career opportunities in the organization are favourable', 'I feel that the organization can provide me with a stimulating job content in the near future', 'I believe that [the organization] will need my competence also in the future' and 'My pay development in this organization is promising'. A 5-point scale from 'strongly disagree' to 'strongly agree' is used for responses.

Huang et al. (2012) include both a four-item scale of cognitive job insecurity developed by Caplan et al. (1975), and a 10-item scale focusing on the affective dimension of job insecurity constructed using a seven-item scale outlined in Huang et al. (2010) with three additional items added to increase reliability. The cognitive job insecurity scale comprises: 'How certain are you about what your future career picture looks like?', 'How certain are you that opportunities for promotion and advancement will exist in the next few years?', 'How certain are you about whether your job skills will be of use and value five years from now?' and 'How certain are you about what your responsibilities will be six months from now?' The affective scale aims to gain insight into the emotional impacts of concern or distress surrounding potential loss, with items including: 'The lack of job security in this company makes me feel nervous', 'I feel uneasy about my chances for remaining with this company' and 'I am worried that this company will fire me any time'. A 5-point scale from 'strongly disagree' to 'strongly agree' is used for responses.

TRAINING, SKILLS AND EDUCATION MATCH

Providing workers with training and making good use of their skills and education is essential to not only the effective operation of an organization, asso-

Rewarding careers 143

ciated with productivity and financial performance (Glaveli and Karassavidou, 2011), but also the well-being of workers. These aspects of work, further, have potentially significant wider macroeconomic implications as skill mismatch and underuse of skills is effectively a waste of human capital and limits productivity across the globe. Given its significance, it is an area of continued political and economic debate (Lawton, 2015; OECD, 2015). Provision of suitable training and career development opportunities is therefore significant at the individual, organizational and societal level. Approaches to job quality and 'good' work emphasize these components of work, including the quality of training provided by employers and opportunities available to workers to utilize their skills and qualifications (Felstead and Green, 2017; Green et al., 2016b; Wheatley and Gifford, 2019). A study of 42 organizations in the UK, reported in Patterson et al. (2004), indicated a strong positive correlation between job satisfaction and the perceptions of workers that their organization has a focus on staff development, although it is also acknowledged that there is a close interconnected relationship between staff development and goals, and career outlook and progression, factors associated with positive impacts on well-being at work discussed later in this chapter.

Training can take different forms from work-based or vocational training (i.e. firm or sector-specific internal training), to financial support provided to employees for externally provided education or training, and individual learning practices (i.e. learning via training and supported education encouraging employees to become more learning oriented and pursue further knowledge and skill development) (Sung and Choi, 2014). Common methods of gauging investment in training and development are to collect data on availability and take-up of training opportunities, hours of training or the ratio of employees trained. At the organizational level, the simplest indicator of commitment to employee training and development is the reported financial investment (i.e. training expenditure) (Cooke et al., 2011; Sung and Choi, 2014). A range of surveys regularly include modules which collect data on training and skill development. For example, the European Social Survey (ESS) and the UK Skills and Employment Survey (SES), amongst others, include training and skills development, as well as lines of questioning focusing on the terms and conditions of employment.

The relative 'match' between a job and the skills of a worker is also highly relevant to workplace well-being. Perceptions of over-qualification or being over-skilled can result in incidence of boredom and lower levels of worker engagement (Piper, 2015), which in turn could have negative implications for earnings and career progression where workers 'check-out', and equally creates difficulties for employers in retaining talent should better matched opportunities be found elsewhere. The under-utilization of skills can be addressed in some cases through better matching of workers with roles, perhaps involving the use of a 'matching panel' to identify and negotiate moving workers between roles and functions relative to the fit of their skills. Equally, match may be poor because of organizational deficiencies, reflecting the presence of poor work organization, job design and/or leadership. In this circumstance, solutions could involve the application of a number of actions associated with the intrinsic components of work. Revisiting job design could enable better employment of the skills and expertise of workers, and improving environmental clarity gives workers a greater sense of purpose and achievement (i.e. providing clearer expectations of the role including task outcomes and position within the wider organizational context) (Hackman and Oldham, 1976; Warr, 2007).

As well as under-utilization there is also the potential problem of workers having a lack of skills or being under-skilled. This is also an important consideration as the presence of a lack of skills can act as a cause of under-performance and work-related stress (Piper, 2015). This could be an outcome of mismatch between worker and job at the point of employment, resulting from adverse selection. Adverse selection is a term used in principal–agent theory within industrial economics to refer to situations where the principal (employer) and agent (prospective employee) have different levels of information, or information asymmetry. In this case, the prospective employee will hold private information over their relative skills and ability that is not known to the employer. Asymmetric information of this nature can lead to the employment of a worker whose skills do not actually match those required by the employer (Laffont and Martimort, 2002, 28–9). Mismatch can also be indicative of a lack of, or poor quality, work-based training being provided by employers. The need for skill development and training has increased as the pace of work accelerates driven by technological change, which continues to impact the content and practice of many jobs. As the analysis of the European Social Survey conducted in Chapter 4 noted, considerable proportions of workers report that their job requires that they keep learning new things. Evidence has further suggested an upward trajectory in recent decades in this aspect of work (Felstead et al., 2007).

The need to acquire new skills can be problematic given the observed unevenness of the distribution of training both across and within organizations (Cooke et al., 2011). In addition, in the UK context at least, a significant reduction in training volume, measured in reference to time spent in training activities, has been identified in the period 1997 to 2012 (Green et al., 2016b). Similar patterns have been recorded in other economies, for example in Sweden, although evidence is mixed as training volumes increased in Eastern Europe during the same period (Markowitsch et al., 2013; Mignon, 2013). Four potential causes of the apparent decline in training volume are considered by Green et al. (2016b, 441). First, it could reflect a reduction in the demand

Rewarding careers

for training at the organizational level, evident of a reduced value being given to work-based training by organizations as they operate in an uncertain environment that drives a focus on numerical flexibility of workers (Raess and Burgoon, 2015). The growth in highly flexible forms of work in this argument results in a reduction in human capital investment and training at the organization level. Casualized and contingent forms of employment shift the cost and responsibility for human capital investment onto the worker and state. Fewer opportunities for work-based training and development are likely to be present for workers on these contracts (Barling et al., 2003). Providing training to employees does represent a risk for the employer should the employee leave, as the investment will be lost, especially where skills gained are more transferable or provide industry/occupation-recognized certification to employees (Acemoglu and Pischke, 2000).

The second cause of changes in training volume posited by Green et al. (2016b) is that as engagement in education has risen, prior education may be acting as a substitute for current work-based training. Third, the change could simply reflect a more efficient application of training, rendering time-focused measures of training less accurate. Finally, and perhaps most positively, it could reflect a structural shift in the nature of training towards 'workplace learning'. Workplace learning reflects the learning obtained through participation in workplace activities, working collaboratively in teams, and through involvement in 'communities of practice' (Green et al., 2016b). Workplace learning offers a potentially cost-effective and successful method for workers to continue developing their knowledge and skills throughout their career and for organizations to ensure a more optimal match between workers and their jobs. This corresponds with other existing evidence, including Felstead et al. (2012) which identified a move towards 'smarter training'. Using the case of the UK during, and in the aftermath of, the 2007–09 global economic crisis, they found that while training volume decreased it was still delivered but in a smarter (more cost-effective and efficient) form. This involves more focused training based around business needs; increasing in-house provision and delivery by existing employees; increasing on-site group training; renegotiating relationships with external training providers; and expanding the use of e-learning.

CAREER DEVELOPMENT AND PROGRESSION

Understanding careers and the factors that influence career success is important as careers have substantial implications for workers, and their households, through influencing identity, psychological and physiological well-being (Greenhaus and Kossek, 2014, 362). Career development and advancement opportunities are incorporated into the majority of models of workplace well-being and job quality. Connell and Burgess (2016) include career development opportunities as a key component of the job prospects dimension of their job quality model, while also acknowledging its links with skills and other job quality dimensions. Barling et al. (2003) identify extensive training as one of three non-pay dimensions of job quality alongside autonomy and task variety. Development opportunities are incorporated, alongside contracts, into the terms of employment amenity dimension of the model developed by Muñoz de Bustillo et al. (2011).

Opportunities for training and development play a role in not only worker well-being, but also the health of organizations linked to organizational performance, and to the progress of society through the advancement of human capital (Greenhaus and Kossek, 2014). Training and development opportunities provided by employers are central to personal and career progression, extending the benefits of education outside of work (Connell and Burgess, 2016). The nature of the career has changed in recent decades in line with wider economic and societal change. Careers have become more diverse in their structures. Hierarchical 'career ladder' structures have been replaced with flatter and more flexible careers (Demel and Mayrhofer, 2010; Dickmann and Baruch, 2011). There has been an observed shift with workers increasingly focusing on the rewards offered by the achievement of work–life balance and higher levels of job satisfaction and happiness as opposed to a solitary focus on career advancement (Dickmann and Baruch, 2011; Hall, 2004). Traditional models of upward progression ordered in a hierarchy of prestige involving a series of related jobs, often within the same organization and associated with age and experience (Greenhaus et al., 2000; Schein, 1978; Wilensky, 1960), are increasingly incompatible with contemporary organizational and career structures.

A range of models have been developed to better reflect the modern career, including the portfolio career, protean career and kaleidoscope career. Emphasizing the greater flexibility and breadth of contemporary careers, a portfolio career is characterized by workers shifting between strategies, organizations and even employment sectors throughout their working lives (Fenwick, 2006). The protean career emphasizes the internal drivers and individual values which influence decisions around careers. In this model, the role of the individual is central, with the worker committed to a profession and the work itself, rather than an organization or employer (Briscoe et al., 2006; Hall, 2004; Hall et al., 2012). The protean career, further, emphasizes the relevance of success linked to well-being such as the achievement of goals and job satisfaction rather than success solely obtained through salary or position. The occupation or industry of employment remains important, as it can act as a career anchor or compass, which influences the identity of the individual, and remains relatively stable throughout their working life (Peel and Inkson, 2004;

Schein, 1978, 1996). Finally, the kaleidoscope career involves an individual evaluating career decisions as if through a kaleidoscope lens in order to arrive at an optimum balance of work at a particular career stage. These decisions reflect the preferences of the individual, but also the demands, constraints and opportunities present, while also incorporating the potential impacts to life, family and relationships. The kaleidoscope career emphasizes the relevance of balance between work and the rest of our lives (Sullivan et al., 2009). A key contribution of the literature base on careers reflects the distinct nature of the careers of men and women, which is discussed further in Box 6.4.

BOX 6.4   GENDER, CAREERS AND REWARD

Evidence continues to show that while there have been increases in labour market participation rates among women since the mid-twentieth century, and a wide range of policy aimed at providing greater equality of opportunity and experience in paid work, the careers of men and women remain distinct. Traditional male-centred career models do not adequately acknowledge the complex nature of the careers of women including challenges in balancing work and family (Arthur, 2008; Peel and Inkson, 2004). Attempts have been made to capture the nature of the careers of women including the concepts of multi-directional (Dickmann and Baruch, 2011), patchwork, boundary-less, or frayed (Peel and Inkson, 2004, 544) careers. The 'typical' female career trajectory is non-linear, complex and dynamic (Arthur, 2008). The kaleidoscope and patchwork career models aim to capture the complexity of women's experiences of work, including career transitions experienced throughout the life course (Sullivan et al., 2009). These contemporary career models (Arthur, 2008, 168) highlight how, for example, '... women shift the pattern of their careers by rotating different aspects of their lives to arrange their roles and relationships in new ways' (Mainiero and Sullivan, 2005, 111). Women's careers are characterized by transition periods with attitudes to work and career aspirations subject to both change and conflict. It should also be acknowledged that these complex career paths, characterized by transitions, also often fit the notion of a protean career.

Labour market participation, for many women, does not simply reflect labour supply preferences but also their unpaid work within the household. Women, more often, fit paid work around household responsibilities (Lundberg and Pollak, 2007), at least at certain points during the life course. Women, for example, are more likely than their male counterparts to quit their job where their partner is overworked (i.e. reports long working hours).

The careers of women within many households are considered secondary, especially where dependent children are present (Cha, 2010, 319–20). A range of demand- and supply-side factors act to influence career trajectories among women including having children, marital status, education level and job availability (Yerkes, 2010, 700). Family-related career breaks, interruptions or reductions in time spent in paid work, or even a move into self-employment, are all potential outcomes among those with dependent children and/or other caring responsibilities (Cabrera, 2007; Hytti, 2010). A strategy adopted by an increasing portion of women is to postpone or forego a family in order to commit to a career (Sturges and Guest, 2004, 17). Meanwhile, at later career stages, some women make the decision to leave senior roles in order to obtain greater balance and flexibility and avoid high-pressure long hours cultures (Anderson et al., 2010).

The career choices of women and realized career success are influenced by occupation (Crompton and Lyonette, 2011) and degree of gender segregation found in the organization and/or industry of employment. Divisions remain present in both vertical and horizontal forms, resulting in gender segregation by industry and occupation (Teasdale, 2013, 400). Household norms and the division of labour, alongside other socio-economic factors, result in an observed divide. 'Career' women are highly educated and command well-paid employment, but are time poor (Jones, 2003, 7; McDowell et al., 2005), while other women find themselves in lower paid and insecure work, some of whom exit the labour market where they cannot afford marketized care (Drinkwater, 2015, 284). Through restricting both participation and commitment (at least that perceived by the employer), at certain stages of the life course, the household division of labour limits career progression and associated benefits including income among women who do not, or are unable to, adhere to full-time career cultures. Commitment linked directly to hours of work remains the primary focus of some employers rather than more effective measures of the performance of workers (Harris et al., 2007a, 501; Lewis and Humbert, 2010). Dependent children, in particular, act to reduce the work-time of women, but increase it among men (Wheatley and Wu, 2014); this is a factor in the continued presence of the gender pay gap.

There has been a recorded improvement in the gender pay gap; however, pay discrimination remains present in the labour market (Kilgour, 2013). Across many economies, including the USA and the UK, estimates suggest an overall gender pay gap close to 20 per cent (Graf et al., 2019; Wheatley et al., 2018). Even after factoring out the differences in relative levels of working hours and human capital (i.e. qualification and professional experience differences) there remains an approximate 10 per cent gap between the wages of men and women (Ausberg et al., 2017). Beyond the effects of the household division of labour, a number of other explanations are offered for this continued pattern. Ausberg et al. (2017) use a multi-factorial experiment approach to collect data in Germany, asking respondents to rate descriptions of fictitious employees. They find support for reward expectation theory, which states that differences in expectations between men and women result in lesser expectations among women regarding how much women should be paid for otherwise equal work. Meanwhile, Fortin et al. (2017) argue that underrepresentation of women in top income brackets, reflecting a glass ceiling at the highest income levels, explains a substantial portion of the gender pay gap present in Canada, Sweden and the UK. It may be that it is not one, but a combination of these different factors which results in the persistence of the gender pay gap and in the continued observed differences in experiences of paid work among men and women.

ACHIEVING SUCCESS IN A CAREER

Career success is influenced by a combination of factors which extend beyond traditional objective concepts of career progression linked to hierarchy and pay, to include more subjective measures of success including balance between work and life and psychological well-being (Hall et al., 2012, 744). Workers exhibit different internal career orientations summarized by Chompookum and Derr (2004, 408) into five categories: *getting ahead* (i.e. career progression through hierarchical advancement); *getting secure* (i.e. job security and commitment to the organization); *getting free* (i.e. autonomy), *getting balanced* (i.e. work–life balance), and *getting high* (i.e. job satisfaction). Getting ahead, or career progression, has traditionally been considered as most important in measuring career success. The accrual of career capital – which comprises three core elements: (1) knowing how (competencies and skills), (2) knowing whom (professional intra- and inter-firm networks), and (3) knowing why (balancing the individual's identity and career choices) as defined by Defillippi and Arthur (1994) – forms an essential component of career progression. While *getting ahead* is undoubtedly relevant to the careers of many individuals, there is increased acknowledgement in contemporary career models of the significance of both *getting balanced* and of *getting high*. The latter is perhaps more commonly referred to as psychological success which reflects a (re)focusing of the career on maintaining and enhancing well-being (Hall, 2004; Hall et al., 2012), and has been defined as 'the feeling of pride and personal accomplishment that comes from achieving one's most

150 *Well-being and the quality of working lives*

important goals in life, be they achievement, family happiness, inner peace, or something else' (Hall, 1996, 8).

It is possible, in principle, for workers to achieve success in all aspects of a career, where a desirable equilibrium between effort (e.g. time pressure), workload, and reward (career progression, job security) is achieved. Career progression is realized alongside satisfactory balance and results in greater work engagement, job satisfaction and work–life enrichment (Gustafson, 2014, 70–1; Hyvönen et al., 2010; Mäkelä et al., 2015, 526). Benefits may also be felt by employers as, for example, workers who are satisfied with their careers contribute more to their organizations (Fleisher et al., 2014; Patterson et al., 2004). In contrast, uncertainty around this aspect of work can act as a source of qualitative job insecurity, as outlined earlier in the chapter (Hellgren et al., 1999).

CASE STUDY: THE CHANGING ROLE OF TRAVEL IN CAREER SUCCESS

Craig Bickerton, Nottingham Trent University.
This case study provides insights into the relationship between career success and travel-for-work. It draws on data from the Travel-for-Work Research Project (see Bickerton, 2019; Wheatley and Bickerton, 2016), and reflects on the findings from the study in the context of the growth in remote working in response to the global pandemic in 2020 and the debates it has prompted around the future of work, including levels of physical mobility. Travel-for-work refers to work-related travel undertaken in order to fulfil tasks of employment, incorporating business travel, and certain forms of teleworking. It is distinct from the commute, and assignments resulting in extended periods of absence including expatriation (Nicholas and McDowall, 2012, 350; see also Gustafson, 2014). It includes meeting colleagues, clients and suppliers, and attending/participating in training, conferences and exhibitions (Nicholas and McDowall, 2012, 336), but is not usually used to refer to short trips, for example a meeting taking place within the same urban area as the main workplace (Jones, 2013, 63). Prior to 2020, business-related travel accounted for substantial portions of national and international mobility, with a significant associated financial value (Wheatley and Bickerton, 2016).

The Travel-for-Work Research Project involved the collection of data from highly skilled workers based in the UK Midlands via an online quantitative-qualitative survey and follow-up face-to-face semi-structured interviews. The findings from the study supported the assertion that travel-for-work forms an integral aspect of career success among highly skilled workers, but also evidenced trade-offs present between intense work routines which reduce balance and present challenges to well-being. Travel-for-work

Rewarding careers 151

enhances skills and professional and client networks, as one survey respondent outlined: 'Travel to other locations allows me to increase my experience and network with people from other organizations' (Survey Respondent 52, male, aged 28, senior development officer, public sector organization). Working with those from elsewhere in the organization and/or building networks aids development of both the knowing how and knowing whom components of career capital (Defillippi and Arthur, 1994; Dickmann and Doherty, 2008):

> It gives me the opportunity to go and understand some of the other sites that we've got around the world. So it gives me an insight into other areas of the business, which I otherwise wouldn't have had. And to meet new people as well … it allows me to make new contacts within the business. (Interviewee 12, female, aged 34, audit manager, engineering)

For many highly skilled workers travel has a significant influence on career development. The evidence is indicative of considerable reward being derived from travel, including career progression benefits such as skill development, enhanced visibility and networking, and broader added value including psychological success. International mobility was reported as providing positive impacts associated with exposure to different cultures and 'getting to see the world'. Travel-for-work is by no means without difficulties, however, as balance and some aspects of psychological success were cited as negatively impacted by more frequent and intense travel-for-work. The most frequent travellers stated impacts on leisure time, family and health as predominantly negative, reflecting the effects of intense schedules and lengthy working hours which create work–life conflict (Nicholas and McDowall, 2012, 350–1). Lower job satisfaction was also reported among those with the most intense travel routines. More frequent overnight stays were reported as having particularly negative impacts on leisure time and family, while effects also spilled over into physical (health) and psychological (overall happiness) well-being among frequent overnight travellers. The interviews provided insight into the challenges of travel involving overnight stays, including limiting exercise, sleeping difficulties and reduced leisure time:

> The more recent [trips] have been about two nights away. Normally you don't get back to the hotel 'til maybe seven o'clock at night and then you go for food, but then you'll be in work in meetings for eight o'clock the next morning. And you're normally there all day, and you normally travel back on the same day as well. So it can be easily eleven o'clock at night when you eventually get home. (Interviewee 5, female, aged 27, technologist, aerospace engineering)

The impacts of travel on career success and life outside of work are challenging to manage. Absence from home, family and the workplace result in significant trade-offs as workers receive substantial career progression benefits, but also have to navigate the negative impacts on balance and psychological success which are exacerbated by greater frequency and time away. More intense travel, including that requiring periods away, is perceived by many highly skilled workers as a necessary trade-off to achieve career progression, including the development of career capital. Impacts on time available for leisure, socializing and family are all important aspects of the trade-offs reported. The presence of flexibility over the timing and location of work including the ability to remote work from home and work flexible hours, reported among some of the interviewees, can help to mediate negative effects, especially when returning from travel (Mäkelä and Kinnunen, 2018). However, some of the interviewees stated that these trade-offs become difficult to manage in the longer term:

> It's allowed me to achieve things in my career that I couldn't have done otherwise. That time has been invaluable in terms of career progression. But, I am starting to get to the point where I'm having to consider how sustainable, I guess that's the best word I can use, how sustainable this model is. And that is just starting to affect how I think I feel about the balance that I have at this moment in time. (Interviewee 14, male, aged 46, principal lecturer, higher education)

The evidence from the Travel-for-Work Research Project is indicative of substantive career development and progression benefits being derived from travel, but also of the ratio of reward to effort falling beyond a particular level of travel, as intense travel reduces balance and reported well-being. The evidence suggests that balance and psychological success may become more central measures of career success for some highly skilled workers when their travel tolerance is reached. This may be particularly relevant for workers whose mobility is more often limited by household responsibilities (Bergström-Casinowsky, 2013; Jeong et al., 2013), resulting in lower travel tolerances. These findings are particularly pertinent given the reduced physical mobility experienced by many workers in 2020–21, including those in previously highly mobile occupations. The findings emphasize the rewards that can be obtained from travel through physically interacting with others and experiencing different cultures. Based on the evidence presented, lesser travel at the individual level could reduce opportunities to develop networks and gain visibility in both the organization and employment sector, while for organizations it could act to limit creativity, knowledge sharing and talent development. This is not to suggest that organizations should return to previous high-intensity routines of travel, but that where organizations intend to continue to limit travel, they will need to seek effective virtual alternatives to previous physical interactions. The findings from the project also evidence the difficulties faced, including for well-being, from frequent and intense routines of travel, and the alternative forms of career success that can be derived where lesser travel is undertaken. Perhaps the most beneficial outcomes for workers and organizations could be realized from more targeted and infrequent travel combined with the use of effective remote working technologies.

EFFORT–REWARD (IM)BALANCE

The effort–reward imbalance (ERI) model, developed by Siegrist et al. (1986), highlights the dangers for workers of a lack of adequate recognition and reward, which go beyond the risk of workers losing motivation and becoming unproductive or leaving the organization, to having significant negative impacts on physical and mental health. Initially developed as a method of predicting and explaining (the onset of) cardiovascular-related outcomes, the ERI model is predicated on the idea that the benefits that can be realized from work are dependent upon a reciprocal relationship between effort and reward (van Vegchel et al., 2005). Effort, in this case, refers to the extrinsic job demands or obligations placed on the worker. Reward, meanwhile, refers to the extrinsic rewards explored in this chapter comprising pay and other benefits, job security, career development opportunities and recognition, which is referred to as esteem. A third, intrinsic, component in the relationship is that of overcommitment, which operates independently of effort and reward. This is a personality characteristic, which as such is person-specific, in contrast to effort and reward, which are situation-specific. Figure 6.3 summarizes the relationship between the three components of the concept.

Source: Siegrist, 1999.

Figure 6.3   Effort–reward imbalance (ERI) model

The assumed relationship in the ERI model is based on that of social exchange theory (i.e. reciprocity) (see a fuller discussion in Chapter 7). Workers put in effort in response to the demands placed upon them and, in turn, expect to receive a reward. However, where a combination of high effort and low reward occurs it reflects an imbalance or deficit in the reciprocal relationship, which generates strain (Siegrist, 1999; Siegrist et al., 1986, 2004). For example, a stressful imbalance occurs if an employee works hard but does not receive adequate pay, development opportunities or praise, or at least perceives this to be the case. The presence of overcommitment acts to exacerbate this imbalance as overcommitted workers either underestimate the level of challenge or overestimate their own abilities, resulting in more strained reactions (Siegrist, 1999). In this way, overcommitment indirectly influences health through employee perceptions of relative effort and reward. However, it is also suggested that overcommitment has a direct effect on employee health as in the long run it can result in exhaustion. The ERI model predicts three outcomes, summarized in Table 6.1 (see van Vegchel et al., 2005).

Table 6.1   Predicted outcomes of the ERI model

Extrinsic ERI hypothesis	The presence of an imbalance in which a worker puts in a high level of extrinsic effort but receives a low reward causes a risk to health which is greater than the risks from the separate high effort and low reward components (i.e. the combined effect is greater than the sum of the component parts)
Intrinsic overcommitment (OVC) hypothesis	High level of overcommitment can increase the risk of poor health, as inflated effort is not met with reward, even where extrinsic ERI is not present
Interaction hypothesis	Extrinsic ERI occurs alongside high levels of overcommitment resulting in the highest risk of poor health

The ERI model is increasingly relevant to experiences of paid work, as technological change and labour market restructuring have generated debates around job quality and good work, including concerns around increased work pressure and intensity, greater job insecurity, uncertain development and progression prospects, and poor pay (Siegrist and Li, 2017). A key conceptual underpinning of the ERI model is that work has a significant role in us fulfilling self-regulatory needs (i.e. enabling the acquisition of self-efficacy through successful performance, self-esteem through recognition, and self-integration from a sense of belonging) (van Vegchel et al., 2005). The presence of imbalance acts to threaten the fulfilment of these needs, by causing 'active distress' with sustained incidence shown to contribute to development of mental (e.g. depression) and physical (e.g. cardiovascular) illness (Siegrist et al., 1986, van Vegchel et al., 2005). As such, the ERI model can be used to predict psychological well-being, as imbalance between effort and reward can generate significant negative emotions. However, it is possible that a worker may not consciously log the negative impacts of ERI as, in some cases, it can be experienced as a regular or 'normal' occurrence. In addition, workers may be subject to ERI for a sustained period where (1) no alternative labour market opportunities exist; (2) they remain in their current job despite ERI for strategic reasons, including expectations of future reward; or (3) where the worker exhibits excessive work-related overcommitment, reflecting a need for approval and esteem (van Vegchel et al., 2005).

The ERI model has been tested extensively using questionnaires containing multi-item scales measuring each of the three components of the ERI model (van Vegchel et al., 2005, 1119). The effort component is measured using a six-item scale with measures reflecting on physical load (suggested for inclusion only where jobs involve relevant physicality), time pressure, interruptions, responsibility, working overtime, and increasing demands. Reward is measured using an 11-item scale, which takes the form of a composite measure with a three-factor structure: financial reward, esteem reward, and reward-related career development opportunities and job security. Finally, the overcommitment component is tested through six items: a five-item scale which focuses on the inability to withdraw from work, and a single-item measure of disproportionate irritability (Siegrist et al., 2004). All items are measured on 5-point scales from 'disagree' to 'agree'. A summary of all 23 items included in the ERI questionnaire is provided in Table 6.2.

Existing evidence supports the predicted outcomes of the ERI model, including emphasizing the role of overcommitment in increasing experiences of ERI and associated job strain (Feldt et al., 2016; Weiß and Süß, 2016). Research employing an ERI questionnaire on a sample of full-time employees in the Caribbean, for example, evidenced that ERI has a direct negative effect on incidence of burnout, reported turnover intention, and overall employee well-being (Devonish, 2018). Evidence has shown, using the case of academic staff in UK higher education, that the use of informal reward mechanisms can reduce ERI (Hamilton, 2019). It is acknowledged, however, that receipt of only informal rewards may result in greater incidence of overcommitment, as employees actively seek informal rewards due to the lack of more formal reward mechanisms being offered by the employer. Other evidence has highlighted the importance of addressing overcommitment given its role in heightening the negative outcomes of ERI, including by providing specific forms of training to employees (Weiß and Süß, 2016). The evidence highlights a range of potential measures available at both the organization and more local level

Table 6.2 Effort–reward imbalance questionnaire

Questionnaire No.	Questionnaire Item
EFFORT	
ERI1	I have constant time pressure due to a heavy workload
ERI2	I have many interruptions and disturbances in my job
ERI3	I have a lot of responsibility in my job
ERI4	I am often pressured to work overtime
ERI5	My job is physically demanding
ERI6	Over the past few years, my job has become more and more demanding
REWARD	
Esteem	
ERI7	I receive the respect I deserve from my superiors
ERI8	I receive the respect I deserve from my colleagues
ERI9	I experience adequate support in difficult situations
ERI10	I am treated unfairly at work
ERI15	Considering all my efforts and achievements, I receive the respect and prestige I deserve at work
Job promotion	
ERI11	My job promotion prospects are poor
ERI14	My current occupational position adequately reflects my education and training
ERI16	Considering all my efforts and achievements, my work prospects are adequate
ERI17	Considering all my efforts and achievements, my salary/income is adequate
Job security	
ER12	I have experienced or I expect to experience an undesirable change in my work situation.
ERI13	My job security is poor
OVERCOMMITMENT	
OC1	I get easily overwhelmed by time pressures at work
OC2	As soon as I get up in the morning I start thinking about work problems
OC3	When I get home, I can easily relax and 'switch off' work
OC4	People close to me say I sacrifice too much for my job
OC5	Work rarely lets me go, it is still on my mind when I go to bed
OC6	If I postpone something that I was supposed to do today I'll have trouble sleeping at night

Note: Siegrist et al., 2004.

for addressing ERI. Recommendations for measures that could be utilized to address ERI are summarized in Figure 6.4 in the context of the framework for workplace well-being. Note that there is a level of overlap with aspects of good job design outlined in Chapter 4 and potential mechanisms that can be used to address ERI, evidencing the interconnectedness of dimensions of workplace well-being and common practice that could therefore be employed. Alongside these recommendations a further consideration for employers is to undertake periodic monitoring of ERI, perhaps administered using the 23-item ERI questionnaire or similar as an alternating module within a regular employee survey.

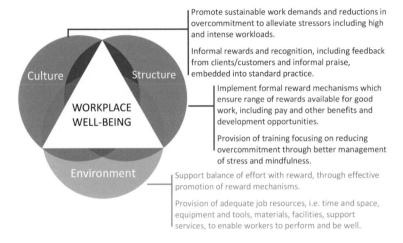

Figure 6.4   Methods for addressing ERI using the framework for workplace well-being

CHAPTER SUMMARY: TOWARDS A REWARDING CAREER

The rewards received from paid work have a considerable impact on our well-being, both in and out of work. Rewards act as a motivational tool for workers, but as this chapter has recognized, a focus on extrinsic motivators such as pay, over intrinsic drivers of motivation, such as autonomy, challenge and purpose, is likely to be less effective in the long run. In addition, the presence of imbalance between effort and reward, or at least the perception of imbalance, can act as a significant source of work-related strain with potentially severe recorded impacts on both mental and physical well-being. Effectively motivating workers to be productive and perform in their roles involves a mix of intrinsic and extrinsic motivating factors, including those explored in this chapter, such as pay and other benefits, job security, and career development and progression opportunities.

Workers and organizations benefit from putting in place, and/or raising awareness of, clearly defined formal reward mechanisms including progression pathways and links to pay scales/increments. This also requires well-defined timelines, and both workers and line managers should have a good understanding of benchmarks and measurable criteria which can be used to identify goals, and gauge progress towards their fulfilment. Awareness and use of employee benefits is often quite limited. Many employee benefits go unused or underused, as they do not meet the needs of workers. As such, efforts to increase awareness and reflect on the relative 'fit' of benefits is also likely to be beneficial. Provision of relevant training provides a method of nurturing talent, and particular benefits may be realized from the application of 'smart' training to ensure both workers and organizations benefit in a cost-effective manner. Effective reward also involves providing workers with secure terms of employment wherever possible, or where this is not available, clarity over employment status to manage worker expectations. Where employment status is insecure workers can benefit from this flexibility, however, this requires organizational-level acceptance that flexibility should work both ways. Employers benefit from lower associated labour costs and workers on these types of contracts should have the flexibility to pursue whatever employment opportunities are available to them including multiple job holding and undertaking training and education.

Finally, essential to a rewarding working life is to create a culture and environment that nurtures intrinsic motivation. A number of factors relevant to intrinsic motivation reflect good job design, as discussed in Chapter 4. Rewarding workers through various extrinsic methods is highly important to both recruitment and retention, but a longer-term focus on effectively embedding a combination of intrinsic and extrinsic rewards will offer the greatest benefits for workers and organizations alike.

7. Relationships

INTRODUCTION

This chapter focuses our attention on the role of relationships with others in our well-being at work. Through work many of us develop complex networks with a variety of different people from colleagues and peers, to line managers and leaders, and clients or customers. As time spent in work forms a core component of our time-use, it may be the case that we spend more time with these individuals than with family and friends outside of work. Those we work with may, equally, be(come) friends or may be family members, potentially blurring the nature of relationships in the work context. We may in turn choose to spend time outside of work in the company of those in our work networks.

The purpose of work for many goes beyond economic factors, extending to benefits associated with developing interpersonal relationships (Jung and Yoon, 2016). Relationships with others at work have an important role in helping to create and maintain social connections (Lancee and Radl, 2012), while occupational and professional networks act as a central source of social capital throughout our lives (McDonald and Mair, 2010). Positive interactions with others can act to create a more positive environment at work, driving the commitment and motivation of workers (Chiaburu and Harrison, 2008). Conflict at work, in contrast, is a potential source of burnout and raises the likelihood of a worker wishing to leave their job (Deery et al., 2011; Wheatley and Gifford, 2019). Also important to relationships at work is that workers, at all levels, wish to be heard and value their opportunities to voice their feelings and be involved in decision-making. Whether these opportunities are realized through formal mechanisms (e.g. trade unions and other employee groups), or informally through interactions with senior colleagues, they have important impacts on the conditions of work encountered and perceptions of them (Connell and Burgess, 2016; Wilkinson et al., 2014). The relationships we have with others at work are, therefore, highly relevant to well-being, both in and outside of work.

This chapter begins with a conceptual discussion of a number of contributions which help our understanding of how relationships impact our lives, drawing on the concepts of social capital (Bourdieu, 1986; McDonald and Mair, 2010; Putnam, 2001), social connectedness (Lancee and Radl, 2012;

Toepoel, 2013) and social exchange theory (Blau, 1964; Ng et al., 2014a). The chapter uses this context to explore the nature of social connections in the workplace, before considering the specific role of trust within organizations, including that held between leaders/managers and employees. The chapter outlines the impacts of conflict at work, between workers and between managers and employees, and potential methods for resolving conflict. The impact of worker relations and employee voice on worker well-being is explored, before the chapter finally considers the role of relationships in fun and playfulness at work, and the interaction between time spent in leisure and work. The chapter ends with a reflection on evidence on the ways to successfully manage relationships at work.

SOCIAL CAPITAL, SOCIAL CONNECTEDNESS AND SOCIAL EXCHANGE THEORY

Human beings exhibit an inherent need to connect with one another. This need acts as the primary motivator of social behaviour (Smith and Mackie, 2007). The need to connect extends into our working lives, influencing our actions and interactions in the work sphere. Various concepts can be usefully employed to explain and provide context for the role of relationships at work in influencing the quality of our working lives. This chapter elaborates the importance of sociability at work using the concepts of social capital, social connectedness and social exchange.

Social Capital

Social capital is a multi-dimensional concept that has been defined in a number of different contexts through the work of Bourdieu (1984, 1986), Coleman (1988), Putnam (2000, 2001) and many others. This has led to what some have argued is a lack of precision as to the exact nature of social capital and how best to empirically investigate it (Nichols et al., 2012). The OECD describe social capital as 'networks together with shared norms, values and understandings that facilitate co-operation within and among groups' (OECD, 2001, 41, cited in Helliwell and Huang, 2010). An alternative definition offered by Nahapiet and Ghoshal (1998, 243) describes it as the 'sum of the actual and potential resources embedded within, available through, and derived from the network of relationships possessed by an individual or social unit'. Notably, these definitions focus their attention on different dimensions of social capital. The OECD (2001) definition emphasizes the groups/network dimension of social capital that leads to beneficial societal outcomes. Nahapiet and Ghoshal (1998), meanwhile, acknowledge the role of resources, and of social capital at both the individual and group (e.g. community) level.

Social capital can, perhaps, be best understood through the work of Pierre Bourdieu (1984, 1986), James Coleman (1988, 1990) and Robert Putnam (2000, 2001), although their approaches to this concept differ notably and are not without criticism. For Bourdieu (1984, 1986), different social position and status results in differences between individuals in terms of the possession of capital, which takes three forms: economic, cultural, and social. Economic capital refers to the material resources (financial assets, property rights) available to an individual. Cultural capital refers to the way an individual is able to employ their cultural knowledge to support their position in society. Social capital, meanwhile, for Bourdieu, refers to the resources, actual or virtual, accrued by an individual (or group) from their network of relationships. The interdependence between the three forms of capital is emphasized as it is argued that capital can be converted from one form to another and that the acquisition of one form of capital is dependent on the others. The concept of social position employed by Bourdieu is relational evidencing the interplay between the social position of an individual with respect to others. Groups who exhibit a similar amount and composition of the three types of capital have the potential to become a social class. Further, the possession of capital determines the relative power of an individual in different social spheres (Bourdieu, 1984).

Coleman (1988), instead, combines insights from the sociology discipline in terms of the role of norms, rules and obligations, and from the mainstream economics rational choice approach in developing his model of social capital. In this model it is argued that social capital is one potential resource available to an individual, alongside their human capital resource (i.e. their skills and expertise), physical capital (i.e. tools, machines), and economic capital (i.e. financial resources). Coleman also suggests that while social capital is a resource available to an individual, it does not necessarily need to be 'owned' by them. For example, we may be able to benefit from the social resource available to us if we work in an environment where work colleagues help each other when work demands are high, but this may not be available to a worker in another organization where relationships are weaker. Coleman's work also notes the importance of social context in understanding social capital, as it is argued that 'a given form of social capital that is valuable in facilitating certain actions may be useless or even harmful for others' (Coleman, 1988, S98). Coleman's contribution is useful as, like Nahapiet and Ghoshal (1998), it acknowledges social capital both at the level of the individual and the group, and also recognizes the role of social context.

Putnam, meanwhile, describes social capital as 'connections among individuals – social networks and the norms of reciprocity and trustworthiness that arise from them' (Putnam, 2000, 19). Putnam's approach is distinct as it conceptualizes social capital in reference to a collective aggregate of resources, norms and reciprocity. This resource, it is argued, is embedded within complex social networks that act as a source of societal benefits, as good-quality relationships facilitate progress. Putnam emphasizes the role of a network of reciprocal social relations in society, noting that 'a society of many virtuous but isolated individuals is not necessarily rich in social capital' (Putnam, 2000, 19). Although Putnam is, arguably, the most well-known for his work on social capital, there have been several criticisms levelled at his work. Where Putnam equates social capital to values and attitudes, it is argued that in essence this treats social capital as a transferrable resource, which can be applied in other areas of life (Nichols et al., 2012). However, this ignores the role of social context as noted by Coleman above. Another criticism focuses on the lack of a clear distinction between sources of social capital, social capital as a resource, and the resources that are obtained because of it (Portes, 1998).

Common to most approaches is that social capital acts as an important social resource that is available from social interaction (Bourdieu, 1984), and that provides access to information, opportunities and support that might otherwise be unavailable (Putnam, 2000, 2001). Resources in this context include ideas, knowledge and information, advice, opportunities, help and support, and goodwill (Adler and Kwon, 2002, cited in Baker and Dutton, 2007, 325). Also common to most approaches is the acknowledged difference between bridging and bonding social capital (Nichols et al., 2012). Bonding social capital (otherwise called homophilic ties) refers to strong ties that are formed between individuals who are similar and/or within close networks, while bridging social capital (otherwise called heterophilic ties) refers to weaker ties between more loosely or sparsely connected individuals and networks. Putnam described the difference as he referred to bonding social capital as 'sociological superglue', whereas bridging social capital is more akin to 'sociological WD-40' (Putnam, 2000) which enables networks among more diverse groups. A further division within the concept of social capital is between structural capital, cognitive capital, and relationship capital (Nahapiet and Ghoshal, 1998; Yu et al., 2013). This division acknowledges that social capital has both a structural component as well as cognitive and relational components reflecting the resources that can be utilized through the network. The structural component refers to the configuration of networks – and the roles, rules and procedures that govern them – and the links between social groups of individuals. The cognitive capital component reflects shared understanding, which can take the form of shared languages, codes, narratives, values, attitudes and beliefs. Finally, relational capital refers to the nature and quality of relationships including norms and obligations, identity and trust (Nahapiet and Ghoshal, 1998). The combination of these three forms of capital acts to motivate collective action and knowledge sharing among individuals. It should be noted, though, that social capital can be both positive and negative. Positive social capital is realized when the means by which social capital is created, and way in which it is used, offer a societal benefit. This is reflected in the expansion of capacity (e.g. an individual or groups' ability to achieve personal and professional goals) and through realized outcomes (e.g. enhanced team performance in the completion of work tasks) (Baker and Dutton, 2007, 326). It can be viewed as negative, though, should a worker use their social capital, for example, to get a job or gain a promotion through relationships with senior managers at the cost of other more deserving candidates.

As well as the more obvious human capital benefits of paid work, in developing and maintaining skills and knowledge, work offers the potential to develop our social capital. Work has an interdependent relationship with social capital, as workplace networks can act as a source of social capital, and at the same time our existing social capital can help us gain opportunities (e.g. a new job or promotion) (McDonald and Mair, 2010). Social capital can both enhance our working lives, and our working lives can enhance our social capital. Social capital has been shown to have an important relationship with well-being. For example, empirical evidence measuring social capital using trust and trustworthiness, marriage and family, relationships with friends and neighbours, and civic engagement, found strong links between these measures and subjective well-being (Helliwell and Putnam, 2004). Other research has similarly shown that individual social capital has a positive relationship with measures of subjective well-being (Arampatzi et al., 2018, 100; Portela et al., 2013).

In the context of work, evidence drawing on a sample of workers in Spain has identified a positive relationship between higher levels of social capital and satisfaction with job and quality of working life (Requena, 2003). Social capital in this case is measured in respect to indicators of trust (in colleagues and management); social relations at work; commitment (willingness to work more than required, pride in organization); communication (ability to communicate opinion); and influence (ability to put ideas into practice). Notably, many of these measures of social capital are also measures of the quality of work, evidencing the interaction between the quality of relationships and the quality of our working lives. In the work context, social capital is also relevant when we consider relationships with colleagues and peers in respect of the operation of teams. Each individual within the team influences the team-level social capital through their individual social interactions. In turn, the team-level social capital influences individual behaviour. The social capital of the team, moreover, is determined not only by its formal boundary, but by a wider social boundary. This reflects that the broader network of the team includes each of the team member's internal ties as well as their external ties within the organization (Yu et al., 2013).

Social Connectedness

Much like social capital, social connectedness is a helpful concept in explaining sociability in societies (Toepoel, 2013, 356). Undoubtedly, connecting with others has a significant role in our well-being. Positive relationships generate benefits through enhancing social connectedness, which can be defined simply as the quantity and quality of social relationships (Lancee and Radl, 2012; Toepoel, 2013, 357). The concept of social connectedness has developed from the body of work exploring belongingness (see Grieve et al., 2013, 604). Belongingness theory suggests that an individual will be motivated to develop and maintain positive social relationships so that they are able to experience a sense of belonging (Baumeister and Leary, 1995). Where we have meaningful relationships and connections with others, it enables us to experience feelings of belonging which can enhance our well-being. Social connectedness comprises the sense of sharing of knowledge and experiences with others, feelings of being involved, and social appraisals (i.e. the response of others to events and actions) (Richter et al., 2020). Other associated but distinct terms reflecting on the role of sociability include social integration, which refers to the presence of social connections with others and social isolation, which refers to a lack of social connections (De Jong Gierveld and van Tilburg, 2006).

Social connectedness simultaneously has both a cause and an effect. The presence of social connections offers us the opportunity to engage in social action, for example participation in leisure activities and the associated positive outcomes including for well-being. At the same time, engaging in social activities acts to create and maintain social connections (Park et al., 2009; Portes, 1998). Social connectedness is important as it has a significant role in enhancing our well-being, while its absence or negative forms of it have been linked to depression. Depression can be the result of what is termed negative reciprocal interpersonal transactions. Where an individual perceives there to be the presence of negative appraisal (i.e. criticism, rejection) and reduced or non-genuine support, this has been suggested to act as a primary driver of depressive responses (Cockshaw and Shochet, 2010). It triggers a greater need for validation which is usually manifest in excessive reassurance seeking and self-denigration behaviours as individuals doubt their self-worth (Coyne, 1976, cited in Cockshaw and Shochet, 2010).

Existing evidence supports the relevance of social connectedness to work. Social connectedness enables us to gather and share knowledge and experiences with others. Further, it can act to nurture trust and cooperation, reduce employee turnover and enhance worker performance (see Richter et al., 2020, for a discussion). Connectedness offers well-being benefits in the form of feelings of closeness and staying in contact, intimacy, sharing and belonging,

Relationships 165

and reduced levels of anxiety (Cockshaw and Shochet, 2010; Ijsselsteijn et al., 2009). An absence of connectedness, meanwhile, produces feelings of distance, difference and isolation, and can make it difficult for individuals to accept social roles and responsibilities. Feelings of social exclusion, alternatively termed ostracism, may reduce productivity levels and potentially increase employee turnover (Robinson et al., 2013). Using a sample of over 200 working adults in Australia, Cockshaw et al. (2014) explored the relationship between general connectedness, workplace connectedness and symptoms of depression. They found a lack of social connectedness to be associated with a rapid increase in the symptoms of depression. Meanwhile, a study of 472 professional IT workers in the USA identified that social connectedness or strong interpersonal relationships at work serve to mitigate the negative effects of workplace stress and burnout (Anthony-McMann et al., 2017). Methods for capturing social connectedness in the workplace are outlined briefly in Box 7.1.

BOX 7.1 MEASUREMENT OF SOCIAL CONNECTEDNESS

Considered objectively, social connectedness can be captured using measures such as the number of social ties someone has at work. However, this simple quantification ignores the relative quality of each of these relationships. Subjective approaches to capturing social connectedness at work aim to capture an employee's perception regarding both their ability to increase the quantity of relationships with co-workers and to improve the quality of these relationships (Ijsselsteijn et al., 2009).

Subjective measurement of social connectedness can be captured in two dimensions (van Bel et al., 2009, cited in Richter et al., 2020):

1. Social appraisals. These measures reflect perceptions of the quantity and quality of connections;
2. Sense of sharing and involvement. This set of measures includes items focusing on relationship salience (or relative importance), shared understanding and knowledge of one another's feelings and experiences.

Examples of items that can be used in the measurement of each of the components of social connectedness include the following (see van Bel et al., 2009, 5):

*   Relationship salience: *'Aside from our contact, I often feel "together" with [individual's name] somehow'*.

- Dissatisfaction with contact quantity: '*I would like to have a larger circle of friends*'.
- Shared understanding: '*I feel that [individual's name] shares my interests and ideas*'.
- Knowing one another's experiences: '*I often know what [individual's name] feels*'.
- Feelings of closeness: '*In comparison with all your other relationships (with both men and women), how close is your relationship with [individual's name]?*'

Social connectedness at work has further been argued as being central to levels of employee engagement (Kahn, 2007). However, positive relationships are argued as only being possible where working environments offer employees feelings of trust and safety (Kahn, 2007). These relationships occur when 'members join together in meaningful ways to share information, solve problems, make sense of their experiences and provide support' (Kahn, 2007, 189). High levels of social connectedness (i.e. the presence of positive relationships at work) can potentially provide greater resilience to employee engagement from factors that could otherwise act to negatively impact it (e.g. feelings of work being under-valued) (Anthony-McMann et al., 2017). Kahn (2007) highlights the importance at all levels of the organization of understanding how to create and foster environments that enable positive relationships at work to develop and flourish. Training for both workers and leaders is identified as a potential route towards achieving this goal.

Social Exchange Theory

A further concept that is highly relevant to relationships in the context of work is social exchange theory, associated with the work of Homans (1958), Blau (1964) and Emerson (1976). This concept asserts that the outcome of the relationship or exchange between two social entities is determined by the extent to which both entities follow explicit and implicit agreements made between them (Ng et al., 2014a). These agreements or interactions are interdependent (i.e. outcomes are based on the combined efforts of both entities) and generate a sense of obligation between the two entities (Blau, 1964; Emerson, 1976; Huang et al., 2016). In the work context, both the workers and organization (represented by leaders/managers) take the role of social entities. Each of these entities has expectations around their relationship, and whether and how these expectations are met determines the ongoing relationship. If the agreements are adhered to, the relationship between the social entities is positive. Where expectations are not met this amounts to the agreement being broken, weakening the relationship. This, however, can lead to adverse outcomes including diminished motivation or turnover intentions (employer breaking agreement), or termination of the employee (employee breaking agreement).

A particular emphasis of social exchange theory is the idea of rules and norms, which act as guidelines of exchange processes. Reciprocity is, perhaps, that which receives the most focus in existing literature (Cropanzano and Mitchell, 2005, 875). Reciprocity refers to the notion that one social entity in a relationship will reciprocate positively (i.e. return the favour), when the other social entity acts to improve the quality of the relationship (Ng et al., 2014a). In addition, it is suggested that a positive cycle can be created wherein the reciprocal exchange generates a self-reinforcing cycle (Molm et al., 2012). As positive reciprocity becomes the norm within an exchange, it results in increasingly stable levels of trust, loyalty, commitment and emotional investment between the social entities involved (Cropanzano and Mitchell, 2005, 875). Negotiated rules can also be present in exchanges. In negotiated exchanges both parties jointly bargain over the terms of the agreement (Molm et al., 2012, 143). Negotiated exchanges or agreements are usually explicit, detailed and understood (i.e. both parties know what they will receive prior to the exchange taking place). These exchanges often continue beyond the short term and can involve binding legal or contractual agreements. Negotiated exchanges are relevant in the work sphere as they often form part of economic transactions. An employee, for example, may negotiate a salary level when joining an organization, while team members may negotiate responsibilities and the distribution of labour within the team (Cropanzano and Mitchell, 2005, 878).

In the organizational context, social exchange theory is also useful for understanding the importance, and impact, of relationships at different levels (Omilion-Hodges et al., 2016). A number of contributions have developed the core concept providing insight into exchanges between workers (co-worker exchanges or CWX), between workers and leaders (leader–member exchanges or LMX), and within teams (team-member exchanges or TMX). Co-worker exchange is used to describe the quality of relationships between an employee and their co-workers (Ng et al., 2014a; Sherony and Green, 2002). Increases in co-worker exchanges assist workers in expanding their internal and external social networks. Employees with more co-worker exchanges put more resources into, and receive more resources from, relationships with co-workers. This can take the form of tangible support (e.g. support in completing work activities from co-workers) and intangible support (e.g. emotional support) (Chiaburu and Harrison, 2008). As co-worker exchanges increase, this may result in the worker becoming less reliant on their organization for resources and support. Existing evidence, for example, suggests that workers who receive more support from co-workers suffer from lower levels of psychological distress when they feel mistreated by their employer (Rousseau et al., 2009).

Leader–member exchange refers to the degree to which a worker with a supervisory or leadership function (leader) develops a quality relationship with their subordinates (employees or members) (Dansereau et al., 1975). Central to this relationship is trust, mutual respect and a sense of obligation (Martin et al., 2016, 71). Leader–member exchanges can be beneficial for workers as evidence has suggested potential career development benefits as supervisors support the expansion of the internal and external social network of the worker (see Ng et al., 2014a, for a discussion). Finally, team-member exchange reflects the sum of relationships within a workgroup, incorporating both relationships with leaders and co-workers. It is argued that the communicative and relational work experience of an employee is the aggregate of these workplace relationships (Omilion-Hodges et al., 2016, 344). Relationships with individuals within the organization also have a wider significance as improvements or reductions in the quality of relationships can spill over into other exchange relationships and overall relationships with the organization (Ng et al., 2014a). Workers can experience quite different exchange relationships with supervisors compared with the relationships they have with co-workers (Rousseau and Aubé, 2010, 323). Equally, if a relationship between an employee and their line manager sours as a result of a loss of trust, the employee may feel a reduction in the quality of their relationship with the organization as a whole, as the employee views the leader as a representative of the organization.

RELATIONSHIPS AT WORK

For the majority of us our time engaged in paid work involves interaction with others (Robertson and Cooper, 2011). For many, these interactions are frequent and extensive reflecting complex networks. As already outlined, work has an important role in developing and maintaining social connectedness (Anthony-McMann et al., 2017; Richter et al., 2020), while occupational networks act as a source of social capital throughout our lives (McDonald and Mair, 2010). Positive relationships have an essential role in supporting our well-being, acting as an important barrier to mental ill health (Aked et al., 2008). Social interactions at work can even influence our physical health through effects on immune, cardiovascular and neuroendocrine systems (Heaphy and Dutton, 2008).

We develop a range of relationships, both with others within our organization including managers and colleagues who can be referred to as insiders, and with those outside of the organization (or outsiders), including clients and customers. Both insider and outsider relationships can be equally significant to our experienced job quality (Deery et al., 2011). The centrality of relationships with colleagues (co-worker exchanges and team-member exchanges) extends beyond the social environment as the quality of relationships has an important function in defining the overall working environment (Chiaburu and Harrison, 2008). The quality of relationships with leaders (i.e. leader–member exchanges outlined in the previous section) has a role in mediating experiences of work. Leaders have a direct influence over the levels of work-related stress and burnout among workers through the imposition of workload, and opportunities for development and progression through supporting and enhancing networks (Ng et al., 2014a; Schyns and Schilling, 2013).

Positive relationships have a significant role in mediating work-stressors, enabling us to successfully manage the demands we face in our working lives. Interactions with others, and the relationships developed through work, have been identified as a source of satisfaction and fulfilment at work (Robertson and Cooper, 2011). Experiences of unemployment lead to a loss of these social networks and can negatively affect our identity (Sparrowe et al., 2001). Research has indicated that the presence of positive interactions with others at work can create positive work attitudes among workers and increase levels of commitment (Chiaburu and Harrison, 2008). Relationships are important, both in the number we have and their relative strength. Stronger social relationships offer benefits in the form of support, encouragement and meaningfulness (Aked et al., 2008). For example, colleagues with whom we have closer relationships can act as a source of considerable support when we attempt to navigate difficulties encountered at work or at home (Robertson and Cooper, 2011). Meanwhile, the presence of broader or more 'superficial' relationships can still provide benefits to well-being associated with enhanced social connectedness, and feelings of familiarity and self-worth in the context of our position in the community. Evidence emphasizes that both strengthening and broadening social networks has the potential to deliver the greatest benefits to well-being (Aked et al., 2008).

While there are a range of benefits derived from our interaction with others, the highly competitive nature of modern society can result in a tendency to compare ourselves to others. Indeed, the social comparisons we make with the outcome–input ratio (i.e. the effort–reward balance) of other employees may have a potentially significant impact on our realized job satisfaction and job performance (Takeuchi et al., 2011). Social comparison theory explains this process. It can take both downward and upward forms. Downward comparison involves comparing ourselves to those we perceive to be worse off, while upward comparison is that which involves us comparing our situation to those we perceive to be better off (Tesser and Collins, 1988). In both cases this behaviour can have positive or negative impacts on our well-being. Downward comparison can generate a self-enhancement effect, for example feeling better about your income level in comparison to peers. However, it can result in a fragile psychological state in which we feel positive through comparing our own situation to the negative circumstances encountered by others. Where these circumstances cease (e.g. a colleague gets a better-paid role), we may feel somewhat more negative about our own lives. Meanwhile, upward comparison can be used as motivation to drive us towards our goals where we see others as role models, but can be damaging to self-esteem and self-efficacy (i.e. our belief in own capabilities) and result in feelings of envy towards others. Fear of missing out (FOMO) is a further potential hazard associated with our interaction with others including work colleagues. It describes a psychological state involving anxiety that others within our professional and/or social spheres are leading more interesting and socially desirable lives (Przybylski et al., 2013). This form of well-being stressor has in recent years often been associated with the use of social media where it has been linked to addictive and destructive behaviours (Buglass et al., 2017).

Where relationships create strain, including those associated with the above behaviours, this can have negative impacts on well-being. Two primary aspects of work are of concern here. First, there is a potential for workers to engage in 'emotional labour' at work (Robertson and Cooper, 2011, 85). Emotional labour is a term used to describe 'the effort, planning, and control needed to express organizationally desired emotions during interpersonal transactions' (Morris and Feldman, 1996, 98). An example would be a worker dealing with a customer or client who is unpleasant towards them. Emotional labour is required, in this case, for the worker to be able to retain composure and avoid responding in an unprofessional manner. Emotional labour extends to interactions with colleagues, co-workers and leaders, and as well as supressing emotions as outlined in the example, it can also involve expressing emotions (e.g. offering a positive reaction), when this is not felt. In all cases, the effort involved in expressing and/or supressing emotion can result in negative well-being implications through emotional exhaustion and burnout (Pisaniello et al., 2012; Robertson and Cooper, 2011, 86). Second, and to some degree extending the concept of emotional labour, workers may encounter conflict at work.

CONFLICT AT WORK

Conflict at work can take various forms from bullying and harassment, to blame cultures and lack of trust between workers, and with leaders. It can be both overt (e.g. a public argument) or covert (e.g. speaking about someone without them being aware) (Meier et al., 2014). Conflict at work is highly important to our relative experience of work; just one experience of conflict can be enough to have a significant detrimental effect (Aselage and Eisenberger, 2003). Conflict at work can be broadly categorized into task conflict (i.e. conflict related to the tasks involved in a job) and relationship conflict (i.e. conflict arising from disagreements associated with differences in personality types) (Pinkley, 1990). A third form of conflict, non-task organizational conflict has been more recently identified, reflecting conflict arising from the culture within the organization, leadership and power relations, employee benefits, recruitment decisions and working conditions (e.g. health and safety) (Bruk-Lee et al., 2013, 340). This distinction is of relevance as different forms of conflict have quite different outcomes.

Not all conflict is bad. The existing evidence base highlights that conflict over a task is generally more positive in its impacts. Debate and disagreement over how to approach or progress a task can lead to a number of benefits including idea generation, skill development, enhanced use of resources, more effective task completion and more accurate understanding of the requirements of the job (see Bruk-Lee et al., 2013; De Wit et al., 2012; Hon and Chan, 2013). In contrast, relationship conflict has been found to have negative impacts on performance (linked to burnout), job and team satisfaction, and turnover intention (Deery et al., 2011; Hon and Chan, 2013). At the individual level, relationship conflict creates several negative affective reactions such as anger, frustration and annoyance that can lead to reduced performance (Bruk-Lee et al., 2013; Rispins and Demerouti, 2016). Workplace bullying, as a form of relationship conflict, refers to interpersonal hostility that is characterized by being deliberate, repeated and causes harm (Suggala et al., 2021). It can be verbal or physical and includes harassment, offensive behaviour, humiliation, social exclusion and purposefully hindering task completion. Bullying has a range of physical and mental well-being impacts at the individual level, such as anxiety, depression, problems sleeping, work-related stress and low self-efficacy (Einarsen and Mikkelsen, 2003, cited in Suggala et al., 2021). It also imposes several organizational costs associated with reduced productivity, employee absenteeism and turnover, compensation and grievance mechanisms, and legal disputes (Rodríguez-Muñoz et al., 2009). Non-task organizational conflict, meanwhile, has also been shown to have negative impacts, as it exhibits a negative relationship with employee engagement, performance and job satisfaction (Bruk-Lee et al., 2013).

Psychological safety is a concept closely linked to both conflict and trust, and refers to our perception regarding the potential outcome of taking interpersonal risks at work (Edmondson and Lei, 2014). It offers us the ability to present ourselves in the workplace (e.g. our own perspectives) without fear of negative outcomes to self-image, status or career (Kahn, 1990). The psychological safety climate within an organization reflects the range of policies, practices and procedures focused on protecting the well-being (physical and mental) of workers (Dollard and Bakker, 2010). The relative level of psychological safety affects our willingness to share ideas and knowledge, raise concerns and suggestions for change, and use our initiative in our actions. It is influenced by perceived levels of support and trust in colleagues regarding the integrity of their actions, and can be negatively impacted by forms of conflict including incidence of blame cultures and being deliberately undermined by colleagues. Existing research suggests that psychological safety has an important interconnection with relationships at work and a range of organizational, team and individual outcomes. For example, experiencing positive relationships at work builds psychological safety and, in turn, this promotes organizational learning (i.e. developing behaviours including critical thinking, problem solving, and failure and error management). Meanwhile, within teams, psychological safety enhances performance through the mechanisms already outlined, and team learning behaviours have been found to mediate this relationship (Edmondson, 1999; Edmondson and Lei, 2014). The psychological safety climate is thus cited as a potentially significant location for intervention to address sources of work stress including conflict at work (Dollard and Bakker, 2010).

BOX 7.2   EVIDENCE ON CONFLICT AT WORK

Both relationship and non-task organizational conflict at work can generally be considered as problematic given the potential negative outcomes. Evidence from the Chartered Institute of Personnel and Development's (CIPD) UK Working Lives Survey (UKWLS) highlights the common incidence of conflict. Almost one third of workers surveyed in 2019 reported experiencing at least one form of conflict and almost one in ten at least two forms, in the 12 months prior to the survey (see Wheatley and Gifford, 2019). Conflict most often recorded in the 2019 UKWLS comprised being undermined or humiliated (14.4 per cent), shouting or heated arguments (12.9 per cent) and verbal abuse or insult (11.3 per cent). Incidence of conflict can lead to a vicious cycle, as relationship conflict can result in depressive symptoms, and individuals who already suffer from depressive symptoms (e.g. feelings of unhappiness, low self-esteem) may be more vulnerable to the negative effects of experiences of conflict (Meier et al., 2014). Resolution of conflict and stemming any further conflict is, therefore, essential to limit negative impacts to workplace well-being. Returning to the UKWLS data, it suggests that a little over half of conflicts are resolved or partly resolved within 12 months. Resolution rates differ by type of conflict; more serious conflict such as forms of sexual harassment are less likely to be resolved quickly, while negative behaviours including undermining or humiliating others and discrimination are only resolved in around one in seven cases. These forms of conflict are by their nature difficult to prove and behaviours often slow to change rendering these more problematic to eradicate within the workplace. Conflict associated with diversity and inclusion in the workplace is discussed in the next section.

Evidence, in the UK context, from the CIPD *Absence Management Annual Survey Report 2016* (Sinclair, 2016) and the *Health and Wellbeing at Work Survey Reports* for 2018 (Sinclair, 2018), 2019 (Sinclair, 2019) and 2020 (Sinclair and Suff, 2020) suggest that relationships at work are important factors contributing to incidence of work-related stress. Outside of workload/volume of work, pressure to meet targets and organizational change, management style and relationships at work are the most prominent work factors reported as acting as causes of work-related stress (Figure 7.1). Management style is also identified as being more relevant to workers in the 2019 and 2020 surveys, with 41 per cent (2019) and 43 per cent (2020) reporting management style as a key work-stressor compared to 32 per cent in 2018. Relationships at work are reported as a significant source of stress at work for more than one in four respondents (23 per cent in 2018; 30 per cent in 2019; and 26 per cent in 2020). A lack of effective employee voice is comparatively a relatively lesser source of work-related stress, perhaps evidencing the good quality of voice mechanisms offered in most organizations. Overall, the CIPD data evidences the impacts of relationships including those with leaders in creating a healthy working environment.

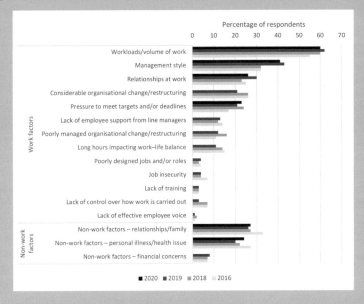

Note: Data available for 2020 limited to only six main factors.
Source: Sinclair, 2016, 2018, 2019; Sinclair and Suff, 2020.

Figure 7.1   Main causes of stress at work

174 *Well-being and the quality of working lives*

CONFLICT AND DIVERSE AND INCLUSIVE WORKPLACES

Workforce diversity centres on the principles of employment without discrimination and equality of opportunity (Jaiswal and Dyaram, 2018, 159). Having a diverse and more inclusive workplace offers a range of documented benefits including access to a wider potential talent pool, greater levels of innovation, improved decision-making, and a broader customer base. However, extracting the benefits of diversity can be challenging. A central distinction when considering diversity in the workplace is between visible and underlying diversity. Visible diversity, alternatively termed surface diversity, reflects more objective or discrete categories of difference such as age, gender, race and ethnicity. Diversity can also be found in 'underlying' or 'knowledge' form where difference reflects characteristics obtained throughout our lives that can change, including education, functional background and organizational tenure (Jaiswal and Dyaram, 2018, 159). A key assumption of this conceptualization is that these diversity characteristics are intrinsic and remain relatively stable for a given individual (Garcia-Prieto et al., 2003). Using simple demographic data, workers can be placed into categories enabling workforce diversity to be measured and monitored using metrics. More recent contributions to this field of research, however, acknowledge that diversity may be subjectively experienced. Nominal categorization of difference focus on the categories into which we 'fall', but diversity can reflect more centrally where we 'feel' difference, and in this case it can be dynamic and context dependent (Garcia-Prieto et al., 2003, 415; Jaiswal and Dyaram, 2018, 159).

Underlying diversity can promote cognitive processes centred on a task, thus leading to positive task-related conflict and, in turn, enhancements in team performance (Garcia-Prieto et al., 2003). Relationship conflict arising from negative behaviours related to visible diversity, such as stereotyping, discrimination and bias, has negative effects on individual and team performance. These negative outcomes can be understood with reference to social categorization theory (Tajfel et al., 1971, cited in Jaiswal and Dyaram, 2018). This concept argues that individuals have a tendency towards the creation of in- and out-groups or an 'us' and 'them' culture. They consider those who they regard to be similar as part of the 'us' or in-group, and those who are dissimilar as 'them' or part of the out-group. This results in colleagues in the in-group having greater levels of trust and support, but can create negative behaviours including prejudice, bias and stereotyping of those in the out-group, limiting team cohesion and performance among workers in the organization.

Not only do these behaviours have negative impacts at the organization-level, but they have significant negative impacts at the individual level including reducing feelings of acceptance and inclusion, support and well-being, and these can have wider impacts outside of work (Jaiswal and Dyaram, 2018, 160). Conflict on the basis of difference is, therefore, legislated against in many countries with policy focusing on a range of diversity characteristics. For example, in the UK, the Equality Act of 2010 prohibits direct or indirect discrimination in the workplace (and in wider society) on the basis of a set of protected characteristics. The Act identifies nine protected characteristics: age, sex, disability, race, religion or belief, sexual orientation, gender reassignment, marriage and civil partnership, and pregnancy and maternity (see Gov.uk, 2015).

Evidence from the UKWLS, reported in Wheatley and Gifford (2019), highlights negative behaviours associated with social categorization; exclusion on the basis of difference is reported by 22.3 per cent of employees. Reported conflict at work, meanwhile, evidences some stark differences in experiences of work by diversity characteristics. Almost one in seven non-white workers compared to only one in twenty white workers report being the victim of discrimination. Sexual orientation offers a further example; one in five LGBT workers report being undermined or humiliated compared with 14 per cent of heterosexual workers, and 11 per cent of LGBT workers reported discrimination compared to only 5 per cent of heterosexual workers. Gender remains a key site of difference with respect to conflict at work. Greater incidence is reported by women related to being undermined or humiliated; non-sexual intimidation/harassment; discrimination on the basis of a protected characteristic (which includes gender); and unwanted attention of a sexual nature. Although uncommon, the latter is more than twice as likely to be reported among women as men. Men more often report conflict involving shouting or heated arguments, verbal abuse or insult, false allegations against them, and physical threats.

LEADERSHIP AND TRUST WITHIN ORGANIZATIONS

The relationships between leaders and workers have already been noted as having a major role in overall experiences of work. Leadership has been argued as being one of the 'single biggest factors contributing to employee perceptions in the workplace and workforce engagement' (Wang and Walumbwa, 2007, 399). The quality of relationships between workers and leaders, including appreciation, support and effective feedback provided by leaders can act to counteract some of the negative impacts of high job demands on employee well-being (Bakker and Demerouti, 2007). High-quality relationships can create a positive and empowering work environment. Employees who have a good relationship with their leaders report having more control and autonomy, greater environmental clarity, experience more challenge, receive more opportunities for development and progression, and exhibit greater occupational self-efficacy or feelings of competence (Schermuly and Meyer, 2016; Syrek et al., 2013).

A number of models attempt to develop our understanding of leadership, with transformational leadership perhaps one of the most prominent. Transformational leadership captures leaders who motivate and empower their employees (Bass, 1985). Transformational leadership achieves this outcome through effective support mechanisms, challenging workers to develop their skills and ability, recognition of good performance, provision of a clearly communicated inspiring mission and/or vision for the organization, and building high-quality personal relationships with employees (Syrek et al., 2013, 253). Transformational leadership offers a number of specific benefits linked to well-being at work. It can help workers to develop skills that enable them to cope with job demands and better manage their work–life balance (Munir et al., 2012), reducing the negative impacts of time pressure (Syrek et al., 2013). Through attending to the needs of employees, this approach to leadership is argued as providing specific benefits through the provision of constructive feedback, creating an environment which is conducive to individual growth.

Often contrasted with transformational leadership, but sometimes argued to be a precondition for it to be effective, transactional leadership can be broadly referred to as leadership that involves the use of social exchanges for transactions (Bass and Avolio, 1993, 1997). A transactional leadership approach involves employees (or followers) performing their roles and assignments in agreement, acceptance or compliance with a leader in exchange for rewards, recognition and resources or in order to avoid disciplinary action (Bass et al., 2003, 208). Consistent with social exchange theory, transactional leadership takes two forms, one more corrective and one more passive. The corrective form, which is referred to as active management by exception, involves a leader setting standards for compliance, including clear indication of ineffective performance. This approach applies punishment to employees who do not meet the standards. As such, it usually involves closer monitoring of employee non-compliance, mistakes and errors, to enable corrective action to take place. However, while aspects of this form of leadership can be effective in extracting work effort, it is contingent on the effort–reward balance (see Chapter 6 for a discussion). Moreover, it could result in a Taylorist work organization being adopted, which negatively impacts worker performance and well-being (see Chapter 5).

The passive form of transactional leadership, meanwhile, involves a leader passively or reactively taking action to resolve problems once they have arisen or avoiding taking any form of action completely (Bass et al., 2003, 208). This form of leadership is referred to as passive management by exception (or passive-avoidant), but can reflect a laissez-faire leadership style in the latter case (Hinkin and Schriesheim, 2008). As well as the more obvious problems arising from destructive or negative leadership outlined later in this section, the existing evidence base highlights the potential negative consequences of laissez-faire leadership or non-leadership (Skogstad et al., 2007). Hinkin and Schriesheim (2008, 1234) describe laissez-faire leadership as a style in which leader behaviour is characterized by avoidance or delay of decision-making, failing to follow up, and being absent (physically and/or emotionally) when needed. Laissez-faire leadership more often reflects an ineffective leadership style, which can lead to lower levels of performance and satisfaction among employees (Judge and Piccolo, 2004). In some circumstances, though, it can operate effectively, for example where workers are highly skilled and highly motivated, including in some highly skilled professional occupations. However, non-leadership, while ineffective, does not result in the same degree of severity of negative impacts as is observed with negative or destructive leadership.

A range of studies have explored the impacts of negative or 'destructive' leadership behaviours (see Schyns and Schilling, 2013, for a discussion). Destructive leadership behaviour has been defined as 'a process in which over a longer period of time the activities, experiences and/or relationships of an individual or the members of a group are repeatedly influenced by their supervisor in a way that is perceived as hostile and/or obstructive' (Schyns and Schilling, 2013, 141). Negative behaviours comprise a range of verbal, non-verbal and even physical forms of abuse towards workers, as well as taking credit for others' work, scapegoating, and isolating individuals amongst other behaviours. These behaviours have potentially severe well-being impacts on workers, including increased incidence of work-related stress, emotional exhaustion and burnout, work–life conflict, turnover intention and reductions in satisfaction with job (Robertson and Cooper, 2011; Schyns and Schilling, 2013). It has also been suggested to potentially promote worker resistance and deviant work behaviour (e.g. malfeasance). Poor leadership behaviours can further hinder the ability of workers to cope with certain pressures at work, including the challenges of daily workloads and lack of resources (Snelgrove, 1998). The impacts of negative leadership behaviour extend to both the organization and society. It can impose significant costs on the organization and in turn to society, through increased employee absenteeism (linked to burnout and associated well-being impacts), employee turnover (linked to satisfaction and well-being), and reduced performance and productivity (linked to resistance/deviant behaviour and well-being).

BOX 7.3   MEASUREMENT OF LEADERSHIP

A comprehensive measurement of leadership can be found in the Multifactor Leadership Questionnaire (MLQ) developed by Bass and Avolio (1993, 1997). Form 5X of the MLQ contains scales that capture transformational leadership (four scales), transactional leadership (three scales) and laissez-faire leadership (one scale). Transformational leadership scales comprise (1) idealized influence; (2) individualized consideration; (3) intellectual stimulation; and (4) inspirational motivation. Transactional leadership scales comprise (1) contingent reward; (2) active management by exception; and (3) passive management by exception. Example items include:

Transformational Leadership	
Idealized influence	I go beyond self-interest for the good of the group
	I consider the moral and ethical consequences of decisions
Individualized consideration	I help others to develop their strengths
Intellectual stimulation	I re-examine critical assumptions to question whether they are appropriate
Inspirational motivation	I talk optimistically about the future
Transactional Leadership	
Contingent reward	I make clear what one can expect to receive when performance goals are achieved
Management by exception: active	I keep track of all mistakes
Management by exception: passive	I wait for things to go wrong before taking action
Laissez-faire Leadership	
Laissez-faire	I avoid making decisions

As well as more comprehensive measurement scales of leadership of the MLQ form that are directed toward the leader, a number of social surveys also include lines of questioning directed toward employees which explore aspects of the quality of leadership and trust in leadership within organizations. For example, the CIPD's UK Working Lives Survey includes several questions that probe the relative quality of relationships with line managers and senior leadership, summarized in Figures 7.2 and 7.3.

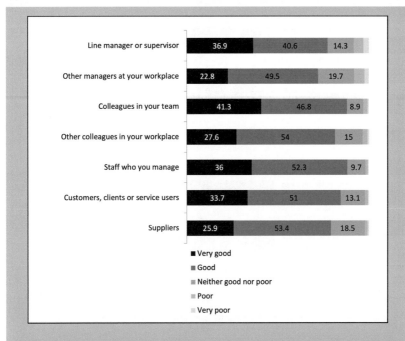

Note: Base: all employees (n = 4414).
Source: UK Working Lives Survey (Wheatley and Gifford, 2019).

Figure 7.2   Relationship quality at work (%)

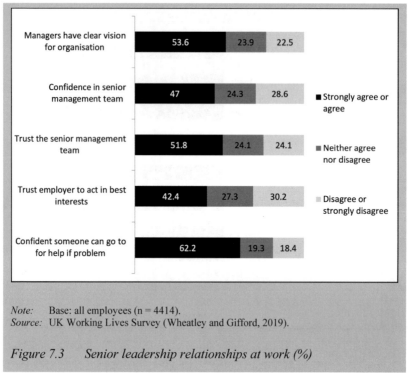

Note: Base: all employees (n = 4414).
Source: UK Working Lives Survey (Wheatley and Gifford, 2019).

Figure 7.3   Senior leadership relationships at work (%)

The role of trust is highly important when we consider, in particular, relationships within hierarchies in workplaces between line managers or leaders and workers. Trust can be defined as a state which occurs under conditions of risk, where the trusting party or 'trustor' develops positive expectations over the behaviours and intentions of the other party or 'trustee'. Importantly, trust involves these expectations becoming adequate to generate 'a willingness to become vulnerable to the trustee's future conduct' (Saunders et al., 2014, 640). As a concept, trust is closely linked to social capital discussed earlier in the chapter. Social capital has a highly interdependent relationship with trust (Lewicki and Brinsfield, 2009). Trust can potentially operate as a foundation, component, and/or outcome of social capital (Nichols et al., 2012). Further, it has been suggested that trust and social capital have a reciprocal relationship; trust is a factor in the creation of social capital, and at the same time use of social capital engenders trust (Nooteboom, 2007). As the measures of leadership within organizations in Box 7.3 evidence, aspects of trust and leadership within organizations are closely connected. Trust in leaders undoubtedly affects the wider relationship a worker has with their organization. Organizational trust refers to employee expectations regarding the intentions and behaviour of the range of stakeholders within the organization (i.e. owners, leaders and other decision makers) in the conduct, motives and objectives of the organization (Cropanzano et al., 2017; Ozyilmaz et al., 2018).

The trust an employee has in their organization is an important internal environmental component of work. Where trust is present it positively influences the expectations we have of our employer, and can foster positive perceptions and attitudes, enhanced performance and relationships including improved team-working (Alfes et al., 2012). This is a result of higher levels of trust increasing employee self-efficacy, leading to a range of potential positive effects on job satisfaction, task performance, and organizational citizenship behaviours. It is noteworthy also that higher levels of employee self-efficacy could increase intention to leave where the organizational environment is characterized by a lack of trust or other unfavourable conditions, further highlighting the importance of trust within the organization (Ozyilmaz et al., 2018). However, it is not only trust that an employee has in their leader or the organization that matters in creating a positive working environment, but also the trust a leader has in their employees. For example, where leaders exhibit a level of trust in their employees – often present where a more general good-quality relationship between leader and employee exists – leaders are likely to reward their employees with greater levels of control and autonomy, and decision-making responsibility (Schermuly and Meyer, 2016), which are central factors in job quality and workplace well-being. Where trust is present between leader and worker it has been shown in various studies to enhance employee engagement resulting from the free exchange of ideas, knowledge and information (see Engelbrecht et al., 2017, 370). Leaders can more easily influence LMX. Those with line management or leadership roles, therefore, have significant influence over the quality of relationships with employees, and through proactive approaches can develop high-quality relationships founded on trust.

WORKER RELATIONS AND EMPLOYEE VOICE

Employee voice and representation is a further relational component of work that impacts on workplace well-being. We all value opportunities to voice our suggestions and feedback in the workplace, either directly through engaging with managers or leaders, or indirectly through employee representatives (Lavelle et al., 2010). Employee voice refers to the ways in which employees can communicate views on work activities or participate in decision-making in an organization. First established in the seminal work by Hirschman (1970) and termed Exit–Voice–Loyalty theory, this concept originally focused on customers rather than employees (Mowbray et al., 2015). Employee voice is often used interchangeably with other terms including participation, engagement, involvement and empowerment (Wilkinson and Fay, 2011), although these terms have differing meanings and a number have been covered elsewhere in this book. Employee voice has both an instrumental and intrinsic value. Influencing the conditions of work we encounter through communicating preferences and concerns, and being able to exert influence and make a difference within the organization reflect the instrumental value of voice (Wilkinson et al., 2014). Meanwhile, our feelings regarding having an influence and being recognized form the intrinsic dimension of job quality (Connell and Burgess, 2016).

A range of potential channels exist for voice. A summary of these is provided in Table 7.1, broadly divided into formal and informal mechanisms (Mowbray et al., 2015). These include direct forms of communication with the most common and frequent usually being one-to-one meetings with line managers (formal or informal), appraisal systems (formal) and team meetings (formal). Other, often less frequently utilized, opportunities for voice include employee focus groups, employee attitude surveys and online forums (Wheatley and Gifford, 2019). All-hands (all-department or all-organization) meetings may offer a further opportunity for voice, but these are often more infrequent and can be more challenging at the individual level to raise concerns or provide feedback where the meetings involve a large number of workers and tend to take more of a briefing format.

Indirect voice, meanwhile, involves a mechanism for collective representation and can take the form of trade unions as well as non-union worker associations. These indirect approaches remain one of the most common forms of employee voice (Lavelle et al., 2010, 396). It should be noted that recent decades have seen a significant movement towards decline in membership of trade unions across many economies (Ebbinghaus et al., 2011; Waddington, 2015). A number of explanations have been offered to explain this decline, ranging from the impacts of the business cycle and changing labour market structure, relationships between political parties and unions, provision of welfare systems (income replacement), and changing individual characteristics of workers. Importantly, these explanations fail to address differences in national rates of decline, the impact of different union organization and strategy, and that among most workers decisions over union membership often reflect their workplace circumstances more so than the national economic or political environment (Waddington, 2015).

Employee voice offers a range of potential benefits for both the individual and the organization. Effective voice strategies can lead to enhanced performance as a result of reductions in absenteeism and improved team-work and cooperation. Also, linked to this, voice should engender improvements in employee behaviour, satisfaction, loyalty and commitment to the organization. Finally, it can lead to enhancements in managerial systems as opportunities for voice enable access to novel ideas and sharing of knowledge and experience (Wilkinson and Fay, 2011, 67). The relative effectiveness of voice, however, is

Relationships 183

Table 7.1   Employee voice mechanisms

Formal voice mechanisms	Informal voice mechanisms
Grievance processes	Informal discussions
One-to-one meetings and appraisals	One-to-one meetings
Speak-Up programme	Word-of-mouth
Email	Email
Open door policy	Open door policy
Empowerment by supervisor	Empowerment by supervisor
Self-managed teams	
Team briefings and meetings	
Employee attitude surveys	
Employee focus groups	
Staff meetings (all-department or all-organization)	
Upward problem-solving groups and quality circles	
Suggestion schemes	
Joint Consultative Committee	
Works Councils	
Continuous improvement teams	
Ombudsman	
Mediation	
Arbitration	
Internal Tribunals	
Online forums	

Source: Adapted from Mowbray et al., 2015, 389.

dependent on how it is approached. Historically, it has been argued, voice was often viewed as a mechanism to avoid labour disputes and collective action (Mowbray et al., 2015). Voice initiatives should aim to avoid the potential pitfalls around lack of longer-term planning, which can lead to one-off surveys of staff or an inconsistent or ever-changing approach to channels available for voice. Employee voice is effective where there is provision of relevant communication regarding outcomes and actions of any voice activities, while the most effective approaches to employee voice focus on embedding voice within the overall organizational strategy.

FUN AND PLAYFULNESS IN THE WORKPLACE

Workplace fun covers a range of different activities and interactions in the workplace. This includes fun derived from social interactions and activities (e.g. celebrations) at work (Tews et al., 2015). Work tasks can themselves be perceived as fun when workers feel engaged in their job (Schaufeli et al., 2008), in this case reflecting a specific form of engagement referred to as 'flow' that includes elements of enjoyment, pleasure and effective performance (Plester and Hutchison, 2016, 340). Gallacher et al. (2015) investigate the provision of physical resources in the form of interactive installations aimed at increasing levels of fun and playfulness within the workplace. They report sustained usage of a set of mood squeeze balls at the entrance to an office workplace, and generally positive impacts on workers including greater reflection and discussion of mood and feelings, and associated increases in social interaction. Other layout and design choices can be utilized to create a more engaging and conducive work environment without directly necessitating 'fun'. This could include, for example, providing a mix of larger open spaces and smaller spaces so that it necessarily creates 'collisions' between workers, promoting greater informal interaction (Gallacher et al., 2015). For a fuller discussion of workplace layout and design, see Chapter 9.

The use of interventions to increase levels of workplace fun has been shown to have potential positive effects. These include enhancements in innovation and productivity, reductions in absenteeism, better physical well-being, organizational citizenship behaviours and greater job satisfaction (Gallacher et al., 2015; Heaphy and Dutton, 2008). Using an ethnographic approach at four organizations in New Zealand, Plester and Hutchison (2016) reported that some methods of introducing fun in the workplace can create positive affect, providing workers with a refreshing break from work tasks. In turn, it is argued that this positive affect drives greater workplace and task engagement. Workplace fun needs to be handled carefully, though, as evidence has shown that where it is perceived to be too management-led, workers may reject and distance themselves from what they consider to be the imposition of 'organized fun' (Bolton and Houlihan, 2009; Plester and Hutchison, 2016). In addition, for some workers, whether management-led or organic, fun can result in feelings of disengagement as it creates distraction (e.g. due to noise and/ or loss of focus), disharmony or difference of opinion that effectively acts as a disruption to work (Plester and Hutchison, 2016). Better approaches provide opportunities to engage in fun and give ownership to workers over how this is implemented and to what degree to engage.

CHAPTER SUMMARY: BUILDING AND MAINTAINING HIGH-QUALITY RELATIONSHIPS AT WORK

Relationships at work are a central facet in the quality of our lives, both inside and outside of work. They can act as a driver for engagement in work, providing social connectedness and acting as a source of social capital. Meanwhile the quality of the relationships we have with our leaders, colleagues and clients/ customers has an important impact on our experiences of work and, in turn, our well-being. The presence of conflict focused on task can be healthy and positive, promoting debate and fresh thinking, and acting as a source of challenge in our jobs. Furthermore, embedding an environment that assists psychological safety promotes the sharing of knowledge and ideas, employee voice (and its associated benefits), and workers using their initiative. Methods that could be employed to engender positive relationships at work are outlined using the framework for workplace well-being in Figure 7.4. Essential to beneficial outcomes for both workers and organization is to put in place relevant mechanisms including training that promote an inclusive and positive working environment.

Figure 7.4   Realizing positive relationships at work for workplace well-being

The role of leadership in workplace well-being, and specifically in promoting good-quality relationships, is significant. It is linked to opportunities for development and progression, evidencing an interaction with the rewarding careers dimension of workplace well-being. Moreover, good-quality relationships with leaders can engender trust and intrinsic motivation among workers. Where leaders are ineffective or even engage in destructive behaviours, it can have significant detrimental impacts on employees with wider impacts felt within organizations and even society. Linked to the quality of leadership, employee voice is a further powerful mechanism for creating and maintaining good-quality relationships at work. Voice involves empowering workers to feed into discussions around the organization, including with leaders, and become involved in decision-making. Where employee voice mechanisms are poor, it can lead to negative behaviours, dissatisfaction and greater levels of employee turnover. An effective employee voice strategy, meanwhile, can offer benefits for both the employee (e.g. satisfaction, commitment) and organization (e.g. performance, retention, idea and knowledge generation and diffusion).

Where relationships fail, conflict at work can occur. Incidence of relationship conflict, including forms of bullying and harassment and/or discrimination, has a number of negative effects at the individual level. It affects our ability to perform in our jobs, for example as conflict with others creates barriers to task completion or even results in sabotage. This, of course, highlights the potential transmission of the negative impacts of conflict through to teams and even extending further throughout (and even beyond) the organization. Further, conflict of this nature influences our wider well-being, acting as a source of work-related stress and potentially resulting in depressive symptoms. Incidence of conflict can also create a vicious cycle where those who find themselves victims of conflict become more likely to become involved in further conflict and, in turn, may be more likely to feel the greatest negative effects. Relationship conflict, as such, should be a subject of significant concern at the level of the organization, given its impact on productivity, recruitment and retention, and imposing costs associated with conflict resolution. Building and maintaining high-quality relationships and evading the potential negative effects of conflict at work is, therefore, highly important to both the health of employees and their organizations.

8. Giving

INTRODUCTION

Giving is an act that most of us engage in on a regular basis. However, its role in creating a positive and successful working environment is not always given adequate consideration including in existing models of well-being at work. In the work context, giving can be defined as involving employees and organizations in philanthropic contributions of time, skills and expertise, support and money (i.e. pay and employer-matching donation schemes), fund-raising and employer grants (Rimes et al., 2019, 828). Debates have long existed over the motivations for giving, with some scholars arguing that giving behaviours can be devolved to self-interest, while others argue that giving reflects altruistic or selfless behaviour (André et al., 2017). Reciprocity (i.e. getting something in return for giving) (explored in Chapter 7 in reference to social exchange theory (Blau, 1964)), offers a third possible explanation for giving. Giving can be engaged with through both formal and informal action, with the former involving acts such as volunteering through an organization, and the latter including a wide range of activities such as giving time (Woolvin and Hardill, 2013) and offering support to colleagues. As such, giving can take many forms from simply taking time to listen to others and providing social support to distributing workload which under more formal arrangements can involve work sharing (e.g. a workforce distributing workload to avoid redundancy) (Crimman et al., 2010). Other methods of giving at work include coaching and developing colleagues as well as offering wider social and mental health support through schemes such as Mental Health First Aiding (Mental Health First Aid England, 2019).

Giving offers a range of potential rewards to both the 'giver' and to the recipient including to well-being. Individuals may enhance their own well-being through caring about the recipients' well-being, gaining enjoyment from the act of giving to others, and from seeing the well-being of others increase. Giving also offers extrinsic benefits, potentially acting as a source of human and social capital. This is important to consider with regard to giving in the workplace. Engaging in this activity helps the giver, and in some cases the recipient, to develop skills and networks (Folbre, 2012; Meier and Stutzer, 2008) which can have broader benefits for their working lives and the working lives of others. This chapter explores the range of ways in which giving intersects with our working lives. The chapter begins with a conceptual discussion of motivations for giving, including consideration of the benefits that may be generated from engaging in these acts. The chapter then turns to a discussion of different forms of giving and their impacts in the work context, including volunteering, charitable giving, social support, workplace helping and mentoring. The chapter ends with a case study which explores the experiences of engaging in a social enterprise.

MOTIVATIONS TO GIVE: SELF-INTEREST, ALTRUISM AND RECIPROCITY

To understand the motivations for giving we can turn to the debate over self-interest and altruism, drawing in part from the discussion on this matter offered by André et al. (2017). Self-interest, as a concept, can be traced back to the work of Adam Smith in his book *An Enquiry into the Nature and Causes of the Wealth of Nations* (1981 [1776]). Smith identifies that the pursuit of self-interest can lead to socially beneficial outcomes. As Smith described, 'It is not from the benevolence of the butcher, the brewer, or the baker, that we expect our dinner, but from their regard to their own interest. We address ourselves, not to their humanity but to their self-love, and never talk to them of our necessities but of their advantages' (*The Wealth of Nations*, Book I, Chapter II). Smith argued that the actions of individuals act to create demand for products and their supply, and that individual self-interest in this form overlaps into the interests of others, and in turn creates unintended wider societal benefits. However, Smith's own later work acknowledges that there may be more to our actions than self-interest. In the *Theory of Moral Sentiments* (1790), Smith acknowledges interest in the fortunes of others, that is, natural sympathy in our nature:

> our sensibility to the feelings of others, so far from being inconsistent with the manhood of self-command, is the very principle upon which that manhood is founded. The very same principle or instinct which, in the misfortune of our neighbour, prompts us to compassionate his sorrow; in our own misfortune, prompts us to restrain the abject and miserable lamentations of our own sorrow. The same principle or instinct which, in his prosperity and success, prompts us to congratulate his joy; in our own prosperity and success, prompts us to restrain the levity and intemperance of our own joy. In both cases, the propriety of our own sentiments and feelings seems to be exactly in proportion to the vivacity and force with which we enter into and conceive his sentiments and feelings. (*The Theory of Moral Sentiments*, Part III, Chapter III)

The argument here is that the behaviour of an individual, while reflecting self-interest, also recognizes the plight of others.

The concept of altruism stands in opposition to that of self-interest in understanding motivations for giving. The term 'altruism' was first coined in the nineteenth century by the philosopher August Comte (1966 [1851]). Altruism centres on the idea of selflessness. It has been defined as an action that is performed intentionally, and for the welfare of others. It is performed without expectation of benefits being received or may even result in loss for the individual engaged in the action (Cropanzano and Mitchell, 2005; Green, 2005, cited in Suzuki and Miah, 2015, 210). It comprises both actions which are performed for the benefit of others and those taken to avoid or prevent harm to them. Altruism does not underlie all seemingly charitable behaviours, though, as Hammond (1975, 115) observes: 'altruism can be invoked to explain any charitable behavior we may observe. But it is not quite obvious that altruism must be invoked to explain all charitable behavior.' Pure altruism (or unconditional altruism) may be the driver of some of this behaviour. Egoism (i.e. altruistic behaviour driven by the belief that it will result in some future benefit, also referred to as reciprocal altruism) could equally act as a driver (Fong, 2007). Warm glow is argued as a further potential motivator, referring to the individual deriving an affect benefit from the act of giving. In this latter case the individual is 'impurely altruistic' as they exhibit both altruistic and egoistic motivations for giving (Andreoni, 1990).

The reciprocal altruism concept links closely to concepts of reciprocity explored in Chapter 7 in reference to social exchange theory (Blau, 1964). Blau (1964, 91) argues that gifts reflect social exchanges based around reciprocity, as individuals give 'by the returns they are expected to bring and typically do in fact bring from others'. The suggested driver for altruistic behaviour in this case evidences clear roots in self-interest, but goes beyond self-interest in the pure sense, reflecting a motivational middle ground of sorts. Conceptualization of reciprocity suggests that we engage in actions which benefit others as we perceive this to be returning the favour for something they have done in the past (André et al., 2017). This can take both positive and negative forms, with individuals repaying gifts or exacting revenge. Moreover, these actions can be engaged in even where the individual gains nothing else from the reciprocal act (Fehr and Gächter, 2000). A further note on the nature of these reciprocal relationships is in their distinction from transactions in the economic sense. Where reciprocity differs is that it creates affect and relationships (good or bad), whereas purely economic transactions do not. It further generates a cycle which does not have a clearly defined ending as does a transaction. In reciprocal giving the 'gift' operates as a method of creating and maintaining the relationship between parties (André et al., 2017; Mauss, 1923).

Existing contributions suggest that only a minority of individuals tend towards being either pure altruistic 'givers' or self-interested 'takers', and rather forms of reciprocal giving behaviour dominate (André et al., 2017). The work of Mauss (1923) is useful in explaining the blurred lines between self-interest and altruism. Mauss (1923) argues that 'the idea that inspires all the economic acts [...] is neither a purely free and gratuitous provision nor a purely interested, utilitarian notion of production and exchange, but a sort of hybrid'. Reciprocal giving is argued as a method for individuals to cultivate and nurture relationships within a society. The act of giving necessarily creates a self-reinforcing cyclical relationship in which the recipient is obliged to give, in turn leading to them becoming a recipient, and again to them giving (André et al., 2017; Molm et al., 2012). The already outlined conceptualizations of reciprocity and social exchange also differ from that of generalized exchange or generalized reciprocity, also termed 'paying it forward'. This refers to giving without expectation of receiving something directly in return from the recipient, but instead with expectation to receive something indirectly from others and/or at another point in time (Molm et al., 2007, 2012). Examples of this type of exchange include donating blood, helping someone in the street, and anonymously reviewing a journal article. By its nature, generalized exchange is a higher risk form of reciprocal giving, as the giver cannot be certain they will receive benefits in return. As may be expected, evidence suggests that giving is lower in this form of social exchange (Molm et al., 2007).

A further explanation of giving distinguishes motivations in reference to associated intrinsic and extrinsic rewards obtained from this action (Folbre, 2012; Meier and Stutzer, 2008). Within the context of volunteering, it is argued that intrinsic motivation to give reflects the notion that helping others produces well-being benefits. This occurs as individuals care about the well-being of recipients; themselves gain enjoyment from the act of giving; and/or derive enjoyment from observing the well-being of others being enhanced through their actions (Meier and Stutzer, 2008). These benefits can be seen as being akin to the warm glow outlined earlier. Meanwhile, where extrinsic reward operates as a motivator, the individual may view the act of giving as an investment in human capital. The giver in this case can develop new or enhance existing skills and knowledge through engaging in voluntary and other giving activities. Equally, giving may be viewed as an investment in a social network, or a method of gaining social approval, reflecting giving behaviours offering potential sources of enhancements to social capital. Where motivation to give is driven by extrinsic reward, it is argued this reflects expectations of future benefit through reciprocation (Bianchi et al., 2008). Important to acknowledge in this approach to understanding the motivation to give is that whether intrinsic or extrinsic drivers predominate, the act of giving can clearly be viewed as generating benefits to the giver, recipient and society more broadly.

Extending the notion of societal benefits acting as a motivator for giving is the concept of prosocial motivation (PSM), which emphasizes the feelings of individuals towards the wider community (Christensen et al., 2018). It can be described as 'general altruistic motivation to serve the interests of a community of people, a state, a nation, or humanity' (Rainey and Steinbauer, 1999, 23). It has further been defined as 'the belief, values and attitudes that go beyond self-interest and organizational interest, that concern the interest of a larger political entity and that motivate individuals to act accordingly whenever appropriate' (Vandenabeele, 2007, 547). The existing evidence base supports PSM as having a positive relationship with engagement in voluntary and philanthropic behaviours (Bekkers and Wiepking, 2011), including in the workplace (Christensen et al., 2018).

GIVING IN THE WORKPLACE

In the work context, acts of giving can take several forms from a worker giving time to listen to the concerns of another, to a line manager offering mentoring support to a new member of staff, to a workplace volunteering programme or local or organization-wide fund-raising (referred to in this book as charitable giving). These forms of giving are undeniably distinct in their actions and outcomes and may, to some degree, be subject to differing drivers although the overall motivation to give will follow the mechanisms already explored in this chapter.

Organizations increasingly engage in giving behaviours and develop workplace giving programmes as part of corporate social responsibility agendas. Hybrid organizations, for example social enterprises (see the case study in this chapter), are more obvious examples of the ways in which organizations can engage with communities and in giving activities (André et al., 2017). However, there are a range of activities that organizations can engage in to combine commercial and social responsibility. Organizations can establish a 'culture of giving' to promote participation in giving behaviours within the workplace (Campione, 2016). Workplace giving programmes – describing a set of organization-driven giving activities including volunteering, charitable financial giving, workplace helping, mentoring schemes and other giving behaviours – provide a framework for giving within the organization that may offer a number of benefits for organizations and their employees, as well as the recipients of their acts of giving (Rimes et al., 2019).

One benefit of workplace giving programmes is that they provide an accessible method for employees to both define and achieve their altruistic goals (Rimes et al., 2019, 830). Giving programmes channel the attention of employees to a narrower set of potential giving activities and recipients, raising awareness while helping to focus their efforts, as well as offering the potential to build relationships with specific recipient organizations or communities. Workplace giving programmes can be particularly effective where organizations offer their employees tangible incentives to engage in giving behaviour (Grodal et al., 2015), including time off (which in some instances could be time allocated specifically for the giving act) or monetary incentives (e.g. a prize draw). At the individual level, workplace giving programmes also offer the potential to reduce transaction costs associated with giving. Specifically, it reduces the opportunity cost incurred from the time spent giving and that involved in gathering information about potential recipient charitable organizations. Reducing these costs is argued to promote greater levels of giving behaviour (Knowles and Servátka, 2015).

Workplace giving programmes can lead to enhanced employee motivation and organizational commitment as workers connect with the prosocial values of their employer (Rimes et al., 2019, 828). Evidence also points towards possible benefits in the form of increasing levels of trust within the organization (and towards the recipient), which may promote other internal giving behaviours including organizational citizenship and workplace helping, explored in this chapter (Lin et al., 2020; Osili et al., 2011, 406). Socially responsible organizations have also been shown to be more attractive to workers, offering potential benefits to recruitment and retention (Grant, 2012). Psychological benefits can also be realized from, and may act as drivers of, giving in the workplace. Workplace giving programmes can engender a sense of pride in employees as part of their organization and can create feelings of team solidarity. Giving alongside others may increase the satisfaction or warm glow obtained from giving and may, in turn, result in enhanced job satisfaction and fulfilment (Campione, 2016).

VOLUNTEERING

A general definition of volunteering describes it as the act of freely choosing to give time to help or benefit others with no direct remuneration (Zappala, 2000). Associated terms used to describe volunteering in the work context include corporate volunteering, workplace volunteering and employee volunteering. Corporate or workplace volunteering is used to describe activities such as community service, outreach, or social responsibility which involve giving time, knowledge or skills. Importantly, corporate volunteering is usually considered to take place on company time and with no additional compensation provided to the volunteer (Grant, 2012). Employee volunteering, meanwhile, has been defined as 'giving time or skills during a planned activity for a volunteer group' (Rodell, 2013, 1274). A further definition, focusing on formal volunteering describes it as 'employed individuals giving time during a planned activity for an external non-profit or charitable group or organization' (Rodell et al., 2016, 57). An alternative definition offers that employee volunteering comprises any voluntary act undertaken by employed individuals. In this definition, corporate volunteering is employee volunteering that is performed through a workplace volunteering programme, consistent with the above definition, while personal volunteering is used to refer to employee volunteering enacted during the employee's own time. Volunteering can be undertaken formally through a volunteer group or organization (e.g. charity, non-profit organization), or on a more informal basis through good neighbouring and/or time giving on a one-to-one basis alternatively referred to as the 'fourth sector' (Williams, 2003, 2011; Woolvin and Hardill, 2013). Most definitions of volunteering in the work context identify it as a formalized and public activity in which the volunteer, prior to undertaking the act, does not personally know the recipient(s) (Wilson, 2000).

Volunteering is distinct from other forms of giving such as charitable giving as it involves giving time as opposed to financial donations. In addition, volunteering involves active participation in an act of giving whereas charitable giving involves only monetary donations which are more passive in form. Finally, volunteering can be considered to be distinct from workplace helping as it is a planned, rather than spontaneous, activity (Rodell et al., 2016). The motivation to engage in volunteering appears to range from the more altruistic, where volunteering is an act that is 'given freely' and/or performed for the benefit of others (Wilson, 2000, 215), to motivations that are more self-interested. Individuals may volunteer as they seek fulfilment of their own values, to develop social connections, and to escape working lives that they feel lack meaning (Rodell et al., 2016). Employee volunteering may also be motivated by efforts to manage expectations (including feelings of obligation) or impressions among colleagues and/or line managers and leaders in the workplace, or as a direct method of attempting to gain recognition at work (Booth et al., 2009). Both intrinsic and extrinsic motivations are, therefore, relevant to employee volunteering behaviours. In most cases the motivators of volunteering are a combination of both intrinsic and extrinsic factors, although extrinsic motivation often delivers fewer benefits to employee well-being (Meier and Stutzer, 2008). Other evidence offers a more nuanced perspective. Self-interested motivation increases volunteering intensity in the work sphere as workers are driven by a combination of human capital investment (learning), expectations around potential career advancement benefits, and social interaction. Meanwhile, personal volunteering intensity is more likely driven by intrinsic factors including improving the well-being of others (Peloza et al., 2009).

Many organizations now incorporate community service activities and civic engagement (i.e. voluntary activities performed by members of the community aimed at enhancing community and society), as optional (or in some instances, required) opportunities to fulfil educational or employment obligations (Hoffman et al., 2010). Many employers offer some form of workplace volunteering programme, acknowledging that volunteering is viewed as generating benefits for employees, employers and society (Rodell et al., 2016). Volunteering programmes can be strategically valuable to the organization providing positive effects on company reputation and attractiveness as a place to work, with associated benefits to recruitment and retention. These programmes build levels of respect and pride among employees, giving them a stronger attachment and commitment to the organization and wider community (Jones, 2010; Kim et al., 2010). In the organizational context, formal volunteering programmes can be integrated into a wider corporate social responsibility strategy. Existing evidence suggests that employees perceive workplace volunteering programmes to offer a more important method of engaging in corporate social responsibility than charitable giving (Grant, 2012; Kim et al., 2010), and that this may be especially valued by newer generations of employees including millennials (Rodell et al., 2016). Volunteering programmes also offer benefits for recipient charity or non-profit organizations including cost savings through economies of scale in recruiting and organizing volunteers (Grant, 2012).

At the individual level, evidence suggests benefits in the form of job meaningfulness and employee morale, both intrinsic components of work (Grant, 2012; Rodell, 2013). Two potential mechanisms are argued here; first, that workers who perceive their jobs to offer good job quality including being interesting and challenging, engage in volunteering as a form of giving back for the good work environment provided by their employer (Rodell et al., 2016). Equally, some workers may use volunteering as a source of meaning where they encounter a lack of meaning in their jobs (Rodell, 2013). Employee volunteering has been suggested to improve task performance and enhance organizational citizenship, while it also acts to reduce counterproductive behaviours in the workplace (Jones, 2010; Rodell, 2013). Second, evidence also suggests volunteering to be positively associated with satisfaction with job, amount of leisure time, and life (Hardill and Wheatley, 2017; Meier and Stutzer, 2008). Meanwhile, personal volunteering may generate positive spillover effects as engaging in volunteering has been found to increase levels of employee engagement and motivation (Rodell, 2013). Further, benefits include voluntary work acting as a method of work recovery (Campione, 2016), as it acts as a use of leisure time that has positive effects on the recovery process (Mojza et al., 2011).

Three forms of leisure time experiences which aid work recovery can be obtained through volunteering. First, volunteers can experience psychological detachment from paid work (i.e. they are able to 'switch off' and be mentally away from paid work, as they fully engage in the voluntary act). Second, volunteering offers community experiences (i.e. the ability to cultivate social contacts and generate feelings of social connectedness and belonging) (Mojza et al., 2010; Sonnentag, 2001; Sonnentag and Fritz, 2007). The volunteer is able to gather social resources, which can be used to restore resources depleted during work-time and offset work strain. Third, volunteers can benefit from mastery experiences. As per potential extrinsic motivations already outlined, volunteering provides the volunteer with the opportunity to develop knowledge and skills (Meier and Stutzer, 2008), including active listening, communication and interpersonal skills (Booth et al., 2009; Mojza et al., 2011). They acquire knowledge and learn new skills and these experiences promote successful work recovery through aiding the accumulation and replenishment of psychological resources including greater resilience, optimism and self-efficacy (Campione, 2016). Through volunteering, a worker feels a sense of accomplishment which enables them to develop and grow (Booth et al., 2009; Mojza et al., 2011).

Engagement in Volunteering

Levels of engagement in volunteering differ relative to several demographics including age, social class, ethnicity and place of residence (Rochester et al., 2010). As already outlined, motivations to volunteer are both complex and dynamic. The concept of the life course provides a useful heuristic for understanding how and why capacities to volunteer fluctuate throughout our lives (Hardill and Baines, 2011). Throughout the life course, the propensity to volunteer takes the form of an inverted U-shape (Hardill and Wheatley, 2017; Musick and Wilson, 2008), although other demographics apart from age also influence the shape of volunteering engagement. Engagement in volunteering may be closely related to key transitions, including time spent in education, movements into and out of paid work, and expansion of caring responsibilities for dependent children (parenting and grandparenting) and ill/elderly relatives/friends.

Patterns evidence the impact of trade-offs present between time spent in these activities. Paid work has been found to act as a particular barrier to volunteering, especially for men (Hardill and Wheatley, 2017). Significant value may therefore be generated, especially for workers, by offering volunteering programmes within the organization. Retirement acts as a specific trigger for personal volunteering, especially for formal volunteering activity among men. Research suggests that women are more likely to engage in voluntary work than men (Hardill and Wheatley, 2017; Rochester et al., 2010). The time available to volunteer may be limited among many women due to childcare and other household responsibilities and caring for ill/elderly friends and relatives. Nevertheless, women are more likely than their male counterparts to devote a greater amount of time to volunteering throughout the middle part of their lives (Hardill and Wheatley, 2017). Employees with dependent children more often engage in volunteering which has links to activities in which their children are involved; for example, parents may volunteer at sports clubs their children attend (Cornwell and Warburton, 2014; Hardill and Wheatley, 2017). Analysis of drivers and barriers to engagement in volunteering is provided in Box 8.1.

BOX 8.1   PATTERNS OF VOLUNTEERING: EVIDENCE FROM THE COMMUNITY LIFE SURVEY

The Community Life Survey (CLS) is conducted in England and is a household survey that captures trends and developments relating to social action and community engagement, including charitable giving and volunteering (DCMS, 2019). Data from the 2018–19 survey offers useful insight into the drivers of participation in volunteering as well as barriers faced. Drivers include: (1) 'I wanted to improve things/help' (47.0 per cent of respondents); (2) 'the cause was really important to me' (32.4 per cent); (3) 'I had spare time to do it' (26.8 per cent); (4) 'I wanted to meet people/make friends' (24.3 per cent); (5) 'I thought it would give me a chance to use my existing skills' (23.0 per cent); and (6) 'I felt there was a need in my community' (22.2 per cent). These responses support the assertion of intrinsic motivators (and rewards) acting as drivers of voluntary work. Extrinsic motivation, including career development (6.7 per cent) or gaining qualifications (2.2 per cent), is less commonly cited as a driver in the survey, although the potential to learn new skills is reported by around one in six (15.7 per cent) individuals.

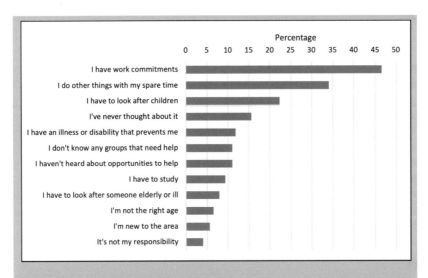

Source: Community Life Survey, 2018–19 (DCMS, 2019).

Figure 8.1   Barriers to volunteering

Barriers to volunteering are summarized in Figure 8.1. The most common barrier to volunteering reported in the CLS is 'I have work commitments', reported by just under half of respondents. This highlights the potential importance of incorporating volunteering at the organizational level through, for example, time out of normal working routines for volunteering. As well as work itself acting as a barrier, household responsibilities can be a barrier, and one that falls more predominantly on women: 'I have to look after children/the home' (26.9 per cent of women compared to 17.2 per cent of men) and 'I have to look after someone elderly or ill' (9.2 per cent of women compared to 6.5 per cent of men). Meanwhile, the response 'I do other things with my spare time' is reported by around one third of respondents (38.4 per cent of men compared to 30.6 per cent of women). A notable portion of respondents indicate, 'I've never thought about it' (15.6 per cent), 'I don't know any groups that need help' (11.0 per cent), or 'I haven't heard about opportunities to help' (11.0 per cent), all of which indicate a lack of awareness which could be addressed through effective signposting as part of corporate volunteering programmes. Among the survey sample only a relatively small proportion of individuals reported that their employer offered a charitable giving programme (13.4 per cent), a volunteering/helping programme (5.8 per cent), or both charitable giving and volunteering/helping programme (6.5 per cent). This data highlights the limited provision that may be present within organizations, and which can limit engagement in these acts and the associated benefits which can be derived from them.

Promoting and supporting volunteering at the organizational level through offering time off (e.g. a day to volunteer per month), modified work schedules and/or the provision of resources has been shown to increase time given to volunteering by employees by up to 45 per cent (Booth et al., 2009). To be most effective, workplace volunteering programmes require sustained employee engagement, but it can be difficult to retain volunteers rendering it important to focus on the long term when developing workplace volunteering programmes (Grant, 2012). This ensures better stakeholder engagement (including recipients) and helps to spread the cost of the training investment involved. Long-term contributors to workplace volunteering programmes tend to engage in multiple different volunteering activities and can become champions of voluntary activities within the organization, generating benefits as these champions can promote others within the organization to become involved and create a culture of workplace volunteering (Muthuri et al., 2009).

CHARITABLE GIVING

Charitable giving (also referred to as philanthropic giving) describes the giving of donations including those that take monetary form (Rimes et al., 2019). As with other forms of giving, patterns of charitable giving can be linked to the concept of reciprocity, which suggests that individuals respond in kind to positive or negative giving acts (Fehr and Gächter, 2000). The relationship between reciprocity and charitable giving can be usefully divided into positive and negative reciprocity; an individual will be compelled to donate more when other members in their group also donate, reflecting in this case positive reciprocity. Meanwhile, an individual will donate less when the contributions of others are also low, reflecting negative reciprocity. The presence of these forms of reciprocity, which are also termed 'matching' or 'conditional cooperation', implies that a level of coordination is present in the act of charitable giving (Ashley et al., 2010). It is also noted that most charitable giving exhibits the properties of a normal good (i.e. levels of charitable giving increase with income) (Evans et al., 2017, 563). In the work context, Christensen et al. (2018) find that prosocial motivation has a positive relationship with charitable giving, and that it also has a positive interaction with organizational commitment (see Chapter 4). Organizational commitment may be increased as workers respond positively to their employer communicating their prosocial values through charitable giving programmes. This, in turn, can have positive effects on employee motivation (Rimes et al., 2019).

Furthermore, the findings of Christensen et al. (2018) suggest that to maximize engagement, and in turn the benefits from charitable giving, employers should focus on ensuring a good match between them and their employees, including prosocial values, during the recruitment process, and should build organizational commitment through the training and team-building provision within the organization. Through including a charitable or non-profit organization in a list of recipients, an employer offers legitimacy and trustworthiness. It generates name recognition and creates awareness of the organizations and their respective needs/causes. Employers can act as a gatekeeper for employees to access recipient organizations with which they may build relationships which extend beyond the workplace (Osili et al., 2011, 395). Existing research suggests charitable giving often follows direct solicitation, and that the propensity to donate is positively associated with the number of solicitations (Rimes et al., 2019). Charitable giving programmes need to be balanced, though, with the potential for 'giving fatigue'. If requests to give are too frequently it could result in feelings of fatigue and fewer donations (Barnes, 2006, cited in Rimes et al., 2019). If a worker feels overwhelmed with requests to give this could even prompt a complete break from giving behaviour. Important also is that employers generate a list of potential recipients that aligns with the values of the organization and the individual workers. Evidence supports that organizations offering a greater variety of choice with respect to giving benefit from higher levels of employee participation and greater absolute values of donations (Rimes et al., 2019).

The evidence on relative levels of workplace charitable giving suggests that industry-specific culture and environment may have an influence on giving behaviours (Osili et al., 2011). At the demographic level, findings are conflicting to some degree, with some studies suggesting higher levels of giving among women and more diverse workforces (Leslie et al., 2013), but other research reporting insignificant differences or conflicting results (Agypt et al., 2012). At the broader societal level, Rimes et al. (2019) suggest that workplace charitable giving can be a powerful method of encouraging giving behaviour among households as charitable giving at work promotes charitable giving at home. In this sense, charitable giving could have a possible reinforcement effect, that is, individuals who give at work may be more likely to engage in giving outside of the workplace (Nesbit et al., 2012).

A potential negative side of charitable giving is that it can lead to reputational damage and psychological costs should workers not engage in donating behaviour (Rimes et al., 2019). Not giving, whether through choice or because of constraint (e.g. household finances limiting charitable giving), could damage the reputation of an individual. Work colleagues may deem them to be 'selfish' when they do not offer donations. Social pressure of this nature can result in relationship difficulties and psychological costs being incurred, with negative implications for worker well-being. Negative effects may be particularly apparent in cases where an individual is part of a group earning a similar salary where giving is common and/or where their employer creates a culture promoting charitable giving which perhaps inadvertently generates a level of institutional and peer pressure to give. The responsibility of the organization is in ensuring that charitable giving remains optional, and while it may be promoted given the number of benefits that can be realized, workers should not be subject to negative consequences if they do not engage in this form of giving.

SOCIAL SUPPORT AT WORK

The levels of social support we experience within the workplace can have a significant impact upon our working lives (Chiaburu and Harrison, 2008). Social support describes the availability of help and assistance that provides feelings of being appreciated and cared for by others (Kossek et al., 2011, 291). It is both given and received through interaction in relationships which consist of actual or perceived exchanges of physical and psychosocial resources that can enhance coping, esteem, belonging and competence (Nielsen et al., 2020, 44). Social support has been more formally defined as 'verbal and nonverbal communication between receiver and provider that reduces uncertainty about a situation, one's self, another, or a relationship' (Sias, 2009, 70). Several forms of social support have been identified. First, instrumental support refers to practical support given to help with the completion of work tasks. This aspect of social support is consistent with the concept of workplace helping which is outlined in the next section. The second form of social support is emotional support, reflecting the expression of care, empathy or esteem, including listening to the challenges faced by a peer and offering consolation or potential solutions. Finally, informational support involves the giving and receiving of advice, information or guidance (Holland and Collins, 2020; Sias, 2009).

Applying the concept of social support to our working lives, workplace social support describes the support that emanates from supervisors, colleagues and the employing organization (Kossek et al., 2011). As such, it includes a range of interpersonal behaviours that can improve worker performance and well-being: assistance with work tasks (i.e. workplace helping, as already noted); giving emotional support; mentoring (discussed later in this chapter); and educating others on the social power structures in the workplace (Harris et al., 2007b). In addition, important to concepts of workplace social support is that it is often defined in reference to the degree to which a worker perceives that workplace sources of social support (supervisors, colleagues and the organization) value and provide help to support their well-being (Eisenberger et al., 2002; Eisenberger and Stinglhamber, 2011). Perceived support, then, is central to consideration of workplace social support. The existing literature refers to this as perceived organizational support (POS), perceived supervisor support (PSS) and perceived colleagues support (PCS). These sources of social support at work have been found to promote positive workplace outcomes including enhanced performance and job satisfaction (Caesens et al., 2020;

Eisenberger and Stinglhamber, 2011). Methods of measuring workplace social support empirically are outlined in Box 8.2.

BOX 8.2   MEASURING SOCIAL SUPPORT AT WORK

A range of measures are available to capture levels of social support in the workplace. Scales have been developed including that by Beehr et al. (1990) which focuses on types of communication between workers during supportive episodes. Each of the statements is measured on a 5-point scale with options comprising (1) never, (2) seldom, (3) occasionally, (4) often, and (5) always. An adapted version of the statements from the Beehr et al. (1990) scale is as follows:

- We discuss things that are happening in our personal lives.
- We talk about off-the-job interests that we have in common.
- We share personal information about our backgrounds and families.
- We talk about off-the-job social events.
- We talk about how we dislike some parts of our work.
- We talk about the bad things about our work.
- We talk about problems in working with [colleagues].
- We talk about how this is a lousy place to work.
- We talk about the good things about our work.
- We share interesting ideas about [our jobs].
- We talk about how this is a good place to work.
- We talk about the rewarding things about this job.

POS describes the overall belief of workers as to whether their organization values its employees, provides adequate resources to support their socio-emotional needs and fulfil job demands, and is concerned with their well-being (Kossek et al., 2011). Organizational support theory is a useful concept to contextualize this aspect of workplace social support. It suggests that workers to some degree personify their organization. Their perception regarding whether their employer values their efforts and cares about their well-being acts as a driver of commitment, well-being, and positive work attitudes and behaviours (Eisenberger and Stinglhamber, 2011). Organizational support theory draws on social exchange theory, and specifically reciprocity, in explaining these behaviours (Caesens et al., 2020). The suggested relationship is that where a worker perceives high levels of organizational support, they are more likely to consider that positive actions by their organization reflect that their employer is committed to them (Kurtessis et al., 2017). The employee, in turn, feels an obligation to reciprocate this behaviour through helping the organization realized through positive work attitudes and behaviours evident in improved performance. Under the assumptions of social exchange theory, existing evidence argues that the rules of exchange govern workplace social support relationships which develop over time and depend on both parties reciprocating support (Cropanzano and Mitchell, 2005; Holland and Collins, 2020).

The existing evidence base highlights the benefits of workplace social support. It has been found to have a positive relationship with job satisfaction and to be related to several positive outcomes in the workplace including enhanced job performance, reduced turnover intention and reductions in the negative effects of social stressors at work including reduction in sickness absence (see Harris et al., 2007b; Nielsen et al., 2020; Sias, 2009). POS, meanwhile, has been identified as enhancing employee performance, organizational commitment and job satisfaction, and potentially aiding reductions in emotional exhaustion, absenteeism and turnover (Caesens et al., 2020). PSS has a significant relationship with job tenure (Harris et al., 2007b) and PCS that takes the form of instrumental support may generate benefits in helping management of workload and reducing role ambiguity and role conflict, providing associated positive effects on job satisfaction and organizational commitment (Chiaburu and Harrison, 2008).

Social support can result, however, in negative outcomes where support is inconsistent. For example, evidence suggests that supervisor support can vary across employees resulting in in- and out- groups as per social categorization theory in Chapter 7, and that employees who are in the 'in-group' may be given greater depth, breadth and quality of support when compared to employees in the 'out-group' (Sias, 2005). In addition, where a worker perceives that they give more social support compared to that which they receive, it can generate feelings of unfairness and the giving of support effectively becomes a burden. Meanwhile, workers who are in receipt of greater support than they give to others can experience feelings of guilt (Bowling et al., 2005). Some research has shown workplace social support to have a significant relationship with several negative outcomes including absenteeism, turnover, burnout, depression and anxiety (Harris et al., 2007b). The consistent link with these outcomes is that workers are more likely to need social support when they are struggling in their jobs, so the higher levels of reported social support in these cases reflects a response to a negative outcome already present. For example, Deelstra et al. (2003) suggest that colleague support might not be positively related to job satisfaction as unhappy or stressed workers have a higher propensity to seek this support. Finally, workplace social support can be problematic for workers who are physically distant from one another, such as teleworkers. In their qualitative study of UK teleworkers, Collins et al. (2016) find teleworkers can become socially isolated where their working pattern is exclusively teleworking. They report that the social support networks of teleworkers often consist only of co-workers with whom they have existing relationships prior to them working at home, and there can be a level of unwillingness and/or inability to build new relationships. This finding is particularly relevant given the rapid growth in remote and homeworking in 2020–21, evidencing the challenges workers and organizations face in supporting one another when working remotely.

WORKPLACE HELPING

Helping others at work is a form of social support termed workplace helping. It is defined as the 'willing devotion of time and attention to assist with the work of others' (Hargadon and Bechky, 2006, 489). It is a voluntary behaviour, not part of the contractual requirements of a job as specified by an organization (Sparrowe et al., 2006). Although clearly overlapping, workplace helping differs slightly in definition from employee organizational citizenship, with the latter specifically referring to helping others within the organization following a generalized exchange process (i.e. without necessarily having an expectation of a direct return from the recipient) (Flynn and Brockner, 2003, 1035). At the individual level the decision to offer help to another involves a cost for the helper, as they have to spend their time and effort supporting the work of others, potentially invoking a short-term cost to their own productivity (Grodal et al., 2015). Evidence suggests that workplace helping is associated with higher levels of performance within teams and organizations and can deliver wider societal benefits through promoting economic growth and dynamism (Sirola and Pitesa, 2017). There remain, however, two opposing perspectives on the impacts of workplace helping for the helper. The enrichment-based perspective argues that workers who help others receive benefits in the form of enhanced meaningfulness and well-being. Meanwhile, the depletion-based perspective suggests that helping is resource depleting, acting as a source of work-related stress, exhaustion, role overload, and reduced task performance and career success (Lin et al., 2020, 386).

Lin et al. (2020) find evidence in support of both the enrichment-based and depletion-based perspectives of workplace helping. Helping is found to be positively related to meaningfulness and psychological safety, but also to levels of emotional exhaustion. These impacts have opposing relationships with job involvement as meaningfulness and psychological safety are related to increases, but exhaustion related to reductions in job involvement. Through its impacts on job involvement, helping behaviour can both stimulate and diminish future helping behaviour. It is argued it is the relative balance of these two opposing impacts that determines whether workers will continue to offer workplace help and the relative effects this act has on their well-being at work. In other research using a series of experiments with US employees, Sirola and Pitesa (2017) find that levels of workplace helping are negatively impacted by economic downturns; workers tend to perceive that success for some necessitates loss for others, and engage in less helping behaviour when the economic outlook is bleak. This response represents a problem not only for organizations but society more broadly, given the documented positive effects of workplace helping. It is, therefore, argued that embedding a strong collaborative culture is important for the health of the organization to negate this outcome. Establishing linked or joint incentives or rewards for tasks could also provide a method of mediating impacts of economic downturn on workplace giving.

The incidence of workplace helping differs relative to job design and the nature of the work being performed as well as the individual characteristics of the workers. Where work tasks are more interdependent, and jobs involve more complex activities, helping others is more common. Workers in these cases often rely on each other to complete tasks; indeed, some tasks may not be feasible to complete in isolation. Helping each other is simply part of the job, and one that generates benefits for all parties. Nevertheless, a number of factors influence the decision to offer help in the workplace (Flynn and Brockner, 2003). The perceptions an individual holds towards the recipient influences the decision to help, as does their interpretation of the value of the help that is to be given. Finally, prior experiences of giving and receiving help from others influence decisions to offer help (Grant and Dutton, 2012). We can return to the concepts of reciprocity and social exchange theory in explaining some of these actions. A worker may be more likely to engage in workplace helping if they have received help themselves from others in the past, reflecting in this case workplace helping as a form of generalized exchange (Molm et al., 2007). Equally, they may be more likely to provide help to a co-worker should they feel that doing so provides them with a bargaining chip for getting help from others in the future to accomplish tasks when they lack the resources to complete the task themselves; an example of reciprocal exchange.

Grodal et al. (2015) provide a useful example of the benefits of workplace helping in the context of innovative and interdependent work environments. Reporting on their study of hardware and software engineers in the USA, they argue that the greatest benefits from workplace helping can be realized when there is a culture within the workplace that embeds and rewards psychological safety around help giving and seeking. Offering intrinsic and/or extrinsic rewards for helping is argued as necessary to positively reinforce these behaviours and avoid workers becoming discouraged from helping. Meanwhile, providing psychological safety around help giving promotes this behaviour as both giving and seeking help are viewed as acceptable and positive behaviours within the organization. Further, it is suggested that the cognitive and emotional engagement present in the act of helping has the potential to generate a self-reinforcing cycle where helping encourages future helping behaviour.

MENTORING

As explored in Chapter 7, relational aspects of work have a key role in determining experiences of work and well-being. Mentoring has been argued as an important relational component of work in this context (Allen et al., 2004) that centres on an act of giving. Drawing on the seminal work of Levinson et al. (1978) and Kram (1985), mentoring is defined as a work relationship in which a more experienced, often older, worker (the mentor) advises, counsels and provides development opportunities to a less experienced, usually younger, protégé or mentee. Bozeman and Feeney (2007, 731) further describe mentoring as 'a process for the informal transmission of knowledge, social capital, and psychosocial support perceived by the recipient as relevant to work, career, or professional development'. The relationship is founded upon the expectation that the mentor has greater knowledge and experience and is willing to share this with the mentee to enhance their career prospects (Janssen et al., 2018). It is often conceptualized as involving a blend of coaching, role modelling, sponsorship, friendship and counselling (Holt et al., 2016, 78).

Where mentoring is successful, this positive connection has the potential to enhance the well-being of workers and their organizations (Murphy, 2012). High-quality mentoring delivers benefits to the mentee with regard to the quality of the relational component of work, while also supporting and influencing perceptions of non-relational aspects such as job properties and careers (Jiang et al., 2020). Mentoring involves the act of giving and reciprocity is argued as a central factor in mentoring as both mentors and mentees enter into mentoring arrangements with an understanding of the benefits that they and the other member of the relationship can obtain from mentoring (Kram, 1985). Mentors provide career and psychosocial support resources to the mentee. Career mentoring support comprises the nomination of the mentee for progression opportunities and assignments (sponsorship); teaching the mentee the most effective approach to accomplish tasks, gain recognition and achieve career goals (coaching); intervening in difficult and potentially career-damaging circumstances and shielding the mentee (protection); supplying new learning opportunities, alongside feedback and technical support (challenging assignments); and introducing the mentee to senior colleagues and stakeholders (exposure and visibility). Psychosocial mentoring support involves treating the mentee like a peer (friendship); engaging in positive social experiences with the mentee (social); acting as a positive and respected influence (role model, parent); helping personal and professional development (counsel); and helping the mentee develop self-efficacy and feelings of competence (acceptance) (Baranik et al., 2010; Kao et al., 2020). These different components of the mentoring role are captured in the mentor role instrument (MRI) developed by Ragins and McFarlin (1990) as a method of measuring the nature and impacts of mentoring relationships, drawing on the seminal work of Kram (1985). A summary of the MRI is included in Box 8.3.

BOX 8.3   MEASUREMENT OF MENTORING USING THE MENTOR ROLE INSTRUMENT

The mentor role instrument (MRI) developed by Ragins and McFarlin (1990) empirically measures 11 mentor roles. It explores perceptions of career mentor roles sub-divided into sponsorship, coaching, protection, challenging assignments and exposure, and psychosocial mentor roles divided into friendship, role modelling, counselling and acceptance. It additionally includes items that focus on parent and social mentor roles to better understand the nature of mentoring relationships and their impacts. The MRI uses a 5-point scale from strongly disagree (5) to strongly agree (1), with questions as follows:

	My mentor:
Career roles	
Sponsor	helps me attain desirable positions
	uses his/her influence in the organization for my benefit
	uses his/her influence to support my advancement in the organization
Coach	suggests specific strategies for achieving career aspirations
	gives me advice on how to attain recognition in the organization
	helps me learn about other parts of the organization
Protect	'runs interference' for me in the organization
	shields me from damaging contact with important people in the organization
	protects me from those who are out to get me
Challenging assignments	provides me with challenging assignments
	assigns me tasks that push me into developing new skills
	gives me tasks that require me to learn new skills
Exposure	helps me be more visible in the organization
	creates opportunities for me to impress important people in the organization
	brings my accomplishments to the attention of important people in the organization
Psychosocial roles	
Friendship	is someone I can confide in
	provides support and encouragement
	is someone I can trust
Social	and I frequently have one-on-one, informal social interactions outside the work setting
	and I frequently socialize one-on-one outside the work setting
	and I frequently get together informally after work by ourselves
Parent	reminds me of one of my parents
	is like a father/mother to me
	treats me like a son/daughter
Role model	serves as a role model for me
	represents who I want to be
	is someone I identify with
Counsel	guides my personal development
	serves as a sounding board for me to develop and understand myself
	guides my professional development
Acceptance	accepts me as a competent professional
	thinks highly of me
	sees me as being competent

Career and psychosocial mentoring is associated with a range of objective (i.e. performance, promotion, and income) and subjective (i.e. job and career satisfaction, organizational commitment) benefits for the mentee (Allen et al., 2004; Harris et al., 2007b; Janssen et al., 2018; Kao et al., 2020; Murphy, 2012). Wanberg et al. (2003, cited in Murphy, 2012, 552) identify three forms of learning benefits generated by mentoring: (1) cognitive learning (i.e. strategic or tacit knowledge related to organizational processes, norms and values); (2) skill-based learning involving technical/motor skills derived from feedback, training and coaching; and (3) affective-based (attitudinal/motivational) learning including self-awareness, diversity awareness, self-efficacy and goal-setting. Furthermore, existing evidence suggests that mentoring positively influences the behaviours of mentees, including work attitudes, motivation and well-being (Allen et al., 2004).

The performance and commitment of the mentor, meanwhile, may be increased as they feel a sense of purpose and worthwhileness in developing the mentee (Chun et al., 2012; Holt et al., 2016). Further benefits for the mentor include increased visibility within the organization and the associated potential for their own advancement, obtaining a loyal base of support and learning from the mentee. Indeed, mentors may be more likely to agree to mentoring someone who they perceive as high performing, given the potential benefits that may be realized by the mentor through associating themselves with a successful mentee, while they may be averse to supporting a worker who is viewed as performing poorly (Holt et al., 2016). The organization stands to benefit from mentoring through increased productivity and performance, derived from both the mentor supporting the task accomplishment of the mentee (Janssen et al., 2018) and the aforementioned enhancements of the mentor. Organizations also benefit from reductions in both mentor and mentee turnover intention (Holt et al., 2016). Together, career-related and psychosocial mentoring support act as a signal that the organization is invested in the development of the mentee (career) and that the organization cares about the mentee (psychosocial), resulting in higher levels of POS (Baranik et al., 2010). However, existing evidence does suggest that the relative benefits from mentoring are dependent on the work environment within the organization, which can act to assist or limit the positive outcomes (Higgins, 2001, cited in Lo and Ramayah, 2011).

Mentoring can take place as a formal or informal arrangement (Allen et al., 2017). A third party (usually the employing organization) initiates formal mentoring programmes, while informal mentoring develops naturally and voluntarily between the mentor and mentee in response to the needs of the individuals (Janssen et al., 2016; Ragins and Cotton, 1999). While both formal and informal mentoring can be beneficial, existing evidence suggests the benefits from informal mentoring may be greater. Informal mentoring relationships tend to me more involved and focus not only on professional, but also personal, development. Informal mentoring may also involve a wider array of career development and psychosocial roles and their benefits in comparison to formal mentoring (Ragins and Cotton, 1999), although evidence is inconsistent. In part, this is because informal mentoring can be less visible, and is not in some cases identified or articulated clearly, or even consciously, as a mentoring relationship. Formal mentoring is also often limited to a specific time period (e.g. six months or one year), whereas informal mentoring relationships may continue for extended periods (in some cases many years) and, in turn, could offer more extensive long-term benefits. The level of participation and quality of information shared may be lower in formal mentoring relationships, especially if mentors feel coerced into mentoring, which can also limit the benefits realized (Allen et al., 2017; Holt et al., 2016; Ragins and Cotton, 1999). As such, Ragins and Cotton (1999) identified formal mentoring as offering a more useful complement, rather than alternative, to informal mentoring. Formal programmes may be more successful where a greater level of similarity can be identified between mentor and mentee. Increased levels of contact time may help to raise perceptions of similarity as both parties are able to build their relationship identifying shared interests and ideas (Holt et al., 2016). Referring to social exchange processes, Holt et al. (2016) argue that where formal leader–member exchange (LMX) is low (i.e. the formal mentoring relationship is of a low quality), workers are more likely to seek out an informal mentor. Adopting a more informal approach and building better quality relationships is likely to render formal mentoring more successful.

While usually viewed as a one-to-one relationship between organizational members of unequal status, mentoring can take place at multiple levels, including peer and group mentoring. A typology of mentoring is provided in Table 8.1. Peer-to-peer or co-mentoring simply involves workers of equal role or status supporting each other in their development. It is also relevant here to mention buddying schemes which usually involve an existing worker acting as a first point of contact for a new starter, although this is often a relatively short-term arrangement. Group mentoring has four main forms (Huizing, 2012): peer group mentoring (PGM), one-to-many mentoring (OTMM), many-to-one mentoring (MTOM), and many-to-many mentoring (MTMM). PGMs can comprise two or more individuals and usually focus on peers providing to each other personal and professional development. Benefits include sharing of knowledge, ideas and understanding, and the development of lifelong learning. This form of peer-to-peer mentoring can suffer from lack of trust between peers, perceptions that peers are less able to aid development, and a lack of training around how to realize benefits from peer-to-peer mentoring. OTMM involves a senior, often older, worker acting as a mentor for a group of junior, usually younger, workers. It enables those in the mentoring relationship to benefit from the experience of the mentor, while also sharing

210 *Well-being and the quality of working lives*

Table 8.1   A typology of mentoring forms

Mentoring form	Descriptor	Source
Senior-to-junior (traditional)	A more experienced, often older, worker acts as a mentor for a less experienced, usually younger, protégé or mentee	Allen et al. (2004) Bozeman and Feeney (2007) Holt et al. (2016) Janssen et al. (2016, 2018) Kram (1985)
Junior-to-senior (reverse)	A junior, usually younger, worker acts as mentor for a senior, usually older, mentee	Chaudhuri and Ghosh (2012) Harvey et al. (2009) Murphy (2012)
Peer-to-peer/co-mentoring	Workers of equal role or status support each other in their development	Fouché and Lunt (2010) Huizing (2012)
Peer group mentoring (PGM)	A group of two or more individuals in which the role of mentor constantly shifts	Huizing (2012)
One-to-many mentoring (OTMM)	One senior, often older, worker acts as a mentor for a group of junior, usually younger, workers	Huizing (2012)
Many-to-one mentoring (MTOM)	More than one senior, often older, workers act as mentors for one junior, often younger, worker	Huizing (2012)
Many-to-many mentoring (MTMM)	A group of less and more experienced workers, in which two or more individuals can be identified as having a mentoring role	Huizing (2012)
Nested mentoring	Non-linear mentoring relationships across a set of workers in which multiple mentoring relationships occur and new mentoring relationships evolve	Fouché and Lunt (2010)

experiences and knowledge with peers. MTOM, meanwhile, involves multiple senior, often older, workers acting as mentors for one junior, often younger, worker. This is extended by Fouché and Lunt (2010) who present the idea of 'nested' mentoring, which is characterized by non-linear mentoring relationships across a set of workers in which multiple mentoring relationships occur and new mentoring relationships flow into existing relationships, offering rich interactions and potentially greater benefits.

Finally, mentoring can take on a reverse form. Jack Welch, CEO of General Electric, formally introduced reverse mentoring in 1999 (Chaudhuri and Ghosh, 2012). It describes a junior, usually younger, worker acting as mentor for a senior, usually older, mentee (Murphy, 2012). Reverse mentoring can be age or experience driven. It allows the mentee to develop skills including the use of new technologies, gain awareness and understanding of diversity in the workplace and work–life balance, gain insight into recent developments in the work discipline, and develop a more global perspective (Chaudhuri and Ghosh, 2012, 57). Benefits for the mentor in reverse mentoring include access to information, gaining the professional respect of the mentee, leadership development, increased morale and job satisfaction, and lower turnover intention associated with higher levels of organizational commitment (Harvey et al., 2009; Murphy, 2012). Specific benefits have also been identified for millennials from reverse mentoring as it provides a method for these workers to gain immediate exposure and impact in their organization, including with leaders (Murphy, 2012). At the organization level, reverse mentoring can improve intergenerational relationships, enhance technology skills, help to build a leadership pipeline and facilitate a diverse workforce.

CASE STUDY: EXPERIENCES OF BALANCING SOCIAL ENTERPRISE WITH WORK IN ACADEMIA

Chris Lawton, Community Development Officer, Skateboard GB, and Visiting Research Fellow, Nottingham Business School, Nottingham Trent University. This case study is a reflection on my experience of the decision to pursue social enterprise and community organizing and the associated reduction in working hours to 60 per cent (three days a week) as a contracted academic. My request to work flexibly, made under the auspices of the 2014 Flexible Working Regulations, was accepted by my employer in April 2017. I maintained this until I accepted an alternative full-time job offer outside academia in April 2021. During the period of working part-time, I was also involved in a number of research projects on the determinants of job quality on behalf of the university's place-based think tank (see Clark et al., 2020), which gave me a personal perspective on some of the issues we were exploring, including overwork, work–life balance and workplace well-being. During this time, I also undertook consultancy research on the potential impacts of enterprise and entrepreneurship education in Higher Education for the Midlands Enterprise Universities (MEU) group (Lawton, 2017a), which provided context on the application of social entrepreneurship in my learning and teaching practice.

In this case study, I reflect on the positive drivers, or 'pull factors' of my decision to pursue a social enterprise project that might also enhance my teaching practice and widen my engagement with the university's external stakeholders, alongside some of the negative 'push factors', including my perception of poor work–life balance and the lack of flexibility of teaching-intensive academic work following bereavement and then starting a family.

The negative 'push factors' driving my request included my experience of a long hours working culture as an academic, requiring frequent weekend working and fairly consistent weeks in excess of 50 hours, with timetabled teaching, administrative responsibility and third-stream revenue generation targets (consultancy research) leaving little time for scholarly activity or the community organizing I wished to pursue with a greater level of commitment. Compounding this challenging work life, was the long period (approximately 11 years) it took for my wife and I to have our daughter, including five miscarriages and multiple courses of IVF. This experience spanned my time with a previous employer, during which compassionate leave was granted; however, this was not available with my university after we lost a pregnancy in 2016. The isolating experience for my wife, who had to spend time alone in hospital while I had to work, was a primary driver for me requesting flexible working arrangements. We fully expected we would lose more pregnancies and felt this would be unbearable without me having the flexibility to be at home at least some of the week. Fortunately, our daughter was born just less than a year after I moved to three days a week.

Community organizing was the primary positive 'pull' factor behind my original request for FWA. This became more purposive social entrepreneurship during my first year of flexible working, on the encouragement of colleagues within the university enterprise support unit, who were at that time working towards a 'social enterprise city' strategy. I incorporated a Community Interest Company (CIC) (a form of non-charitable limited company that has clearly stated social objectives), with two friends as co-founders in July 2017.

The CIC, Skate Nottingham, attempted to build on the informal community organizing that my friends and I, all lifelong skateboarders, had been undertaking following multiple summer holiday trips to Malmö (Sweden). We had observed the significant role the skaters had in the economic, social and cultural regeneration of their city, starting with co-designing and project-managing a large, public outdoor skatepark in the former shipbuilding district of the city and culminating in a high school, social development organization and place-making vehicle, with place-making referring to activities that seek to enhance a local area's social, cultural, commercial and physical assets, stretching across planning and design of public realm to projects that develop residents' skills, employability, health and well-being. The place-making vehicle in this example, Bryggeriet (a non-profit based in a former brewery in Malmö), engages young people directly as an education provider, but also delivers major international events, such as the Vans Pro Skate Park Series (an Olympics qualifying event), builds and maintains skateparks and a multifunctional active public realm, and works in partnership with the municipality to communicate Malmö's assets to a global skateboarding audience as a tourism, study or work destination and a location for inward investment (Lawton, 2017b). Finding out about Bryggeriet had a significant impact on us, as we were all from economic development backgrounds (I had worked in regional development, friends had worked in regeneration teams in local government and in homelessness and domestic violence support roles) and saw similarities between Nottingham and Malmö in population size and experiences of post-industrialization – while both have large, internationally notable skateboarding communities. Skate Nottingham quickly grew to deliver skateboarding sessions to hundreds of children, young people and adults (beneficiaries total almost 3,000 at the time of writing), along with large-scale National Lottery-funded alternative education programmes, such as skate-photography and film making courses, and built environment and STEM outreach activities, including participatory design projects for a new generation of public skateparks around the city.

This had several benefits for my learning and teaching practice as an academic. Through Skate Nottingham I developed a large network of contacts amongst local government policymakers and other stakeholders in the public, private and charitable sectors. Since the inception of Skate Nottingham, I was invited to speak at the quasi-academic 'Pushing Boarders' conference at The Bartlett, UCL and London House of Vans in 2018 to an audience of 1,700 and have since delivered talks for the EU-funded Sport4Values project and invitational addresses to the Forum for the Built Environment and the Landscape Institute in 2020 (Lawton, 2020a, 2020b, 2020c). I was thus able to approach these contacts in my teaching role, as external contributors to a series of applied economics projects undertaken in a final year Leadership and Employability module. In the 2019–20 academic year, Skate Nottingham worked with the Finnish Embassy to the UK and the University of Tampere, with a team of skateboarders and community organizers from Tampere visiting in July–August 2019 for the National Lottery-funded 'Skateboarding in the City' festival (a nine-day event with more than 600 participants that included skateboarding competitions, film screenings and public talks). These contacts became collaborators for the final iteration of the Leadership and Employability module, in which my final year economics students investigated the applicability to Nottingham of alternatives to GDP as a measure of national progress, with the Finnish connection being particularly relevant and inspiring, given Finland's frequent top ranking in the World Happiness Index (e.g. Helliwell et al., 2019). The richness of the problem-based learning environments, the wide range of external collaborators (who helped identify the 'problems' for each year's group coursework and provided feedback as guests at the students' poster exhibitions) and some of the incentives and rewards for student attainment (including funded trips to Tampere) were entirely a result of my social entrepreneurship activities. It also enabled me to widen my scholarly activity, including being a co-investigator in a successful research funding application for research into the experiences of female skateboarders in Nottingham and Manchester, partly focusing on beneficiaries of Skate Nottingham's programmes.

The partial success of the social enterprise project had the ironic outcome of worsening the work–life balance that contributed to my original request to work part-time. The project has been only partially successful in that it has not directly created any full-time roles for me, other founding directors or regular volunteers and sessional workers – and remains firmly within the voluntary and community sector. The benefits to my learning and teaching practice and scholarly work also proved challenging to codify. Although the Leadership and Employability module was a key case study in successful international accreditation applications made by my employer, it was discontinued in the 2020–21 academic year due to concerns about differential experiences of students on different programmes and was replaced by a more uniform cross-discipline employability module. I was able to publish significantly in non-academic titles (e.g. Lawton, 2020d), including an article for The Conversation (Lawton, 2019) that was republished by The Atlantic's (now Bloomberg's) CityLab and Newsweek Japan, but have not been able to transfer my social entrepreneurship experiences into peer-reviewed output. Perhaps predictably, it also became the case that my teaching responsibilities quickly extended well beyond my contracted three days per week, with obligatory engagements such as Exam Boards and Course Committees frequently falling outside the three days I was at the university; while responsibilities and opportunities generated by Skate Nottingham also quickly grew beyond that which could realistically be performed within two days a week. This led to a situation in 2021 that was much the same in terms of working hours as had prompted my original FWA request to reduce my hours, with significant impacts on time spent with my young family. However, the achievements of the social enterprise were hugely fulfilling and provided intrinsic motivation, offsetting some of the more difficult aspects of academic life.

Focusing on these benefits and remaining resilient in this case has delivered a considerable pay-off as I have been offered a newly created full-time role as Community Development Officer for the National Governing Body for skateboarding, Skateboard GB, as the sport joined the Olympics for the first time. Skate Nottingham had become one of, if not the, pre-eminent place-based social skateboarding organizations in the UK, which gave me a significant advantage in a competitive recruitment process. I accepted this role and have since left academia as an employee, although I remain a Visiting Research Fellow. Only months into my new role, my work–life balance significantly improved, enabling me to more seamlessly combine my community organizing with my main employment to better protect and enjoy time with my family. It is also beneficial in terms of well-being and self-efficacy, as I have been explicitly recruited on the basis of my social entrepreneurship achievements, meaning that I can share my learning with new and emerging community organizations all over the UK, including how to incorporate a social enterprise, good practice in grant capture and project delivery and monitoring, business development and sustainability, and strategies for effective engagement with local government. This work is also creating significant opportunities for further independent and collaborative scholarly activity.

CHAPTER SUMMARY: GIVING WELL AT WORK

The significance of giving at work is perhaps not as well recognized as some of the other dimensions of workplace well-being. This is evident in existing models which incorporate it into broader dimensions that focus on social, relational and/or community aspects of work. But, giving is a central dimension of well-being at work and one that has a vital role in the health of workers, organizations and society more broadly. Giving can have altruistic intention or reflect expectations around reciprocation. In practice, much giving may reflect a blurred middle ground in which those giving do so consciously for the benefit of the recipient(s), but also take some form of reward from this act, whether this is through obtaining human or social capital receiving help or support from those we have previously helped (or from a more generalized exchange), or gaining well-being benefits from helping others. Mechanisms for successfully embedding giving at work using the framework for workplace well-being are summarized in Figure 8.2.

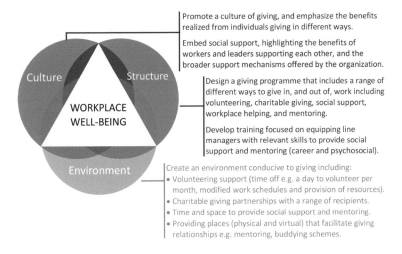

Figure 8.2   *Giving well at work using the framework for workplace well-being*

Volunteering offers many of the benefits of giving more generally, including extrinsic rewards (e.g. human and social capital development) and intrinsic rewards (e.g. satisfaction from seeing the well-being of others increase). Corporate volunteering programmes can be used to achieve these benefits and at the same time enhance the corporate social responsibility agenda of the organization. Charitable giving is also to be encouraged, although the evidence does suggest that the relative benefits of this form of giving are more limited and fatigue can set in should requests become too frequent. There is also the potential for it to create undesirable social and relational impacts should stigma be attached to those who do not engage in philanthropic behaviour. It is, perhaps, best used alongside other forms of giving to develop a giving culture within the organization.

Social support at work takes several forms comprising support that is provided by peers, supervisors (and leaders), and the organization. Perception of support is highly important, and as such, social support is most effective where an environment is created and maintained in which workers perceive that they are being supported throughout the organization. Workplace helping focuses, specifically, on support in the completion of tasks. Giving of this nature generates benefits in relation to productivity and performance and is more commonly found where workers engage in complex and interdependent tasks. This is not to say that workplace helping is not beneficial in other cases, but rather that it offers the greatest benefits where there are networks of activity that are interconnected, a characteristic of many contemporary occupations and organizations. As workers support each other, workplace helping enhances knowledge and skills, aids team building, and has positive effects on workplace relationships. It is, however, integral to ensure that helping is not one way and that there is either direct or generalized exchange, to avoid potential negative outcomes including stress and work overload.

Finally, mentoring is a relational form of giving which can provide a wide range of benefits to workers and organizations including supporting talent identification and development, and succession planning processes. Existing evidence suggests that mentoring relationships that are more informal in their relationship nature and longer term are likely to be those that are most beneficial to mentor, mentee and the organization. Mentoring should also be considered in multiple forms as traditional mentoring can be extended to peer-to-peer (including buddying schemes), group, and reverse mentoring. Whatever form(s) it takes, giving is central to the well-being of workers, organizations and society.

9. Physical space and activity

INTRODUCTION

The physical spaces and environments in which we work, our interaction with them and our broader levels of physical activity at work, form the sixth dimension of workplace well-being. The physical space component of the dimension incorporates the physical structures, fixtures and fittings and physical resources (i.e. equipment), available to us (Elsbach and Pratt, 2007). As such, it has a close relevance to health and safety. The physical workspace is not only integral to our physical health but also to our psychological experiences of work (Greenaway et al., 2016). The physical environment influences the way we interact with others at work impacting social bonding and feelings of connectedness (Sander et al., 2019). Relevant to the spaces in which we work are physical characteristics including comfortable and ergonomic furnishings (Haynes, 2008), thermal comfort (Lamb and Kwok, 2016), lighting and air quality (Elsbach and Pratt, 2007), noise levels (Ryherd et al., 2008), and access to green space and nature (Lee et al., 2015). A core debate over the physical working environment has centred on workplace designs and layouts, and specifically the benefits or otherwise of open plan workplaces (Kim and de Dear, 2013; Kim et al., 2016), and lean versus personalized or enriched workplaces (Greenaway et al., 2016). Increasing emphasis has also been placed on the natural environment, prompting growth in green buildings and sustainability in workplace design (Nieuwenhuis et al., 2014; World Green Building Council, 2016). Meanwhile, employers are turning to flexible and agile approaches to the organization of work and workplace (Babapour et al., 2020) and increasing proportions of workers are undertaking their jobs in multiple locations and/or from the home.

The physical work environment has a close relationship with physical activity at work through workplace design and physical resources (e.g. workstations) (MacEwan et al., 2015; Shrestha et al., 2018; Torbeyns et al., 2017). Physical activity is an important factor in our well-being (Kavetsos, 2011; Taylor et al., 2015). Opportunities for physical activity at work vary depending on the nature and location of work. Some work is inherently physically demanding and can involve high levels of physical health risks and implications. The growth of employment in services and use of information and communication technology (ICT), and development of labour-saving technologies in traditionally more physically demanding work (e.g. manufacturing) has led to a greater proportion of work taking on a more sedentary form (Brierley et al., 2019; Kazi et al., 2014; Renaud et al., 2020). Being active at work offers several benefits to worker physical and mental well-being (Jackson et al., 2014; Knight and Baer, 2014) and to the organization (e.g. through enhanced creativity and productivity) (Oppezzo and Schwartz, 2014). The commute is also a site of potential physical activity, with evidence supportive of the benefits of active commutes (Dinu et al., 2019; Neumeier et al., 2020). This chapter focuses on the physical work environment and physical activity. The chapter begins by outlining the changing nature of workplace, extending themes explored in Chapter 5, before considering meaning, identity and territoriality in the workplace. It then explores workplace layout and design including the well-being impacts of its physical characteristics. The chapter moves to how we physically interact with our workplace, exploring what it means to be active at work and reflecting on methods for workplaces and the commute to become more active. The chapter ends with a case study exploring a workplace intervention focused on physical space and activity.

WORKPLACE IN CONTEXT

Prior to the Industrial Revolution the home acted as a key location of work. The expansion of employment and population centres throughout the Industrial Revolution centralized economic activity and created a large-scale separation of home and work. The period from the late eighteenth to mid-nineteenth centuries witnessed substantial population shifts in industrializing countries from rural and small town locations to urban centres, as well as emerging patterns of daily movement enabled by technological advancements including the rail transport network (Wheatley, 2020). Workplace for many individuals shifted to fixed spatial settings, separate from the home, including factories, mills and offices (Bienefeld, 1972; Horrell and Humphries, 1995).

Centralizing workplace location (i.e. co-locating workers in a single workplace setting) offers organizational benefits including those relating to efficiency gains from mass production and the division of labour (Smith, 1981 [1776]), and by enabling employers to enact greater control and monitoring of employees (Marglin, 1974). Centralization and growth of economic activity continued throughout the late nineteenth and into the twentieth centuries, as further developments impacted the structure of work including Taylorism, named after Frederick Taylor (Taylor, 1967) and Fordism, named after Henry Ford. Taylorism and Fordism acted to extend the division of labour through routinized mass production involving low-skilled employees working on an assembly line (Figart, 2001). The institutional arrangements present in indus-

Physical space and activity 219

try during the twentieth century promoted fixed workplace locations and the continued separation of home and work (Figart and Golden, 1998, 412).

During the latter half of the twentieth century there was a shift towards flexible specialization in industrialized economies, involving production of smaller batches of products with a focus on greater diversity and generating efficiencies through economies of scope (e.g. common use of machinery to manufacture different products). The change was driven by increasing competition from newly industrializing economies. Large-scale deindustrialization and a shift to services occurred across many developed societies, with the service sector accounting for three out of four workers by the end of the twentieth century (O'Mahoney, 1999). The move to services across many economies impacted workplace. Further automation occurred in industry accompanied by movements of businesses out of urban centres to industrial parks. At the same time there was a continued growth of offices in urban and suburban locations. Office environments have undergone a series of changes, most notably the move from private to open plan designs (Jenkins et al., 2010).

The digital age has led to greater flexibility and diversity in workplace and the expansion of virtual and location-independent work (Green, 2017; Hislop and Axtell, 2009; Moos and Skaburskis, 2007). Among highly skilled and certain other service occupations workplace has extended beyond office-style settings to include client sites, business incubators, co-working spaces, a range of public spaces, and the home (Wheatley, 2020). Information and communication technology (ICT), including cloud computing, wireless technology and smartphones, enable location-independent working and provide 24/7 connectivity (Moos and Skaburskis, 2007). Notwithstanding these changes, the majority of paid work has continued to take place in centralized workplace locations in urban centres and industrial parks (Zhu, 2013), but with greater fluidity and diversity in workplace as workers increasingly fulfil their tasks of employment in more than one location.

Debates remain over the relative benefits of centralized, decentralized and hybrid models of workplace (Shearmur, 2018). The term 'hybrid workspace' was proposed by Halford (2005) to capture workers who combine work at a co-located organizational workplace and at home facilitated by ICT. The rapid expansion of remote working in 2020 represented a considerable and sudden change in workplace location for a portion of workers, with home-based remote work peaking at around two in five workers in many developed economies (ILO, 2020). It should be acknowledged, however, that many workers had already been working in locations outside of a co-located employer or business premise, combining a main workplace with time spent in other locations. Changes to workplace have been occurring in a gradual manner for a number of years (Felstead and Henseke, 2017; Wheatley, 2020). Workplace environments have been reshaped through developments in digital technologies and agendas around sustainability (Arup, 2020; World Green Building Council, 2016), although it has been argued that some of these changes have reflected an emphasis towards cost reduction and rationalization rather than a focus on flexibility for the benefit of the worker (Walker, 2020). Nevertheless, there has been a growth in homeworking, mobile working and teleworking. Note should also be made of the self-employed who have long been characterized by a greater diversity in workplace, with many working at home or using home as a base, and others working in multiple locations including client sites (Felstead and Henseke, 2017; Wheatley, 2020).

Flexibility and diversity in workplace offers a number of benefits from the employer perspective, not least cost reduction where office space can be rationalized (Walker, 2020; Wheatley, 2020). For the worker, benefits can be realized in the form of job satisfaction, greater flexibility over the structure of the working day/week, and time savings from avoiding the commute when working at home (Vartiainen and Hyrkkänen, 2010; Wheatley, 2017a). Locating workers in a single location, though, continues to provide certain benefits for employers, including agglomeration through labour market pooling and knowledge spillovers, and enabling greater economies of scale and scope (Zhu, 2013, 2441). Employees may benefit from co-location through greater social connectedness and physical and mental separation between home and work. This extends to the commute where existing evidence has found that some workers enjoy the transitional feature of the journey to work (LaJeunesse and Rodríguez, 2012). The nature of workplace continues to evolve with the development of more flexible and agile designs to the physical work environment (Babapour et al., 2020; Hesselberg, 2018). It has been suggested that if there is continued greater application of home-based remote work following the rapid expansion in 2020, the focus of co-located workplaces is likely to move towards multifunctional space and shared hubs designed for interaction between colleagues, acting as a site to form social and professional networks, create corporate culture, host clients and attract talent (Green and Riley, 2021).

MEANING AND IDENTITY IN WORKPLACE

Whether a co-located workplace or a private office in the home, physical workspaces and places hold a psychological significance. Our work environment is more than simply a physical space as it can have meaning and reflect identity (Greenaway et al., 2016). Where workplace offers meaning and identity it is argued to lead to potential performance enhancements (Knight and Haslam, 2010) as a workplace that provides meaning has the potential to support, communicate and channel identity at work (Relph, 1976). However, the notion of workplace as identity has long been debated with different perspectives on the role of workplace reflected in different workplace designs and layouts. At the centre of this conflict is the debate over personalized versus non-personalized workplaces. This debate can be traced back to the work of Taylor (1967) who advocated a high degree of managerial control over workspace, and as these ideas developed this led to lean approaches to the management of space in organizations towards the end of the twentieth century (Nieuwenhuis et al., 2014, 199). The lean approach conflicts with notions of workplace as a source of identity as it strips out personalization to focus on optimum space utilization and cost minimization (Bodin Danielsson, 2013, 171). Doing so enables greater flexibility over the use of the workspace and the ability to accommodate changing numbers of workers/workstations (Nieuwenhuis et al., 2014). A lean approach, however, may limit the level of both instrumental (i.e. function-related) and symbolic (i.e. identity-related) control workers have over the physical work environment (Greenaway et al., 2016, 36). Advocates of workplace as identity would maintain that this negatively impacts on worker well-being and performance.

In contrast to a lean approach, enriched workspaces are those that have been furnished such that workers are able to realize identities and take meaning from their physical work environment. Enriched workspaces have been found to improve the performance of workers when compared to lean workspaces, suggesting potential organizational benefits from an enriched approach (Knight and Haslam, 2010; Nieuwenhuis et al., 2014). Several studies have explored this proposed relationship including Knight and Haslam (2010) and Greenaway et al. (2016). Knight and Haslam (2010) conducted two experiments in the UK where participants were asked to complete a productivity task in one of four office environments: (1) a lean workspace (i.e. minimal decoration), (2) an enriched workspace (i.e. decorated with pictures and plants), (3) an empowered workspace (i.e. decorated by the participants), and (4) a disempowered workspace (i.e. decorated by the participants but then redecorated). They found the lowest levels of productivity in the lean environment, higher levels in the enriched workspace, and the highest levels in the empowered workspace. Meanwhile, Australian evidence reported in Greenaway et al. (2016) found that spaces that signal worker identity offer greater psychological benefits, and identity-enriched spaces that provide meaning to workers through decoration have a positive effect on both team functioning and productivity.

Workspace within the home is also important to consider in this context. In principle, an individual should take greater meaning and identify more within a home workspace, as they have greater control over the layout and design of their working environment (Hislop et al., 2015). However, they face limitations resulting from provision of physical resources, or lack of them, by employers, and due to the physical limits of the space available to them within the home (Mustafa and Gold, 2013). If resources provided do not meet the preferences of the worker or there is a lack of provision from their employer, the home workspace may be inappropriately or inadequately equipped. In addition, the personalization of space for work could create conflict with others within the home, either due to differences over preferences for the design and layout of the space, or that arising from space being used for multiple purposes (e.g. a dining room used as a home office during working hours). While the home workspace is one that should offer benefits associated with meaning and identity this may not always be realized.

WORKSPACE TERRITORIALITY

The personalization of co-located workplaces can generate benefits; however, it can also result in conflict associated with workspace territoriality. Workspace territoriality refers to feelings of psychological ownership that are applied to organizational workspaces (Brown et al., 2005, cited in Brown and Zhu, 2016). These behaviours are performed by the worker to define their personal territory and create meaning and comfort in their workspace (Greenaway et al., 2016; Roskams and Haynes, 2019). Workspace territoriality can have both positive and negative effects. For example, workers may feel the need to defend their workspace which can positively act to motivate them to perform in their work tasks (Brown, 2009). However, territoriality over workspace can have undesirable effects. This behaviour may be viewed negatively by others, potentially impacting their perception of the performance of the worker (Brown and Zhu, 2016). It can consume the time and energy of the worker reducing their ability to complete tasks. Finally, it can lead to disengagement and discomfort should others, including colleagues or managers, infringe upon the workspace or attempt to alter or control it in some way (Brown, 2009, 46; Greenaway et al., 2016).

Non-territorial flexible or agile workplaces counter territorial behaviours as they limit personalization of workspace. Instead of having an assigned space, workers use different workspaces, often in an ad hoc manner although some form of booking system may be employed (Roskams and Haynes, 2019). However, territorial behaviours may still occur in non-territorial workspaces as evidence has been found of hiding favourite equipment and taking over communal spaces (e.g. barring doors, taking over meeting rooms) (Nathan, 2002, cited in Brown and Zhu, 2016). Evidently there are strengths and weaknesses with the adoption of either a lean, non-territorial, or enriched/empowered, approach to workplace, and Haynes (2012) emphasizes that perhaps most central is the need to align the physical characteristics of the workplace environment with the psychological characteristics and working routines of its workers.

WORKPLACE LAYOUT AND DESIGN

A central debate over the physical work environment is that of the relative benefits of private and shared workspace. Since the latter part of the twentieth century there has been a concerted move towards greater flexibility in the design and layout of workplaces, while industrial environments have long adopted lean approaches to workplace design. Designs that afford greater control over personal space such as the ability to adjust equipment and decorate the workspace to some degree, and those that provide access to private space can enhance job satisfaction and perceived group cohesiveness (Lee and Brand, 2005; Kim et al., 2016). Open plan or shared designs, meanwhile, provide greater flexibility in terms of how the space is used and offer opportunities for interaction and knowledge sharing between workers. However, these designs face problems associated with lack of privacy and potential distractions (Kim and de Dear, 2013).

Shared physical spaces present within the workplace can act as a source of social connectedness at work (see Chapter 7), reflecting a form of 'social affordance' (i.e. the space offers properties which promote social actions) (Fayard and Weeks, 2007). This includes the classic notion of 'watercooler chat' and the printer/photocopier room, which provide a mechanism for bringing workers into close proximity and promote informal interactions with others, including those we may not have to directly interact with to complete our job tasks. Benefits extend to spaces such as cafeterias, lunch and break rooms; spaces that all encourage workers to come together informally to communicate with each other and bond socially (Kniffin et al., 2015).

Regardless of workplace design and layout, it is almost certain that workers will identify preferences for certain workstations or spaces, and this can create territorial behaviours, as already outlined. The realities of the space available and factors such as proximity to windows, break rooms, and other amenities will create a hierarchy of desirability of workspace in most workplaces (Babapour et al., 2020). The presence of desirable or undesirable characteristics can lead to competition between workers for what are considered 'good' workspaces (Babapour et al., 2020). Where first come, first served approaches to the allocation of space such as flexi-desking are employed, it can create inequality where some workers are unable to arrive early at work (e.g. due to performing the school run), or where an individual stakes a claim for use of the same workspace even where spaces are in principle shared. The cultural resistance to accepting a more flexible or agile working environment has to be broken for shared and flexible designs to be most effective (Kim et al., 2016).

Shared Space, Open Plan and Non-territorial Designs

Open plan spaces can be usefully identified, as per Di Blasio et al.'s (2019) definition, as those in which more than five workers share a space, whereas shared spaces usually involve fewer workers (two to five) sharing a workspace (e.g. a more traditional office shared between two or three colleagues). In the latter shared space design, it is often the case that workstations will be 'owned' by individuals. Non-territorial open plan or shared workplace layouts differ in that they utilize flexi-desking which involves shared workstations and spaces, thus dissolving the link between employee and workstation (Kim et al., 2016). A non-territorial workplace layout creates a more agile working environment and enables the workplace to adapt to changes in team and organizational structures and size. It can also provide greater opportunities for team-working as the shared nature of the space promotes collaboration. These arrangements usually involve the workspace being designed so that only around seven in ten workers can fit into the space at any one time, offering the employer a more efficient and cost-effective facilities strategy (Bodin Danielsson, 2013, 171). This approach minimizes the time where workstations are left unused (e.g. when an individual is meeting clients outside of the workplace, on annual or sick leave, or attending a training course) (Kim et al., 2016). Flexible designs do not, however, always exhibit the same characteristics. Lean designs, for example, can have clean desk policies (Bodin Danielsson, 2013, 171), but more team-focused or enriched designs may allow personalization, at least at the team level.

Problems associated with lean or shared workplace designs include lack of desk availability if a higher than planned portion of workers are present in the workplace, and loss of ability to define boundaries or display identity in the workspace (Kim et al., 2016). The latter can lead to workers feeling that there is a lack of privacy in their work environment which could increase levels of emotional exhaustion (Kim and de Dear, 2013). Linked to this problem is that of personal hygiene as the sharing of workspace can act as a source of stress where workers display differing hygiene standards. Clean desk policies are a solution to this, but impose their own costs as keeping space clean necessarily creates a loss of time used in setting and packing up equipment at the start and end of each working day. Enforcement of clean desk policies is also difficult, potentially leading to some workers following these requirements and others not. A lack of space to keep personal belongings can also present a challenge, often solved using lockers or similar storage areas, although the physical detachment of workers from their belongings can have detrimental impacts including those already noted around privacy, meaning/identity, and time being spent going to access belongings.

Activity-based Flexible Offices

Activity-based flexible offices (AFOs) are configured as a predominantly open plan workspace with additional collaborative (i.e. breakout spaces and meeting rooms) and private workspaces (Babapour et al., 2020). AFOs usually have desk sharing policies in order to enable workers to engage in flexible use of the workspace, and to provide a cost-effective design which ensures that workspaces are available but within a smaller overall space (Rolfö, 2018). Evidence highlights a number of factors that influence the relative success of AFOs including the effectiveness of the design and layout, but also the frequency that workers switch workstations, and the change management and planning processes employed (Babapour et al., 2018; Rolfö, 2018). Research into the use of AFOs at two public sector organizations in Sweden, reported in Babapour et al. (2020), identified several characteristics influencing the preferences of workers for use of certain workspaces and workstations: (1) functional characteristics reflecting ability to personalize the equipment; (2) social characteristics including closeness to desired others (e.g. work friends); (3) ambient characteristics such as lighting (see section on physical characteristics); and (4) emotional characteristics including feeling energetic from interacting with others. The aesthetics of the workplace were argued as less relevant, although clearly these are linked to a number of the ambient and emotional characteristics.

A common failure in the implementation of AFOs is not providing workers with enough choice over workstation design and location (Babapour et al., 2018). Non-use of space, either linked to lack of variation in workstations or some spaces having a combination of undesirable attributes is a further problem. For example, in their study exploring the design of AFOs, Babapour et al. (2020) found that the AFOs in the studied organizations did not actually fulfil the desired motive of optimal use of space. Problems faced in AFOs can include: (1) undesirable functional characteristics of workstations such as a lack of easily adjustable chair or screen; (2) problems with environmental ambience including poor lighting, uncomfortable temperature, lack of views (e.g. no window with view outside); (3) exposure to negative stimuli such as noise or distracting movement due to proximity to busy thoroughfares or breakout spaces; (4) feelings of alienation and loneliness even in open spaces, where there is a lack of meaning and identity or exclusion from the group of workers in the locale; and (5) symbolic attributes including territoriality resulting in implicit ownership of workspace (Babapour et al., 2020; Greenaway et al., 2016).

Green Workplaces and Sustainable Design

Green workplaces and sustainability in workplace design are by no means new concepts in debates around workplace design and well-being at work. In the 1950s, the German Bürolandschaft or office landscaping movement aimed to provide enrichment and privacy in workplace design using indoor plants and partitions to create a more efficient, collaborative and humane working environment (Vischer, 2005, cited in Nieuwenhuis et al., 2014). Sustainability in workplace design has risen in profile in recent decades alongside wider societal awareness of climate change and the environment (World Green Building Council, 2016). Common characteristics associated with green designs include the use of indoor plants and views of nature. However, a focus on green design and sustainability goes beyond these measures and requires consideration of building materials, energy efficiency, workspace layout and other aspects of the physical environment (Ornetzeder et al., 2016). At the organizational level, consideration needs to be given to such factors as the impact of workers commuting to the workplace and logistics involved in operations and associated carbon footprints. Use of green designs have been shown to enrich the workplace, with benefits from the use of indoor plants and views of nature for productivity, collaboration and the well-being of workers (Nieuwenhuis et al., 2014). While the environmental benefits can be clearly measured, the evidence base on the specific benefits to worker productivity and well-being of green buildings is less certain (see Ornetzeder et al., 2016). More central is the provision of, and worker response to, certain physical characteristics of the workplace.

PHYSICAL CHARACTERISTICS OF THE WORKPLACE

A number of common physical characteristics have impacts on our experiences of work having long been identified as potential environmental stressors (Broadbent, 1971, cited in Lamb and Kwok, 2016). Where these physical characteristics are inadequate or poorly designed it can have detrimental effects on physical health and result in stress being placed on the cognitive reserves, concentration levels and attention of workers, leaving fewer resources to direct towards work performance (Lamb and Kwok, 2016, 104). These factors are equally relevant to work taking place within the home, explored later in this chapter. A note should also be made of the impact of subjective reactions to the physical work environment rather than simply the objective characteristics of the environment itself (Hackman and Oldham, 1975). Evidence has indicated that offering greater control to workers over the physical work environment including lighting, temperature and seating can offset some of the otherwise detrimental effects of these environmental characteristics (Lee and Brand,

2005). This is not to suggest that these factors should not be given adequate consideration or effort be made to design workplaces for well-being. Rather, these factors must be considered in the wider context of worker well-being acknowledging the objective and subjective nature of our relationship with workplace.

Ergonomic Workspaces

Ergonomics in the context of the workplace reflects design which aims to optimize the health and safety, comfort and effectiveness of human occupants (Brand, 2008). Ergonomic workplace design is recognized as important to an effective and productive work environment (Kroemer and Robinette, 1969). It incorporates physical resources, and our interactions with them, including tools, machinery, desks, chairs and other equipment (e.g. visual display equipment, keyboards, tablet PCs), as well as wider physical characteristics of the workplace. It also incorporates the ways in which work is performed such as methods of lifting and carrying and performance of repetitive tasks. Poor ergonomics in workplace design is a primary cause of work-related musculo-skeletal disorders (MSD) (Brand, 2008; Brandt et al., 2004), which represent a significant cost to the world economy (Otto et al., 2017). It can also result, for example, in eye strain associated with the use of visual display equipment (Coles-Brennan et al., 2019; Toomingas et al., 2014). Considerations for effective workspace setup to minimize MSD and eye strain in the context of office work can be found from research reported in Coles-Brennan et al. (2019) and Jaschinski et al. (1998), and from sources such as the UK Health and Safety Executive (2020) which offers a useful display screen equipment checklist.

Evidence has highlighted that a well-designed ergonomic setup, for example, in an office environment the provision of a desk with an adequately sized flat surface and an ergonomic chair, can help workers to minimize MSD such as muscle strain, back injury and tendonitis (Brand, 2008). This needs to be administered alongside guidance on how to use equipment in a safe and effective way, for example methods of lifting heavy equipment in a factory environment, or optimal distances and angles from visual displays in an office environment. Although the provision of ergonomic furniture and equipment represents a cost to the employer, it is one which is likely to be more than repaid. An ergonomic working environment not only has positive effects in improving the well-being of workers, but also enables substantive cost savings associated with reductions in medical costs and absenteeism, and higher levels of productivity (Brand, 2008; Otto et al., 2017).

Lighting

Evidence identifies lighting as having an important influence on worker well-being. Where workers report satisfaction with lighting this has a positive relationship with general levels of comfort and happiness in the workplace (Boyce et al., 2003). Access to natural light (and fresh air) from windows aligns physical and mental activity with our body clock, and is associated with higher overall levels of satisfaction with lighting and wider well-being benefits including better sleep (Borisuit et al., 2015; Boubekri et al., 2014). However, not all work is performed during the day or in bright conditions, nor do all workers operate in environments with windows. The quality of artificial light is, therefore, a consideration. Working in environments that are too dark or bright can be detrimental to both performance and well-being (Sithravel and Ibrahim, 2019). Control over lighting, such as dimmer switches and functioning blinds, has been shown to have positive impacts on satisfaction with working environment and self-reported productivity (Boyce et al., 2003). Dynamic lighting systems, meanwhile, aim to replicate the changes in light which occur during the day through varying colour temperature and illuminance (i.e. brightness). While evidence suggests workers report satisfaction with these technologies, impacts on aspects of physical (e.g. eye strain) and psychological well-being (e.g. need for recovery associated with attention fatigue and stress) are less conclusive (de Kort and Smolders, 2010). These considerations are all the more challenging given the differing tolerances and preferences of individuals towards illuminance (Borisuit et al., 2015), something that should be factored into design so that spaces offer different levels of light and/or control over lighting levels.

Temperature

The temperature of the working environment is associated with several human responses including thermal comfort, perceptions of air quality and sick building syndrome (SBS) symptoms such as headaches, irritation (skin, eyes), cough, nausea and difficulty concentrating (Redlich et al., 1997). Thermal comfort has been identified as impacting performance and well-being, and research suggests that workers often show dissatisfaction with the temperature of the workplace (Lamb and Kwok, 2016; Oseland and Hodsman, 2018). For example, using a series of experiments of environments at different temperatures, Cui et al. (2013) reported learning rates were hindered by environments that were too warm or cold or had frequently changing temperatures. Tanabe et al. (2015), meanwhile, considered the relationship between worker performance and levels of thermal satisfaction using field measurements of simulated office work (e.g. multiplication, proof reading tasks) and a survey.

Physical space and activity

They found that worker performance in simulated tasks increased with greater individual thermal satisfaction. Their results also suggested that perceived thermal satisfaction may be more strongly correlated with self-estimated performance than the actual air temperature in the work environment, suggesting that subjective response to temperature may be an important factor. Evidence suggests an optimal temperature of around 21°C to 25°C (Cui et al., 2013; Fassoulis and Alexopoulos, 2015). However, existing research regarding the relative impact of air temperature remains inconsistent. In part, this reflects that, consistent with other environmental characteristics of the workplace, individuals differ in their relative sensitivity to changes in environmental stressors including temperature and sound (Clausen and Wyon, 2008). This adds further to the complexity of identifying an optimal and inclusive working environment (Box 9.1).

BOX 9.1 MEASURING THE IMPACT OF THE PHYSICAL CHARACTERISTICS OF THE WORKPLACE

A wide array of both objective and subjective measures exist for capturing data on the impact of physical characteristics of the work environment. Lamb and Kwok (2016), for example, employ a series of measures to capture the subjective responses of workers to thermal comfort, lighting and noise.

Thermal comfort is captured using the 7-point ASHRAE scale (ASHRAE, 1966) where 1 = cold, 2 = cool, 3 = slightly cool, 4 = neutral, 5 = slightly warm, 6 = warm, and 7 = hot.

Satisfaction with light levels are captured using a similar 7-point scale, where 1 = much too dark, 2 = too dark, 3 = comfortably dark, 4 = comfortable, 5 = comfortably bright, 6 = too bright, and 7 = much too bright.

Noise annoyance is captured through questions developed by Fields et al. (2001). They recommend using two questions together, one that captures responses on a verbal scale and one on a numerical scale. The verbal scale question asks, 'How much does noise from [source] bother, disturb, or annoy you?' Answer options comprise: extremely, very, moderately, slightly or not at all. The numerical question asks, 'What number from zero to ten best shows how much you are bothered, disturbed, or annoyed by [source] noise?' Responses are captured on a 10-point scale, where 0 = not at all and 10 = extremely.

Noise

Both the level and type of noise encountered at work has impacts on well-being. In certain environments, such as factories, evidence has long identified that noise can represent a significant risk to physical health where noise levels exceed exposure limits, resulting in damage to, and loss of, hearing (Smith, 1989). Even in office and other 'quieter' working environments poor acoustics and ambient noise can have considerable impacts. It acts as a distraction resulting in difficulties with concentration, communication and productivity (Di Blasio et al., 2019). Noise also has several specific effects on well-being at work, acting as a source of annoyance, stress, anxiety, emotional exhaustion and burnout, and dissatisfaction (Lamb and Kwok, 2016). Existing studies have found acoustics to be one of the greatest sources of dissatisfaction alongside temperature (Oseland and Hodsman, 2018).

Co-worker speech is identified as one of the most common sources of dissatisfaction with noise (Haapakangas et al., 2017). Research reported in Di Blasio et al. (2019) explores the impact of noise distraction from irrelevant (i.e. non-essential) speech. Surveying a sample of workers in Italy, they found that around two thirds of respondents felt that the main impact of noise was to reduce levels of concentration. Furthermore, around one in ten workers in open plan offices reported physical health symptoms (e.g. headaches, tiredness), or negative emotional and social feelings (annoyance with colleagues). Research by Oseland and Hodsman (2018) explores existing methods for resolving noise distraction in offices and presents design guidance for employers presented within the DARE acronym (Figure 9.1). Lee and Aletta (2019, 212) provide more technical guidance through a set of 19 practical measures under four key performance indicators (KPIs) following their exploration of noise impacts on well-being in a study of open plan offices in the USA.

Displace	Avoid	Reduce	Educate
Work environments should be designed to accommodate and separate activities which generate noise from those that are quieter.	Workplace layouts should provide separate meeting and private working zones and locate noisy teams away from more subdued ones.	Control size and density of workstations to reduce speech carrying across open-plan areas and noise transference between spaces.	Introduce etiquette to be considerate towards colleagues and expectations around behaviours in shared work environments.

Source: Adapted from Oseland and Hodsman, 2018.

Figure 9.1   DARE noise distraction guidance

Air Quality

Air quality is a further factor to consider in workplace layout and design. It is strongly linked to incidence of SBS, characterized by a particular building producing non-specific symptoms in workers that are not the product of an illness (Redlich et al., 1997). Evidence has suggested that the health risks associated with exposure to indoor air pollution could represent a greater risk than outdoor pollution (Cincinelli and Martellini, 2017). The causes of SBS have been recognized as being driven by efforts to make buildings more energy-efficient including use of mechanical ventilation systems to circulate fresh air, temperature and humidity control. It is also linked to synthetic materials being used in construction and furnishing of workplaces. The Taylorization of office work (i.e. standardization and regimentation), and the associated increase in work stress, could also be a factor in the increase in SBS (Redlich et al., 1997). Methods for reducing air-quality problems in workplaces include better ventilation which has been shown to improve perceived air quality and work performance and reduce SBS symptoms (Sundell et al., 2011). Reduction of environmental contamination is also integral in addressing SBS, including through selection of low-pollutant construction and furnishing materials (Redlich et al., 1997; Wargocki et al., 1999).

Access to Nature and Green Space

Access to nature from views through windows and greenery both within and outside of the workplace also impacts our experiences of work. Theoretical explanations have been posited over the influence of nature, including the biophilia hypothesis which suggests that nature has a calming effect for humans as it has a historic link to survival. Meanwhile, the attentional restoration theory (ART) asserts that exposure to nature has a restorative effect on cognitive resources (e.g. problem solving and concentration) (Kaplan, 1995, cited in Largo-Wight et al., 2017). A range of studies have explored the impact of nature in the workplace, identifying associations with productivity through restoration of resources, job satisfaction, self-reported health and well-being, and reductions in stress and absenteeism (Kaplan, 1993; Largo-Wight et al., 2011, 2017; Lee et al., 2015). Being able to connect to nature through access to outdoor green spaces may have positive effects on levels of stress and help workers to avoid potential health effects of working in indoor environments, especially in sedentary occupations, through providing opportunities to be active (Largo-Wight et al., 2017). The presence of indoor plants can generate well-being benefits through perceptions of comfort and a more pleasing aesthetic (Kaplan, 1993; Largo-Wight et al., 2011). Views through windows can provide benefits, but these are primarily realized when views are of natural environments and elements (Largo-Wight et al., 2017). Windowless environments not only have negative well-being effects associated with the lack of natural light, as noted earlier (Sithravel and Ibrahim, 2019), but also extend to feelings of claustrophobia, isolation and restriction as they leave workers without the presence of views or connection to nature.

THE HOMEWORKING ENVIRONMENT

The homeworking environment has become increasingly relevant following the large-scale rapid adoption of remote working in 2020 (see Chapter 5). While existing research identifies working at home as having a series of potential advantages, the evidence for the physical working environment is more conflicting. For a fuller discussion of themes related to the physical work environment of the home, see Sander et al. (2021). In principle, the home environment may offer a more comfortable work location including providing better air quality, noise levels, and control over temperature (Montreuil and Lippel, 2003). Some employers will undertake a formal health and safety check of the home workspace, and physical resources may be provided by the employer, such as ICT, desks, chairs, and other equipment (Ng, 2010). However, this is not always the case, especially where workers are involved in a more hybrid model involving work at both an organizational workplace and at home. In these cases, homeworking arrangements can shift the costs of physical resources onto the worker (Moos and Skaburskis, 2008, 336). Where resourcing is the responsibility of the worker they may, either through lack of finances or preferences regarding the use of household incomes, not adequately equip their homeworking environment leading to potential hazards for physical health such as musculoskeletal problems and eye strain. Challenges identifying adequate space for working within the home can result in potential conflict with family and blurring of boundaries between home and work. Practical limitations of the home as a working space also include insufficient storage space, and inability to adequately address ergonomics (Ng, 2010).

It is often the case that when working from home we will try to replicate elements of the physical working environment of the workplace including creating separate workspaces where space is available, and through use of similar equipment such as desks, computers and visual displays (Ng, 2010). These actions help to transform the private space of the home into a working environment. In some cases, employers may provide specific symbols and artefacts of the workplace to help the worker to adjust to working remotely (Halford, 2005). However, the shared spaces of a co-located workplace, such as photocopier rooms, cafeterias and break rooms have a significant role in promoting belonging and connectedness, as discussed earlier in the chapter. Working remotely and in virtual teams necessarily results in a lack of, or reduced, presence of opportunities to interact with others in these physical shared spaces diminishing informal and emotional exchanges (Sander et al., 2021). This has potentially negative impacts reflected in concerns around isolation when working at home (Bentley et al., 2016; Tietze et al., 2009).

THE OFFICE CONCEPTS FRAMEWORK

A useful conceptual framework for understanding the relationship between the physical work environment and worker performance and well-being is presented by de Croon et al. (2005). The model highlights the relationship between the physical space and arrangement of work, referred to as office concepts, and both physical and mental well-being at work. Office concepts are divided into three dimensions: (1) office location (i.e. a co-located employer workplace or home office); (2) office layout (i.e. workspace openness (open plan or private) and distance between workplaces (referring to distance between workstations)); and (3) office use (i.e. single fixed workstation or desk-sharing arrangement).

The model proposes that office concepts can drive several short-term physiological and psychological reactions (Figure 9.2). These occur either directly or indirectly through work conditions (i.e. job demands and job resources), which are conceptualized in terms of the job demands-resources (JD-R) model outlined in Chapter 3 (Bakker and Demerouti, 2007). Job demands in this context come in two forms; first, the demands on cognitive-attentional processes resulting from office stimuli (e.g. noise), and second, working hours including non-standard or irregular patterns of work. Job resources, meanwhile, are positive factors which act to offset job demands, categorized in the office concepts model as (1) communication (i.e. the extent that the workplace stimulates interactions and communication); (2) work autonomy (i.e. levels of autonomy afforded by the work arrangement, such as control over schedule); (3) psychological privacy (i.e. the level of privacy experienced in the workplace environment); and (4) interpersonal relations at work (i.e. social support experienced) (de Croon et al., 2005, 121–2).

Responses to the workplace environment take physical and psychological forms with physiological short-term responses including increased blood pressure and cortisol levels (stress hormone), and psychological short-term responses including impacts on job satisfaction and crowding stress (i.e. a psychological state reflecting the inadequacy of space). Short-term responses can accumulate leading to longer-term negative impacts to health in the form of burnout, chronic fatigue and MSD, and to job performance (de Croon et al., 2005, 121–2). The systematic review conducted by de Croon et al. (2005) to test the model found evidence of the impact of workplace layout on work conditions and short-term reactions. Open plan workplaces were found to be associated with lower levels of job satisfaction and privacy. Close distance between workstations was also found to create a more intense working environment, increasing cognitive workload and reducing privacy. A positive relationship was identified between more flexible arrangements in the form of desk-sharing and communication between workers, indicative of flexible workplace design enhancing opportunities for interaction with others (and with different others) at work.

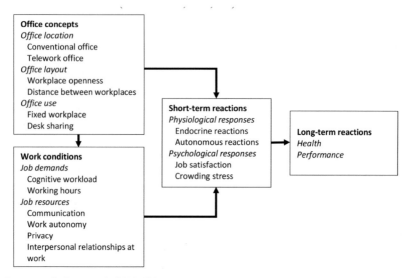

Source: de Croon et al., 2005, 121.

Figure 9.2   Conceptual model linking office concepts via demands and resources to short- and long-term reactions

Ng (2010) applies an adapted version of the office concepts framework to consider the design and physical conditions of home offices. It is identified that home-based teleworkers display similar preferences for the home workspace as they do in employer premises, specifically a private office space with good-quality lighting and relevant equipment, and that it is preferably located separately from private areas of the home to avoid conflict and disruption including noise. Prior to 2020, many home-based teleworking practices involved working at home in a more flexible or ad hoc way (Wheatley, 2020), with workers engaging in only certain activities (e.g. computer-based tasks such as word processing and reading), when working at home. Home-based teleworking all the time presents a different set of challenges regarding the physical setup within the home, requiring greater investment of physical resources including space and equipment. This has implications as job satisfaction, job performance, personal (e.g. MSD, eye strain, work-related stress) and family well-being, and broader quality of life can all be negatively affected by working conditions in the home (Ng, 2010; Russell et al., 2009).

PHYSICAL WELLNESS AND WORK

Levels of physical activity differ considerably between occupations. Physical activity at work has significant implications for our well-being as evidence shows that for many in the working population physical activity at work accounts for a substantial portion of total daily physical activity (Reis et al., 2005). It is also relevant given the wider context of growth in the prevalence levels of overweight and obesity which increased by a combined 28 per cent among adults in the period 1980 to 2013 (Ng et al., 2014b, cited in Zhu et al., 2020, Broadbent, 1971). It has further relevance as it has been estimated that the annual global cost of physical inactivity to healthcare systems equates to $53.8 billion (Ding et al., 2016).

Occupational physical activity can present multiple health risks, particularly in manual jobs, including tasks such as lifting and carrying (Maes et al., 2020). Of increasing concern is the level of inactivity involved in many occupations. In recent decades, there has been a significant growth in the proportions of workers whose jobs involve low-activity or sedentary routines (Chau et al., 2012). Sedentary behaviour can be defined as 'any waking behavior characterized by an energy expenditure ≤ 1.5 metabolic equivalents (METs), while in a sitting, reclining or lying posture' (Tremblay et al., 2017, 9). Evidence shows that over half of the time at work can be spent sitting, and this can amount to more time than is spent sleeping among many workers (Kazi et al., 2014). Total sedentary time is closely linked to potential health effects, as is how sedentary time is broken up through workers moving between locations or taking breaks involving physical activity (Zhu et al., 2020).

Sedentary behaviour can have detrimental effects on physical health and well-being (Brierley et al., 2019; Kazi et al., 2014; Renauld et al., 2020), including increasing risk of all-cause and cardiovascular mortality (Maes et al., 2020; Zhu et al., 2020) and reduced life expectancy (Katzmarzyk, 2010; Levine, 2010). Effects can extend to psychological impacts associated, for example, with body image. It also has clear links with health problems discussed earlier in the chapter associated with the physical work environment, such as MSD and eye strain, where workers are sitting for long periods and/or exposed to poor ergonomics (Brand, 2008). Potential methods for capturing and monitoring levels of physical activity at work are summarized in Box 9.2.

BOX 9.2 METHODS FOR CAPTURING PHYSICAL ACTIVITY LEVELS AT WORK

Measures of physical activity can be captured using either objective or subjective methods. Objective measurement of physical activity at work can be performed using various techniques. Most involve the use of wearable devices that capture aspects of physical activity. Posture measurement tools capture whether individuals are stood, seated and so on. Pedometers and accelerometers can be used to measure levels of physical movement and are commonly employed methods of monitoring physical activity used both in research and by employers in well-being programmes. Pedometers capture the number of steps taken which can be used to calculate distance, while accelerometers offer more advanced data collection as they measure acceleration as a more accurate log of movement.

Subjective measures usually involve self-report surveys, such as the Occupational Physical Activity Questionnaire (OPAQ) (see Reis et al., 2005), the MONICA Optional Study on Physical Activity Questionnaire (MOSPA-Q) developed by the World Health Organization, and the Occupational Sitting and Physical Activity Questionnaire (OSPAQ). The OSPAQ is a modified version of the MOSPA-Q and was developed by Chau et al. (2012). It is a simple and brief survey tool to capture data on time spent sitting, standing, walking and performing heavy labour at work. Unlike the OPAQ it separates sitting and standing so that measures can be taken of each activity. Compared with objective measurement, survey tools of this nature are a much lower cost method of monitoring physical activity levels at work. Evidence suggests a reasonable level of validity in the OSPAQ relative to objective measurement tools in more sedentary professional work environments; however, measurement in other contexts may not be as reliable and objective measurement tools are therefore promoted as a more accurate method of data collection (Maes et al., 2020). The version of the OSPAQ reported in Chau et al. (2012) is as follows:

Occupational Sitting and Physical Activity Questionnaire (OSPAQ)
1. How many hours did you work in the last 7 days? _____ hours
2. During the last 7 days, how many days were you at work? _____ days
3. How would you describe your typical work day in the last 7 days? (This involves only your work day, and does not include travel to and from work, or what you did in your leisure time.)

(a) Sitting (including driving)	____%
(b) Standing	____%
(c) Walking	____%
(d) Heavy labour or physically demanding tasks	____%
Total	____%

Example:

Jane is an administrative officer. Her work day involves working on the computer at her desk, answering the phone, filing documents, photocopying, and some walking around the office. Jane would describe a typical work day in the last 7 days like this:

(a) Sitting (including driving)	90%
(b) Standing	5%
(c) Walking	5%
(d) Heavy labour or physically demanding tasks	0%
Total	100%

Scoring:

Minutes sitting at work per week = Item 1*Item 3a.

Minutes sitting per work day = (Item 1/Item 2)*Item 3a.

Similar calculations can be done for standing, walking and heavy labour.

INCREASING PHYSICAL ACTIVITY AT WORK

Interventions to increase levels of physical activity among workers fall into two primary forms, those focused on education and behaviours, and those focused on the physical work environment.

Education and Behaviours

Many interventions focus on educating workers to change behaviours and less so on exploring how the physical work environment could be used and/or adapted to enhance levels of physical activity (Zhu et al., 2020). Mechanisms which fall broadly under the umbrella of education and behaviours include promoting the taking of breaks that involve socializing and light exercise which may help us experience greater positive emotions at work (Taylor et al., 2016; Trougakos et al., 2014). Use of computer prompts to act as a reminder to take a break may reduce sitting time by anywhere between 14 and 96 minutes per day based on existing studies (Shrestha et al., 2018).

Evidence has suggested a preference among workers for walking, swimming, gym (fitness centre), cycling and exercise classes as forms of physical activity at work (Hunter et al., 2018). Implementing well-being programmes involving forms of physical activity such as yoga has been shown to improve well-being and increase resilience among employees (Hartfiel et al., 2011). Different types of physical activity may provide different well-being benefits as lower intensity activities may have greater mental well-being benefits, and more intense activity provides greater benefits to physical health (Downward and Dawson, 2016). It has also been demonstrated, for example, that walking enhances creativity in thinking (Oppezzo and Schwartz, 2014).

Existing evidence, however, suggests that interventions focused solely on educational and behavioural change may have relatively smaller and shorter-term impacts (see Chu et al., 2016). A potential reason for this is offered by Ryde et al. (2020). They argue that often interventions target increases in physical activity in discretionary time such as lunch hours, but these may be limited in their success as they suffer from low participation rates. Conducting focus groups in three organizations in Scotland, they report a general acknowledgement among workers that physical activity offers benefits to physical and mental health and extending to productivity and favourable perceptions of employers. However, in their research they also identify potential barriers that can act to limit engagement in physical activity at work: (1) the nature of certain jobs such as those that are customer facing, and the structure of the working day including problems around high workloads; (2) practical considerations around the provision of facilities (e.g. to shower and change clothes before/after taking exercise); (3) workplace culture including presence of a no break culture and/or resentment from workers who do not take part in activities; and (4) organizational barriers including concerns around the cost of lost work-time and public perceptions of the use of organization funds in this manner. Further considerations for employers include the timing and location of scheduled opportunities for physical activity (e.g. group-based exercise classes), in order to avoid potential conflicts with work commitments (e.g. common meeting times), and life commitments such as taking children to, and picking them up from, school (Kinnafick et al., 2018).

The Physical Work Environment

Moving to the physical work environment, Zhu et al. (2020) emphasize from the findings of their systematic literature review the importance of considering the different spatial scales of physical activity at work when developing strategy and designing interventions to increase physical activity and reduce sedentary behaviours. They separate the physical work environment into three spatial levels: (1) the workstation, the location in which many workers sit for the majority of their working day; (2) spaces within or around the workplace where workers engage in movement such as space between buildings, break spaces, cafeterias, rooftop gardens; and (3) the neighbourhood around the workplace in which workers may walk during breaks and take other exercise such as jogging, and this extends to active methods of commuting such as walking or cycling considered later in the chapter.

The evidence base on the physical work environment suggests several potential benefits. Knight and Baer (2014) conducted an experiment using students in a US university to explore the impacts of non-sedentary workspaces by comparing group meetings conducted in a sedentary space (i.e. seated meeting) against those conducted in a standing format. They found that non-sedentary meeting arrangements improved group performance as they help to stimulate those involved, promote collaborative working and indirectly reduce territoriality over the ownership of ideas. Active workstations enable physical activity to be incorporated into work tasks that would otherwise take a sedentary form. They include combining working at a desk with walking on a treadmill, pedalling a bicycle or using an elliptical trainer, and sit-stand desks allow work to be performed while standing using a height-adjustable desk (Torbeyns et al., 2014). Based on a review of 34 existing studies, Shrestha et al. (2018) found that use of sit-stand desks can reduce total sitting time during a working day by between 84 and 116 minutes. Positive impacts on physical health and broader well-being have been reported in studies of the use of treadmill and bicycle desks (MacEwan et al., 2015; Torbeyns et al., 2017). While the potential health benefits may be clear, the impact on performance is less certain. Ojo et al. (2018) review evidence on the impact of active workstations on productivity and performance. They report that existing evidence is relatively clear in showing no detrimental impacts; however, evidence equally does not suggest any definite increase in performance from use of active workstations.

Active Workplace Design

Taking the role of the physical work environment a step further is active design (see Engelen, 2020). An active workplace design is a holistic approach combining structural design choices with the adoption of an active culture and workplace policies. It includes recommendations for the design and placement of stairs, elevators, lobbies, internal walking routes, and amenities such as break rooms and cafeterias. Active design also includes the provision of on-site facilities that enable engagement in physical activity prior to, and during, the working day such as bicycle storage, locker rooms and showers, and access to exercise rooms or equipment (Kahn et al., 2002). The design and provision of these physical elements of the workplace act to encourage, and in some cases demand, physical activity. In a study of over 3,000 workers across more than 300 organizations in the UK captured using online survey techniques, Knox et al. (2017) reported that provision of on-site facilities and opportunities for physical activity (e.g. exercise classes), are particularly effective interventions in improving physical activity behaviours.

The active design concept has gained some traction and has featured in public health and urban planning guidelines such as those provided by the Center for Active Design (2021) in the USA, Sport England (2015), and the Heart Foundation (2017) in Australia. In a review of existing studies, Engelen (2020) finds evidence of positive effects from active workplace design on sitting (reductions) and standing (increases) time. Wider evidence of well-being impacts such as reductions in MSD and increases in step counts have been reported, although the evidence base is relatively limited. An extension of the active design concept is that of active biophilic design, which incorporates nature into an active workplace design through natural lighting, ventilation, greenery, views of nature and use of natural and recycled materials (Wallmann-Sperlich et al., 2019). In doing so, the design not only promotes and provides opportunities to be active, but also offers the benefits outlined earlier in the chapter with respect to access to nature in the physical work environment.

Social and Group-based Physical Activity

Being active at work also has a function with respect to social connectedness and relationships. Existing studies have suggested, for example, that engagement in group-based workplace physical exercise can increase levels of social capital and relatedness among working teams (Andersen et al., 2015; Kinnafick et al., 2018). Workplace initiatives focusing on group-based physical activity may be more successful in promoting engagement in physical activity (Hunter et al., 2018; Jakobsen et al., 2017), especially among less physically active individuals (Kassavou et al., 2013). In addition, physical activity interventions may be more successful where conducted in groups that interact, feel a level of group identity, and where there is cohesiveness within the group towards the accomplishment of goals (Burke et al., 2006). Interventions of this nature may also benefit from efforts to make the activity enjoyable or fun (see Chapter 7). Kinnafick et al. (2018) report on the use of a high-intensity interval training (HIIT) programme among a group of workers in the UK, with the group dynamic acting as a driver of commitment to the programme, and group members benefitting from feelings of comfort and confidence from engaging in physical activity with others.

ACTIVE COMMUTING

The commute is often cited as one of the least enjoyable activities performed during the working day, but this primarily reflects the experiences of those travelling by car (Kahneman et al., 2004; Wheatley, 2014). In contrast, active forms of commuting such as cycling and walking can have significant benefits for physical health and wider well-being (Woodcock et al., 2009). Active commuting is associated with lower incidence of a range of health problems including cardiovascular disease, with benefits for those who walk, and especially those who cycle, to work (Celis-Morales et al., 2017; Dinu et al., 2019).

Mytton et al. (2016) explored the impacts of cycling and walking to work from a small-scale survey (n = 801) conducted in the UK. They found lower reported sickness absence, equating to one less day per year, among those cycling to work, as well as higher mental well-being scores. They did not, however, find significant benefits among those who walked to work. Neumeier et al. (2020) collected data from workers in Austria to assess the effects of active commuting on health-related quality of life (HRQoL) and sickness absence from work. Utilizing the 36-item short-form health survey (SF-36), which offers a subjective measurement tool consisting of questions relating to physical and mental well-being, the study compared workers in two active commuting groups: (1) cycling and (2) walking combined with use of public transport, against a control group. Positive changes were observed in physical functioning, mental health, vitality and general health, and in the physical health summary score. They also found the benefits for the cycling group to be more pronounced. Page and Nilsson (2017) report the findings of a pilot intervention in a UK organization involving the use of electrically assisted bikes (e-bikes). They compare workers who adopted active commuting using an e-bike with those engaged in passive commuting modes using subjective measures including the short 12-item General Health Questionnaire (GHQ12). They found active commuters reported positive affect and better physical health, and more positive organizational behaviour measured in relation to the reported ability to connect with others, and willingness to help others at work.

While active commuting benefits appear clear, most workers continue to commute using more passive modes of transport. Data for Great Britain from 2017 suggest travel by car accounts for 68 per cent and travel using public transport for 18 per cent of commutes, while active forms of transport – walking or cycling – together account for only around 12 per cent of commutes (Department for Transport, 2017). In part, these patterns reflect practical challenges that limit adoption of cycling and walking to work. Active commuting is not feasible for some workers due to their commuting distance, at least not without combining it with another form of transport (e.g. cycling to a train station). Some workers, meanwhile, will need to combine their journey to work with other activities such as the school run, necessitating certain forms of transport (Wheatley, 2013). Safety concerns could also act to limit engagement in some forms of active commuting, especially at night or in certain locations (Pooley et al., 2005, 140). Poor weather, road conditions and road safety can also act as barriers to cycling to work (Page and Nilsson, 2017). Effectively embedding active commuting also requires the provision of on-site facilities, such as bicycle storage and showers that act as enablers of active commuting (Engelen, 2020; Knox et al., 2017). Active commuting is somewhat of a moot point for homeworkers, a consideration that has greater significance since the shift to homeworking witnessed during 2020 due to the global pandemic. However, the time that would otherwise be used for commuting could very usefully be employed to engage in physical activity.

CASE STUDY: THE CARDIFF UNIVERSITY LIFESTYLE LEADERSHIP APPROACH

Helen Spittle and Rhian Roberts, Cardiff University, UK.
Can changing your physical state bring positive changes to your mental well-being? How do our working environments drive our physical behaviours at work, and affect our mental states? This case study outlines an approach to support staff to discover the benefits of proactively managing physical work-spaces for their well-being and performance.

Within the case study organization staff surveys had identified dissatisfaction with work–life balance, and leaders were keen to address this holistically. In response, we implemented a new approach through a seven-month 'Lifestyle Leadership Programme' undertaken by 20 managers in the College of Arts, Humanities and Social Sciences. The impact has been felt across the College as these leaders 'cast a positive shadow' through observable behaviours and implement interventions in their staff teams. The programme promotes a synergistic understanding of work–life balance, encouraging the formation of good habits whether at work or at home, with practical approaches to transitioning between the two. Benefits realized include an improved quality of life at work and at home; mental and physical benefits via the application of psychological interventions and exercise; reduction in stress-related absence; greater resilience (both individual and team); and a stronger collegiate team-working with confidence.

Is Sitting the New Smoking?

A key element of the programme has been a focus on the physical working environment, which for most staff was an office. 'Sitting is the new smoking' became a popular catch phrase during this period; on average we sit more than we sleep, and a study by Diaz et al. (2019) of almost 8,000 people found that even light-intensity movement for 30 minutes a day may reduce the risk of death incurred by sitting, and that replacing sitting with only minutes of movement provides health benefits. In addition to the physical benefits of movement, the impact on staff mental health was a key driver of this work. Mental health problems are one of the main causes of the overall disease burden worldwide (Vos et al., 2013), with one in four people in the UK experiencing a mental health problem in any given year (McManus et al., 2009). Research has shown a strong link between exercise and mental health (Sharma et al., 2006), by reducing anxiety, depression and negative moods. We were keen to put this to the test with staff through the Lifestyle Leadership approach.

The Lifestyle Leadership Approach

The programme was delivered off-site through a series of mixed theory and practical sessions, allowing managers to experience a new way of working while learning. As a result, managers re-evaluated their approach to the physical workplace environment and the interaction of staff with it, through a series of interventions:

1. *Remodelling offices to encourage less sitting.*
   Standing desks, or 'desk risers' encourage staff to spend more time on their feet while working, and while meeting people in offices.
2. *Adopting 'active meetings'.*
   One-to-one meetings, or team meetings were held outside while walking wherever possible.
3. *Encouraging physical activity at work.*
   Wearing trainers at lunchtime, or to walk between meetings was another visible way of managers role modelling. We also held exercise classes at lunchtimes, from yoga to high-intensity interval training.

In evaluating the impact of these interventions over time, leaders observed a number of changes in team behaviours. First, staff were moving more. There was a visible difference in the clothing and footwear staff were choosing to wear at work or to change into, enabling them to move around more freely. This led to a greater willingness to participate in active meetings and spend more time outdoors. An unintended benefit of a meeting involving physical activity is similar to that of travelling in a car; because you are not directly facing the person as you talk, difficult conversations become easier. This was

244 *Well-being and the quality of working lives*

particularly helpful in one-to-one meetings when discussing performance or personal issues.

> Our professional services team have adopted several new and improved working practices, to promote health and well-being. These vary from walking team meetings to altering the way staff utilize their working space by adopting new ideas such as standing desks. This year's professional services staff away day has been organized to continue with the health and well-being theme, covering areas such as work–life balance, the effects of exercise, mindfulness, habit breaking and yoga. All areas that will have a positive impact on our working lives. (Technical Services Manager, Cardiff University)

Second, people were standing up more, and sitting down less. Meetings held standing up tended to be shorter and more effective, as well as reducing the sitting time of staff. Many managers invested in experimenting with standing desks of different types, and even in changing the whole workspace to reflect the values of the Lifestyle Leadership Programme. Figure 9.3 shows a 'before and after' in the office of one of the managers. This is almost a metaphor for the change that the programme was intending to bring about; being active (through standing, moving), letting in the light, decluttering, focus, creativity and well-being.

Changes in transport behaviours included more walking or cycling to work, as well as walking between meetings across campus. As well as the health benefits of active commuting, there was an environmental and cost impact as people were using cars and taxis less.

> The lifestyle leadership initiative is explicitly addressing work–life balance, providing real solutions to perennial office life issues. The School and College has a tradition of social and developmental events, but this is different, providing a healthier and more holistic approach to leadership development. (Director of PGR Studies, Cardiff University)

Changes in the self-confidence of staff were also observed within the teams. Having watched the TED talk by Amy Cuddy on the benefits of power posing, based on her 2010 research, managers applied this in the workplace. Standing and moving more enables more expressive body language and managers reported feeling more confident in their interactions with staff and at meetings after employing these techniques (Figure 9.4).

> The lifestyle leadership initiative has played a big part in building staff resilience, by helping people to attain better mental and physical health, and by developing a common language and common practices among leaders in the College. (School Manager, Cardiff University)

Source: Photos by Helen Spittle.

Figure 9.3   Workspace layouts before and after the Lifestyle Leadership Approach

Source: Photo by Emma Howells-Davies.

Figure 9.4   Power posing on a lunchtime Lifestyle Leadership session

As well as these benefits, the statistics on sickness absence within the College reflected a reduction in stress-related absence. Empowering our leaders to fundamentally review their leadership styles by linking academic research with practical application has worked well for the College. The personal and organizational benefits of the programme have given them the confidence to put the tools and theory into practice in their teams and in the wider university. Ultimately, we believe that this holistic approach to well-being has enabled a more resilient and effective workforce.

CHAPTER SUMMARY: A HEALTHY AND ACTIVE WORK ENVIRONMENT

The physical work environment has impacts on both our physical and psychological well-being. In recent years there has been a move towards more flexible workplace design and a growth in location-based flexibility including expansion of work from home, even prior to the rapid expansion in 2020. Key developments such as activity-based flexible working environments, acknowledgement of the role of sustainability in workplace design, and expanded scope for technology-enabled location-independent working in a wide range of organizations are reshaping the physical work environment. For some workers, activities requiring concentration are likely to be performed more often at home, while co-located workplaces will become more focused on collaborative working and social interaction. A key debate moves to whether individuals have the space available at home to achieve an effective division between home and work. A lack of workspace within the home, due to sharing space with family or housemates, could leave some workers demanding quiet space in employer work premises. Wider adoption of home-based remote working also necessitates adequate resources to be provided by employers for the purpose of health and safety and productivity; the costs of resourcing a suitable homeworking environment should not be borne by the employee. Regardless of whether the workplace is at a co-located employer premise, home, a co-working space, other location or a combination of any or all of these, several common characteristics are important to physical and psychological well-being. These include the ergonomics of the workspace, lighting, temperature, air quality, noise levels, access to nature and green space, shared spaces for collaborating and socializing, and private spaces to aid concentration.

Levels of physical activity at work are also central, as trends towards sedentary working routines have generated an increased need for intervention at the individual, organizational and societal levels. Evidence suggests the most effective interventions combine education and behaviour change with changes to the physical work environment, including active workstations and provision of active-enabling facilities. Providing opportunities for workers to engage in group-based physical activity either face-to-face or virtually with colleagues also offers an effective method of promoting engagement and building and maintaining relationships at work. Workers can also benefit from engaging in more active forms of commuting, such as cycling or walking. Remote working at home has distinct implications for physical activity, with the potential to be quite hazardous as the tendency to work longer, take fewer breaks, and always be in one workspace exacerbates problems of sedentary working routines. The social dimension of physical activity may increase in relevance if workers continue to work more at home, experiencing fewer opportunities to interact face-to-face with colleagues, clients and others. Well-being programmes such as that outlined in the case study in this chapter become all the more central to the health of workers and organizations. Key factors to consider in creating a healthy and active work environment are outlined using the framework for workplace well-being in Figure 9.5.

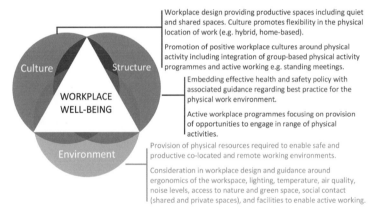

Figure 9.5   *Creating a healthy and active work environment for workplace well-being*

PART III

Enhancing the quality of working lives

10. Conclusions: ways to working well

INTRODUCTION

This book has contributed to our understanding of well-being at work, highlighting its multifaceted influence on the quality of our working lives. The book has explored different conceptualizations of well-being and existing contributions that have applied understanding of well-being in the work context. These contributions support the notion of work having a complex and interdependent relationship with well-being. Well-being at work is multi-dimensional and the chapters of this book have outlined a new approach to understanding the relationship between work and well-being and the range of factors that influence it, using the lens of job quality. Key distinctions have been drawn between the relevance of intrinsic aspects of work (that is, the nature of the work that we undertake) and extrinsic hygiene factors such as pay. We have considered the importance of control over our working lives, what it means to achieve balance between work and life, and the role of motivation in navigating work and a career. The book has reflected on the significance of the connections we have with others throughout our working lives and the social capital we draw from them, whether our actions at work reflect altruistic, self-interested or reciprocal behaviours, and how we derive identity from our working environment and interact with it physically and mentally.

This final chapter of the book draws together the dimensions of workplace well-being, linking each of the six dimensions presented in the framework for workplace well-being and highlighting the importance of taking a holistic approach when considering the influences and impacts of work on well-being. One of the main purposes of the chapter is to outline methods of measuring outcomes and impacts of well-being programmes and interventions. Consideration is given to objective and subjective methods of measurement, with the former including measures of performance and occupational health statistics, and the latter including measures of job satisfaction, levels of engagement and turnover intention. Furthermore, the chapter considers the usefulness to understanding well-being at work of broader measures of well-being. The chapter offers guidance pertaining to how we can measure the impacts of the various elements of paid work that influence experienced job quality and well-being. In this sense, the chapter is helpful to researchers

250 *Well-being and the quality of working lives*

investigating aspects of well-being at work. The content extends to practical advice on how to measure the impacts and effectiveness of policies and programmes focusing on worker well-being at the organization level. The chapter also provides overall recommendations to organizations and workers on ways of building and maintaining healthy working lives, including reflecting on relevant concepts of resilience and mindfulness amongst other considerations. The chapter and book end with a brief discussion of the future of well-being at work, reflecting on the range of potential influences including changes in technology and the lasting effects of the global pandemic.

LINKING THE DIMENSIONS OF WORKPLACE WELL-BEING

Within this book a new framework has been presented for approaching well-being at work. The framework captures the interdependencies and distinctions between the dimensions of work that comprise workplace well-being. It is formed around three strategic elements, namely the culture of the organization and its workers, the structures that govern their activities, and the physical and psychological work environment. Underpinning these strategic elements are six dimensions of work that have been informed by an extensive review of existing models and approaches to workplace well-being and job quality (Chapter 3), that itself was informed by an exploration of broader approaches to understanding well-being (Chapter 2). The six dimensions – job properties, flexibility, rewarding careers, giving, relationships, and physical space and activity – and their fluid relationship with the strategic elements of the framework are summarized in Figure 10.1. Each of the dimensions has been considered in detail within the preceding chapters of the book including reflection on existing conceptualizations and evidence, as well as more practically focused exploration of methods of measuring the sub-dimensions of each of the six dimensions of workplace well-being.

Job Properties

The job properties dimension of workplace well-being was explored in Chapter 4 and incorporates the wide array of intrinsic characteristics of work that influence our experiences of paid work. These characteristics of work reflect the nature of the work we undertake comprising the different components which collectively make up a job. They include levels of control and autonomy over the tasks we complete, the way we complete them, and when and where we complete them; the relative intensity of work, that is, how hard we have to work to complete the tasks in our jobs; the resources we have at our disposal including time and space, equipment and tools, materials, facilities,

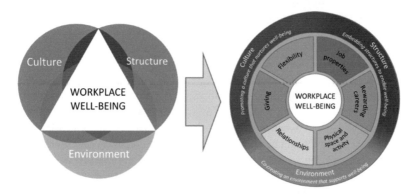

Figure 10.1   The framework for workplace well-being

and support services; the variety, complexity and level of challenge present in tasks; the meaning and purpose we take from our jobs; and the clarity we have over our responsibilities and position within an organizational structure.

The intrinsic characteristics that comprise the job properties dimension have a central role in our experiences of paid work, influencing the quality of our working lives. They are also heavily driven by job design reflecting a key organizational role in this dimension of workplace well-being. The presence of greater levels of control and autonomy, manageable workloads, adequate and suitable resources, meaning, variety, challenge and environmental clarity, have all been found to have benefits to job quality and well-being at work. These characteristics are also highly interconnected which renders it important to consider each in the broader context of the job properties dimension. A number of these characteristics are more subjective in nature, or at least often are measured as such, which does need to be factored into the design of jobs and development of policies and practices to enhance worker well-being. Nevertheless, existing evidence emphasizes the role of intrinsic factors to our experiences of paid work. The close relationship with job design also presents a potential barrier to enhancements in the intrinsic characteristics of work. When embarking on well-being programmes, organizations are often hesitant to engage in more substantive change. This is not to suggest that it is not possible to make improvements through small and iterative change, for example increasing the level of control workers have over certain aspects of their job. However, more significant structural and cultural change may deliver greater benefits. Refocusing jobs towards task and outputs, as opposed to time, is increasingly appropriate in many sectors and occupations, as is providing workers with the ability to craft their jobs, something that is returned to later

252 *Well-being and the quality of working lives*

in this chapter. Enacting change of this nature does impose a short-term cost for the organization; however, significant benefits can be realized including enhanced performance and reduced employee turnover and absence.

Flexibility

Flexibility is the second dimension of workplace well-being and was explored in Chapter 5. This dimension focuses on how we achieve a desirable and effective balance between work and the rest of our lives, and includes aspects of work such as working hours and overwork, work recovery and breaks, availability and experiences of the use of both formal and informal flexible working arrangements, and the application of agile approaches to work. Flexibility is important as it permeates throughout our jobs and influences the relationship between work and the rest of our lives. When employee-led, flexibility, for example over the start and end time of the working day or the ability to remote work at home, reflects a form of autonomy (schedule control) and can enable the achievement of balance between work and life. The evidence explored in the book indicates that employee-focused flexibility offers several positive outcomes for well-being. Embedding flexibility within organizations can take the form of effective management and monitoring of working hours, embedding cultures that promote good practice in working routines including taking breaks, and through the availability and widespread use of both formal and informal flexible working arrangements, including ensuring a good level of awareness of, and access to, arrangements across the organization.

However, flexibility has become an increasingly contentious subject in recent years as the flexibilization of work has presented benefits and challenges for workers and organizations. Potential difficulties associated with flexibility include gaps between provision and use of flexible working arrangements, often due to lack of awareness and/or buy-in from line managers and leaders. Many of the problems associated with flexibility, though, centre on the application of employer-focused flexibility including flexible contracting such as zero hours and gig working. A focus on cost reduction and numerical flexibility can be successful and offer benefits to workers and the organizations employing their labour. However, evidence suggests that many workers involved in these forms of employment (or self-employment) report low job quality, and gains obtained by the organization from this course of action may well be limited to the short term as workers become less productive and seek alternative employment where they are able. Meanwhile, where flexibility means there is lesser time spent at a co-located workplace, resulting in distance between workers and with their employer, this can reduce feelings of connectedness and coherency and can create problems with communications

Conclusions: ways to working well 253

and the monitoring of job activity, factors linked to the relationships dimension of workplace well-being.

Rewarding Careers

The rewards we receive from work have considerable relevance to the quality of our working lives. Chapter 6 of the book recognized that rewards act as a motivational tool for workers. However, a focus on extrinsic drivers, sometimes called hygiene factors such as pay and other benefits, over intrinsic drivers of motivation, such as autonomy, challenge and purpose, is likely to be less effective in achieving beneficial outcomes for organization and worker. The discussion of this dimension of workplace well-being nevertheless highlighted the benefits of well-designed, and communicated, formal reward mechanisms including progression pathways linked to pay scales/increments. While these components of work act more as hygiene factors, remuneration from work supports our well-being through its influence on realized standards of living. This extends to awareness and use of employee benefits, which can be quite limited. Increasing awareness and improving the 'fit' of benefits is essential to avoid benefits going unused or underused. Moreover, the provision of a clear progression pathway for workers, including timescales, benchmarks and measurable criteria used to identify goals and gauge progress towards their fulfilment, can act as both a motivator and offer wider benefits where workers gain intrinsic motivation including meaning and challenge.

The chapter also emphasized the role of training, and the relative benefits of 'smart' training which can be used to increase human capital for the benefit of workers and organizations in a cost-effective manner. Levels of job security are a further aspect of this dimension of workplace well-being. The flexibilization of the labour market discussed in Chapter 5 has important consequences for relative job security as increasing portions of workers engage in fixed or short term, zero hours and other forms of employment. Employers benefit from being able to more easily increase/decrease the size of the workforce and avoid other costs associated with permanent employees, such as paid leave. In return, workers should benefit from these forms of flexibility to pursue opportunities available to them including multiple job holding and undertaking training and education. This requires an organizational-level culture change focused on acceptance that flexibility should deliver benefits to both worker and organization. The sub-dimensions of the rewarding careers dimension of workplace well-being influence our well-being, in part given the potential for the presence of imbalance between effort and reward (i.e. a gap between the effort given and the reward received) or at least the perception of imbalance. Rewarding workers through extrinsic factors is undoubtedly important to both recruitment and retention and worker well-being, but a longer-term focus on

254 *Well-being and the quality of working lives*

effectively embedding both intrinsic and extrinsic rewards will deliver the greatest benefits for workers and organizations.

Relationships

Relationships at work are highly important to our lives and are recognized as such in many existing models of well-being at work and broader approaches to understanding well-being. Chapter 7 considered how relationships can act as a driver for engagement in work, providing social connectedness, enhancing social capital and participation in leisure. A further consideration is the social exchanges that take place within the work sphere with expectations around fulfilment of obligations of respective roles (e.g. leader and worker) determining the ongoing relationship. The quality of the relationships we have with our leaders, as well as co-workers and clients/customers has impacts on our experiences of work and, in turn, our well-being. The presence of conflict at work can be healthy and positive where it is focused on task, through promoting debate and fresh thinking, and acting as a source of challenge. Furthermore, embedding an environment that assists psychological safety promotes the sharing of knowledge and ideas, employee voice, and workers using their initiative. Essential to beneficial outcomes is to put in place a culture and appropriate structures including policies and provision of training, which promote an inclusive and positive working environment. The role of good leadership in this dimension of workplace well-being is integral, through promoting high-quality relationships. It is linked to opportunities for development and progression and mentoring, emphasizing the links with the rewarding careers and giving dimensions of workplace well-being. Good-quality relationships with leaders can engender trust and intrinsic motivation among workers and provide opportunities for employees to have an input in decision-making and be heard, whereas ineffectiveness or even destructive behaviours from leaders can have significant negative effects on the health of workers and the organization.

A particular concern for well-being at work is the failure of relationships and incidence of conflict at work. This includes incidence of forms of bullying and harassment and/or discrimination, lack of trust and lack of opportunities to be heard. In Chapter 7, existing evidence highlighted how conflict affects job performance, with impacts felt at the level of the individual and the team, and extending throughout the organization. Conflict negatively affects performance, recruitment and retention, and imposes costs associated with conflict resolution and worker absence. Conflict at work not only influences well-being at work but also our broader well-being, acting as a source of stress and depressive symptoms. Co-creating a positive and safe working environment that is

Conclusions: ways to working well 255

free from the negative effects of conflict is central to the quality of working lives and the health of organizations.

Giving

Giving at work is not given a central role in many existing models of well-being at work, often being incorporated into other dimensions that focus on social, relational and/or community aspects of work. It is acknowledged in broader approaches to well-being such as the Five Ways to Well-being outlined in Chapter 2. Giving has a vital role in the health of workers, organizations and society. In Chapter 8, drivers of giving behaviours were considered with the debate centring on whether giving reflects altruistic intention, self-interest or expectations around reciprocation. In practice, giving behaviours may reflect a blurred middle ground in which those giving do so consciously for the benefit of the recipient(s), but also take a reward from this act, through obtaining human or social capital, gaining satisfaction from helping others, or receiving some form of benefit in kind in future, evidencing a reciprocal component.

In the work context, giving takes a number of forms, from volunteering and charitable giving, to more relational aspects including social support, workplace helping and mentoring. Volunteering can generate many of the broader benefits of giving, including human and social capital development, and enhanced satisfaction levels from seeing the well-being of others increase. Corporate volunteering programmes can be used to achieve these benefits and at the same time enhance corporate social responsibility agendas. Charitable giving (i.e. monetary and other donations) is another form of giving that many organizations engage in successfully, although evidence indicates that its relative benefits are more limited and fatigue can set in, while it can also create undesirable impacts where stigma is attached to those who do not engage in philanthropic behaviour. It is, perhaps, best applied as part of a package of interventions as a method of embedding a giving culture. Social support at work takes several forms including support provided by peers, line managers, leaders and the broader organization. Perceived organizational support (POS) emphasizes the need to create and maintain an environment in which workers perceive that they are being supported. Workplace helping, which involves support in the completion of tasks, is particularly relevant where workers engage in complex and interdependent tasks. It enhances knowledge and skills, aids team building, and has positive effects on workplace relationships, productivity and performance. Helping must not be one way, though, to avoid negative outcomes for more diligent individuals including work-related stress and work overload. Finally, mentoring is an important component of this dimension of workplace well-being that overlaps with both the rewarding careers and relationships dimensions. It provides a range of benefits including

256   *Well-being and the quality of working lives*

supporting talent identification and development, and succession planning, with existing evidence suggesting that more informal and longer-term mentoring relationships are likely to be most beneficial.

Physical Space and Activity

The final dimension of workplace well-being, considered in the book in Chapter 9, is physical space and activity. The physical work environment has impacts on physical and psychological well-being. It is closely connected to health and safety, while it also acts as a significant source of meaning and identity for the worker. The physical spaces in which we work continue to evolve through more flexible workplace design and the growth in location-based flexibility including work from home, even prior to the rapid expansion witnessed in 2020. Key developments such as activity-based flexible working environments, acknowledgement of the role of sustainability in workplace design including green buildings, and expanded scope for technology-enabled location-independent working in a wide range of locations are reshaping the physical work environment. Regardless of whether the workplace is at a co-located employer premise, at home, a co-working space, other location or a combination of any or all of these, several common physical characteristics influence experienced well-being at work. These include the ergonomics of the workspace which has particular impacts on physical health related to musculoskeletal disorders. This aspect of the physical environment extends to mental health through its impacts on comfort. Other characteristics that influence well-being comprise lighting, temperature, air quality (which is linked to incidence of sick building syndrome), noise levels, access to nature and green space, and the balance between shared and private spaces.

Levels of physical activity at work form the second core component of this final dimension. Recent decades have witnessed a growth in sedentary working routines that impact both physical and mental health, generating an increased need for intervention at both the individual and organization level to increase levels of physical activity. Evidence suggests that the most effective interventions combine education and behaviour change with changes to the physical work environment, linking closely the components of this dimension. This can be performed through the use of active workstations and provision of active-enabling facilities such as changing rooms. Workplace design and layout also plays a role here, effectively requiring movement from workers to interact and meet. Providing opportunities for workers to engage in group-based physical activity either face-to-face or virtually also offers an effective method of promoting engagement in physical activity, while building and maintaining relationships at work, evidencing the connection between this and the relationships dimension of workplace well-being. Engaging in more active forms of commuting, such as cycling or walking, provides further opportunities to enhance physical and mental well-being at work.

Through the exploration of each of the dimensions of workplace well-being in the preceding chapters of the book it is clear that while each dimension is distinct there are many connections between the six broad dimensions, and the three overarching strategic principles, culture, structure and environment. While the coverage of each dimension provides a high degree of understanding and in turn offers significant opportunity for enhancements in workplace well-being to be realized for workers and organizations, developing strategies and implementing well-being programmes requires consideration of all of the components of the framework for workplace well-being to be most effective. The chapters of the book have provided a range of examples of methods of capturing objective and subjective understanding of current experiences of work. In this chapter, the discussion now turns to our understanding of the outcomes of workplace well-being and the identification of methods for measuring impacts, such that we can manage and enhance the quality of our working lives.

UNDERSTANDING THE OUTCOMES OF WORKPLACE WELL-BEING

Existing research and evidence on job quality and well-being at work employs a wide-ranging set of empirical methods for capturing outcomes and measuring impacts. These include objective and subjective measures, single-item and multi-item or composite indicators, and consider individual elements of our working lives through to overall measures of well-being. As it would be near impossible to provide an exhaustive list here given the breadth of measures available, several of the most popular tried and tested methods for capturing outcomes and measuring impacts are outlined in this section.

Productivity and Performance

Performance is often used interchangeably with productivity although the terms are distinct (Ojo et al., 2018). In the context of the work performed by an individual, performance can be defined as 'the proficiency with which individuals perform the core substantive or technical tasks central to their job' (Koopmans et al., 2016, 610). Productivity, meanwhile, is usually defined and measured relative to output in a specified period (or at the organization level output per worker). Notwithstanding these definitional differences, there is a high degree of overlap practically in the measurement of worker performance and productivity. It can be challenging to quantify in an objective way, especially for knowledge work where outputs are intangible and involve hard-to-quantify elements including creativity. Laihonen et al. (2012) discuss the complexities of measuring productivity among knowledge workers, outlining guidelines for the design of performance measurement systems. Productivity at the individual level is also challenging to measure objectively where work is structured around teams and tasks are interdependent, characteristics that are increasingly present in many jobs. Evidence on the relative comparability of objective and subjective measures of productivity suggests that these measures should not be used interchangeably, and rather that measures should be chosen based on the purpose of the measurement exercise and suitability to the work being performed (Bommer et al., 1995).

Objective measures of productivity include, but are not limited to: (1) classic piece-rate measures such as outputs in a specified period (e.g. the number of sales per month); (2) completion of defined performance goals (e.g. targets/deliverables), which may be linked to department or organization key performance indicators (KPIs), and can be quantitative or qualitative in nature; (3) productivity loss measures such as the number of hours/days or output lost due to illness/absence; and (4) supervisor ratings. Example measures of supervisor ratings include that reported in Sears et al. (2013), where the overall job performance of a worker is rated on a 5-point scale ranging from 'unacceptable' to 'exceptional'. Yam et al. (2014), meanwhile, capture supervisor ratings using a single-item scale, asking the supervisor to respond to the statement, *'This employee always completes the duties specified in his or her job description'*, using a 7-point scale from strongly disagree = 1 to strongly agree = 7. Supervisor ratings, it should also be noted, could be argued as being subjective at least to a degree.

Subjective measures of productivity, as per other outcome measures, can be captured using single-item or multi-item scales. A useful multi-item example is the Health and Work Questionnaire (HWQ) developed in partnership with GlaxoSmithKline by Shikiar et al. (2004). It contains 24 items which capture work quality, quantity, efficiency, concentration/focus, impatience/irritability, supervisor relations, work satisfaction and non-work satisfaction. Of the 24 questions, 11 have been found, using factor analysis, to effectively capture productivity. Three of these questions have three parts (a, b and c), asked relative to self, supervisor and co-workers, thus accounting for nine items in total. All nine are assessed on a 10-point scale from 'My worst ever' to 'My best possible'. The items are as follows:

How would you and the following people describe your efficiency this week?
How would you and the following people describe the overall quality of your work this week?
How would you and the following people describe the overall amount of work you did this week?

The two remaining productivity-focused items ask respondents to rate their overall efficiency – *Rate your highest level of efficiency this week; Rate your lowest level of efficiency this week* – with responses again on a 10-point scale from 'My worst ever' to 'My best possible'.

A second example is the Individual Work Performance Questionnaire (IWPQ), developed by Koopmans et al. (2013, cited in Koopmans et al., 2016). Originally in the Dutch language and since converted to English, the IWPQ aims to capture all aspects of performance at work using individual worker self-report. It comprises 18 items structured into three sub-sections covering task performance (TP), contextual performance (CP) and counterproductive work behaviour (CWB). Task performance is defined in relation to the proficiency of a worker to complete the core tasks of the job, contextual performance refers to worker behaviours that act to support the organizational, social and psychological work environment, and counterproductive work behaviour captures behaviours that negatively impact the health of the organization (Koopmans et al., 2016, 610). All items use a common 5-point scale ranging from seldom = 0 to always = 4. The questionnaire items are as follows:

Task performance (TP)
TP1 *I was able to plan my work so that I finished it on time.*
TP2 *I kept in mind the work result I needed to achieve.*
TP3 *I was able to distinguish main issues from side issues.*
TP4 *I was able to carry out my work well with minimal time and effort.*
TP5 *I planned my work optimally.*

Contextual performance (CP)

CP6 *On my own initiative, I started new tasks when my old tasks were completed.*

CP7 *I took on challenging tasks when these were available.*

CP8 *I worked on keeping my job-related knowledge up-to-date.*

CP9 *I worked on keeping my work skills up-to-date.*

CP10 *I came up with creative solutions for new problems.*

CP11 *I took on extra responsibilities.*

CP12 *I continually sought new challenges in my work.*

CP13 *I actively participated in meetings and/or consultations.*

Counterproductive work behaviour (CWB)

CWB14 *I complained about unimportant issues at work.*

CWB15 *I made problems at work bigger than they were.*

CWB16 *I focused on the negative aspects of a situation at work instead of the positive aspects.*

CWB17 *I talked to colleagues about the negative aspects of my work.*

CWB18 *I talked to people outside of the organization about the negative aspects of my work.*

Presenteeism and Productivity Loss

Presenteeism is a term used to refer to workers continuing to engage in tasks of employment despite ill health that would normally require absence (Karanika-Murray et al., 2015). The definition is usually extended to acknowledge impaired performance at work as a product of a range of different factors both directly health related (e.g. illness/injury) and those which reflect the impact of other elements of the dimensions of well-being at work such as lack of resources (Sears et al., 2013). An alternative, and to some degree distinct, term is 'psychological presenteeism' which refers to being at work physically but being psychologically absent (Karanika-Murray et al., 2015). A further use of the term is to define it as the opposite of absenteeism, that is, working long hours and feeling pressure to be physically present at work, with this latter definition closely linked to concepts of long hours cultures discussed in Chapter 5. Presenteeism is increasingly considered to be a major component of productivity measurement associated with the costs of workers attending work unwell, resulting in reduced work output and on-the-job errors (Schultz and Edington, 2007). The World Health Organization's Health and

Work Performance Questionnaire (HPQ) includes a measure of overall job performance relative to the worst and best potential performance to give an indication of the impacts of presenteeism on worker performance, where 'Worst Performance' = 0 and 'Top Performance' = 10 (Kessler et al., 2003). A simple yes/no measure of presenteeism is included in the Chartered Institute of Personnel and Development's (CIPD) UK Working Lives Survey, which asks, '*In the last three months have you ever worked in your main job despite not feeling well enough to perform your duties?*' The Work Productivity and Impairment Questionnaire (WPAIQ) also includes a single-item measure of productivity loss. The WPAIQ is designed to measure the effects of health problems on work productivity and other activities (Reilly et al., 1993; Reilly Associates, 2004). The productivity loss question within the questionnaire asks respondents to indicate how their health has affected productivity at work using an 11-point scale as follows:

During the past seven days, how much did health problems affect your productivity *while you were working*?

Think about days you were limited in the amount or kind of work you could do, days you accomplished less than you would like, or days you could not do your work as carefully as usual. If health problems affected your work only a little, choose a low number. Choose a high number if health problems affected your work a great deal.

Consider only how much *health problems* affected productivity *while you were working*.											
Health problems had no effect on my work	0	1	2	3	4	5	6	7	8	9	10	Health problems completely prevented me from working

Existing evidence has suggested that the Work Limitations Questionnaire (WLQ) (see Lerner et al., 2003) offers a relatively comprehensive method of capturing lost productivity resulting from presenteeism (Sanderson et al., 2007). The WLQ comprises 25 items split into four sub-scales that cover (1) time and scheduling demands (e.g. ability to complete work without stopping to take breaks); (2) physical demands (e.g. ability to walk or move around work locations, use handle-held equipment, and sit, stand or stay in one position for longer than 15 minutes); (3) mental-interpersonal demands (e.g. ability to keep mind on work, think clearly when working, and speak with people in-person, in meetings or on the phone); and (4) output demands (e.g. ability to handle workload, work fast enough, and work without making mistakes) (Lerner et al., 2003, 659). The questionnaire is formed around multi-item questions that each contain items from the different sub-scales. All are asked using a 5-point scale from 'All of the time' to 'None of the time'. An example question from the WLQ is as follows:

In the past 2 weeks, how much of the time did your physical health or emotional problems make it difficult for you to do the following?

	(Mark one box on each line a. through e.)					
	All of the Time (100%)	Most of the Time	Some of the Time (about 50%)	A Slight Bit of the Time	None of the Time (0%)	Does Not Apply to My Job
a. do your work without stopping to take breaks	$\square_1$	$\square_2$	$\square_3$	$\square_4$	$\square_5$	$\square_0$
b. stick to a routine or schedule	$\square_1$	$\square_2$	$\square_3$	$\square_4$	$\square_5$	$\square_0$
c. keep your mind on your work	$\square_1$	$\square_2$	$\square_3$	$\square_4$	$\square_5$	$\square_0$
d. speak with people in-person, in meetings or on the phone	$\square_1$	$\square_2$	$\square_3$	$\square_4$	$\square_5$	$\square_0$
e. handle the workload	$\square_1$	$\square_2$	$\square_3$	$\square_4$	$\square_5$	$\square_0$

In their research into the impacts of well-being on productivity and retention, Sears et al. (2013) utilize the Well-being Assessment for Productivity (WAP) tool. The WAP includes an 11-item questionnaire capturing the factors that can impair work performance. Respondents answer the question '*During the past 4 weeks (28 days), how often have you had trouble at work concentrating or doing your best because of:*' with responses comprising two sub-scales representing personal factors (e.g. caring for others, financial issues, feeling depressed/stressed), and work-related factors (e.g. lack of resources, issues with supervisor or co-workers, lack of training). Reponses are scored on a scale comprising 'not at all', 'some' and 'a lot' (see Prochaska et al., 2011) to capture impacts of different barriers to performance.

Absenteeism

Absenteeism is a further indicator of worker well-being. Absenteeism refers to time lost to physical and/or mental health in the form of unscheduled absences from work. It can be captured using several different objective measures, including the number of attendance interruptions (i.e. periods of continuous absence, number of days absent in a specified period such as a month or year) and the number of lost working hours due to absence. It is often captured by

Conclusions: ways to working well 263

organizations as part of occupational health monitoring; however, several tools also exist that enable questioning at the level of the worker. The WPAIQ includes lines of questioning on both working hours and days absent (Reilly et al., 1993; Reilly Associates, 2004) as follows:

During the past seven days, how many hours did you miss from work because of your health problems? Include hours you missed on sick days, times you went in late, left early, etc., because of your health problems. Do not include time you missed to participate in this study.
_____ HOURS

During the past seven days, how many hours did you miss from work because of any other reason, such as vacation, holidays, time off to participate in this study?
_____ HOURS

Occupational Health Referrals

Occupational health data captured by organizations is a useful source of insight into the relative levels of physical and mental well-being present within the organization. While often captured within absence data, in some cases well-being concerns do not result in absence but can impact performance and require referrals. Examples include musculoskeletal disorders that could require referral to physiotherapists, and mental health difficulties that could require referral to an employee assistance programme (EAP).

Work Engagement

Kahn's (1990) seminal work identifies work engagement as reflecting a situation where the employee finds work meaningful and invests effort in the pursuit of personal and career benefits. Work engagement has further been defined as a work-related state of mind that is positive and fulfilling and is characterized by vigour, dedication and absorption (Schaufeli et al., 2002, 74). Work vigour reflects an individual feeling energetic and mentally resilient in their work, even where work presents challenge. Dedication is used to describe a high degree of involvement in work and is associated with feelings of significance, enthusiasm, inspiration, pride and challenge. Finally, absorption refers to a state of full concentration and engrossment in work, such that time feels as though it passes quickly, and it can be difficult to detach from work (Schaufeli et al., 2006, 702).

Kahn (1990) identifies three psychological conditions which influence work engagement: psychological meaningfulness, psychological safety and psychological resource availability. In Kahn's model, psychological meaningfulness refers to an employee deriving meaning from their work, that is, they feel they receive 'a return on investments of one's self in a currency of physical, cognitive, or emotional energy' (Kahn, 1990, 703–4). Psychological safety describes whether a worker feels 'able to show and employ one's self without fear of negative consequences to self-image, status, or career' (Kahn, 1990, 708). Psychological resource availability, meanwhile, is used to describe the level to which an employee feels that they have the physical, emotional and/ or psychological resources required to invest themselves at work. Job involvement, which has been defined as 'a positive and relatively complete state of engagement of core aspects of the self in the job' is argued as a key indicator of work engagement (Brown, 1996, 235). Various factors have been shown to promote work engagement including effective leadership and high-quality relationships with co-workers which are central components of the work environment, as well as stimulating tasks, availability of resources and effective reward mechanisms (Brunetto et al., 2012, 430).

The Utrecht Work Engagement Scale (UWES) developed by Schaufeli et al. (2006) offers a useful method of empirically measuring engagement in work. It uses a 17-item scale which captures three components of work engagement: vigour (denoted VI in the list of questions below), dedication (DE) and absorption (AB). Questions are answered using a 7-point scale where Never = 0, Sometimes = 3 and Always = 6. The scale is presented as follows:

1. *At my work, I feel bursting with energy. (VI1)*
2. *I find the work that I do full of meaning and purpose. (DE1)*
3. *Time flies when I am working. (AB1)*
4. *At my job, I feel strong and vigorous. (VI2)*
5. *I am enthusiastic about my job. (DE2)*
6. *When I am working, I forget everything else around me. (AB2)*
7. *My job inspires me. (DE3)*
8. *When I get up in the morning, I feel like going to work. (VI3)*
9. *I feel happy when I am working intensely. (AB3)*
10. *I am proud of the work that I do. (DE4)*
11. *I am immersed in my work. (AB4)*
12. *I can continue working for very long periods at a time. (VI4)*
13. *To me, my job is challenging. (DE5)*
14. *I get carried away when I am working. (AB5)*
15. *At my job, I am very resilient, mentally. (VI5)*
16. *It is difficult to detach myself from my job. (AB6)*
17. *At my work, I always persevere, even when things do not go well. (VI6)*

Conclusions: ways to working well 265

An alternative approach is to measure disengagement from work and exhaustion. A useful measurement tool in this case is the Oldenburg-Burnout Inventory (OLBI). The OLBI is a 16-item instrument that uses a 4-point scale from 'strongly agree' = 1 to 'strongly disagree' = 4. It asks respondents to rate their agreement with eight negative and eight positive statements (see Demerouti et al., 2010). Note that at the end of each statement in parentheses, D denotes a disengagement measure, E an exhaustion measure, and R an item scored in reverse (i.e. a higher score indicates a greater degree of burnout). The scale is presented as follows:

Below you find a series of statements with which you may agree or disagree. Using the scale, please indicate the degree of your agreement by selecting the number that corresponds with each statement.

1. *I always find new and interesting aspects in my work. (D)*
2. *There are days when I feel tired before I arrive at work. (E.R)*
3. *It happens more and more often that I talk about my work in a negative way. (D.R)*
4. *After work, I tend to need more time than in the past in order to relax and feel better. (E.R)*
5. *I can tolerate the pressure of my work very well. (E)*
6. *Lately, I tend to think less at work and do my job almost mechanically. (D.R)*
7. *I find my work to be a positive challenge. (D)*
8. *During my work, I often feel emotionally drained. (E.R)*
9. *Over time, one can become disconnected from this type of work. (D.R)*
10. *After working, I have enough energy for my leisure activities. (E)*
11. *Sometimes I feel sickened by my work tasks. (D.R)*
12. *After my work, I usually feel worn out and weary. (E.R)*
13. *This is the only type of work that I can imagine myself doing. (D)*
14. *Usually, I can manage the amount of my work well. (E)*
15. *I feel more and more engaged in my work. (D)*
16. *When I work, I usually feel energized. (E)*

Organizational Commitment

Organizational commitment is the psychological attachment a worker has to their organization that is reflected in a strong belief in the goals and values of the organization, willingness to put in work effort, and desire to stay with the organization (Meyer et al., 2012; Mowday et al., 1979). Organizational commitment is useful in understanding the attachment workers have to their organization, as it provides a global affective response to the organization, and as such is argued to be more stable over time than other indicators of well-being at work such as job satisfaction. One of the most widely recognized methods for measuring organizational commitment is the Organizational Commitment Questionnaire (OCQ) developed by Mowday et al. (1979). The OCQ contains 15 items each scored on a 7-point scale from 'strongly disagree' = 1 to 'strongly agree' = 7. The responses to the items are summed and then divided by 15 to generate a summary indicator of commitment. Note that some of the items are negatively scored, denoted by R.

1. *I am willing to put in a great deal of effort beyond that normally expected in order to help this organization be successful.*
2. *I talk up this organization to my friends as a great organization to work for.*
3. *I feel very little loyalty to this organization. (R)*
4. *I would accept almost any type of job assignment in order to keep working for this organization.*
5. *I find that my values and the organization's values are very similar.*
6. *I am proud to tell others that I am part of this organization.*
7. *I could just as well be working for a different organization as long as the type of work was similar. (R)*
8. *This organization really inspires the very best in me in the way of job performance.*
9. *It would take very little change in my present circumstances to cause me to leave this organization. (R)*
10. *I am extremely glad that I chose this organization to work for over others I was considering at the time I joined.*
11. *There's not too much to be gained by sticking with this organization indefinitely. (R)*
12. *Often, I find it difficult to agree with this organization's policies on important matters relating to its employees. (R)*
13. *I really care about the fate of this organization.*
14. *For me this is the best of all possible organizations for which to work.*
15. *Deciding to work for this organization was a definite mistake on my part. (R)*

A second common measure of organizational commitment employed in both research and practice is the Affective Commitment Scale developed by Meyer and Allen (1997). This six-item scale asks respondents to signal agreement with three positive and three negative statements using a 5-point scale from 'Strongly Agree' = 1 to 'Strongly Disagree' = 5, with statements comprising:

1. *This organization has a great deal of personal meaning for me.*
2. *I do not feel emotionally attached to this organization.*
3. *I really feel as if this organization's problems are my own.*

4. *I do not feel part of a family in my organization.*
5. *I do not feel strong sense of belongingness to my organization.*
6. *I would be very happy to spend the rest of my career with this organization.*

Alternative indicators of organizational commitment and wider meaning/sense of belonging derived from work are captured in the UK Working Lives Survey using four items. All statements use a 5-point scale from 'strongly agree' = 1 to 'strongly disagree' = 5, as follows:

1. *I am willing to work harder than I have to in order to help my employer or organization.*
2. *I have the feeling of doing useful work for my organization/client(s).*
3. *I have the feeling of doing useful work for society.*
4. *I am highly motivated by my organization's core purpose.*

Turnover Intention and Actual Turnover

Through influencing well-being, a range of different aspects of experienced job quality including job demands (Alfes et al., 2018; Burke et al., 2010; Greenhaus et al., 2012), rewards (Kuvaas et al., 2017) and relationships (Deery et al., 2011; Richter et al., 2020) impact the intention to stay with or leave an organization, and actual worker turnover rates. Measures of turnover intention can focus on gauging intention to stay or intention to leave a job. An example question which focuses on intention to leave from the UK Working Lives Survey is as follows: *How likely do you think it is that you will voluntarily quit your job in the next 12 months?* Responses are given on a 5-point scale from 'very likely' to 'very unlikely'. Actual turnover levels, meanwhile, can be captured in both voluntary and involuntary forms (Sears et al., 2013). Voluntary turnover reflects workers leaving the organization of their own volition (e.g. to retire, for another job, and/or as a way to address well-being problems), whereas involuntary turnover captures workers who are terminated, for example, due to poor performance which itself could be a product of negative well-being influences at work.

Job Satisfaction

Job satisfaction is a measure of an individual's overall evaluative judgement of their job (Mérida-López et al., 2019). It captures the level of favourability towards a job and is usually presented along a continuum of satisfaction (positive) to dissatisfaction (negative) (Judge et al., 2017). While existing evidence has identified that job satisfaction has a statistically reliable relationship with the sub-dimensions of subjective well-being (i.e. life satisfaction, happiness, and the presence of positive and absence of negative affect), the existing evidence base suggests that the strength of these relationships, often measured in terms of correlations between job satisfaction and sub-dimensions of subjective well-being, may vary considerably across individuals and sub-dimensions (Bowling et al., 2010).

There is a distinction to note between overall or global satisfaction with job and satisfaction with facets or components of a job including pay (or income), working hours, work tasks, opportunities for development and progression, supervisors and co-workers. An example here is the single-item subjective measure of pay included in the European Social Survey, 'Considering all my efforts and achievements in my job, I feel I get paid appropriately' with responses on a 5-point scale from 'agree strongly' = 1 to 'disagree strongly' = 5. While it might be assumed that overall satisfaction is a simple composite product of satisfaction with job facets, evidence has indicated that the general attitude towards a job can be distinct from attitudes about various features of the job (i.e. you may feel satisfied overall with your job but be dissatisfied with working hours or pay received) (Judge et al., 2017). Research has also shown that global job satisfaction has a stronger relationship with subjective well-being than specific job satisfaction facets. Existing evidence on the causal relationship between overall measures of well-being and job satisfaction (i.e. whether overall well-being influences job satisfaction, or job satisfaction influences overall well-being) is inconsistent (Bowling et al., 2010). This may be indicative of a reciprocal relationship, to some degree, in which either can influence the other at certain points throughout our working lives. Single-item scales of global job satisfaction take a common form, although the exact wording and nature of the answer scale can differ. The UK Understanding Society survey, for example, includes a single-item scale as follows:

7	6	5	4	3	2	1
Completely satisfied	Mostly satisfied	Somewhat satisfied	Neither satisfied or dissatisfied	Somewhat dissatisfied	Mostly dissatisfied	Completely dissatisfied

Q. On a scale of 1 to 7 where 1 means 'Completely dissatisfied' and 7 means 'Completely satisfied', how dissatisfied or satisfied are you with your job overall?

A range of multi-item or composite measures also exist, such as the Gallup Q12 scale of employee job satisfaction, which is also considered as a useful measure of engagement (Harter et al., 2013). The Gallup Q12 comprises 12 questions with responses on a 5-point 'strongly disagree' to 'strongly agree' scale, which ask about different components or facets of job quality and worker well-being, including environmental clarity, job resources, recognition, relationships with

Conclusions: ways to working well 269

supervisors and colleagues, development and progression, employee voice, meaning and worthwhileness, and personal growth. Items include:

1. *Do you know what is expected of you at work?*
2. *Do you have the materials and equipment to do your work right?*
3. *In the last seven days, have you received recognition or praise for doing good work?*
4. *At work, do your opinions seem to count?*
5. *Does the mission/purpose of your company make you feel your job is important?*
6. *In the last six months, has someone at work talked to you about your progress?*

An alternative measurement tool linked to Deci and Ryan's (2000) self-determination theory (SDT), outlined in Chapter 6, is the Basic Psychological Needs Satisfaction at Work Scale (see Deci et al., 2001). This is a 21-item scale that aims to capture the extent to which three basic needs outlined in SDT – *relatedness*, *competence* and *autonomy* – are met at work. All statements are answered on a 7-point scale from 'Not at all true' = 1 to 'Very true' = 7, with items comprising the following:

1. *I feel like I can make a lot of inputs to deciding how my job gets done.*
2. *I really like the people I work with.*
3. *I do not feel very competent when I am at work.*
4. *People at work tell me I am good at what I do.*
5. *I feel pressured at work.*
6. *I get along with people at work.*
7. *I pretty much keep to myself when I am at work.*
8. *I am free to express my ideas and opinions on the job.*
9. *I consider the people I work with to be my friends.*
10. *I have been able to learn interesting new skills on my job.*
11. *When I am at work, I have to do what I am told.*
12. *Most days I feel a sense of accomplishment from working.*
13. *My feelings are taken into consideration at work.*
14. *On my job I do not get much of a chance to show how capable I am.*
15. *People at work care about me.*
16. *There are not many people at work that I am close to.*
17. *I feel like I can pretty much be myself at work.*
18. *The people I work with do not seem to like me much.*
19. *When I am working I often do not feel very capable.*
20. *There is not much opportunity for me to decide for myself how to go about my work.*
21. *People at work are pretty friendly towards me.*

Work-related Stress

Work-related stress can be captured using several different measurement scales. These include the ASSET (an organizational stress screening tool) stress measurement instrument (Johnson and Cooper, 2003) outlined in Chapter 3, which offers a comprehensive method of understanding work-related stress and psychological well-being. Measures within the job demand-control model (JD-C) (Karasek, 1979) outlined in Chapter 3, and the effort–reward imbalance (ERI) model (Siegrist, 1999; Siegrist et al., 1986; Siegrist et al., 2004) detailed in Chapter 6 also provide useful insight into work-stressors. All items in the ERI are outlined in Chapter 6. Example items from Bell et al. (2017) employed to capture the demands component of the JD-C model are summarized below, with each usually measured on a 5-point scale (e.g. 'totally disagree' to 'totally agree').

1. *My job requires working very hard.*
2. *My job requires working very fast.*
3. *I have enough time to get the job done.*
4. *I am free from conflicting demands that others make.*
5. *I am not asked to do an excessive amount of work.*

Understanding of work overload and work-related stress can also be obtained using single-item scales, such as that used in the UK Working Lives Survey which asks for responses to the statement '*At my work I feel under excessive pressure*' using a 5-point scale from 'Always' = 1 to 'Never' = 5.

Other Well-being Outcome Measures

In addition to measures of job satisfaction, both domains and overall measures of well-being can be employed to understand the outcomes and impacts of well-being at work. Within the UK Understanding Society survey, for example, a multi-item question is used to capture domain level and overall life satisfaction using a 7-point scale from 'completely dissatisfied' = 1 to 'completely satisfied' = 7, as follows:

Here are some questions about how you feel about your life.
Please choose the number which you feel best describes how dissatisfied or satisfied you are with the following aspects of your current situation.

Health.
The income of your household.
The amount of leisure time you have.
Your life overall.

Conclusions: ways to working well 271

An alternative measure, which focuses on global positive and negative affect is the Institute of Work Psychology (IWP) Multi-affect Indicator (see Warr and Parker, 2016). It comprises 16 items that each capture emotions at work (eight negative and eight positive) including feeling 'enthusiastic', 'depressed', 'relaxed', 'excited', 'worried' and 'hopeless'. It uses a 7-point scale from 'Never' = 0 to 'Always' = 6. Another commonly used tool for measuring mental health is the General Health Questionnaire (GHQ). Initially comprising 60 items, the GHQ was developed by Goldberg in the 1970s (Goldberg, 1972) and has since been shortened into different forms comprising between 30 and 12 items in total. The shortened version of the GHQ (GHQ-12) contains 12 questions, summarized in Table 10.1, which provide a measure of mental health that can be used in detection of psychiatric disorders.

Table 10.1   Shortened version of the General Health Questionnaire (GHQ-12)

Have you recently …				
1. Been able to concentrate on what you're doing?	Better than usual	Same as usual	Less than usual	Much less than usual
2. Lost much sleep over worry?	Not at all	No more than usual	Rather more than usual	Much more than usual
3. Felt you were playing a useful part in things?	More so than usual	Same as usual	Less useful than usual	Much less useful
4. Felt capable of making decisions about things?	More so than usual	Same as usual	Less so than usual	Much less capable
5. Felt constantly under strain?	Not at all	No more than usual	Rather more than usual	Much more than usual
6. Felt you couldn't overcome your difficulties?	Not at all	No more than usual	Rather more than usual	Much more than usual
7. Been able to enjoy your normal day-to-day activities?	More so than usual	Same as usual	Less so than usual	Much less than usual
8. Been able to face up to your problems?	More so than usual	Same as usual	Less so than usual	Much less able
9. Been feeling unhappy and depressed?	Not at all	No more than usual	Rather more than usual	Much more than usual
10. Been losing confidence in yourself?	Not at all	No more than usual	Rather more than usual	Much more than usual
11. Been thinking of yourself as a worthless person?	Not at all	No more than usual	Rather more than usual	Much more than usual
12. Been feeling reasonably happy, all things considered?	More so than usual	About same as usual	Less so than usual	Much less than usual

LINKING THE DIMENSIONS AND OUTCOMES OF WORKPLACE WELL-BEING

The discussion in this chapter has outlined the breadth of outcomes and impacts of workplace well-being and methods for measuring them. Each of the dimensions and sub-dimensions of the framework for workplace well-being explored throughout the preceding chapters influence our experiences of work, and in turn has outcomes on the quality of our working lives. Figure 10.2 provides a summary of the core sub-dimensions within each of the six dimensions of the framework and in the centre the range of associated outcomes that can be measured to understand and evaluate the impacts of work on our well-being.

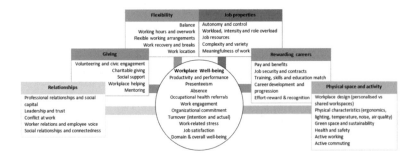

Figure 10.2   Dimensions and outcomes of workplace well-being

A comprehensive approach to well-being at work will seek to incorporate measures of all outcomes. However, the exact combination of measures employed will be dependent on the nature and context of the measurement exercise and, in some cases, practicalities associated with data collection and availability. For research purposes often exercises are more focused and concentrate on specific outcomes or dimensions, although broader attempts to measure job quality and worker well-being can offer greater insight where they incorporate many of the outcome measures covered in this chapter. Limitations can be faced when drawing on data from large-scale social surveys where questions may be limited to single-item measures and some outcomes not directly measured. At the organizational level, practicalities around data collection through staff surveys or other mediums (e.g. limited resources, risk of survey fatigue) will likely mean limited lines of questioning can be included (or collected through other mechanisms), thus restricting the outcomes that can be captured. Key to effective understanding and monitoring of well-being outcomes within organizations is capturing a combination of outcomes that offers suitable insight given the context of the organization and the constraints

Conclusions: ways to working well

faced. An example could be to gather subjective data on performance, work engagement, organizational commitment and job satisfaction, and combine this with objective data on presenteeism, absence, occupational health referrals and actual turnover.

BUILDING AND MAINTAINING A THRIVING WORKPLACE

Within this book a new approach to understanding well-being in the context of work – the framework for workplace well-being – has been presented. The model can be employed as a framework for well-being within organizational settings. To build and maintain a thriving workplace, organizations should consider the following recommendations.

Understand Worker Well-being Within the Organizational Setting

Benchmarking of well-being within the organization can be performed using, for example, staff surveys to provide a baseline for any well-being strategy or programmes. Many organizations already capture data from staff providing scope for job quality and well-being-focused lines of questioning to be added either as regular elements or periodic inclusions. Monitoring of worker well-being is recommended through different forms including surveys, focus groups, appraisal systems and other methods of data collection, to gauge the effectiveness of job quality and well-being enhancement programmes and inform future strategy development. It is important to time data collection carefully and/or embed well-being data capture within existing surveys or other staff touchpoints to avoid survey fatigue and disengagement.

Combine Proactive and Reactive Approaches

One of the potential barriers to the enhancement of worker well-being is a focus on solely reactive interventions, including the provision of mental health support and EAP. While this type of support is integral to maintaining the well-being of workers, organizations need to consider more proactive approaches to workplace well-being focusing on creating a culture, designing suitable structures, and providing an environment that promotes good work and well-being as outlined in the chapters of this book. Combining proactive and reactive initiatives (i.e. a combination of well-being enhancers and well-being supporters) is likely to be most effective in delivering beneficial outcomes for worker and organization.

Smaller Iterative Change or Comprehensive Strategy?

When approaching workplace well-being it can be challenging to generate awareness and receive buy-in from certain stakeholders within an organization and this can limit the desire for a central or overarching strategy. Smaller-scale initiatives focusing on iterative change can be effective, both in terms of costs/resourcing and in generating awareness/buy-in to inform larger-scale well-being programmes (including piloting initiatives). Smaller-scale interventions can also serve a valuable purpose in enhancing individual aspects or sub-dimensions of workplace well-being where need is identified. A comprehensive strategy, though, should be a longer-term target to guide the overall approach, avoid silos of activity that could lead to potential negative outcomes such as inequality in experience, or replication of effort where there is a lack of coordination.

Avoid a Stimulate and Abandon Outcome

A potential risk in delivering a well-being programme or strategy is a stimulate and abandon outcome, that is, engaging workers through collecting data and increasing awareness of well-being at work but taking no action (or at least being perceived not to) as an outcome of this work. Where action is taken it is necessary to communicate what this action is, and to report its impacts within the organization. It is also important to provide opportunities for all stakeholders to feed back and input into decision-making and further strategy development to close the loop.

Prioritize the Intrinsic Through Job Crafting

Existing evidence supports the argument that intrinsic factors and rewards from work are those that have the greatest potential to enhance well-being. While it remains important to put in place relevant extrinsic 'hygiene' factors, organizations should focus their attention on the intrinsic characteristics of work. A potential way to improve the intrinsic is to empower workers to input into the design of their job. As outlined in Chapter 4, job crafting provides the opportunity for a worker to shape, mould, and redefine their job, in doing so increasing levels of engagement, satisfaction, meaning, and job performance (Brewster and Holland, 2021).

Flexibility Should Be Employee Focused

Increased flexibility has been a key feature of the changes in paid work in recent decades, as acknowledged in Chapters 5 and 9. Evidence is clear in identifying the relative benefits to worker and organizational well-being of an approach centred on employee-focused flexibility, including the provision of greater levels of autonomy and use of formal and informal flexible working arrangements, and contrastingly the relative longer-term costs, including to the health of workers and organizations, of a sole focus on employer-focused flexibility centred on contract flexibility and cost reduction.

Create a Well-being Culture Through Leadership Buy-in

Effective well-being programmes require an inclusive culture which values well-being and is supported by leaders within the organization. This includes the provision of adequate resource to support well-being programmes as well as 'leading by example' being evident in the actions of the organization and its leaders. As the content of this book has emphasized, well-being is multifaceted and leaks into all aspects of our working lives, therefore necessitating a workplace culture that acknowledges this throughout all levels of an organization.

Develop a Tailored Approach Acknowledging the Diversity of Workers

Well-being strategy and programmes should be developed that offer a degree of tailoring that acknowledges the diversity of workers and their preferences. One-size-fits-all policies rarely suit the needs of all workers, and while external influences such as legislation may determine the nature and content of certain workplace policies, it is likely to be most effective to provide different mechanisms of engaging with, and realizing positive outcomes in, each of the dimensions of workplace well-being.

ADDITIONAL MECHANISMS FOR MANAGING AND SUPPORTING WORKER WELL-BEING

Aside from many of the specific actions that can be taken to enhance each of the dimensions of workplace well-being and their constituent sub-dimensions outlined throughout the book, a number of more general mechanisms are available in the management and support of worker well-being. Some of these measures are more reactive in nature (e.g. mental health first aid), while others are more proactive, such as resilience training. Equally, some of the measures involve the organization taking the initiative, while others are more focused on empowering workers to take ownership of the management of their own well-being.

Mental Health First Aid

First aiders for physical injuries are a common feature in organizations. Mental Health First Aid (MHFA) adopts a similar approach but for mental health. MHFA was first developed in Australia in 2001 and has since gained traction in several countries (see Kitchener and Jorm, 2008). It provides a mechanism for early intervention that involves line managers and other staff being trained to identify the signs and symptoms of common mental health concerns, offer support, and provide guidance to where further support can be found. Existing evidence suggests that MHFA increases recognition and awareness of mental health, promotes helping behaviours within the organization, and supports the mental health of recipients (Hadlaczky et al., 2014).

Employee Assistance Programmes

Many organizations lack the capacity and/or expertise to provide their workers with adequate support on the range of different well-being challenges they face. Organizations in some cases, therefore, pay for an EAP which is provided by external organizations who offer a range of confidential services from mental health support to financial advice and even well-being monitoring through apps. Sometimes referred to as an employee benefit, existing evidence is mixed on the relative success of EAPs. More successful cases have been found to reduce the severity of mental health concerns (Richmond et al., 2017); however, less successful applications often reflect the organization using an EAP as a method of individualizing well-being concerns rather than addressing them at the organizational level (Kirk and Brown, 2003). EAPs are perhaps best employed as one element of a more comprehensive well-being strategy.

Building Resilience

Defined as the capacity of an individual to demonstrate successful adaptation, recovery and bounce back in the presence of social disadvantage, adversity or change (Noble and McGrath, 2012; Windle, 2002, 163), building resilience among workers offers a further mechanism for enhancing well-being through increasing the ability of workers to cope with well-being challenges. Resilience is a coping component of well-being (Noble and McGrath, 2012), associated most closely with the positive psychology approach to well-being developed by Seligman (see Chapter 2). Approaches to understanding what makes us resilient focus on the nexus between 'individual' and 'environmental' factors. Individual factors refer to more stable individual personality traits including self-efficacy, the level of control we feel over our lives, our awareness of and ability to manage emotions, ability to problem-solve, perseverance, perspective, how optimistic we are and the presence of a sense of humour (CIPD, 2011; Rees et al., 2015). Environmental factors are more dynamic and dependent on the experiences we have with our environment, including family, work and the community, such as the level of social support we receive. Different perspectives suggest 'individual' or 'environmental' factors may predominate in determining resilience, but research also suggests it is the combination of the two (Richardson, 2002, cited in CIPD, 2011). A wide range of resources outlining methods for building resilience are available, such as those by the CIPD (2011) and Roffey Park (see Lucy et al., 2014). Example methods for enhancing resilience include at the individual level use of personal rewards which can be small and should focus on recognition rather than materialism. Key to becoming more resilient is to learn from and share experiences. One method for achieving this is the resilience regimen (see Margolis and Stoltz, 2010). It asserts the benefits of workers and leaders reframing negative events in productive ways through responding to questions under four sets: (1) control (e.g. *what features of the situation can I (even potentially) improve?*); (2) impact (e.g. *what sort of positive impact can I personally have on what happens next?*); (3) breadth (e.g. *how can I contain the negatives of the situation and generate currently unseen positives?*); and (4) duration (e.g. *what can I do to begin addressing the problem now?*). Building confidence and self-esteem is a further method for enhancing resilience (e.g. through self-efficacy training). Self-efficacy can be developed through a strengths-based approach using humour and optimism that encourages identification of positive aspects of a situation, referred to as 'positive tracking', and teaches coping skills (Noble and McGrath, 2005). Finally, resilience can be increased by taking control of the present (e.g. through mindfulness techniques). A potential criticism of resilience building, as per EAPs, is that it can reflect an organization pushing the responsibility for well-being onto the individual, while not addressing the demands and work-stressors that create well-being challenges. Nevertheless, building resilience is an effective method of navigating well-being challenges.

Mindfulness Techniques

Mindfulness is a form of meditation that involves the use of relaxation techniques to monitor and observe moment-by-moment sensory and psychic events (LaJeunesse and Rodríguez, 2012, 197). Use of mindfulness techniques, including breathing exercises and guided imagery, promotes acceptance rather than change and value-based actions (Bond and Flaxman, 2006). Through providing peaceful and restorative experiences, evidence has shown it to enhance mental health and social engagement, and to help us to manage our energy, emotions, attention and behaviours (Brown et al., 2007). Mindfulness can be usefully applied in the work context. For example, Langer and Moldoveanu

(2000) identify that mindfulness techniques can be used to positively alter worker perceptions of their job tasks and, combined with the collaborative rearrangement of tasks by workers and employers, increase worker engagement. Mindfulness may also increase bonds between individuals in certain contexts and levels of empathic concern for others (Lecchi et al., 2019). LaJeunesse and Rodríguez (2012), meanwhile, explore the benefits of mindfulness techniques during time spent commuting. Based on their findings they argue that through increasing engagement in the activity, mindfulness breathing techniques can be used to enhance commuting experiences.

THE FUTURE OF WELL-BEING AT WORK

Work continues to evolve as changes in society, including those driven by technology and other agendas such as climate change, create new opportunities, demand for new knowledge and skills, and new ways of working. At the same time, these changes render other areas of employment obsolete due to, for example, the automation of tasks. Most recently, the changes witnessed in 2020 highlighted the potential for paid work to take place in different spatial settings and be performed through different mechanisms. The positive experiences of many workers and organizations to the unprecedented rapid expansion of remote working in response to the global pandemic reinforce the mutual benefits for workers and organizations including performance, job satisfaction and work–life balance, which can be realized from increased levels of flexibility. These recent developments also highlight the importance of workers having control over the timing, and where possible, location of work. They have emphasized the potential of remote working at home, but also a number of beneficial dimensions of work that are more easily realized in a co-located or face-to-face environment including aspects of building and maintaining relationships with others. Acknowledging these outcomes and their relevance to several of the dimensions of well-being at work, and thinking towards the future of work, the application of more flexible agile and hybrid work models may be particularly attractive to both workers and organizations. Employed correctly they have potential to offer benefits for workers, in terms of balancing work and life and managing well-being, and for organizations through providing a cost-effective and performance-maximizing model of work.

To generate the greatest mutually beneficial outcomes for workers, organizations and society requires the application of a comprehensive approach to well-being that acknowledges and responds to the dimensions of workplace well-being explored throughout this book. It is essential that a proactive approach is taken to the development of policies, strategy and initiatives with a focus on good work and well-being enablers as opposed to only responding

Conclusions: ways to working well 279

to poor mental and/or physical health. Organizational policy that is reactive in nature may appear easier and/or cheaper to implement; however, it will impose greater costs on the organization as lost productivity, sickness absence and other outcomes negatively impact performance. Being ignorant of or lacking adequate resources and processes to support workers who face well-being difficulties is likely to result in exacerbation of problems. To support and enhance job quality and well-being at work requires a commitment at the individual, organizational and societal level. While much remains uncertain regarding the future of work, and developments will likely continue to be fluid and organic in nature, it is undoubtedly the case that well-being should be placed firmly at the centre of a healthy and successful workplace.

References

Acemoglu, D. and Pischke, J.-S. (2000). Certification of training and training outcomes. *European Economic Review*, 44(4–6), 917–27.

Adema, W., Clarke, C., Frey, V., Greulich, A., Kim, H., Rattenhuber, P. and Thévenon, O. (2017). Work/life balance policy in Germany: promoting equal partnership in families. *International Social Security Review*, 70(2), 31–55.

Adler, P.S. and Kwon, S. (2002). Social capital: prospects for a new concept. *Academy of Management Review*, 27(1), 17–40.

Agosti, M.T., Bringsén, Å. and Andersson, I. (2017). The complexity of resources related to work–life balance and well-being – a survey among municipality employees in Sweden. *The International Journal of Human Resource Management*, 28(16), 2351–74.

Agypt, B., Christensen, R. and Nesbit, R. (2012). A tale of two charitable campaigns: longitudinal analysis of employee giving at a public university. *Nonprofit and Voluntary Sector Quarterly*, 41(5), 802–25.

Aked, J., Marks, N., Cordon, C. and Thompson, S. (2008). *Five Ways to Wellbeing* [online]. Available at: https://neweconomics.org/uploads/files/8984c5089d5c2285ee_t4m6bhqq5.pdf.

Alfes, K., Shantz, A.D. and Ritz, A. (2018). A multilevel examination of the relationship between role overload and employee subjective health: the buffering effect of support climates. *Human Resource Management*, 57(2), 659–73.

Alfes, K., Shantz, A. and Truss, C. (2012). The link between perceived HRM practices, performance and well-being: the moderating effect of trust in employer. *Human Resource Management Journal*, 22(4), 409–27.

Allen, T., Chao, G., Eby, L. and Bauer, T. (2017). Taking stock of two relational aspects of organizational life: tracing the history and shaping the future of socialization and mentoring research. *Journal of Applied Psychology*, 102(3), 324–37.

Allen, T., Poteet, M., Lentz, E. and Lima, L. (2004). Career benefits associated with mentoring for protégés. *Journal of Applied Psychology*, 89(1), 127–36.

Aloisi, A. (2016). Commoditized workers: case study research on labor law issues arising from a set of on-demand/gig economy platforms. *Comparative Labor Law and Policy Journal*, 37(3), 653–90.

Andersen, L.L., Poulsen, O.M., Sundstrup, E., Brandt, M., Jay, K., Clausen, T., Borg, V., Persson, R. and Jakobsen, M.D. (2015). Effect of physical exercise on workplace social capital: cluster randomized controlled trial. *Scandinavian Journal of Public Health*, 43(8), 810–18.

Anderson, D., Vinnicombe, S. and Singh, V. (2010). Women partners leaving the firm: choice, what choice? *Gender in Management: An International Journal*, 25(3), 170–83.

André, K., Bureau, S., Gautier, A. and Rubel, O. (2017). Beyond the opposition between altruism and self-interest: reciprocal giving in reward-based crowdfunding. *Journal of Business Ethics*, 146, 313–32.

References

Andreoni, J. (1990). Impure altruism and donations to public goods: a theory of warm-glow giving. *Economic Journal*, 100(401), 464–77.

Anthony-McMann, P., Ellinger, A., Astakhova, M. and Halbesleben, J. (2017). Exploring different operationalizations of employee engagement and their relationships with workplace stress and burnout. *Human Resource Development Quarterly*, 28(2), 163–95.

Arampatzi, E., Burger, M. and Novik, N. (2018). Social network sites, individual social capital and happiness. *Journal of Happiness Studies*, 19(1), 99–122.

Arrowsmith, J. (2001). *Government Calls for Better Work–Life Balance* [online]. European Industrial Relations Observatory. Available at: http://www.eurofound.europa.eu/eiro/2001/02/feature/uk0102115f.htm.

Arrowsmith, J. and Marginson, P. (2010). The decline of incentive pay in British manufacturing. *Industrial Relations Journal*, 41(4), 289–311.

Arthur, M. (2008). Examining contemporary careers: a call for interdisciplinary inquiry. *Human Relations*, 61(2), 163–86.

Arup (2020). *Future of Offices: In a Post-Pandemic World* [online]. Arup. Available at: https://www.arup.com/-/media/arup/files/publications/f/future-of-offices-in-a-post-pandemic-world.pdf.

Aselage, J. and Eisenberger, R. (2003). Perceived organisational support and psychological contracts: a theoretical integration. *Journal of Organisational Behavior*, 24(5), 491–509.

Ashley, R., Ball, S. and Eckel, C. (2010). Motives for giving: a reanalysis of two classic public goods experiments. *Southern Economic Journal*, 77(1), 15–26.

ASHRAE (1966). *Thermal Comfort Conditions*. Standard 55.66. New York: ASHRAE.

Atherton, A., Faria, J., Wheatley, D., Wu, D. and Wu, Z. (2016). Financial hardship and the decision to moonlight: second job holding by the self-employed. *Industrial Relations Journal*, 47(3), 279–99.

Atkinson, C. and Hall, L. (2009). The role of gender in varying forms of flexible working. *Gender, Work and Organization*, 16(6), 650–66.

Ausberg, K., Hinz, T. and Sauer, C. (2017). Why should women get less? Evidence on the gender pay gap from multifactorial survey experiments. *American Sociological Review*, 82(1), 179–210.

Babapour, M.C., Harder, M. and Danielsson, C.B. (2020). Workspace preferences and non-preferences in activity-based flexible offices: two case studies. *Applied Ergonomics*, 83. https://doi.org/10.1016/j.apergo.2019.102971.

Babapour, M.C., Karlsson, M. and Osvalder, A.-L. (2018). Appropriation of an activity-based flexible office in daily work. *Nordic Journal of Working Life Studies*, 8(S3). https://doi.org/10.18291/njwls.v8iS3.105277.

Badger, A. and Woodcock, J. (2019). Ethnographic methods with limited access: assessing quality of work in hard to reach jobs. In D. Wheatley (ed.), *Handbook of Research Methods on the Quality of Working Lives*, 135–46. Cheltenham, UK, and Northampton, MA, USA: Edward Elgar Publishing.

Bailey, A. and French, J. (2018). *Future of Wellbeing at Work: Applying the PERMA Model*. Available at: https://www.linkedin.com/pulse/future-wellbeing-work-applying-perma-model-alex-bailey/.

Bailey, D. and Kurland, N. (2002). A review of telework research: findings, new directions, and lessons for the study of modern work. *Journal of Organizational Behavior*, 23(4), 383–400.

Baird, M. (2011). The state, work and family in Australia. *The International Journal of Human Resource Management*, 22(18), 3742–54.

Baker, W. and Dutton, J.E. (2007). Enabling positive social capital in organizations. In J.E. Dutton and B.R. Ragins (eds), *Exploring Positive Relationships at Work*, 325–45. New York: Psychology Press.

Bakker, A.B. and Demerouti, E. (2007). The job demands-resources model: state of the art. *Journal of Managerial Psychology*, 22, 309–28.

Bakker, A.B. and Schaufeli, W.B. (2008). Positive organizational behavior: engaged employees in flourishing organizations. *Journal of Organizational Behavior*, 29(2), 147–54.

Baranik, L., Roling, E. and Eby, L. (2010). Why does mentoring work? The role of perceived organizational support. *Journal of Vocational Behavior*, 76(3), 366–73.

Barling, J., Kelloway, E.K. and Iverson, R.D. (2003). High-quality work, job satisfaction, and occupational injuries. *Journal of Applied Psychology*, 88(2), 276–83.

Barnes, M. (2006). Reducing donor fatigue syndrome. *Nonprofit World*, 24(2), 1–8.

Bass, B.M. (1985). *Leadership and Performance Beyond Expectations*. New York: Free Press.

Bass, B.M. and Avolio, B.J. (1993). *Multifactor Leadership Questionnaire*. Palo Alto, CA: Consulting Psychologists Press.

Bass, B.M. and Avolio, B.J. (1997). *Full Range Leadership Development: Manual for the Multifactor Leadership Questionnaire*. Palo Alto, CA: Mindgarden.

Bass, B.M., Avolio, B.J., Jung, D.I. and Berson, Y. (2003). Predicting unit performance by assessing transformational and transactional leadership. *Journal of Applied Psychology*, 88(2), 207–18.

Batt, R. and Valcour, P.M. (2003). Human resources practices as predictors of work–family outcomes and employee turnover. *Industrial Relations*, 42(2), 189–220.

Baumeister, R.F. and Leary, M.R. (1995). The need to belong: desire for interpersonal attachments as a fundamental human motivation. *Psychological Bulletin*, 117(3), 497–529.

Beehr, T.A., King, L.A. and King, D.W. (1990). Social support and occupational stress: talking to supervisors. *Journal of Vocational Behavior*, 36(1), 61–81.

Beehr, T.A., Walsh, J.T. and Taber, T.D. (1976). Relationships of stress to individually and organizationally valued states: higher order needs as a moderator. *Journal of Applied Psychology*, 61(1), 41–7.

Bekkers, R. and Wiepking, P. (2011). A literature review of empirical studies of philanthropy: eight mechanisms that drive charitable giving. *Nonprofit and Voluntary Sector Quarterly*, 40(5), 924–73.

Bell, C., Johnston, D., Allan, J., Pollard, B. and Johnston, M. (2017). What do demand-control and effort–reward work stress questionnaires really measure? A discriminant content validity study of relevance and representativeness of measures. *British Journal of Health Psychology*, 22(2), 295–329.

Benedetti, A., Diefendorff, J., Gabriel, A. and Chandler, M. (2015). The effects of intrinsic and extrinsic sources of motivation on well-being depend on time of day: the moderating effects of workday accumulation. *Journal of Vocational Behavior*, 88, 38–46.

Bentley, T.A., Teo, S.T.T., McLeod, L., Tan, F., Bosua, R. and Gloet, M. (2016). The role of organisational support in teleworker wellbeing: a sociotechnical systems approach. *Applied Ergonomics*, 52, 207–15.

Bergström-Casinowsky, G. (2013). Working life on the move, domestic life at standstill? Work-related travel and responsibility for home and family. *Gender, Work and Organization*, 20(3), 311–26.

Bianchi, S.M., Hotz, V.J., McGarry, K. and Seltzer, J.A. (2008). Intergenerationalities: theories, trends, and challenges. In A. Booth, A. Crouter, S. Bianchi and J. Seltzer (eds), *Intergenerational Caregiving*, 3–44. Washington, DC: Urban Institute.

Bickerton, C. (2019). Conducting small scale primary mixed methods research into the impacts of work-related travel. In D. Wheatley (ed.), *Handbook of Research Methods on the Quality of Working Lives*, 268–81. Cheltenham, UK, and Northampton, MA, USA: Edward Elgar Publishing.

Biddle, J.H. and Ekkekakis, P. (2005). Physically active lifestyles and wellbeing. In F. Huppert, N. Baylis and B. Keveme (eds), *The Science of Well-being*, 141–70. Oxford: Oxford University Press.

Bielenski, H., Bosch, G. and Wagner, A. (2002). *Working Time Preferences in Sixteen European Countries*. Luxembourg: Office for Official Publications of the European Communities.

Bienefeld, M.A. (1972). *Working Hours in British Industry*. London: Weidenfeld and Nicolson.

Black, P., Burton, S., Hunter, J., Lawton, C., Pickford, R. and Wheatley, D. (2017). *Out of the Ordinary: Exploring the Lives of Ordinary Working Families*. Nottingham: Nottingham Civic Exchange, Nottingham Trent University. Available at: https://www.ntu.ac.uk/media/documents/about-ntu/Out-of-the-Ordinary-final-report-reduced.pdf.

Blau, P.M. (1964). *Exchange and Power in Social Life*. New York: John Wiley.

Block, R., Malin, M., Kossek, E. and Holt, A. (2013). The legal and administrative context of work and family leave and related policies in the USA, Canada and the European Union. In F. Jones, R. Burke and M. Westman (eds), *Work–Life Balance: A Psychological Perspective*, 39–67. Hove: Psychology Press.

Bodin Danielsson, C. (2013). An explorative review of the lean office concept. *Journal of Corporate Real Estate*, 15(3–4), 167–80.

Boell, S., Cecez-Kecmanovic, D. and Campbell, J. (2016). Telework paradoxes and practices: the importance of the nature of work. *New Technology, Work and Employment*, 31(2), 114–31.

Bolton, S.C. and Houlihan, M. (2009). Are we having fun yet? A consideration of workplace fun and engagement. *Employee Relations*, 31(6), 556–68.

Bommer, W., Johnson, J., Rich, G., Podsakoff, P. and MacKenzie, S. (1995). On the interchangeability of objective and subjective measures of employee performance: a meta-analysis. *Personnel Psychology*, 48(3), 587–605.

Bond, F.W. and Flaxman, P.E. (2006). The ability of psychological flexibility and job control to predict learning, job performance, and mental health. *Journal of Organisational Behaviour Management*, 26(1–2), 113–30.

Booth, J., Won Park, K. and Glomb, T. (2009). Employer-supported volunteering benefits: gift exchange among employers, employees, and volunteer organizations. *Human Resource Management*, 48(2), 227–49.

Borisuit, A., Linhart, F., Scartezzini, J.L. and Münch, M. (2015). Effects of realistic office daylighting and electric lighting conditions on visual comfort, alertness and mood. *Lighting Research & Technology*, 47(2), 192–209.

Bortolotti, L. and Antrobus, M. (2015). Costs and benefits of realism and optimism. *Current Opinion in Psychiatry*, 28(2), 194–8.

Boubekri, M., Cheung, I., Reid, K., Wang, C. and Zee, P. (2014). Impact of windows and daylight exposure on overall health and sleep quality of office workers: a case-control pilot study. *Journal of Clinical Sleep Medicine*, 10(6), 603–11.

Bouncken, R. and Reuschl, A. (2018). Co-working-spaces: how a phenomenon of the sharing economy builds a novel trend for the workplace and for entrepreneurship. *Review of Managerial Science*, 12(1), 317–34.

Bourdieu, P. (1984). *Distinction: A Social Critique of the Judgement of Taste*. London: Routledge & Kegan Paul.

Bourdieu, P. (1986). The forms of capital. In J. Richardson (ed.), *Handbook of Theory and Research for the Sociology of Education*. New York: Greenwood, 241–58.

Bowles, S. and Polanía-Reyes, S. (2012). Economic incentives and social preferences: substitutes or complements? *Journal of Economic Literature*, 50(2), 368–425.

Bowling, N.A., Beehr, T.A. and Swader, W.M. (2005). Giving and receiving social support at work: the roles of personality and reciprocity. *Journal of Vocational Behavior*, 67(3), 476–89.

Bowling, N.A., Eschleman, K.J. and Wang, Q. (2010). A meta-analytic examination of the relationship between job satisfaction and subjective well-being. *Journal of Occupational and Organizational Psychology*, 83(4), 915–34.

Boxall, P. and Macky, K. (2014). High-involvement work processes, work intensification and employee well-being. *Work, Employment & Society*, 28(6), 963–84.

Boyce, P.R., Veitch, J.A., Nesham, G.R., Myer, M. and Hunter, C. (2003). *Lighting Quality and Office Work: A Field Simulation Study*. Richmond, WA: Pacific Northwest National Laboratory.

Bozeman, B. and Feeney, M.K. (2007). Toward a useful theory of mentoring: a conceptual analysis and critique. *Administration & Society*, 39(6), 719–39.

Bradburn, N. (1969). *The Structure of Psychological Well-being*. Chicago, IL: Aldine.

Brand, J.L. (2008). Office ergonomics: a review of pertinent research and recent developments. *Reviews of Human Factors and Ergonomics*, 4(1), 245–82.

Brandt, L.P.A., Andersen, J.H., Lassen, C.F., Kryger, A., Overgaard, E. and Vilstrup, I. (2004). Neck and shoulder symptoms and disorders among Danish computer workers. *Scandinavian Journal of Work, Environment and Health*, 30(5), 399–409.

Brandth, B. and Kvande, E. (2009). Norway: the making of the Father's Quota. In S. Kamerman and P. Moss (eds), *The Politics of Parental Leave Policies: Children, Parenting, Gender and the Labour Market*, 191–206. Bristol: Policy Press.

Branine, M. (2004). Job sharing and equal opportunities under the new public management in local authorities. *International Journal of Public Sector Management*, 17(2), 136–52.

Brannen, J. (2005). Time and the negotiation of work–family boundaries: autonomy or illusion? *Time & Society*, 14(1), 113–31.

Braverman, H. (1974). *Labor and Monopoly Capital: The Degradation of Work in the Twentieth Century*. New York and London: Monthly Review Press.

Breagh, J.A. (1999). Further investigations of the work autonomy scales: two studies. *Journal of Business and Psychology*, 13(3), 357–73.

Brewster, C. and Holland, P. (2021). Redesigning work as a response to the global pandemic: possibilities and pitfalls. In D. Wheatley, S. Buglass and I. Hardill (eds), *Handbook of Research on Remote Work and Worker Well-being in the Post-COVID-19 Era*, 104–21. Hersey, PA: IGI Global.

Brierley, M.L., Chater, A.M., Smith, L.R. and Bailey, D.P. (2019). The effectiveness of sedentary behaviour reduction workplace interventions on cardiometabolic risk markers: a systematic review. *Sports Medicine*, 49, 1739–67.

Briscoe, J., Hall, D. and Frautschy DeMuth, R. (2006). Protean and boundaryless careers: an empirical exploration. *Journal of Vocational Behavior*, 69(1), 30–47.

Broadbent, D. (1971). *Decision and Stress*. New York: Academic Press.

Brown, A., Charlwood, A. and Spencer, D. (2012). Not all that it might seem: why job satisfaction is worth studying despite it being a poor summary measure of job quality. *Work Employment & Society*, 26, 1007–18.

Brown, G. (2009). Claiming a corner at work: measuring employee territoriality in their workspaces. *Journal of Environmental Psychology*, 29(1), 44–52.

Brown, G., Lawrence, T. and Robinson, S. (2005). Territoriality in organizations. *Academy of Management Review*, 30(3), 577–94.

Brown, G. and Zhu, H. (2016). 'My workspace, not yours': the impact of psychological ownership and territoriality in organizations. *Journal of Environmental Psychology*, 48(1), 54–64.

Brown, K.W., Ryan, R.M. and Creswell, D.J. (2007). Mindfulness: theoretical foundations and evidence for its salutary effects. *Psychological Inquiry*, 18(4), 211–37.

Brown, M. (2012). Responses to work intensification: does generation matter? *The International Journal of Human Resource Management*, 23(17), 3578–95.

Brown, S. (1996). A meta-analysis and review of organizational research on job involvement. *Psychological Bulletin*, 120(2), 235–55.

Bruk-Lee, V., Nixon, A.E. and Spector, P.E. (2013). An expanded typology of conflict at work: task, relationship and non-task organizational conflict as social stressors. *Work & Stress*, 27(4), 339–50.

Brunetto, Y., Teo, S., Shacklock, K. and Farr-Wharton, R. (2012). Emotional intelligence, job satisfaction, well-being and engagement: explaining organisational commitment and turnover intentions in policing. *Human Resource Management Journal*, 22(4), 428–41.

Bryson, A., Forth, J. and Stokes, L. (2014). *Does Worker Wellbeing Affect Workplace Performance?* Department for Business, Innovation and Skills. Available at: https://assets.publishing.service.gov.uk/government/uploads/system/uploads/attachment_data/file/366637/bis-14-1120-does-worker-wellbeing-affect-workplace-performance-final.pdf.

Bryson, A. and MacKerron, G. (2016). Are you happy while you work? *The Economic Journal*, 127(599), 106–25.

Buglass, S., Binder, J., Betts, L. and Underwood, J. (2017). Motivators of online vulnerability: the impact of social network site use and FOMO. *Computers in Human Behavior*, 66(1), 248–55.

Bulger, C., Matthews, R. and Hoffman, M. (2007). Work and personal life boundary management: boundary strength, work/personal life balance, and the segmentation - integration continuum. *Journal of Occupational Health Psychology*, 12(4), 365–75.

Burchell, B. (2002). The prevalence and redistribution of job insecurity and work intensification. In B. Burchell, D. Ladipo and F. Wilkinson (eds), *The Prevalence and Redistribution of Job Insecurity and Work Intensification: Job Insecurity and Work Intensification*, 61–76. London: Routledge.

Burke, R.J., Singh, P. and Fiksenbaum, L. (2010). Work intensity: potential antecedents and consequences. *Personnel Review*, 39(3), 347–60.

Burke, S., Carron, A.V., Eys, M.A., Ntoumanis, N. and Estabrooks, P.A. (2006). Group versus individual approach? A meta-analysis of the effectiveness of interventions to promote physical activity. *International Review of Sport and Exercise Psychology*, 2(1), 1–39.

Butler, J. and Kern, M.L. (2016). The PERMA-Profiler: a brief multidimensional measure of flourishing. *International Journal of Wellbeing*, 6(3), 1–48.

Cabrera, E. (2007). Opting out and opting in: understanding the complexities of women's career transitions. *Career Development International*, 12(3), 218–37.

Caesens, G., Gillet, N., Morin, A., Houle, S. and Stinglhamber, F. (2020). A person-centred perspective on social support in the workplace. *Applied Psychology: An International Review*, 69(3), 686–714.

Caillier, J. (2012). The impact of teleworking on work motivation in a U.S. federal government agency. *American Review of Public Administration*, 42(4), 461–80.

Callaghan, G. and Thompson, P. (2001). Edwards revisited: technical control and call centres. *Economic and Industrial Democracy*, 22(1), 13–37.

Campione, W.A. (2016). Volunteer work experience: can it help millennials to find meaning and interest in their work and to negotiate their role within the workplace? *Journal of Leadership, Accountability and Ethics*, 13(3), 11–27.

Cant, C. (2019). *Working for Deliveroo, Resistance in the New Economy*. Cambridge: Polity.

Caplan, R.D., Cobb, S., French Jr, J.R.P., Van Harrison, R.V. and Pinneau, Jr, S.R. (1975). *Job Demands and Worker Health: Main Effects and Occupational Differences*. Washington, DC: U.S. Department of Health, Education, and Welfare.

Carlson, D.S., Hunter, E.M., Ferguson, M. and Whitten, D. (2014). Work–family enrichment and satisfaction: mediating processes and relative impact of originating and receiving domains. *Journal of Management*, 40(3), 845–65.

Carmichael, F., Hulme, C., Sheppard, S. and Connell, G. (2008). Work–life imbalance: informal care and paid employment in the UK. *Feminist Economics*, 14(2), 3–35.

Carney, D.R., Cuddy, A.J.C. and Yap, A.J. (2010). Power posing: brief nonverbal displays affect neuroendocrine levels and risk tolerance. *Psychological Science*, 21(10), 1363–8.

Celis-Morales, C., Lyall, D., Welsh, P., Anderson, J., Steel, L., Guo, Y., Maldonado, R., Mackay, D., Pell, J., Sattar, N. and Gill, J. (2017). Association between active commuting and incident cardiovascular disease, cancer, and mortality: prospective cohort study. *BMJ*, 357, j1456.

Center for Active Design (2021). *Active Design Guidelines* [online]. Available at: https://centerforactivedesign.org/guidelines/.

Cha, Y. (2010). Reinforcing separate spheres: the effect of spousal overwork on men's and women's employment in dual-earner households. *American Sociological Review*, 75(2), 303–29.

Cha, Y. and Weeden, K. (2014). Overwork and the slow convergence in the gender gap in wages. *American Sociological Review*, 79(3), 457–84.

Chandola, T. and Zhang, N. (2018). Re-employment, job quality, health and allostatic load biomarkers: prospective evidence from the UK Household Longitudinal Study. *Journal of Epidemiology*, 47(1), 47–57.

Chang, A., McDonald, P. and Burton, P. (2010). Methodological choices in work–life balance research 1987 to 2006: a critical review. *The International Journal of Human Resource Management*, 21(13), 2381–413.

Chari, R., Chang, C.C., Sauter, S.L., Petrun Sayers, E.L., Cerully, J.L., Schulte, P., Schill, A.L. and Uscher-Pines, L. (2018). Expanding the paradigm of occupational safety and health: a new framework for worker well-being. *Journal of Occupational and Environmental Medicine*, 60(7), 589–93.

Chau, J.Y., van der Ploeg, H.P., Dunn, S., Kurko, J. and Bauman, A.E. (2012). Validity of the occupational sitting and physical activity questionnaire. *Medicine and Science in Sports and Exercise*, 44(1), 118–25.

Chaudhuri, S. and Ghosh, R. (2012). Reverse mentoring: a social exchange tool for keeping the boomers engaged and millennials committed. *Human Resource Development Review*, 11(1), 55–76.

Cheng, T., Mauno, S. and Lee, C. (2014). Do job control, support, and optimism help job insecure employees? A three-wave study of buffering effects on job satisfaction, vigor and work–family enrichment. *Social Indicators Research*, 18, 1269–91.

Chiaburu, D.S. and Harrison, D.A. (2008). Do peers make the place? Conceptual synthesis and meta-analysis of co-worker effects on perceptions, attitudes, OCBs and performance. *Journal of Applied Psychology*, 93(5), 1082–103.

Choi, S., Leiter, J. and Tomaskovic-Devey, D. (2008). Contingent autonomy technology, bureaucracy, and relative power in the labor process. *Work and Occupations*, 35(4), 422–55.

Chompookum, D. and Derr, C. (2004). The effects of internal career orientations on organizational citizenship behavior in Thailand. *Career Development International*, 9(4), 406–23.

Christensen, R., Nesbit, R. and Stritch, J. (2018). The role of employees' public service motives and organizational commitment in workplace giving campaigns. *American Review of Public Administration*, 48(7), 644–58.

Chu, A.H.Y., Ng, S.H.X., Tan, C.S., Win, A.M., Koh, D. and Müller-Riemenschneider, F. (2016). A systematic review and meta-analysis of workplace intervention strategies to reduce sedentary time in white-collar workers. *Obesity Reviews*, 17(5), 467–81.

Chun, J.U., Sosik, J.J. and Yun, N.Y. (2012). A longitudinal study of mentor and protégé outcomes in formal mentoring relationships. *Journal of Organizational Behavior*, 33(8), 1071–94.

Cincinelli, A. and Martellini, T. (2017). Indoor air quality and health. *International Journal of Environmental Research and Public Health*, 14(11), 1286.

CIPD [Chartered Institute of Personnel and Development] (2011). *Developing Resilience: An Evidence-Based Guide for Practitioners*. London: Chartered Institute of Personnel and Development. Available at: https://www.cipd.co.uk/Images/developing-resilience_2011-evidence-based_tcm18-10079.pdf.

CIPD [Chartered Institute of Personnel and Development] (2019). *Flexible Working Taskforce* [online]. Available at: https://www.cipd.co.uk/about/media/press/flexible-working-taskforce.

Clark, A.E., Frijters, P. and Shields, M.A. (2008). Relative income, happiness, and utility: an explanation for the Easterlin paradox and other puzzles. *Journal of Economic Literature*, 46(1), 95–144.

Clark, I., Lawton, C., Stevenson, C., Vickers, T. and Dahill, D. (2020). A 'place based' approach to work and employment: the end of reciprocity, ordinary working families and 'giggers' in a place. *Economic and Industrial Democracy*. https://doi.org/10.1177/0143831X20946374.

Clark, S.C. (2000). Work/family border theory: a new theory of work/family balance. *Human Relations*, 53(6), 747–70.

Clausen, G. and Wyon, D. (2008). The combined effects of many different indoor environmental factors on acceptability and office work performance. *HVAC&R Research*, 14(1), 103–13.

Clear, F. and Dickson, K. (2005). Teleworking practice in small and medium-sized firms: management style and worker autonomy. *New Technology, Work and Employment*, 20(3), 218–33.

Clutterbuck, D. (2003). *Managing Work–life Balance: A Guide for HR in Achieving Organisational and Individual Change*. London: CIPD.

288 *Well-being and the quality of working lives*

Coats, D. and Lekhi, R. (2008). *'Good Work': Job Quality in a Changing Economy*. London: The Work Foundation. Available at: http://www.employabilityinscotland .com/media/82671/good-work-job-quality-in-a-changing-economy.pdf.

Cobb, J. and Daly, H. (1989). *For the Common Good: Redirecting the Economy toward Community, the Environment and a Sustainable Future*. Boston, MA: Beacon Press.

Cockshaw, W.D. and Shochet, I.M. (2010). The link between belongingness and depressive symptoms: an exploration in the workplace interpersonal context. *Australian Psychologist*, 45(4), 283–9.

Cockshaw, W.D., Shochet, I.M. and Obst, P.L. (2014). Depression and belonging-ness in general and workplace contexts: a cross-lagged longitudinal investigation. *Journal of Social and Clinical Psychology*, 33(5), 448–62.

Coleman, J. (1988). Social capital in the creation of human capital. *American Journal of Sociology*, 94, Supplement: Organizations and Institutions: Sociological and Economic Approaches to the Analysis of Social Structure, S95–S120.

Coleman, J.S. (1990). *The Foundations of Social Theory*. Cambridge, MA: Harvard University Press.

Coles-Brennan, C., Sulley, A. and Young, G. (2019). Management of digital eye strain. *Clinical and Experimental Optometry*, 102(1), 18–29.

Collins, A., Hislop, D. and Cartwright, S. (2016). Social support in the workplace between teleworkers, office-based colleagues and supervisors. *New Technology, Work and Employment*, 31(2), 161–75.

Combs, G.M. and Milosevic, I. (2016). Workplace discrimination and the wellbeing of minority women: overview, prospects, and implications. In M.L. Connerley and J. Wu (eds), *Handbook on Well-being of Working Women*, 17–31. Dordrecht: Springer.

Comte, A. (1966 [1851]). *System of Positive Polity, Volume 1: Containing the General View of Positivism and Introductory Principles*. New York: Burt Franklin.

Connell, J. and Burgess, J. (2016). Strategic HRM and its influence on quality of work: evidence from nine Australian organisations in HRM and Organisational Effectiveness. In A. Nankervis, C. Rowley and N.M. Salleh (eds), *Asia Pacific Human Resource Management and Organisational Effectiveness*, 171–92. Amsterdam: Elsevier.

Cooke, G.B., Chowhanand, J. and Brown, T. (2011). Declining versus participating in employer-supported training in Canada. *International Journal of Training and Development*, 15(4), 271–89.

Cornwell, B. and Warburton, E. (2014). Work schedules and community ties. *Work and Occupations*, 41(2), 139–74.

Coyne, J.C. (1976). Towards an interactional description of depression. *Psychiatry*, 39(1), 28–40.

Crawford, E.R., LePine, J.A. and Rich, B.L. (2010). Linking job demands and resources to employee engagement and burnout: a theoretical extension and meta-analytic test. *Journal of Applied Psychology*, 95(5), 834–48.

Crimman, A., Wiener, F. and Bellman, L. (2010). *The German Work-Sharing Scheme: An Instrument for the Crisis*. International Labour Organization, Conditions of Work and Employment Series No. 25. Available at: https://www.ilo.org/wcmsp5/groups/ public/---ed_protect/---protrav/---travail/documents/publication/wcms_145335.pdf.

Crompton, R. and Lyonette, C. (2011). Women's career success and work–life adap-tations in the accountancy and medical professions in Britain. *Gender, Work and Organization*, 18(2), 231–54.

Cropanzano, R., Anthony, E.L., Daniels, S.R. and Hall, A.V. (2017). Social exchange theory: a critical review with theoretical remedies. *Academy of Management Annals*, 11(1), 1–38.

Cropanzano, R. and Mitchell, M.S. (2005). Social exchange theory: an interdisciplinary review. *Journal of Management*, 31(6), 874–900.

Cui, W., Cao, G., Park, J.H., Ouyang, Q. and Zhu, Y. (2013). Influence of indoor air temperature on human thermal comfort, motivation and performance. *Building and Environment*, 68, 114–22.

Dagenais-Desmarais, V., Leclerc, J.-S. and Londei-Shortall, J. (2018). The relationship between employee motivation and psychological health at work: a chicken-and-egg situation? *Work & Stress*, 32(2), 147–67.

Dagenais-Desmarais, V. and Savoie, A. (2012). What is psychological well-being, really? A grassroots approach from the organizational sciences. *Journal of Happiness Studies*, 13(4), 659–84.

Dansereau, F., Graen, G. and Haga, W.J. (1975). A vertical dyad linkage approach to leadership within formal organizations: a longitudinal investigation of the role making process. *Organizational Behavior and Human Performance*, 13(1), 46–78.

Day, L. and Clements, L. (2019). *Personal Well-being in the UK: April 2018 to March 2019*. Office for National Statistics, Statistical Bulletin.

DCMS [Department for Culture, Media and Sport] (2019). *Community Life Survey, 2018–2019* [data collection]. UK Data Service. SN: 8584. http://doi.org/10.5255/UKDA-SN-8584-1.

de Bustillo, R.M., Fernández-Macías, E., Esteve, F. and Antón, J.-I. (2011). *E pluribus unum*? A critical survey of job quality indicators. *Socio-Economic Review*, 9(3), 447–75.

de Croon, E., Sluiter, J., Kuijer, P. and Frings-Dresen, M. (2005). The effect of office concepts on worker health and performance: a systematic review of the literature. *Ergonomics*, 48(2), 119–34.

De Jong Gierveld, J. and van Tilburg, T. (2006). A 6-item scale for overall, emotional, and social loneliness: confirmatory tests on survey data. *Research on Aging*, 28(5), 582–98.

de Kort, Y. and Smolders, K. (2010). Effects of dynamic lighting on office workers: first results of a field study with monthly alternating settings. *Lighting Research & Technology*, 42(3), 345–60.

De Stefano, V. (2016). The rise of the just-in-time workforce: on-demand work, crowd-work, and labor protection in the gig-economy. *Comparative Labor Law & Policy*, 37, 471–504.

De Stefano, V. and Aloisi, A. (2019). Fundamental labour rights, platform work and human rights protection of non-standard workers. In J.R. Bellace and B. ter Haar (eds), *Research Handbook on Labour, Business and Human Rights Law*, 359–79. Cheltenham, UK, and Northampton, MA, USA: Edward Elgar Publishing.

De Wit, F.R.C., Greer, L.L. and Jehn, K.A. (2012). The paradox of intragroup conflict: a meta-analysis. *Journal of Applied Psychology*, 97(2), 360–90.

Deakin, S. and Morris, G. (2012). *Labour Law*, 6th edn. Oxford: Hart.

Deci, E.L. and Ryan, R.M. (2000). The 'what' and 'why' of goal pursuits: human needs and the self-determination of behavior. *Psychological Inquiry*, 11(4), 227–68.

Deci, E.L., Ryan, R.M., Gagné, M., Leone, D.R., Usunov, J. and Kornazheva, B.P. (2001). Need satisfaction, motivation, and well-being in the work organizations of a former eastern bloc country: a cross-cultural study of self-determination. *Personality and Social Psychology Bulletin*, 27(8), 930–42.

Deelstra, J., Peeters, M., Schaufeli, W., Stroebe, W., Zijlstra, F. and van Doornen, L. (2003). Receiving instrumental support at work: when help is not welcome. *Journal of Applied Psychology*, 88(2), 324–31.

Deery, J., Walsh, J. and Guest, D. (2011). Workplace aggression: the effects of harassment on job burnout and turnover intentions. *Work, Employment and Society*, 25(4), 742–59.

Defillippi, R. and Arthur, M. (1994). The boundaryless career: a competency-based perspective. *Journal of Organisational Behaviour*, 15(4), 307–24.

Delanoeije, J., Verbruggen, M. and Germeys, L. (2020). Boundary role transitions: a day-to-day approach to explain the effects of home-based telework on work-to-home conflict and home-to-work conflict. *Human Relations*, 72(12), 1843–68.

Demel, B. and Mayrhofer, W. (2010). Frequent business travelers across Europe: career aspirations and implications. *Thunderbird International Business Review*, 52(4), 301–11.

Demerouti, E., Mostert, K. and Bakker, A. (2010). Burnout and work engagement: a thorough investigation of the independency of both constructs. *Journal of Occupational Health Psychology*, 15(3), 209–22.

Department for Transport (2017). *Transport Statistics: Great Britain 2018* [online]. Crown Copyright. Available at: https://assets.publishing.service.gov.uk/government/uploads/system/uploads/attachment_data/file/787488/tsgb-2018-report-summaries .pdf.

Devonish, D. (2018). Effort–reward imbalance at work: the role of job satisfaction. *Personnel Review*, 47(2), 319–33.

Di Blasio, S., Shtrepi, L., Puglisi, G.E. and Astolfi, A. (2019). A cross-sectional survey on the impact of irrelevant speech noise on annoyance, mental health and well-being, performance and occupants' behavior in shared and open-plan offices. *International Journal of Environmental Research and Public Health*, 16(2), 280.

Diaz, K.M., Duran, A.T., Colabianchi, N., Judd, S.E., Howard, V.J. and Hooker, S.P. (2019). Potential effects on mortality of replacing sedentary time with short sedentary bouts or physical activity: a national cohort study. *American Journal of Epidemiology*, 188(3), 537–44.

Dickmann, M. and Baruch, Y. (2011). *Global Careers*. Abingdon: Routledge.

Dickmann, M. and Doherty, N. (2008). Exploring the career capital impact of international assignments within distinct organisational contexts. *British Journal of Management*, 19(2), 145–61.

Diener, E. (2013). The remarkable changes in the science of subjective well-being. *Perspectives on Psychological Science*, 8(6), 663–6.

Diener, E., Emmons, R.A., Larsen, R.J. and Griffin, S. (1985). The satisfaction with life scale. *Journal of Personality Assessment*, 49(1), 71–5.

Diener, E., Suh, E.M., Lucas, R.E. and Smith, H.L. (1999). Subjective well-being: three decades of progress. *Psychological Review*, 125(2), 276–302.

Diener, E. and Tay, L. (2015). Subjective well-being and human welfare around the world as reflected in the Gallup World Poll. *International Journal of Psychology*, 50(2), 135–49.

Dikkers, J., van Engen, M. and Vinkenburg, C. (2010). Flexible work: ambitious parents' recipe for career success in the Netherlands. *Career Development International*, 15(6), 562–82.

Ding, D., Lawson, K.D., Kolbe-Alexander, T.L., Finkelstein, E.A., Katzmarzyk, P.T., van Mechelen, W. and Pratt, M. (2016). The economic burden of physical inactivity: a global analysis of major non-communicable diseases. *The Lancet*, 388, 1311–24.

Dinu, M., Pagliai, G., Macchi, C. and Sofi, F. (2019). Active commuting and multiple health outcomes: a systematic review and meta-analysis. *Sports Medicine*, 49, 437–52.

Dodge, R., Daly, A., Huyton, J. and Sanders, L. (2012). The challenge of defining wellbeing. *International Journal of Wellbeing*, 2(3), 222–35.

Dolan, P., Peasgood, T. and White, M. (2006). *Review of Research on the Influences on Personal Well-being and Application to Policy Making*. London: Defra. Available at: http://randd.defra.gov.uk/Document.aspx?Document=SD12005_4017_FRP.pdf.

Dolan, P., Peasgood, T. and White, M. (2008). Do we really know what makes us happy? A review of the economic literature on the factors associated with subjective wellbeing. *Journal of Economic Psychology*, 29(1), 94–122.

Dollard, M. and Bakker, A. (2010). Psychosocial safety climate as a precursor to conducive work environments, psychological health problems, and employee engagement. *Journal of Occupational and Organizational Psychology*, 83(3), 579–99.

Dougherty, D. (2012). The maker movement. *Innovations*, 7(3), 11–14.

Downward, P. and Dawson, P. (2016). Is it pleasure or health from leisure that we benefit from most? An analysis of well-being alternatives and implications for policy. *Social Indicators Research*, 126(1), 443–65.

Downward, P. and Rasciute, S. (2011). Does sport make you happy? An analysis of the well-being derived from sports participation. *International Review of Applied Economics*, 25(3), 331–48.

Drinkwater, S. (2015). Informal caring and labour markets outcomes within England and Wales. *Regional Studies*, 49(2), 273–86.

Ducharme, L. and Martin, J. (2000). Unrewarding work, coworker support, and job satisfaction: a test of the buffering hypothesis. *Work and Occupations*, 27(2), 223–43.

Durbin, S. and Tomlinson, J. (2010). Female part-time managers: networks and career mobility. *Work, Employment & Society*, 24(4), 621–40.

Dye, R.A. (1984). The trouble with tournaments. *Economic Inquiry*, 22(1), 14–49.

Dye, R.A. (1992). Relative performance evaluation and project selection. *Journal of Accounting Research*, 30(1), 27–52.

Easterlin, R. (1974). Does economic growth improve the human lot? Some empirical evidence. In P. David and M. Reder (eds), *Nations and Households in Economic Growth*, 89–126. New York: Academic Press.

Easterlin, R.A. (2001). Income and happiness: towards a unified theory. *The Economic Journal*, 111(473), 465–84.

Ebbinghaus, B., Göbel, C. and Koos, S. (2011). Social capital, 'Ghent' and workplace contexts matter: comparing union membership in Europe. *European Journal of Industrial Relations*, 17(2), 107–24.

Edgell, S. (2012). *The Sociology of Work: Continuity and Change in Paid and Unpaid Work*. London: Sage.

Edmondson, A.C. (1999). Psychological safety and learning behavior in work teams. *Administrative Science Quarterly*, 44(2), 350–83.

Edmondson, A.C. and Lei, Z. (2014). Psychological safety: the history, renaissance, and future of an interpersonal construct. *Annual Review of Organizational Psychology and Organizational Behavior*, 1, 23–43.

Egan, S.J., Wade, T.D. and Shafran, R. (2011). Perfectionism as a transdiagnostic process: a clinical review. *Clinical Psychology Review*, 31(2), 203–12.

Ehrenreich, B. (2001). *Nickle & Dimed: Undercover in Low Wage USA*. London: Granta.

Einarsen, S. and Mikkelsen, E.G. (2003). Individual effects of exposure to bullying at work. In S. Einarsen, H. Hoel, D. Zapf and C.L. Cooper (eds), *Bullying and Emotional Abuse in the Workplace: International Perspectives in Research and Practice*, 127–44. London: Taylor and Francis.

Eisenberger, R. and Stinglhamber, F. (2011). *Perceived Organizational Support: Fostering Enthusiastic and Productive Employees*. Washington, DC: APA Books.

Eisenberger, R., Stinglhamber, F., Vandenberghe, C., Sucharski, I. and Rhoades, L. (2002). Perceived supervisor support: contributions to perceived organizational support and employee retention. *Journal of Applied Psychology*, 87(3), 565–73.

Elsbach, K.D. and Pratt, M.G. (2007). The physical environment in organizations. *The Academy of Management Annals*, 1, 181–224.

Emerson, R.M. (1976). Social exchange theory. *Annual Review of Sociology*, 2, 335–62.

Employment Rights Act (1996). Section 230: employees, workers, etc. [online]. Available at: https://www.legislation.gov.uk/ukpga/1996/18/section/230.

Engelbrecht, A., Heine, G. and Mahembe, B. (2017). Integrity, ethical leadership, trust and work engagement. *Leadership & Organization Development Journal*, 38(3), 368–79.

Engelen, E. (2020). Does active design influence activity, sitting, wellbeing and productivity in the workplace? A systematic review. *International Journal of Environmental Research and Public Health*, 17(24), 9228.

Erikson, E.H. (1959). Identity and the life cycle: selected papers. *Psychological Issues*, 1, 1–171.

ESS Round 3: European Social Survey Round 3 Data (2006). Data file edition 3.7. NSD – Norwegian Centre for Research Data, Norway – Data Archive and distributor of ESS data for ESS ERIC. http://dx.doi.org/10.21338/NSD-ESS3-2006.

ESS Round 5: European Social Survey Round 5 Data (2010). Data file edition 3.4. NSD – Norwegian Centre for Research Data, Norway – Data Archive and distributor of ESS data for ESS ERIC. http://dx.doi.org/10.21338/NSD-ESS5-2010.

ESS Round 6: European Social Survey Round 6 Data (2012). Data file edition 2.4. NSD – Norwegian Centre for Research Data, Norway – Data Archive and distributor of ESS data for ESS ERIC. http://dx.doi.org/10.21338/NSD-ESS6-2012.

ESS Round 9: European Social Survey Round 9 Data (2018). Data file edition 3.1. NSD – Norwegian Centre for Research Data, Norway – Data Archive and distributor of ESS data for ESS ERIC. http://dx.doi.org/10.21338/NSD-ESS9-2018.

Eurofound [European Foundation for the Improvement of Living and Working Conditions] (2012). *Trends in Job Quality in Europe: 5th European Working Conditions Survey*. Luxembourg: Publications Office of the European Union. Available at: https://www.eurofound.europa.eu/sites/default/files/ef_publication/field_ef_document/ef1228en_0.pdf.

Eurofound [European Foundation for the Improvement of Living and Working Conditions] (2013a). *Employment Polarisation and Job Quality in the Crisis: European Jobs Monitor 2013*. Dublin: Eurofound.

Eurofound [European Foundation for the Improvement of Living and Working Conditions] (2013b). *Quality of Employment Conditions and Employment Relations in Europe*. Dublin: Eurofound. Available at: https://www.eurofound.europa.eu/publications/report/2013/working-conditions/quality-of-employment-conditions-and-employment-relations-in-europe.

References

Eurofound [European Foundation for the Improvement of Living and Working Conditions] (2020). *Working During COVID-19* [online]. Available at: https://www.eurofound.europa.eu/data/COVID-19/working-teleworking.

European Commission (2005). *Working Time Directive* [online]. Available at: http://www.cec.org.uk/info/pubs/bbriefs/bb28.htm.

European Social Survey (2015). *Measuring and Reporting on Europeans' Wellbeing: Findings from the European Social Survey*. London: ESS ERIC.

Eustace, E. (2012). Speaking allowed? Workplace regulation of regional dialect. *Work, Employment & Society*, 26(2), 331–48.

Evans, C., Evans, G. and Mayo, L. (2017). Charitable giving as a luxury good and the philanthropic sphere of influence. *Voluntas*, 28(2), 556–70.

Fagan, C., Lyonette, C., Smith, M. and Saldaña-Tejeda, A. (2012). *The Influence of Working Time Arrangements on Work–Life Integration or 'Balance': A Review of the International Evidence*. Conditions of Work and Employment No. 32: International Labour Organization.

Faragher, E.B., Cooper, C.L. and Cartwright, S. (2004). A shortened stress evaluation tool (ASSET). *Stress and Health*, 20, 189–201.

Fassoulis, K. and Alexopoulos, N. (2015). The workplace as a factor of job satisfaction and productivity: a case study of administrative personnel at the University of Athens. *Journal of Facilities Management*, 13(4), 332–49.

Fayard, A.L. and Weeks, J. (2007). Photocopiers and water-coolers: the affordances of informal interaction. *Organization Studies*, 28(5), 605–34.

Fehr, E. and Gächter, S. (2000). Fairness and retaliation: the economics of reciprocity. *The Journal of Economic Perspectives*, 14(3), 159–81.

Feldman, F. (2002). The good life: a defence of attitudinal hedonism. *Philosophy and Phenomenological Research*, 65(3), 604–28.

Feldt ,T., Hyvönen, K., Mäkikangas, A., Rantanen, J., Huhtala, M. and Kinnunen, U. (2016). Overcommitment as a predictor of effort–reward imbalance: evidence from an 8-year follow-up study. *Scandinavian Journal of Work and Environmental Health*, 42(4), 309–19.

Felstead, A., Gallie, D., Green, F. and Henseke, G. (2019). Conceiving, designing and trailing a short form measure of job quality: a proof-of-concept study. *Industrial Relations Journal*, 50(1), 2–19.

Felstead, A., Gallie, D., Green, F. and Zhou, Y. (2007). *Skills at Work 1986 to 2006*. ESRC Centre for Skills, Knowledge and Organisational Performance.

Felstead, A. and Green, F. (2017). Working longer and harder? A critical assessment of work effort in Britain in comparison to Europe. In D. Grimshaw, C. Fagan, G. Hebson and I. Tavor (eds), *Making Work More Equal: A New Labour Market Segmentation Approach*, chapter 10. Manchester: Manchester University Press.

Felstead, A., Green, F. and Jewson, N. (2012). An analysis of the impact of the 2008–9 recession on the provision of training in the UK. *Work, Employment and Society*, 26(6), 968–86.

Felstead, A. and Henseke, G. (2017). Assessing the growth of remote working and its consequences for effort, well-being and work–life balance. *New Technology, Work and Employment*, 32(3), 195–212.

Fenwick, T. (2006). Contradictions in portfolio careers: work design and client relations. *Career Development International*, 11(1), 65–79.

Fenwick, T. (2012). Negotiating networks of self-employed work: strategies of minority ethnic contractors. *Urban Studies*, 49(3), 595–612.

Fielding, A. (1999). Why use arbitrary points scores? Ordered categories in models of educational progress. *Journal of the Royal Statistical Society: Series A (Statistics in Society)*, 162(3), 303–28.

Fielding, S.L. (1990). Physician reactions to malpractice suits and cost containment in Massachusetts. *Work and Occupations*, 17(3), 302–19.

Fields, J.M., De Jong, R.G., Gjestland, T., Flindell, I.H., Job, R.F.S., Kurra, S., Lercher, P., Vellet, M., Yano, T., Guski, R., Felscher-Suhr, U. and Schumer, R. (2001). Standardized general-purpose noise reaction questions for community noise surveys: research and a recommendation. *Journal of Sound and Vibration*, 242(4), 641–79.

Figart, D. (2001). Wage-setting under Fordism: the rise of job evaluation and the ideology of equal pay. *Review of Political Economy*, 13(4), 405–25.

Figart, D. and Golden, L. (1998). The social economics of work time: introduction. *Review of Social Economy*, 56(4), 411–24.

Financial Times (2011). Case study: Walmart [online]. Available at: http://www.ft .com/cms/s/0/b28b8dcc-5580-11e0-a2b1-00144feab49a.html#axzz1loB4G0Ea.

Findlay, P., Warhurst, C., Keep, E. and Lloyd, C. (2017). Opportunity knocks? The possibilities and levers for improving job quality. *Work and Occupations*, 44(1), 3–22.

Fleisher, C., Khapova, S. and Jansen, P. (2014). Effects of employees' career competencies development on their organizations. *Career Development International*, 19(6), 700–17.

Flett, G.L. and Hewitt, P.L. (2002). *Perfectionism: Theory, Research, and Treatment*. Washington, DC: American Psychological Association.

Flynn, F.J. and Brockner, J. (2003). It's different to give than to receive: predictors of givers' and receivers' reactions to favor exchange. *Journal of Applied Psychology*, 88(6), 1034–45.

Folbre, N. (2012). Should women care less? Intrinsic motivation and gender inequality. *British Journal of Industrial Relations*, 50(4), 597–619.

Fong, C.M. (2007). Evidence from an experiment on charity to welfare recipients: reciprocity, altruism, and the empathic responsiveness hypothesis. *The Economic Journal*, 117(522), 1008–24.

Fortin, N., Bell, B. and Böhm, M. (2017). Top earnings inequality and the gender pay gap: Canada, Sweden, and the United Kingdom. *Labour Economics*, 47, 107–23.

Foster, D. (2007). Legal obligation or personal lottery? Employee experiences of disability and the negotiation of adjustments in the public sector workplace. *Work, Employment & Society*, 21(1), 67–84.

Fouché, C. and Lunt, N. (2010). Nested mentoring relationships: reflections on a practice project for mentoring research capacity amongst social work practitioners. *Journal of Social Work*, 10(4), 391–406.

Friedman, G. (2014). Workers without employers: shadow corporations and the rise of the gig economy. *Review of Keynesian Economics*, 4(1), 171–88.

Fuzi, A. (2015). Co-working spaces for promoting entrepreneurship in sparse regions: the case of South Wales. *Regional Studies, Regional Science*, 2(1), 461–8.

Gable, S. and Haidt, J. (2005). What (and why) is positive psychology? *Review of General Psychology*, 9(2), 103–10.

Gallacher, S., O'Connor, J., Bird, J., Rogers, Y., Capra, L., Harrison, D. and Marshall, P. (2015). Mood squeezer: lightening up the workplace through playful and lightweight interactions. *Technologies in the Workplace*, 891–902. https:// research-information.bris.ac.uk/en/publications/mood-squeezer-lightening-up-the -workplace-through-playful-and-lig.

Galletta, M., Portoghese, I. and Battistelli, A. (2011). Intrinsic motivation, job autonomy and turnover intention in Italian healthcare: the mediating role of affective commitment. *Journal of Management Research*, 3(2), 1–19.

Gallie, D. (2007). *Employment Regimes and the Quality of Work*. Oxford: Oxford University Press.

Gallie, D., Felstead, A. and Green, F. (2012). Job preferences and the intrinsic quality of work: the changing attitudes of British employees, 1992–2006. *Work, Employment and Society*, 26(5), 806–21.

Gallie, D., Felstead, A., Green, F. and Inanc, H. (2014). The quality of work in Britain over the economic crisis. *International Review of Sociology*, 24(2), 207–24.

Galloway S., Bell, D., Hamilton, C. and Scullion, A. (2006). *Quality of Life and Wellbeing: Measuring the Benefits of Culture and Sport: Literature Review and Thinkpiece*. Edinburgh: Scottish Executive Education Department.

Garcia-Prieto, P., Bellard, E. and Schneider, S.C. (2003). Experiencing diversity, conflict, and emotions in teams. *Applied Psychology: An International Review*, 52(3), 413–40.

Garthwaite, K. (2016). *Hunger Pains: Inside Foodbank Britain*. Bristol: Policy Press.

Gibbs, C. (2020). *Coronavirus and the Latest Indicators for the UK Economy and Society: 16 July 2020* [online]. Available at: https://www.ons.gov.uk/peoplepop ulationandcommunity/healthandsocialcare/conditionsanddiseases/bulletins/ coronavirustheukeconomyandsocietyfasterindicators/16july2020.

Gifford, J. (2018). *UK Working Lives: The CIPD Job Quality Index Survey Report 2018*. London: Chartered Institute of Personnel and Development. Available at: https://www.cipd.co.uk/knowledge/work/trends/uk-working-lives.

Glaveli, N. and Karassavidou, E. (2011). Exploring a possible route through which training affects organizational performance: the case of a Greek bank. *International Journal of Human Resource Management*, 22(14), 2892–923.

Glavin, P. (2013). The impact of job insecurity and job degradation on the sense of personal control. *Work and Occupations*, 40(2), 115–42.

Glavin, P. and Schieman, S. (2012). Work–family role blurring and work–family conflict: the moderating influence of job resources and job demands. *Work and Occupations*, 39(1), 71–98.

Goldberg, D.P. (1972). *The Detection of Psychiatric Illness by Questionnaire*. New York: Oxford University Press.

Golden, L. (2009). Flexible daily work schedules in U.S. jobs: formal introductions needed? *Industrial Relations: A Journal of Economy and Society*, 48(1), 27–54.

Goodman, F., Disabato, D., Kashdan, T. and Kauffman, S. (2018). Measuring well-being: a comparison of subjective wellbeing and PERMA. *The Journal of Positive Psychology*, 13(4), 321–32.

Gov.uk (2015). *Equality Act 2010 Guidance* [online]. Available at: https://www.gov .uk/guidance/equality-act-2010-guidance#overview.

Graf, N., Brown, A. and Patten, E. (2019). *The Narrowing, But Persistent, Gender Gap in Pay* [online]. Pew Research Centre. Available at: https://www.pewresearch.org/ fact-tank/2019/03/22/gender-pay-gap-facts/.

Grant, A. (2012). Giving time, time after time: work design and sustained employee participation in corporate volunteering. *Academy of Management Review*, 37(4), 589–615.

Grant, A. and Dutton, J. (2012). Beneficiary or benefactor: are people more prosocial when they reflect on receiving or giving? *Psychological Science*, 23(9), 1033–9.

Green, A. (2017). Implications of technological change and austerity for employability in urban labour markets. *Urban Studies*, 54(7), 1638–54.

Green, A. and Riley, R. (2021). Implications for places of remote working. In D. Wheatley, I. Hardill and S. Buglass (eds), *Handbook of Research on Remote Work and Worker Well-being in the Post-COVID-19 Era*, 161–80. Hersey, PA: IGI Global.

Green, F. (2001). It's been a hard day's night: the concentration and intensification of work in late twentieth-century Britain. *British Journal of Industrial Relations*, 39(1), 53–80.

Green, F. (2004). Work intensification, discretion, and the decline in well-being at work. *Eastern Economic Journal*, 30(4), 615–25.

Green, F. (2006). *Demanding Work: The Paradox of Job Quality in the Affluent Society*. Princeton, NJ: Princeton University Press.

Green, F. (2008). Work effort and worker well-being in the age of affluence. In C. Cooper and R. Burke (eds), *The Long Work Hours Culture: Causes, Consequences and Choices*, 115–36. Bingley: Emerald.

Green, F. (2009). *Job Quality in Britain*. UK Commission for Education and Skills, November.

Green, F. (2011). Unpacking the misery multiplier: how employability modifies the impacts of unemployment and job insecurity on life satisfaction and mental health. *Journal of Health Economics*, 30(2), 265–76.

Green, F., Felstead, A. and Gallie, D. (2015). The inequality of job quality. In A. Felstead, D. Gallie and F. Green (eds), *Unequal Britain at Work*, chapter 1. Oxford: Oxford University Press.

Green, F., Felstead, A., Gallie, D. and Inanc, H. (2016a). Job-related well-being through the Great Recession. *Journal of Happiness Studies*, 17(1), 389–411.

Green, F., Felstead, A., Gallie, D., Inanc, H. and Jewson, N. (2016b). The declining volume of workers' training in Britain. *British Journal of Industrial Relations*, 54(2), 422–48.

Green, W.S. (2005). Introduction: altruism and the study of the religion. In J. Nuesner and B. Chilton (eds), *Altruism in World Religions*, 11–22. Washington, DC: Georgetown University Press.

Greenaway, K., Thai, H., Haslam, S. and Murphy, S. (2016). Spaces that signal identity improve workplace productivity. *Journal of Personnel Psychology*, 15(1), 35–43.

Greenhalgh, L. and Rosenblatt, Z. (1984). Job insecurity: toward conceptual clarity. *Academy of Management Review*, 9(3), 438–48.

Greenhaus, J.H., Callanan, G. and Godshalk, V. (2000). *Career Management*, 3rd edn. Mason, OH: Thomson-South-Western.

Greenhaus, J.H. and Kossek, E. (2014). The contemporary career: a work-home perspective. *Annual Review of Organizational Psychology and Organizational Behavior*, 1, 361–88.

Greenhaus, J.H. and Powell, G.N. (2006). When work and family are allies: a theory of work–family enrichment. *Academy of Management Review*, 31(1), 72–92.

Greenhaus, J.H., Ziegert, J.C. and Allen, T.D. (2012). When family-supportive supervision matters: relations between multiple sources of support and work–family balance. *Journal of Vocational Behavior*, 80(2), 266–75.

Gregory, A. and Milner, S. (2009). Trade unions and work–life balance: changing times in France and the UK? *British Journal of Industrial Relations*, 47(1), 122–46.

Gregory, K. (2020). 'My life is more valuable than this': understanding risk among on-demand food couriers in Edinburgh. *Work, Employment and Society*, 35(2), 316–31.

Gregory, M. and Connolly, S. (2008). Feature: the price of reconciliation: part-time work, families and women's satisfaction. *The Economic Journal*, 118(526), F1–F7.

Grieve, R., Indian, M., Witteveen, K., Tolan, G.A. and Marrington, J. (2013). Face-to-face or Facebook: can social connectedness be derived online? *Computers in Human Behavior*, 29(3), 604–9.

Grodal, S., Nelson, A. and Siino, R. (2015). Help-seeking and help-giving as an organizational routine: continual engagement in innovative work. *Academy of Management Journal*, 58(1), 136–68.

Grönlund, A. (2007). More control, less conflict? Job demand-control, gender and work–family conflict. *Gender, Work and Organization*, 14(5), 476–97.

Guardian (2019). 'Go back to work': outcry over deaths on Amazon's warehouse floor [online]. Available at: https://www..com/technology/2019/oct/17/amazon -warehouse-worker-deaths. theguardian.

Guest, D. (2002). Perspectives on the study of work–life balance. *Social Science Information*, 41(2), 255–79.

Gustafson, P. (2014). Business travel from the traveller's perspective: stress, stimulation and normalization. *Mobilities*, 9(1), 63–83.

Haapakangas, A., Hongisto, V., Eerola, M. and Kuusisto, T. (2017). Distraction distance and perceived disturbance by noise: an analysis of 21 open-plan offices. *The Journal of the Acoustical Society of America*, 141(1), 127–36.

Hackman, J.R. and Oldham, G.R. (1975). Development of the job diagnostic survey. *Journal of Applied Psychology*, 60(2), 159–70.

Hackman, J.R. and Oldham, G.R. (1976). Motivation through the design of work: test of a theory. *Organizational Behavior and Human Performance*, 16(2), 250–79.

Hadlaczky, G., Hökby, S., Mkrtchian, A., Carli, V. and Wasserman, D. (2014). Mental health first aid is an effective public health intervention for improving knowledge, attitudes, and behaviour: a meta-analysis. *International Review of Psychiatry*, 26(4), 467–75.

Halford, S. (2005). Hybrid workspace: re-spatialisations of work, organisation and management. *New Technology, Work and Employment*, 20(1), 19–33.

Hall, D. (1996). Protean careers of the 21st century. *Academy of Management Perspectives*, 10(4), 8–16.

Hall, D. (2004). The protean career: a quarter-century journey. *Journal of Vocational Behavior*, 65(1), 1–13.

Hall, D., Lee, M.D., Kossek, E.E. and Heras, M.L. (2012). Pursuing career success while sustaining personal and family well-being: a study of reduced-load professionals over time. *Journal of Social Issues*, 68(4), 742–66.

Hall, L. and Atkinson, C. (2006). Improving working lives: flexible working and the role of employee control. *Employee Relations*, 28(4), 374–86.

Hamilton, J. (2019). Cash or kudos: addressing the effort–reward imbalance for academic employees. *International Journal of Stress Management*, 26(2), 193–203.

Hammond, P. (1975). Charity: altruism or cooperative egoism? In S.P. Edmund (ed.), *Altruism, Morality, and Economic Theory*, 115–31. New York: Russell Sage.

Handel, M. (2005). Trends in perceived job quality, 1989 to 1998. *Work and Occupations*, 32(1), 66–94.

Hardill, I. (2012 paperback, 2002 hardback). *Gender, Migration and the Dual Career Household*. International Studies of Women and Place Series. London: Routledge.

Hardill, I. and Baines, S. (2011). *Enterprising Care? Unpaid Voluntary Action in the 21st Century*. Bristol: Policy Press.

Hardill, I. and Wheatley, D. (2017). Care and volunteering: the feel good Samaritan? In D. Wheatley, *Time Well Spent: Subjective Well-being and the Organization of Time*, chapter 6. London: Rowman and Littlefield International.

Hargadon, A. and Bechky, B. (2006). When collections of creatives become creative collectives: a field study of problem solving at work. *Organization Science*, 17(4), 484–500.

Harpaz, I. and Fu, X. (2002). The structure of the meaning of work: a relative stability amidst change. *Human Relations*, 55(6), 639–67.

Harris, J.I., Winskowski, A.M. and Engdahl, B.E. (2007b). Types of workplace social support in the prediction of job satisfaction. *The Career Development Quarterly*, 56(2), 150–6.

Harris, L., Foster, C. and Whysall, P. (2007a). Maximising women's potential in the UK's retail sector. *Employee Relations*, 29(5), 492–505.

Harsanyi, J.C. (1996). Utilities, preferences, and substantive goods. *Social Choice and Welfare*, 14, 129–45.

Harter, J.K., Schmidt, F.L., Agrawal, S. and Plowman, S.K. (2013). *The Relationship Between Engagement at Work and Organizational Outcomes: 2012 Q12 Meta Analysis*. Washington, DC: Gallup.

Hartfiel, N., Havenhand, J., Khalsa, S., Clarke, G. and Krayer, A. (2011). The effectiveness of yoga for the improvement of well-being and resilience to stress in the workplace. *Scandinavian Journal of Work, Environment & Health*, 37(1), 70–6.

Harvey, M., McIntyre, N., Heames, J. and Moeller, M. (2009). Mentoring global female managers in the global marketplace: traditional, reverse, and reciprocal mentoring. *International Journal of Human Resource Management*, 20(6), 1344–61.

Häusser, J.A., Mojzisch, A., Niesel, M. and Schulz-Hardt, S. (2010). Ten years on: a review of recent research on the job demand-control (-support) model and psychological well-being. *Work & Stress*, 24, 1–35.

Haynes, B. (2008). The impact of office comfort on productivity. *Journal of Facilities Management*, 6(1), 37–51.

Haynes, B. (2012). Corporate real estate asset management: aligned vision. *Journal of Corporate Real Estate*, 14(4), 244–54.

Headey, B. (2008). Life goals matter to happiness: a revision of set-point theory. *Social Indicators Research*, 88(2), 213–31.

Health and Safety Executive [HSE] (2020). *Working Safely with Display Screen Equipment* [online]. Available at: https://www.hse.gov.uk/msd/dse/.

Heaphy, E.D. and Dutton, J.E. (2008). Positive social interactions and the human body at work: linking organizations and physiology. *Academy of Management Review*, 33(1), 137–62.

Heart Foundation (2017). *Healthy Active by Design Training Resource* [online]. Available at: https://www.healthyactivebydesign.com.au/healthy-active-by-design -training-resource/.

Hellgren, J., Sverke, M. and Isaksson, K. (1999). A two-dimensional approach to job insecurity: consequences for employee attitudes and well-being. *European Journal of Work and Organizational Psychology*, 8(2), 179–95.

Helliwell, J.F. and Huang, H. (2010). How's the job? Well-being and social capital in the workplace. *Industrial and Labor Relations Review*, 63(2), 205–27.

Helliwell, J.F., Layard, R. and Sachs, J.D. (eds) (2015). *World Happiness Report 2015* [online]. New York: Sustainable Development Solutions Network. Available at: http://worldhappiness.report/wp-content/uploads/sites/2/2015/04/WHR15-Apr29 -update.pdf.

Helliwell, J.F., Layard, R. and Sachs, J.D. (eds) (2019). *World Happiness Report 2019* [online]. New York: Sustainable Development Solutions Network. Available at: https://s3.amazonaws.com/happiness-report/2019/WHR19.pdf.

Helliwell, J.F. and Putnam, R. (2004). The social context of well-being. *Philosophical Transactions of the Royal Society, B (Biological Sciences)*, 359(1449), 1435–46.

Herzberg, F., Mausner, B. and Snyderman, B. (1959). *The Motivation to Work*. New York: John Wiley.

Hesselberg, J. (2018). *Unlocking Agility: An Insider's Guide to Agile Enterprise Transformation*. Harlow: Pearson Education.

Hicks, S., Tinkler, L. and Allin, P. (2013). Measuring subjective well-being and its potential role in policy: perspectives from the UK Office for National Statistics. *Social Indicators Research*, 114(1), 73–86.

Higgins, M.C. (2001). Reconceptualizing mentoring at work: a developmental network perspective. *Academy of Management Review*, 26(2), 254–88.

Hinkin, T.R. and Schriesheim, C.A. (2008). An examination of 'nonleadership': from laissez-faire leadership to leader reward omission and punishment omission. *Journal of Applied Psychology*, 93(6), 1234–48.

Hirschman, A.O. (1970). *The Workplace Within: Psychodynamics of Organizational Life*. Cambridge, MA: MIT Press.

Hislop, D. and Axtell, C. (2009). To infinity and beyond? Workspace and the multi-location worker. *New Technology, Work and Employment*, 24(1), 60–75.

Hislop, D., Axtell, C., Collins, A., Daniels, K., Glover, J. and Niven, K. (2015). Variability in the use of mobile ICTs by homeworkers and its consequences for boundary management and social isolation. *Information and Organization*, 25(4), 222–32.

HM Government (2018). *Good Work: A Response to the Taylor Review of Modern Working Practices*. London: Department for Business, Energy and Industrial Strategy.

Hoffman, A., Wallach, J. and Sanchez, E. (2010). Community service work, civic engagement, and 'giving back' to society: key factors in improving interethnic relationships and achieving 'connectedness' in ethnically diverse communities. *Australian Social Work*, 63(4), 418–30.

Holland, P. and Collins, A. (2020). Supporting and retaining employees with rheumatoid arthritis: the importance of workplace social support. *The International Journal of Human Resource Management*. https://doi.org/10.1080/09585192.2020.1737175.

Holman, D. (2013). Job types and job quality in Europe. *Human Relations*, 66(4), 475–502.

Holt, D., Markova, G., Dhaenens, A., Marler, L. and Heilmann, S. (2016). Formal or informal mentoring: what drives employees to seek informal mentors? *Journal of Managerial Issues*, 28(1–2), 67–82.

Homans, G.C. (1958). Social behavior as exchange. *American Journal of Sociology*, 63(6), 597–606.

Hon, A. and Chan, W. (2013). The effects of group conflict and work stress on employee performance. *Cornell Hospitality Quarterly*, 54(2), 174–84.

Hoque, K., Earls, J., Conway, N. and Bacon, N. (2017). Union representation, collective voice and job quality: an analysis of a survey of union members in the UK finance sector. *Economic and Industrial Democracy*, 38(1), 27–50.

Horrell, S. and Humphries, J. (1995). Women's labour force participation and the transition to the male breadwinner family, 1790–1865. *Economic History Review*, 48(1), 89–117.

Houlihan, M. (2002). Tensions and variations in call centre management strategies. *Human Resource Management Journal*, 12(4), 67–85.

Howcroft, D. and Bergvall-Kåreborn, B. (2019). A typology of crowdwork platforms. *Work, Employment and Society*, 33(1), 21–38.

HR Magazine (2017). Glassdoor's top employers for work/life balance revealed [online]. Available at: http://www.hrmagazine.co.uk/article-details/glassdoors-top -employers-for-work-life-balance-revealed-1.

Huang, G., Lee, C., Ashford, S., Chen, Z. and Ren, X. (2010). Affective job insecurity: a mediator of the cognitive job insecurity and employee outcomes relationships. *International Studies of Management and Organizations*, 40(1), 20–39.

Huang, G.H., Niu, X., Lee, C. and Ashford, S.J. (2012). Differentiating cognitive and affective job insecurity: antecedents and outcomes. *Journal of Organizational Behavior*, 33(6), 752–69.

Huang, Y.H., Lee, J., McFadden, A., Murphy, L., Robertson, M., Cheung, J. and Zohar, D. (2016). Beyond safety outcomes: an investigation of the impact of safety climate on job satisfaction, employee engagement and turnover using social exchange theory as the theoretical framework. *Applied Ergonomics*, 55, 248–57.

Huizing, R. (2012). Mentoring together: a literature review of group mentoring. *Mentoring & Tutoring: Partnership in Learning*, 20(1), 27–55.

Humphrey, S.E., Nahrgang, J.D. and Morgeson, F.P. (2007). Integrating motivational, social, and contextual work design features: a meta-analytic summary and theoretical extension of the work design literature. *Journal of Applied Psychology*, 92, 1332–56.

Hunt, J. (2013). Flexible work time in Germany: do workers like it and how have employers exploited it over the cycle? *Perspektiven der Wirtschaftspolitik*, 14(1–2), 67–98.

Hunter, J.R., Gordon, B.R., Bird, S.R. and Benson, A.C. (2018). Perceived barriers and facilitators to workplace exercise participation. *International Journal of Workplace Health Management*, 11(5), 349–63.

Huppert, F.A. (2009). Psychological well-being: evidence regarding its causes and consequences. *Applied Psychology: Health and Well-being*, 1(2), 137–64.

Hytti, U. (2010). Contextualizing entrepreneurship in the boundaryless career. *Gender in Management: An International Journal*, 25(1), 64–81.

Hyvönen, K., Feldt, T., Tolvanen, A. and Kinnunen, U. (2010). The role of goal pursuit in the interaction between psychosocial work environment and occupational well-being. *Journal of Vocational Behavior*, 76, 406–18.

Iasiello, M., Bartholomaeus, J., Jarden, A. and Kelly, G. (2017). Measuring PERMA+ in South Australia, the state of wellbeing: a comparison with national and international norms. *Journal of Positive Psychology and Wellbeing*, 1(2), 53–72.

Ijsselsteijn, W., van Baren, J., Markopoulos, P., Romero, N. and de Ruyter, B. (2009). Measuring affective benefits and costs of mediated awareness: development and validation of the abc-questionnaire. In P. Markopoulos, B. De Ruyter and W. Mackay (eds), *Awareness Systems*, 473–88. Heidelberg: Springer.

ILO [International Labour Organization] (2013). *Decent Work Indicators: Guidelines for Producers and Users of Statistical and Legal Framework Indicators: ILO Manual*. Geneva, Switzerland: ILO. Available at: http://www.ilo.org/wcmsp5/ groups/public/---dgreports/---integration/documents/publication/wcms_229374.pdf.

ILO [International Labour Organization] (2020). *Working from Home: Estimating the Worldwide Potential*. Geneva, Switzerland: ILO. Available at: https://www.ilo.org/ global/topics/non-standard-employment/publications/WCMS_743447/lang--en/ index.htm.

Jackson, C., Lewis, K., Conner, M., Lawton, R. and McEachan, R.R.C. (2014). Are incremental changes in physical activity and sedentary behaviours associated with improved employee health? A 12-month prospective study in five organisations. *International Journal of Workplace Health Management*, 7(1), 16–39.

Jaiswal, A. and Dyaram, L. (2018). Towards well-being: role of diversity and nature of work. *Employee Relations*, 41(1), 158–75.

Jakobsen, M.D., Sundstrup, E., Brandt, M. and Andersen, L.L. (2017). Psychosocial benefits of workplace physical exercise: cluster randomized controlled trial. *BMC Public Health*, 17(1), 798.

Jang, J.S., Park, R. and Zippay, A. (2011). The interaction effects of scheduling control and work–life balance programs on job satisfaction and mental health. *International Journal of Social Welfare*, 20, 135–43.

Janssen, S., Tahitu, J., van Vuuren, M. and de Jong, M. (2018). Coworkers' perspectives on mentoring relationships. *Group & Organization Management*, 43(2), 245–72.

Janssen, S., van Vuuren, M. and de Jong, M. (2016). Informal mentoring at work: a review and suggestions for future research. *International Journal of Management Reviews*, 18(4), 498–517.

Jaschinski, W., Heuer, H. and Kylian, H. (1998). Preferred position of visual displays relative to the eyes: a field study of visual strain and individual differences. *Ergonomics*, 41(7), 1034–49.

Jefferson, A., Bortolotti, L. and Kuzmanovic, B. (2017). What is unrealistic optimism? *Consciousness and Cognition*, 50, 3–11.

Jeffrey, K., Mahony, S., Michaelson, J. and Abdallah, S. (2014). *Well-being at Work: A Review of the Literature*. New Economics Foundation (NEF). Available at: https://www.nuffieldhealth.com/downloads/wellbeing-at-work-a-review-of-the-literature.

Jenkins, S., Delbridge, R. and Roberts, A. (2010). Emotional management in a mass customised call centre: examining skill and knowledgeability in interactive service work. *Work, Employment and Society*, 24(3), 546–64.

Jeong, Y.-J., Zvonkovic, A., Sano, Y. and Acock, A. (2013). The occurrence and frequency of overnight job travel in the USA. *Work, Employment and Society*, 27(1), 138–52.

Jiang, Z., Di Milia, L., Jiang, Y. and Jiang, X. (2020). Thriving at work: a mentoring-moderated process linking task identity and autonomy to job satisfaction. *Journal of Vocational Behavior*, 118, 103373.

Johns, T. and Gratton, L. (2013). The third wave of virtual work. *Harvard Business Review*, 91(1), 66–73.

Johnson, S. and Cooper, C. (2003). The construct validity of the ASSET stress measure. *Stress and Health*, 19(3), 181–5.

Jones, A. (2003). *About Time for Change*. London: The Work Foundation.

Jones, A. (2013). Conceptualising business mobilities: towards an analytical framework. *Research in Transportation Business & Management*, 9, 58–66.

Jones, D. (2010). Does serving the community also serve the company? Using organizational identification and social exchange theories to understand employee responses to a volunteerism programme. *Journal of Occupational and Organizational Psychology*, 83(4), 857–78.

Jorgensen, B., Jamieson, R. and Martin, F. (2010). Income, sense of community and subjective well-being: combining economic and psychological variables. *Journal of Economic Psychology*, 31(4), 612–23.

Judge, T.A. and Piccolo, R.F. (2004). Transformational and transactional leadership: a meta-analytic test of their relative value. *Journal of Applied Psychology*, 89(5), 755–68.

Judge, T.A., Weiss, H.M., Kammeyer-Mueller, J.D. and Hulin, C.L. (2017). Job attitudes, job satisfaction, and job affect: a century of continuity and of change. *Journal of Applied Psychology*, 102(3), 356–74.

Jung, C.G. (1933). *Modern Man in Search of a Soul*. Translated by W.S. Dell and C.F. Baynes. New York: Harcourt, Brace & World.

Jung, H.S. and Yoon, H.H. (2016). What does work meaning to hospitality employees? The effects of meaningful work on employees' organizational commitment: the mediating role of job engagement. *International Journal of Hospitality Management*, 53, 59–68.

Kafka, G.J. and Kozma, A. (2002). The construct validity of Ryff's Scales of Psychological Well-Being (SPWB) and their relationship to measures of subjective well-being. *Social Indicators Research*, 57, 171–90.

Kahn, E.B., Ramsey, L.T., Brownson, R.C., Heath, G.W., Howze, E.H., Powell, K.E., Stone, E.J., Rajab, M.W. and Corso, P (2002). The effectiveness of interventions to increase physical activity: a systematic review. *American Journal of Preventative Medicine*, 22(4 suppl.), 73–107.

Kahn, W.A. (1990). Psychological conditions of personal engagement and disengagement at work. *Academy of Management Journal*, 33(4), 692–724.

Kahn, W.A. (2007). Meaningful connections: positive relationships and attachments at work. In J.E. Dutton and B.R. Ragins (eds), *Exploring Positive Relationships at Work*, 189–206. New York: Psychology Press.

Kahneman, D. and Krueger, A. (2006). Developments in the measurement of subjective well-being. *Journal of Economic Perspectives*, 20(1), 3–24.

Kahneman, D., Krueger, A.B., Schkade, D., Schwartz, N. and Stone, A. (2004). Toward national well-being accounts. *The American Economic Review*, 94, 429–34.

Kahneman, D., Krueger, A.B., Schkade, D., Schwarz, N. and Stone, A. (2006). Would you be happier if you were richer? A focusing illusion. *Science*, 312(5782), 1908–10.

Kalleberg, A.L. (2009). Precarious work, insecure workers: employment relations in transition. *American Sociological Review*, 74(1), 1–22.

Kalleberg, A.L. (2011). *Good jobs, Bad Jobs: The Rise of Polarized and Precarious Employment Systems in the United States, 1970s–2000s*. New York: Russell Sage Foundation.

Kalleberg, A.L. (2012). Job quality and precarious work: clarifications, controversies, and challenges. *Work and Occupations*, 39(4), 427–48.

Kalleberg, A.L., Nesheim, T. and Olsen, K.M. (2009). Is participation good or bad for workers? *Acta Sociologica*, 52(2), 99–116.

Kao, K.-Y., Hsu, H.-H., Rogers, A., Lin, M.-T., Lee, H.-T. and Lian, R. (2020). I see my future! Linking mentoring, future work selves, achievement orientation to job search behaviors. *Journal of Career Development*. http://doi.org/10.1177/0894845320926571.

Kaplan, R. (1993). The role of nature in the context of the workplace. *Landscape and Urban Planning*, 26(1–4), 193–201.

Kaplan, S. (1995). The restorative benefits of nature: toward an integrative framework. *Journal of Environmental Psychology*, 15(3), 169–82.

Karanika-Murray, M., Pontesa, H.M., Griffiths, M.D. and Biron, C. (2015). Sickness presenteeism determines job satisfaction via affective-motivational states. *Social Science & Medicine*, 139, 100–106.

References 303

Karapinar, P.B., Camgöz, S.M. and Ekmekci, O.T. (2019). Reviewing measurement instruments in job insecurity research: perceived job insecurity and the gender lens perspective. In D. Wheatley (ed.), *Handbook of Research Methods on the Quality of Working Lives*, 46–61. Cheltenham, UK, and Northampton, MA, USA: Edward Elgar Publishing.

Karasek, R.A. (1979). Job demands, job decision latitude, and mental strain: implications for job redesign. *Administrative Science Quarterly*, 24(2), 285–306

Karasek, R.A. and Theorell, T. (1990). *Healthy Work: Stress, Productivity, and the Reconstruction of Working Life*. New York: Basic Books.

Kassavou, A., Turner, A. and French, D.P. (2013). Do interventions to promote walking in groups increase physical activity? A systematic literature review with meta-analysis. *International Journal of Behavioral Nutrition and Physical Activity*, 10(1), 18.

Katzmarzyk, P.T. (2010). Physical activity, sedentary behavior, and health: paradigm paralysis or paradigm shift? *Diabetes*, 59(11), 2717–25.

Kavetsos, G. (2011). Physical activity and subjective wellbeing: an empirical analysis. In P. Rodriguez, S. Kesenne and B.R. Humphreys (eds), *The Economics of Sport, Health and Happiness: The Promotion of Wellbeing through Sporting Activities*, 213–22. Cheltenham, UK, and Northampton, MA, USA: Edward Elgar Publishing.

Kazi, A., Duncan, M., Clemes, S. and Haslam, C.A. (2014). A survey of sitting time among UK employees. *Occupational Medicine*, 64(7), 497–502.

Keith, M., Harms, P. and Tay, L. (2019). Mechanical Turk and the gig economy: exploring differences between gig workers. *Journal of Managerial Psychology*, 34(4), 286–306.

Kelly, E.L., Moen, P. and Tranby, E. (2011). Changing workplaces to reduce work–family conflict: schedule control in a white-collar organization. *American Sociological Review*, 76(2), 265–90.

Kesebir, P. and Diener, E. (2008). In defense of happiness. In L. Bruni, F. Comim and M. Pugno (eds), *Capabilities and Happiness*, 60–80. Oxford: Oxford University Press.

Kessler, R.C., Barber, C., Beck, A., Berglund, P., Cleary, P.D., McKenas, D., Pronk, N., Simon, G., Stang, P., Üstün, T.U. and Wang, P. (2003). The World Health Organization health and work performance questionnaire (HPQ). *Journal of Occupational and Environmental Medicine*, 45(2), 156–74.

Kilgour, J.G. (2013). The pay gap in perspective. *Compensation & Benefits Review*, 45(4), 200–209.

Kim, H.R., Lee, M., Lee, H.T. and Kim, N.M. (2010). Corporate social responsibility and employee–company identification. *Journal of Business Ethics*, 95, 557–69.

Kim, J., Candido, C., Thomas, L. and de Dear, R. (2016). Desk ownership in the workplace: the effect of non-territorial working on employee workplace satisfaction, perceived productivity and health. *Building and Environment*, 103, 203–14.

Kim, J. and de Dear, R. (2013). Workspace satisfaction: the privacy–communication trade-off in open-plan offices. *Journal of Environmental Psychology*, 36, 18–26.

King, M. (2014). Protecting and representing workers in the new gig economy: the case of the Freelancers Union. In R. Milkman and E. Ott (eds), *New Labor in New York: Precarious Workers and the Future of the Labour Movement*, chapter 7. Ithaca, NY: Cornell University Press.

King, S. (2017). Co-working is not about workspace – it's about feeling less lonely. *Harvard Business Review*. Available at: https://hbr.org/2017/12/coworking-is-not -about-workspace-its-about-feeling-less-lonely.

Kinnafick, F.E., Thøgersen-Ntoumani, C., Shepherd, S.O., Wilson, O.J., Wagenmakers, A.J.M. and Shaw, C.S. (2018). In it together: a qualitative evaluation of participant experiences of a 10-week, group-based, workplace HIIT program for insufficiently active adults. *Journal of Sport and Exercise Psychology*, 40(1), 10–19.

Kirk, A.K. and Brown, D.F. (2003). Employee assistance programs: a review of the management of stress and wellbeing through workplace counselling and consulting. *Australian Psychologist*, 38(2), 138–43.

Kirkham, R., Mellor, S., Green, D., Lin, J.S., Ladha, K., Ladha, C., Jackson, D., Olivier, P., Wright, P. and Plotz, T. (2013). The break-time barometer – an exploratory system for workplace break-time social awareness. Proceedings of the 2013 ACM International Joint Conference on Pervasive and Ubiquitous Computing (Ubicomp'13), ACM.

Kitchener, B.A. and Jorm, A.F. (2008). Mental health first aid: an international programme for early intervention. *Early Intervention in Psychiatry*, 2(1), 55–61.

Kitterød, H. and Vatne Pettersen, S. (2006). Making up for mother's employed working hours? Housework and childcare among Norwegian fathers. *Work, Employment and Society*, 20(3), 473–93.

Kitterød, R. and Rønsen, M. (2012). Non-traditional dual earners in Norway: when does she work at least as much as he? *Work, Employment and Society*, 26(4), 657–75.

Kjeldstad, R. and Nymoen, E. (2012). Part-time work and gender: worker versus job explanations. *International Labour Review*, 151(1–2), 85–107.

Kniffin, K.M., Wansink, B., Devine, C.M. and Sobal, J. (2015). Eating together at the firehouse: how workplace commensality relates to the performance of firefighters. *Human Performance*, 28(4), 281–306.

Knight, A.P. and Baer, M. (2014). Get up, stand up: the effects of a non-sedentary workspace on information elaboration and group performance. *Social Psychological and Personality Science*, 5(8), 910–17.

Knight, C. and Haslam, S. (2010). The relative merits of lean, enriched, and empowered offices: an experimental examination of the impact of workspace management strategies on wellbeing and productivity. *Journal of Experimental Psychology: Applied*, 16(2), 158–72.

Knowles, S. and Servátka, M. (2015). Transaction costs, the opportunity cost of time and procrastination in charitable giving. *Journal of Public Economics*, 125, 54–63.

Knox, A., Warhurst, C. and Pocock, B. (2011). Job quality matters. *Journal of Industrial Relations*, 53(1), 5–11.

Knox, E.C.L., Musson, H. and Adams, E.J. (2017). Workplace policies and practices promoting physical activity across England: what is commonly used and what works? *International Journal of Workplace Health Management*, 10(5), 391–403.

Kodz, J., Harper, H. and Dench, S. (2002). *Work–life Balance: Beyond the Rhetoric*. IES report 384. London: Institute for Employment Studies.

Koopmans, L., Bernaards, C.M., Hildebrandt, V.H., van Buuren, S., van der Beek, A.J. and de Vet, H.C.W. (2013). Development of an individual work performance questionnaire. *International Journal of Productivity and Performance Management*, 62(1), 6–28.

Koopmans, L., Bernaards, C.M., Hildebrandt, V.H., Lerner, D., de Vet, H.C.W. and van der Beek, A.J. (2016). Cross-cultural adaptation of the Individual Work Performance Questionnaire. *Work*, 53(3), 609–19.

Kossek, E., Pichler, S., Bodner, T. and Hammer, L. (2011). Workplace social support and work–family conflict: a meta-analysis clarifying the influence of general and work–family-specific supervisor and organizational support. *Personnel Psychology*, 64(2), 289–313.

Kram, K.E. (1985). *Mentoring at Work: Developmental Relationships in Organizational Life*. Glenview, IL: Scott Foresman.

Kroemer, K.H. and Robinette, J.C. (1969). Ergonomics in the design of office furniture: a review of European literature. *International Journal of Industrial Medicine and Surgery*, 38(4), 115–25.

Kühnel, J., Zacher, H., de Bloom, J. and Bledow, R. (2017). Take a break! Benefits of sleep and short breaks for daily work engagement. *European Journal of Work and Organizational Psychology*, 26(4), 481–91.

Kurtessis, J., Eisenberger, R., Ford, M., Buffardi, L., Stewart, K. and Adis, C. (2017). Perceived organizational support: a meta-analytic evaluation of organizational support theory. *Journal of Management*, 43(6), 1854–84.

Kuvaas, B., Buch, R., Weibel, A., Dysvik, A. and Nerstad, C. (2017). Do intrinsic and extrinsic motivation relate differently to employee outcomes? *Journal of Economic Psychology*, 61, 244–58.

Laffont, J.-J. and Martimort, D. (2002). *The Theory of Incentives: The Principal–Agent Model*. Princeton, NJ: Princeton University Press.

Laihonen, H., Jääskeläinen, A., Lönnqvist, A. and Ruostela, J. (2012). Measuring the productivity impacts of new ways of working. *Journal of Facilities Management*, 10(2), 102–13.

LaJeunesse, S. and Rodríguez, D.A. (2012). Mindfulness, time affluence, and journey-based affect: exploring relationships. *Transportation Research Part F*, 15(2), 196–205.

Lamb, S. and Kwok, K.C.S. (2016). A longitudinal investigation of work environment stressors on the performance and wellbeing of office workers. *Applied Ergonomics*, 52, 104–11.

Lancee, B. and Radl, J. (2012). Social connectedness and the transition from work to retirement. *The Journals of Gerontology, Series B: Psychological Sciences and Social Sciences*, 67(4), 481–90.

Langer, E.J. and Moldoveanu, M. (2000). Mindfulness research and the future. *Journal of Social Issues*, 56(1), 129–39.

Largo-Wight, E., Chen, W.W., Dodd, V. and Weiler, R. (2011). Healthy workplaces: the role of nature contact office exposures on employee stress and health. *Public Health Reports*, 126(suppl. 1), 124–30.

Largo-Wight, E., Wlyudka, P., Merten, J. and Cuvelier, E. (2017). Effectiveness and feasibility of a 10-minute employee stress intervention: outdoor booster break. *Journal of Workplace Behavioral Health*, 32(3), 159–71.

Lavelle, J., Gunnigle, P. and McDonnell, A. (2010). Patterning employee voice in multinational companies. *Human Relations*, 63(3), 395–418.

Lawton, C. (2015). *How Job and Skill Shortages Affect the UK*. London: BBC. Available at: https://www.bbc.co.uk/news/business-34297368.

Lawton, C. (2017a). *Enterprise and Entrepreneurship Education and Support in the Midlands Enterprise Universities. Report 1: Literature Review and Baseline Data Analysis*. Nottingham: Nottingham Business School, Nottingham Trent University.

Lawton, C. (2017b). *Malmö: Using Skateboarding to Transform Your Hometown*. London, Caught in the Crossfire. Available at: http://www.caughtinthecrossfire .com/skate/malmo-using-skateboarding-to-transform-your-hometown/.

Lawton, C. (2019). *Skateboarding's DIY Ethos Is Kick-Starting a New Wave of Urban Regeneration*. London, The Conversation. Available at: https://theconversation

.com/skateboardings-diy-ethos-is-kick-starting-a-new-wave-of-urban-regeneration-122304.

Lawton, C. (2020a). Skateboarding landscapes – designing for diverse and active cities. Landscape Institute East Midlands network conference, December.

Lawton, C. (2020b). FBE East Midlands – skateboarding – research, practice and design for inclusive and active cities. Presentation at the Forum for the Built Environment East Midlands Network Branch Networking Event, October.

Lawton, C. (2020c). Skate urbanism – imagining towns and cities for wheeled urban sports. Presentation at the final European Commission Sport4Values Conference, online, September.

Lawton, C. (2020d). Can skateboarders in Nottingham be good partners to the city without being 'shock troops of gentrification'? *Urban Pamphleteer*, 8, University College London, 34–6.

Lawton, C., Pickford, R., Rendall, J. and Wheatley, D. (2019). *Laying the Foundations of a Good Work City: Mapping Nottingham's Employment* [online]. Nottingham: Nottingham Civic Exchange, Nottingham Trent University. Available at: http://irep.ntu.ac.uk/id/eprint/36257/1/13686_Lawton.pdf.

Lawton, C. and Wheatley, D. (2018). The quality of work among older workers. In V. Caven and S. Nachmias (eds), *Hidden Inequalities in the Workplace*, 91–126. London: Palgrave Macmillan.

Lazear, E.P. (1989). Pay, equality and industrial politics. *Journal of Political Economy*, 97(3), 561–80.

Lazear, E.P. and Rosen, S. (1981). Rank-order tournaments as optimum incentive labor contracts. *Journal of Political Economy*, 89(5), 841–64.

Leach, L., Butterworth, P., Rodgers, B. and Strazdins, L. (2010). Deriving an evidence-based measure of job quality from the HILDA survey. *Australian Social Policy Journal*, 9, 67–86.

Leaker, D. and Nigg, W. (2019). *Sickness Absence in the UK Labour Market: 2018.* Newport, South Wales: Office for National Statistics (ONS). Crown Copyright. Available at: https://www.ons.gov.uk/employmentandlabourmarket/peopleinwork/labourproductivity/articles/sicknessabsenceinthelabourmarket/2018.

Leana, C., Appelbaum, E. and Shevchuk, I. (2009). Work process and quality of care in early childhood education: the role of job crafting. *Academy of Management Journal*, 52(6), 1169–92.

Lecchi, T., da Silva, K., Giommi, F. and Leong, V. (2019). Using dual-EEG to explore therapist client interpersonal neural synchrony. *PsyArXiv*. https://doi.org/10.31234/osf.io/ebkpv.

Lee, B. and DeVoe, S. (2012). Flextime and profitability. *Industrial Relations: A Journal of Economy and Society*, 51(2), 298–316.

Lee, K., Williams, K., Sargent, L., Williams, N. and Johnson, K. (2015). 40-second green roof views sustain attention: the role of micro-breaks in attention restoration. *Journal of Environmental Psychology*, 42, 182–9.

Lee, S.Y. and Brand, J.L. (2005). Effects of control over office workspace on perceptions of the work environment and work outcomes. *Journal of Environmental Psychology*, 25(3), 323–33.

Lee, Y. and Aletta, F. (2019). Acoustical planning for workplace health and well-being: a case study in four open-plan offices. *Building Acoustics*, 26(3), 207–20.

Lee, Y.H. and Lin, H. (2011). 'Gaming is my work': identity work in internet-hobbyist game workers. *Work, Employment & Society*, 25(3), 451–67.

Lerner, D., Amick, B.C., Lee, J.C., Rooney, T., Rogers, W.H., Chang, H. and Berndt, E.R. (2003). Relationship of employee-reported work limitations to work productivity. *Medical Care*, 41(5), 649–59.

Leslie, L.M., Snyder, M. and Glomb, T. (2013). Who gives? Multilevel effects of gender and ethnicity on workplace charitable giving. *Journal of Applied Psychology*, 98(1), 49–62.

Levine, J. (2010). Health-chair reform: your chair: comfortable but deadly. *Diabetes*, 59(11), 2715–16.

Levinson, D.J., Darrow, C.M., Klein, E.G., Levinson, M.H. and McKee, B. (1978). *Seasons of a Man's Life*. New York: Knopf.

Lewicki, R.J. and Brinsfield, C.T. (2009). Trust, distrust and building social capital. In V.O. Bartkus and J.H. Davis (eds), *Social Capital: Reaching Out, Reaching In*. Cheltenham, UK, and Northampton, MA, USA: Edward Elgar Publishing.

Lewis, J. and Campbell, M. (2008). What's in a name? 'Work and family' or 'work and life' balance policies in the UK since 1997 and the implications for the pursuit of gender equality. *Social Policy and Administration*, 42(5), 524–41.

Lewis, J. and Plomien, A. (2009). 'Flexicurity' as a policy strategy: the implications for gender equality. *Economy and Society*, 38(3), 433–59.

Lewis, S. and Humbert, L. (2010). Discourse or reality? Work–life balance, flexible working policies and the gendered organization. *Equality, Diversity and Inclusion: An International Journal*, 29(3), 239–54.

Lin, W., Koopmann, J. and Wang, M. (2020). How does workplace helping behavior step up or slack off? Integrating enrichment-based and depletion-based perspectives. *Journal of Management*, 46(3), 385–413.

Lo, M.-C. and Ramayah, T. (2011). Mentoring and job satisfaction in Malaysian SMEs. *Journal of Management Development*, 30(4), 427–40.

Locke, E.A. and Latham, G.P. (2004). What should we do about motivation theory? Six recommendations for the twenty-first century. *Academy of Management Review*, 29(3), 388–403.

Lucy, D., Poorkavoos, M. and Thompson, A. (2014). *Building Resilience: Five Key Capabilities* [online]. Roffey Park Institute. Available at: https://www.roffeypark.ac .uk/wp-content/uploads/2020/07/Building-Resilience-Report-with-covers.pdf.

Lundberg, S. and Pollak, R. (2007). The American family and family economics. *Journal of Economic Perspectives*, 21(2), 3–26.

Lupton, B., Rowe, A. and Whittle, R. (2015). *Show Me the Money! The Behavioural Science of Reward*. London: Chartered Institute of Personnel and Development. Available at: http://www.cipd.co.uk/knowledge/culture/behaviour/reward-report.

Lyness, K., Gornick, J., Stone, P. and Grotto, A. (2012). It's all about control: worker control over schedule and hours in cross-national context. *American Sociological Review*, 20(10), 1–27.

Lyness, K.S. and Kropf, M.B. (2005). The relationships of national gender equality and organizational support with work–family balance: a study of European managers. *Human Relations*, 58(1), 33–60.

MacEwan, B., MacDonald, D. and Burr, J. (2015). A systematic review of standing and treadmill desks in the workplace. *Preventive Medicine*, 70, 50–8.

MacKerron, G. (2012). Happiness economics from 35,000 feet. *Journal of Economic Surveys*, 26(4), 705–35.

Maes, I., Ketels, M., Van Dyck, D. and Clays, E. (2020). The occupational sitting and physical activity questionnaire (OSPAQ): a validation study with accelerometer-assessed measures. *BMC Public Health*, 20(1072). Available at: https://bmcpublichealth.biomedcentral.com/articles/10.1186/s12889-020-09180-9.

Mainiero, L. and Sullivan, S. (2005). Kaleidoscope careers: an alternate explanation for the 'opt-out' revolution. *Academy of Management Executive*, 19(1), 106–23.

Mäkelä, L. and Kinnunen, U. (2018). International business travelers' psychological well-being: the role of supportive HR practices. *The International Journal of Human Resource Management*, 29(7), 1285–306.

Mäkelä, L., Kinnunen, U. and Suutari, V. (2015). Work-to-life conflict and enrichment among international business travelers: the role of international career orientation. *Human Resource Management*, 54(3), 517–31.

Mandl, I., Curtarelli, M., Riso, S., Vargas, O. and Gerogiannis, E. (2015). *New Forms of Employment in Europe*. Dublin: Eurofound.

Marglin, S. (1974). What do bosses do? The origins and functions of hierarchy in capitalist production. *Review of Radical Political Economics*, 6(2), 60–112.

Margolis, J.D. and Stoltz, P. (2010). How to bounce back from adversity. *Harvard Business Review*, 88(1–2), 86–92.

Mariotti, I., Pacchi, C. and Di Vita, S. (2017). Co-working spaces in Milan: location patterns and urban effects. *Journal of Urban Technology*, 24(3), 47–66.

Markowitsch, J., Käpplinger, B. and Hefler, G. (2013). Firm-provided training in Europe and the limits of national skills strategies. *European Journal of Education*, 48(2), 281–91.

Martel, J.P. and Dupuis, G. (2006). Quality of work life: theoretical and methodological problems, and presentation of a new model and measuring instrument. *Social Indicators Research*, 77(2), 333–68.

Martin, R., Guillaume, Y., Thomas, G., Lee, A. and Epitropaki, O. (2016). Leader-member Exchange (LMX) and performance: a meta-analytic review. *Personnel Psychology*, 69(1), 67–121.

Martínez-Tur, V., Peiró, J.M. and Ramos, J. (2005). Linking situational constraints to customer satisfaction in a service environment. *Applied Psychology: An International Review*, 54(1), 25–36.

Maslow, A.H. (1968). *Toward a Psychology of Being*, 2nd edn. New York: Van Nostrand.

Mauss, M. (1923). Essai sur le don: forme et raison de l'échange dans les sociétés archaïques. *L'Anneé Sociologique*, 1, 30–186.

Mazzetti, G., Schaufeli, W.B. and Guglielmi, D. (2014). Are workaholics born or made? Relations of workaholism with person characteristics and overwork climate. *International Journal of Stress Management*, 21(3), 227–54.

McCarthy, A., Darcy, C. and Grady, G. (2010). Work–life balance policy and practice: understanding line manager attitudes and behaviors. *Human Resource Management Review*, 20(2), 158–67.

McCrate, E. (2012) Flexibility for whom? Control over work schedule variability in the US. *Feminist Economics*, 18(1), 39–72.

McDonald, P., Bradley, L. and Brown, K. (2009). 'Full-time is a given here': part-time versus full-time job quality. *British Journal of Management*, 20(2), 143–57.

McDonald, S. and Mair, C. (2010). Social capital across the life course: age and gendered patterns of network resources. *Sociological Forum*, 25(2), 335–59.

McDowell, L., Perrons, D., Fagan, C., Ray, K. and Ward, K. (2005). The contradictions and intersections of class and gender in a global city: placing working women's lives on the research agenda. *Environment & Planning A*, 37(3), 441–61.

McManus, S., Meltzer, H., Brugha, T., Bebbington, P. and Jenkins, R. (2009). *Adult Psychiatric Morbidity in England, 2007: Results of a Household Survey*. The Health and Social Care Information Centre, Social Care Statistics. Available at: https://digital.nhs.uk/data-and-information/publications/statistical/adult-psychiatric -morbidity-survey/adult-psychiatric-morbidity-in-england-2007-results-of-a -household-survey.

Meier, L.L., Semmer, N.K. and Gross, S. (2014). The effect of conflict at work on well-being: depressive symptoms as a vulnerability factor. *Work & Stress*, 28(1), 31–48.

Meier, S. and Stutzer, A. (2008). Is volunteering rewarding in itself? *Economica*, 75(297), 39–59.

Mental Health First Aid England (2019). *Mental Health First Aid* [online]. Available at: https://mhfaengland.org/.

Mentzakis, E. and Moro, M. (2009). The poor, the rich and the happy: exploring the link between income and subjective well-being. *The Journal of Socio-Economics*, 38(1), 147–58.

Mérida-López, S., Extremera, N., Quintana-Orts, C. and Rey, L. (2019). In pursuit of job satisfaction and happiness: testing the interactive contribution of emotion-regulation ability and workplace social support. *Scandinavian Journal of Psychology*, 60(1), 59–66.

Messenger, J.C. (2011). Working time trends and developments in Europe. *Cambridge Journal of Economics*, 35(2), 295–316.

Meyer, J.P. and Allen, N.J. (1991). A three-component conceptualization of organizational commitment. *Human Resource Management Review*, 1(1), 64–89.

Meyer, J.P. and Allen, N.J. (1997). *Commitment in the Workplace: Theory, Research, and Application*. Thousand Oaks, CA: Sage.

Meyer, J.P., Stanley, L.J. and Parfyonovaa, N.M. (2012). Employee commitment in context: the nature and implication of commitment profiles. *Journal of Vocational Behavior*, 80(1), 1–16.

Mignon, J.-F. (2013). Continuing training for employees in Europe: the differences between countries continue to narrow. *Training & Employment*, 106, 1–4.

Milasi, S., González-Vázquez, I. and Fernández-Macías, E. (2020). *Telework in the EU Before and After the COVID-19: Where We Were, Where We Head To*. European Commission: Science for Policy Briefs. Available at: https://ec.europa.eu/jrc/sites/ jrcsh/files/jrc120945_policy_brief_-_covid_and_telework_final.pdf.

Milkman, R., Elliott-Negri, L., Griesbach, K. and Reich, A. (2020). Gender, class, and the gig economy: the case of platform-based food delivery. *Critical Sociology*, 1–16. https://doi.org/10.1177/0896920520949631.

Moeller, J., Ivcevic, Z., White, A.E., Menges, J.I. and Brackett, M.A. (2017). Highly engaged but burned out: intra-individual profiles in the US workforce. *Career Development International*, 23(1), 86–105.

Mojza, E., Sonnentag, S. and Bornemann, C. (2011). Volunteer work as a valuable leisure time activity: a day level study on volunteer work, non-work experiences, and well-being at work. *Journal of Occupational and Organizational Psychology*, 84(1), 123–52.

Mokhtarian, P., Collantes, G. and Gertz, C. (2004). Telecommuting, residential location, and commute-distance traveled: evidence from State of California employees. *Environment and Planning A*, 36(10), 1877–97.

Molm, L.D., Collett, J.L. and Schaefer, D.R. (2007). Building solidarity through generalized exchange. *American Journal of Sociology*, 113(1), 205–42.

Molm, L.D., Whitham, M.M. and Melamed, D. (2012). Forms of exchange and integrative bonds: effects of history and embeddedness. *American Sociological Review*, 77(1), 141–65.

Montania, F. and Dagenais-Desmarais, V. (2018). Unravelling the relationship between role overload and organizational citizenship behaviour: a test of mediating and moderating effects. *European Management Journal*, 36(6), 757–68.

Montreuil, S. and Lippel, K. (2003). Telework and occupational health: a Quebec empirical study and regulatory implications. *Safety Science*, 41(4), 339–58.

Moore, P. and Joyce, S. (2020). Black box or hidden abode? The expansion and exposure of platform work managerialism. *Review of International Political Economy*, 27(4), 926–48.

Moos, A. and Skaburskis, M. (2007). The characteristics and location of home workers in Montreal, Toronto and Vancouver. *Urban Studies*, 44(9), 1781–808.

Moos, M. and Skaburskis, A. (2008). The probability of single-family dwelling occupancy: comparing home workers and commuters in Canadian cities. *Journal of Planning Education and Research*, 27(3), 319–40.

Morgan, J., Dill, J. and Kalleberg, A. (2013). The quality of healthcare jobs: can intrinsic rewards compensate for low extrinsic rewards? *Work, Employment and Society*, 27(5), 802–22.

Morganson, V.J., Major, D.A., Oborn, K.L., Verive, J.M. and Heelan, M.P. (2010). Comparing telework locations and traditional work arrangements. *Journal of Managerial Psychology*, 25(6), 578–95.

Morris, J.A. and Feldman, D.C. (1996). The dimensions, antecedents, and consequences of emotional labour. *Academy of Management Review*, 21(4), 986–1010.

Morrison, J. (2011). Case study: shining a spotlight on working conditions at China's Foxconn. In J. Morrison, *The Global Business Environment*, 3rd edn, 424–5. Basingstoke: Palgrave Macmillan.

Mottaz, C.J. (1988). Determinants of organizational commitment. *Human Relations*, 41(6), 467–82.

Mowbray, P.K., Wilkinson, A. and Tse, H.H.M. (2015). An integrative review of employee voice: identifying a common conceptualization and research agenda. *International Journal of Management Reviews*, 17(3), 382–400.

Mowday, R.T., Steers, R.M. and Porter, L.W. (1979). The measurement of organizational commitment. *Journal of Vocational Behavior*, 14(2), 224–47.

Munir, F., Nielsen, K., Garde, A.H., Albertsen, K. and Carneiro, I.G. (2012). Mediating the effects of work–life conflict between transformational leadership and health-care workers' job satisfaction and psychological wellbeing. *Journal of Nursing Management*, 20(4), 512–21.

Muñoz de Bustillo, R., Fernández-Macías, E., Esteve, F. and Antón, J. (2011). *Measuring More Than Money: The Social Economics of Job Quality*. Cheltenham, UK, and Northampton, MA, USA: Edward Elgar Publishing.

Murphy, W.M. (2012). Reverse mentoring at work: fostering cross-generational learning and developing millennial leaders. *Human Resource Management*, 51(4), 549–74.

Musick, M. and Wilson, J. (2008). *Volunteers: A Social Profile*. Bloomington, IN: Indiana University Press.

Mustafa, M. and Gold, M. (2013). Chained to my work? Strategies to manage temporal and physical boundaries among self-employed teleworkers. *Human Resource Management Journal*, 23(4), 419–23.

Muthuri, J., Matten, D. and Moon, J. (2009). Employee volunteering and social capital: contributions to corporate social responsibility. *British Journal of Management*, 20(1), 75–89.

Mytton, O., Panter, J. and Ogilvie, D. (2016). Longitudinal associations of active commuting with wellbeing and sickness absence. *Preventive Medicine*, 84, 19–26.

Nahapiet, J. and Ghoshal, S. (1998). Social capital, intellectual capital, and the organizational advantage. *Academy of Management Review*, 23(2), 242–66.

Nalebuff, B. and Stiglitz, J. (1983). *Prizes and Incentives: Toward a General Theory of Compensation and Competition*. Research Memorandum, 293, Princeton University.

Nathan, M. (2002). *Space SIG*. Peter Runge House. England: The Work Foundation.

Nätti, J., Tammelin, M., Anttila, T. and Ojala, S. (2011). Work at home and time use in Finland. *New Technology, Work and Employment*, 26(1), 68–77.

Nesbit, R., Christensen, R. and Gossett, L. (2012). Charitable giving in the public workplace. *Public Performance and Management Review*, 35(3), 449–74.

Neugarten, B. (1968). The awareness of middle age. In B.L. Neugarten (ed.), *Middle Age and Aging*, 93–8. Chicago, IL: University of Chicago Press.

Neugarten, B., Havighurst, R. and Tobin, S. (1961). The measurement of life satisfaction. *Journal of Gerontology*, 16(2), 134–43.

Neumeier, L., Loidl, M., Reich, B., Fernandez La Puente de Battre, M., Kissel, C., Templin, C., Schmied, C., Niebauer, J. and Niederseer, D. (2020). Effects of active commuting on health-related quality of life and sickness-related absence. *Scandinavian Journal of Medicine and Science in Sports*, 30(S1), 31–40.

Ng, C.F. (2010). Teleworker's home office: an extension of corporate office? *Facilities*, 28(3–4), 137–55.

Ng, M., Fleming, T., Robinson, M., Thomson, B., Graetz, N., Margono, C. et al. (2014b). Global, regional, and national prevalence of overweight and obesity in children and adults during 1980–2013: a systematic analysis for the Global Burden of Disease Study 2013. *The Lancet*, 384 (9945), 766–81.

Ng, T.W.H., Feldman, D.C. and Butts, M.M. (2014a). Psychological contract breaches and employee voice behaviour: the moderating effects of changes in social relationships. *European Journal of Work and Organizational Psychology*, 23(4), 537–53.

NHS (2018). *Workforce Health and Wellbeing Framework*. Available at: https://www.nhsemployers.org/-/media/Employers/Publications/Health-and-wellbeing/NHS-Workforce-HWB-Framework_updated-July-18.pdf.

Nicholas, H. and McDowall, A. (2012). When work keeps us apart: a thematic analysis of the experience of business travellers. *Community, Work and Family*, 15(3), 335–55.

Nichols, G., Tacon, R. and Muir, A. (2012). Sports clubs' volunteers: bonding in or bridging out? *Sociology*, 47(2), 350–67.

Nielsen, M., Christensen, J., Finne, L. and Knardahl, S. (2020). Workplace bullying, mental distress, and sickness absence: the protective role of social support. *International Archives of Occupational and Environmental Health*, 93, 43–53.

Nieuwenhuis, M., Knight, C., Postmes, T. and Haslam, S. (2014). The relative benefits of green versus lean office space: three field experiments. *Journal of Experimental Psychology: Applied*, 20(3), 199–214.

Noble, T. and McGrath, H. (2005). Emotional growth: helping children and families 'bounce back'. *Australian Family Physician*, 34(9), 749–52.

Noble, T. and McGrath, H. (2012). Wellbeing and resilience in young people and the role of positive relationships. In S. Roffey (ed.), *Positive Relationships*, 17–33. Dordrecht: Springer.

Nooteboom, B. (2007). Social capital, institutions and trust. *Review of Social Economy*, 65(1), 29–53.

Nussbaum, M. (2003). Capabilities as fundamental entitlements: Sen and social justice. *Feminist Economics*, 9(2), 33–59.

O'Mahoney, M. (1999). *Britain's Productivity Performance, 1950–1996: An International Perspective*. London, National Institute of Economic and Social Research.

O'Reilly, J. and Bothfeld, S. (2002). What happens after working part time? Integration, maintenance or exclusionary transitions in Britain and western Germany. *Cambridge Journal of Economics*, 26(4), 409–39.

O'Toole, J. and Lawler, E. (2006). *The New American Workplace*. New York: Palgrave Macmillan.

Oates, W.E. (1971). *Confessions of a Workaholic: The Facts About Work Addiction*. New York: World.

OECD (2001). *The Well-being of Nations: The Role of Human and Social Capital*. Paris: Organisation for Economic Co-operation and Development. Available at: http://www.oecd.org/site/worldforum/33703702.pdf.

OECD (2013). *Measuring Well-being and Progress* [online]. Paris: Organisation for Economic Co-operation and Development. Available at: https://www.oecd.org/sdd/OECD-Better-Life-Initiative.pdf.

OECD (2015). *The Future of Productivity* [online]. Paris: Organisation for Economic Co-operation and Development. Available at: https://www.oecd.org/eco/OECD -2015-The-future-of-productivity-book.pdf.

OECD (2020). *How's Life? 2020: Measuring Well-being* [online]. Paris: Organisation for Economic Co-operation and Development. Available at: https://doi.org/10.1787/9870c393-en.

Ogbonna, E. and Harris, L.C. (2004). Work intensification and emotional labour among UK university lecturers: an exploratory study. *Organization Studies*, 25(7), 1185–203.

Ojo, S.O., Bailey, D.P., Chater, A.M. and Hewson, D.J. (2018). The impact of active workstations on workplace productivity and performance: a systematic review. *International Journal of Environmental Research and Public Health*, 15(3), 417.

Omilion-Hodges, L.M., Ptacek, J.K. and Zerilli, D.H. (2016). A comprehensive review and communication research agenda of the contextualized workgroup: the evolution and future of leader-member exchange, co-worker exchange, and team-member exchange. *Annals of the International Communication Association*, 40(1), 343–77.

ONS [Office for National Statistics] (2014). *Measuring National Well-being* [online]. Available at: http://www.ons.gov.uk/ons/guide-method/user-guidance/well-being/index.html.

ONS [Office for National Statistics] (2020). *Coronavirus and the Latest Indicators for the UK Economy and Society: 2 July 2020* [online]. Available at: https://www .ons.gov.uk/peoplepopulationandcommunity/healthandsocialcare/conditionsan ddiseases/bulletins/coronavirustheukeconomyandsocietyfasterindicators/latest #business-impact-of-the-coronavirus.

Oppezzo, M. and Schwartz, D.L. (2014). Give your ideas some legs: the positive effect of walking on creative thinking. *Journal of Experimental Psychology: Learning, Memory, and Cognition*, 40(4), 1142–52.

Organisation for Economic Co-operation and Development (OECD) (2015). *The Future of Productivity*. Paris: OECD. Available at: https://www.oecd.org/eco/OECD-2015-The-future-of-productivity-book.pdf.

Ornetzeder, M., Wicherb, M. and Suschek-Bergerba, J. (2016). User satisfaction and well-being in energy efficient office buildings: evidence from cutting-edge projects in Austria. *Energy and Buildings*, 118, 18–26.

Oseland, N.A. and Hodsman, P. (2018). A psychoacoustical approach to resolving office noise distraction. *Journal of Corporate Real Estate*, 20(4), 260–80.

Osili, U., Hirt, D. and Raghavan, S. (2011). Charitable giving inside and outside the workplace: the role of individual and firm characteristics. *International Journal of Nonprofit and Voluntary Sector Marketing*, 16(4), 393–408.

Osnowitz, D. and Henson, K. (2016). Leveraging limits for contract professionals: boundary work and control of working time. *Work and Occupations*, 43(3), 326–60.

Otto, A., Boysen, N., Scholl, A. and Walter, R. (2017). Ergonomic workplace design in the fast pick area. *OR Spectrum*, 39, 945–75.

Ozyilmaz, A., Erdogan, B. and Karaeminogullari, A. (2018). Trust in organization as a moderator of the relationship between self-efficacy and workplace outcomes: a social cognitive theory-based examination. *Journal of Occupational and Organizational Psychology*, 91(1), 181–204.

Page, N. and Nilsson, V. (2017). Active commuting: workplace health promotion for improved employee well-being and organizational behavior. *Frontiers in Psychology*, 7, article 1994.

Pal, I., Galinsky, E. and Kim, S. (2020). *2020 Effective Workplace Index: Creating a Workplace That Works for Employees and Employers* [online]. Families and Work Institute. Available at: https://www.familiesandwork.org/research/2020/2020 -effective-workplace-index.

Parfit, D. (1984). *Reasons and Persons*. Oxford: Clarendon Press.

Park, N., Kee, K.F. and Valenzuela, S. (2009). Being immersed in social networking environment: Facebook groups, uses and gratifications, and social outcomes. *CyberPsychology & Behavior*, 12(6), 729–33.

Parsonage, M. and Saini, G. (2017). *Mental Health at Work: The Business Costs 10 Years On*. Centre for Mental Health. Available at: https://www.centreforme ntalhealth.org.uk/sites/default/files/2018-09/CentreforMentalHealth_Mental_health _problems_in_the_workplace.pdf.

Pascall, G. (2008). Gender and New Labour: after the male breadwinner model? In T. Maltby, P. Kennett and K. Rummery (eds), *Social Policy Review 20: Analysis and Debate in Social Policy*. Bristol: Policy Press, 215–40.

Patterson, M., Warr, P. and West, M. (2004). Organizational climate and company productivity: the role of employee affect and employee level. Journal of Occupational and Organizational Psychology, 77(2), 193–216.

Pavot, W. and Diener, E. (2013). Happiness experienced: the science of subjective well-being. In S. David, I. Boniwell and A. Conley Ayers (eds), *The Oxford Handbook of Happiness*, 134–54. Oxford: Oxford University Press.

Peel, S. and Inkson, K. (2004). Contracting and careers: choosing between self and organizational employment. *Career Development International*, 9(6), 542–58.

Peloza, J., Hudson, S. and Hassay, D. (2009). The marketing of employee volunteerism. *Journal of Business Ethics*, 85, 371–86.

Perrons, D., Fagan, C., McDowell, L., Ray, K. and Ward, K. (2005). Work, life and time in the new economy. *Time and Society*, 14(1), 51–64.

Peters, L.H. and O'Connor, E.J. (1980). Situational constraints and work outcomes: the influences of a frequently overlooked construct. *Academy of Management Review*, 5(3), 391–7.

Petrou, P., Demerouti, E., Peeters, M.C., Schaufeli, W.B. and Hetland, J. (2012). Crafting a job on a daily basis: contextual correlates and the link to work engagement. *Journal of Organizational Behavior*, 33(8), 1120–41.

Philp, B., Harvie, D. and Slater, G. (2005). Preferences, power and the determination of working hours. *Journal of Economic Issues*, 39 (1), 75–90.

Philp, B. and Wheatley, D. (2013). European work time regulation and underemployment: a quantitative Marxist analysis. *Economic Issues*, 19(1), 57–74.

Piasna, A. (2017). *'Bad jobs' recovery? European Job Quality Index, 2005–2015.* ETUI Working Paper 2017.06. Brussels: European Trade Union Institute.

Piasna, A. (2018). Scheduled to work hard: the relationship between non-standard working hours and work intensity among European workers (2005–2015). *Human Resource Management Journal*, 28(1), 167–81.

Piasna, A., Burchell, B., Sehnbruch, K. and Agloni, N. (2017). Job quality: conceptual and methodological challenges for comparative analysis. In D. Grimshaw, C. Fagan, G. Hebson and I. Tavora (eds), *Making Work More Equal: A New Labour Market Segmentation Approach*, 168–87. Manchester: Manchester University Press.

Pinkley, R.L. (1990). Dimensions of conflict frame: disputant interpretations of conflict. *Journal of Applied Psychology*, 75(2), 117–26.

Piper, A. (2015). Heaven knows I'm miserable now: overeducation and reduced life satisfaction. *Education Economics*, 23(6), 677–92.

Pisaniello, S.L., Winefield, H.R. and Delfabbro, P.H. (2012). The influence of emotional labour and emotional work on the occupational health and wellbeing of South Australian hospital nurses. *Journal of Occupational Behavior*, 80(3), 579–91.

Plantenga, J. and Remery, C. (2010). *Flexible Working Time Arrangements and Gender Equality: A Comparative Review of Thirty European Countries.* Luxembourg: Official Publications of the European Communities.

Plester, B. and Hutchison, A. (2016). Fun times: the relationship between fun and workplace engagement. *Employee Relations*, 38(3), 332–50.

Poelmans, S. and Beham, B. (2008). The moment of truth: conceptualizing managerial work–life policy allowance decisions. *Journal of Occupational and Organizational Psychology*, 81(3), 393–410.

Pogge, T. (2002). Can the capability approach be justified? *Philosophical Topics*, 30(2), 167–228.

Pooley, C.G., Turnbull, J. and Adams, M. (2005). *A Mobile Century? Changes in Everyday Mobility in Britain in the Twentieth Century.* Farnham: Ashgate Publishing.

Portela, M., Neira, I. and del Mar Salinas-Jiménez, M. (2013). Social capital and subjective wellbeing in Europe: a new approach on social capital. *Social Indicators Research*, 114(2), 493–511.

Portes, A. (1998). Social capital: its origins and applications in modern sociology. *Annual Review of Sociology*, 24, 1–24.

Preenen, P., Vergeer, R., Kraan, K. and Dhondt, S. (2017). Labour productivity and innovation performance: the importance of internal labour flexibility practices. *Economic and Industrial Democracy*, 38(2), 271–93.

Prochaska, J.O., Evers, K.E., Johnson, J.L., Castle, P.H., Prochaska, J.M., Sears, L.E., Rula, E.Y. and Pope, J.E. (2011). The well-being assessment for productivity: a well-being approach to presenteeism. *Journal of Occupational and Environmental Medicine*, 53(7), 735–42.

Przybylski, A., Murayama, K., DeHaan, C. and Gladwell, V. (2013). Motivational, emotional, and behavioral correlates of fear of missing out. *Computers in Human Behavior*, 29(4), 1841–8.

Pugno, M. (2015). Capability and happiness: a suggested integration from a dynamic perspective. *Journal of Happiness Studies*, 16, 1383–99.

Putnam, R. (2000). *Bowling Alone: The Collapse and Revival of American Community*. New York: Simon & Schuster.

Putnam, R. (2001). Social capital: measurement and consequences. *Canadian Journal of Policy Research*, 2(1), 41–51.

Pyöriä, P. (2011). Managing telework: risks, fears and rules. *Management Research Review*, 34(4), 386–99.

Raess, D. and Burgoon, B. (2015). Flexible work and immigration in Europe. *British Journal of Industrial Relations*, 53(1), 94–111.

Ragins, B.R. and Cotton, J.L. (1999). Mentor functions and outcomes: a comparison of men and women in formal and informal mentoring relationships. *Journal of Applied Psychology*, 84(4), 529–50.

Ragins, B.R. and McFarlin, D.B. (1990). Perceptions of mentor roles in cross-gender mentoring relationships. *Journal of Vocational Behavior*, 37(3), 321–39.

Rainey, H. and Steinbauer, P. (1999). Galloping elephants: developing elements of a theory of effective government organizations. *Journal of Public Administration Research and Theory*, 9(1), 1–32.

Redlich, C., Sparer, J. and Cullen, M. (1997). Sick-building syndrome. *The Lancet*, 349(9057), 1013–16.

Rees, C.S., Breen, L.J., Cusack, L. and Hegney, D. (2015). Understanding individual resilience in the workplace: the international collaboration of workforce resilience model. *Frontiers in Psychology*, 6(73), 1–7.

Reilly, M.C., Zbrozek, A.S. and Dukes, E.M. (1993). The validity and reproducibility of a work productivity and activity impairment instrument. *Pharmacoeconomics*, 4(5), 353–65.

Reilly Associates (2004). *The Work Productivity and Impairment (WPAI) Questionnaire* [online]. Available at: http://www.reillyassociates.net/WPAI_GH.html.

Reis, J.P., Dubose, K.D., Ainsworth, B.E., Macera, C.A. and Yore, M.M. (2005). Reliability and validity of the occupational physical activity questionnaire. *Medicine and Science in Sports and Exercise*, 37(12), 2075–83.

Relph, E. (1976). *Place and Placelessness*. London: Pion.

Renaud, L., Jelsma, J., Huysmans, M., van Nassau, F., Lakerveld, J., Speklé, E., Bosmans, J., Stijnman, D., Loyen, A., van der Beek, A. and van der Ploeg, H. (2020). Effectiveness of the multi-component dynamic work intervention to reduce sitting time in office workers – results from a pragmatic cluster randomised controlled trial. *Applied Ergonomics*, 84, 103027.

Requena, F. (2003). Social capital, satisfaction and the quality of life in the workplace. *Social Indicators Research*, 61, 331–60.

Richardson, G. (2002). The metatheory of resilience and resiliency. *Journal of Clinical Psychology*, 58(3), 307–21.

Richmond, M.K., Pampel, F.C., Wood, R.C. and Nunes, A.P. (2017). The impact of employee assistance services on workplace outcomes: results of a prospective, quasi-experimental study. *Journal of Occupational Health Psychology*, 22(2), 170–9.

Richter, A., Leyer, M. and Steinhüser, M. (2020). Workers united: digitally enhancing social connectedness on the shop floor. *International Journal of Information Management*, 52. https://doi.org/10.1016/j.ijinfomgt.2020.102101.

Rimes, H., Nesbit, R. and Christensen, R. (2019). Giving at work: exploring connections between workplace giving campaigns and patterns of household charitable giving in the USA. *Voluntas*, 30, 828–40.

Rispins, S. and Demerouti, E. (2016). Conflict at work, negative emotions, and performance: a diary study. *Negotiation and Conflict Management Research*, 9(2), 103–19.

Robertson, I. and Cooper, C. (2011). *Well-being, Productivity and Happiness at Work*. Basingstoke: Palgrave Macmillan.

Robeyns, I. (2016). The capability approach. In E.N. Zalta (ed.), *The Stanford Encyclopedia of Philosophy (Winter 2016 Edition)*. Available at: https://plato .stanford.edu/archives/win2016/entries/capability-approach/.

Robinson, S., O'Reilly, J. and Wang, W. (2013). Invisible at work: an integrated model of workplace ostracism. *Journal of Management*, 39(1), 203–31.

Rochester, C., Ellis Paine, A., Howlett, S. and Zimmeck, M. (2010). *Volunteering and Society in the 21st Century*. Basingstoke: Palgrave Macmillan.

Rodell, J. (2013). Finding meaning through volunteering: why do employees volunteer and what does it mean for their jobs? *Academy of Management Journal*, 56(5), 1274–94.

Rodell, J., Breitsohl, H., Schröder, M. and Keating, D. (2016). Employee volunteering: a review and framework for future research. *Journal of Management*, 42(1), 55–84.

Rodríguez-Muñoz, A., Baillien, E., De Witte, H., Moreno-Jiménez, B. and Pastor, J.C. (2009). Cross-lagged relationships between workplace bullying, job satisfaction and engagement: two longitudinal studies. *Work and Stress*, 23(3), 225–43.

Rolfö, L.V. (2018). Relocation to an activity-based flexible office – design processes and outcomes. *Applied Ergonomics*, 73, 141–50.

Rosenblat, A. (2019). *Uberland: How Algorithms Are Rewriting the Rules of Work*. Berkeley, CA: University of California Press.

Roskams, M. and Haynes, B. (2019). Employee-workplace alignment: employee characteristics and perceived workplace requirements. *Facilities*, 38(3–4), 282–97.

Rousseau, V. and Aubé, C. (2010). Social support at work and affective commitment to the organization: the moderating effect of job resource adequacy and ambient conditions. *The Journal of Social Psychology*, 150(4), 321–40.

Rousseau, V., Salek, S., Aube, C. and Morin, E.M. (2009). Distributive justice, procedural justice, and psychological distress: the moderating effect of coworker support and work autonomy. *Journal of Occupational Health Psychology*, 14, 305–17.

RSA (n.d.). *Legal Employment Statuses: Applicable in the Gig Economy* [online]. Available at: https://www.thersa.org/globalassets/images/infographics/rsa-gig -economy-chart.pdf.

Russell, H., O'Connell, P. and McGinnity, F. (2009). The impact of flexible working arrangements on work–life conflict and work pressure in Ireland. *Gender, Work and Organization*, 16(1), 73–97.

Ryan, R.M. and Deci, E.L. (2000). Self-determination theory and the facilitation of intrinsic motivation, social development and well-being. *American Psychologist*, 55(1), 68–78.

Ryde, G., Atkinson, P., Stead, M., Gorely, T. and Evans, J. (2020). Physical activity in paid work time for desk-based employees: a qualitative study of employers' and employees' perspectives. *BMC Public Health*, 20(460). https://doi.org/10.1186/s12889-020-08580-1.

Ryff, C.D. (1982). Successful aging: a developmental approach. *The Gerontologist*, 22(2), 209–14.

Ryff, C.D. (1989). Happiness is everything, or is it? Explorations on the meaning of psychological well-being. *Journal of Personality and Social Psychology*, 57(6), 1069–81.

Ryff, C.D. and Keyes, C.L.M. (1995). The structure of psychological well-being revisited. *Journal of Personality and Social Psychology*, 69(4), 719–27.

Ryff, C.D. and Singer, B. (2008). Know thyself and become what you are: a eudaimonic approach to psychological wellbeing. *Journal of Happiness Studies*, 9, 13–39.

Ryherd, E.E., Waye, K.P. and Ljungkvist, L. (2008). Characterizing noise and perceived work environment in a neurological intensive care unit. *The Journal of the Acoustical Society of America*, 123(2), 747–56.

Sallaz, J. (2015). Permanent pedagogy: how post-Fordist firms generate effort but not consent. *Work and Occupations*, 42(1), 3–34.

Sander, E.J., Caza, A. and Jordan, P.J. (2019). Psychological perceptions matter: developing the reactions to the physical work environment scale. *Building and Environment*, 148, 338–47.

Sander, E., Jordan, P.J. and Rafferty, A. (2021). Escaping the cubicle: exploring the physical work environment of the home. In D. Wheatley, S. Buglass and I. Hardill (eds), *Handbook of Research on Remote Work and Worker Well-being in the Post-COVID-19 Era*, 181–201. Hersey, PA: IGI Global.

Sanderson, K., Tilse, E., Nicholson, J., Oldenburgd, B. and Graves, N. (2007). Which presenteeism measures are more sensitive to depression and anxiety? *Journal of Affective Disorders*, 101, 65–74.

Sato, A. (2019). Telework and its effects in Japan. In J. Messenger (ed.), *Telework in the 21st Century: An Evolutionary Perspective*, 76–127. Cheltenham, UK, and Northampton, MA, USA: Edward Elgar Publishing.

Saunders, M.K., Dietz, G. and Thornhill, A. (2014). Trust and distrust: polar opposites, or independent but co-existing? *Human Relations*, 67(6), 639–65.

Schaufeli, W.B., Bakker, A.B. and Salanova, M. (2006). The measurement of work engagement with a short questionnaire: a cross-national study. *Educational and Psychological Measurement*, 66(4), 701–16.

Schaufeli, W.B., Salanova, M., González-Romá, V. and Bakker, A.B. (2002). The measurement of engagement and burnout: a two sample confirmatory factor analytic approach. *Journal of Happiness Studies*, 3(1), 71–92.

Schaufeli, W.B., Taris, T.W. and Bakker, A.B. (2008). It takes two to tango: workaholism is working excessively and working compulsively. In R.J. Burke and C.L. Cooper (eds), *The Long Work Hours Culture: Causes, Consequences and Choices*, 203–26. Bingley: Emerald.

Schein, E. (1978). *Career Dynamics: Matching Individual and Organizational Needs*. London: Addison-Wesley.

Schein, E. (1996). Career anchors revisited: implications for career development in the 21st century. *Academy of Management Executive*, 10(4), 80–8.

Schermuly, C. and Meyer, B. (2016). Good relationships at work: the effects of leader-member exchange and team-member exchange on psychological empowerment, emotional exhaustion, and depression. *Journal of Organizational Behavior*, 37(5), 673–91.

Scholz, T. (2016). *Uberworked and Underpaid*. Cambridge: Polity.

Schor, J.B., Fitzmaurice, C., Carfagna, L.B., Attwood-Charles, W. and Poteat, E.D. (2016). Paradoxes of openness and distinction in the sharing economy. *Poetics*, 54, 66–81.

Schueller, S.M. and Seligman, M.E.P. (2010). Pursuit of pleasure, engagement, and meaning: relationships to subjective and objective measures of well-being. *The Journal of Positive Psychology*, 5(4), 253–63.

Schultz, A.B. and Edington, D.W. (2007). Employee health and presenteeism: a systematic review. *Journal of Occupational Rehabilitation*, 17(3), 547–79.

Schyns, B. and Schilling, J. (2013). How bad are the effects of bad leaders? A meta-analysis of destructive leadership and its outcomes. *The Leadership Quarterly*, 24, 138–58.

Sears, L.E., Shi, Y., Coberley, C.R. and Pope, J.E. (2013). Overall well-being as a predictor of health care, productivity, and retention outcomes in a large employer. *Population Health Management*, 16(6), 397–405.

Seashore, S.E. (1975). Defining and measuring the quality of working life. In L.E. Davis and A.B. Cherns (eds), *The Quality of Working Life*, 105–18. New York: Free Press.

Seligman, M.E.P. (2011). *Flourish: A Visionary New Understanding of Happiness and Well-being*. New York: Simon and Schuster.

Seligman, M.E.P. (2018). PERMA and the building blocks of well-being. *The Journal of Positive Psychology*, 13(4), 333–5.

Seligman, M.E.P. and Czikszentmihalyi, M. (2000). Positive psychology: an introduction. *American Psychologist*, 55(1), 5–14.

Sen, A.K. (1987). The standard of living. In G. Hawthorn (ed.), *The Standard of Living*, 1–38. Cambridge: Cambridge University Press.

Sen, A.K. (2008). The economics of happiness and capability. In L. Bruni, F. Comim and M. Pugno (eds), *Capability and Happiness*, chapter 1. New York: Oxford University Press.

Sharma, A., Madaan, V. and Petty, F.D. (2006). Exercise for mental health. *The Primary Care Companion to the Journal of Clinical Psychiatry*, 8(2), 106. http://doi.org/10.4088/pcc.v08n0208a.

Shearmur, R. (2018). The millennial urban space economy: dissolving workplaces and the de-localization of economic value creation. In M. Moos, D. Pfeiffer and T. Vinodrai (eds), *The Millennial City: Trends, Implications, and Prospects for Urban Planning and Policy*, 65–80. London: Routledge.

Shepperd, J., Pogge, G. and Howell, J. (2017). Assessing the consequences of unrealistic optimism: challenges and recommendations. *Consciousness and Cognition*, 50, 69–78.

Sherony, K.M. and Green, S.G. (2002). Coworker exchange: relationships between coworkers, leader-member exchange, and work attitudes. *Journal of Applied Psychology*, 87(3), 542–8.

Shikiar, R., Halpern, M.T., Rentz, A.M. and Khan, Z.M. (2004). Development of the Health and Work Questionnaire (HWQ): an instrument for assessing workplace productivity in relation to worker health. *Work*, 22(3), 219–29.

Schimmack, U. (2008). The structure of subjective well-being. In M. Eid and R.J. Larsen, (eds), *The Science of Subjective Well-being*, 97–123. New York: Guildford.

Shin, D. and Johnson, D. (1978). Avowed happiness as an overall assessment of the quality of life. *Social Indicators Research*, 5(1), 475–92.

Shrestha, N., Kukkonen-Harjula, K.T., Verbeek, J.H., Ijaz, S., Hermans, V. and Pedisic, Z. (2018). Workplace interventions for reducing sitting at work (review). *Cochrane*

Database of Systematic Reviews, 6. http://doi.org/10.1002/14651858.CD010912.pub4.

Sias, P.M. (2005). Workplace relationship quality and employee information experiences. *Communication Studies*, 56(4), 375–95.

Sias, P.M. (2009). *Organizing Relationships: Traditional and Emerging Perspectives on Workplace Relationships*. Thousand Oaks, CA: Sage.

Siegrist, J. (1999). Occupational health and public health in Germany. In P.M. le Blanc, M.C.W. Peeters, A. Büssing and W.B. Schaufeli (eds), *Organizational Psychology and Healthcare: European Contributions*, 35–44. Munich: Rainer Hampp Verlag.

Siegrist, J. and Li, J. (2017). Work stress and altered biomarkers: a synthesis of findings based on the effort–reward imbalance model. *International Journal of Environmental Research and Public Health*, 14(11), 1373. http://doi.org/10.3390/ijerph14111373.

Siegrist, J., Siegrist, K. and Weber, I. (1986). Sociological concepts in the etiology of chronic disease: the case of ischemic heart disease. *Social Science & Medicine*, 22(2), 247–53.

Siegrist, J., Starke, D., Chandola, T., Godin, I., Marmot, M., Niedhammer, I. and Peter, R. (2004). The measurement of effort–reward imbalance at work: European comparisons. *Social Science & Medicine*, 58(8), 1483–99.

Siegrist, J., Wahrendorf, M., von dem Knesebeck, O., Jürges, H. and Börsch-Supan, A. (2006). Quality of work, well-being, and intended early retirement of older employees – baseline results from the SHARE Study. *European Journal of Public Health*, 17(1), 62–8.

Simmons, J.P. and Massey, C. (2012). Is optimism real? *Journal of Experimental Psychology: General*, 141(4), 630–4.

Sinclair, A. (2016). *Absence Management Annual Survey Report 2016*. London: CIPD. Available at: https://www.cipd.co.uk/Images/absence-management_2016_tcm18-16360.pdf.

Sinclair, A. (2018). *Health and Well-being at Work Survey Report 2018*. London: CIPD. Available at: https://www.cipd.co.uk/Images/health-and-well-being-at-work_tcm18-40863.pdf.

Sinclair, A. (2019). *Health and Well-being at Work Survey Report 2019*. London: CIPD. Available at: https://www.cipd.co.uk/Images/health-and-well-being-at-work-2019.v1_tcm18-55881.pdf.

Sinclair, A. and Suff, R. (2020). *Health and Well-being at Work Survey Report 2020*. London: CIPD. Available at: https://www.cipd.co.uk/Images/health-and-well-being-2020-report_tcm18-73967.pdf.

Sirola, N. and Pitesa, M. (2017). Economic downturns undermine workplace helping by promoting a zero-sum construal of success. *Academy of Management Journal*, 60(4), 1339–59.

Sithravel, R. and Ibrahim, R. (2019). Identifying supportive daytime lighting characteristics for enhancing individuals' psychophysiological wellbeing in windowless workplace in tropical Malaysia. *Indoor and Built Environment*. https://doi.org/10.1177/1420326X19889656.

Skogstad, A., Einarsen, S., Torsheim, T., Aasland, M.S. and Hetland, H. (2007). The destructiveness of laissez-faire leadership behavior. *Journal of Occupational Health Psychology*, 12(1), 80–92.

Small Business Labs (2018). *U.S. Co-working Forecast: 2018 to 2022* [online]. Available at: http://www.smallbizlabs.com/2018/01/us-co-working-forecast-2018-to-2022.html.

Smith, A. (1981 [1776]). *An Inquiry into the Nature and the Causes of the Wealth of Nations*, Book I, chapters 1–4. Indianapolis, IN: Liberty Fund.

Smith, A. (2016). 'The Magnificent 7[am]?' Work–life articulation beyond the 9[am] to 5[pm] 'norm'. *New Technology, Work and Employment*, 31(3), 209–22.

Smith, A.P. (1989). A review of the effects of noise on human performance. *Scandinavian Journal of Psychology*, 30(3), 185–206.

Smith, C. and Exton, C. (2013). *OECD Guidelines for Measuring Subjective Well-being* [online]. OECD Better Life Initiative. Available at: https://www.oecd.org/statistics/oecd-guidelines-on-measuring-subjective-well-being-9789264191655-en.htm.

Smith, E.R. and Mackie, D.M. (2007). *Social Psychology*, 3rd edn. New York: Hove.

Smith, M., Burchell, B., Fagan, C. and O'Brien, C. (2008). Job quality in Europe. *Industrial Relations Journal*, 39(6), 586–603.

Snelgrove, S.R. (1998). Occupational stress and job satisfaction: a comparative study of health visitors, district nurses and community psychiatric nurses. *Journal of Nursing Management*, 6(2), 97–104.

Sonnentag, S. (2001). Work, recovery activities, and individual well-being: a diary study. *Journal of Occupational Health Psychology*, 6(3), 196–210.

Sonnentag, S. and Fritz, C. (2007). The recovery experience questionnaire: development and validation of a measure for assessing recuperation and unwinding from work. *Journal of Occupational Health Psychology*, 12(3), 204–21.

Sparrowe, R.T., Liden, R.C., Wayne, S.J. and Kraimer, M.L. (2001). Social networks and the performance of individuals and groups. *Academy of Management Journal*, 44(2), 316–25.

Sparrowe, R.T., Soetjipto, B.W. and Kraimer, M.L. (2006). Do leaders' influence tactics relate to members' helping behavior? It depends on the quality of the relationship. *Academy of Management Journal*, 49(6), 1194–208.

Spencer, D.A. (2009). *The Political Economy of Work*. London: Routledge.

Spinuzzi, C. (2012). Working alone together: co-working as emergent collaborative activity. *Journal of Business and Technical Communication*, 26(4), 399–411.

Sport England (2015). *Active Design: Planning for Health and Wellbeing through Sport and Physical Activity* [online]. Public Health England. Available at: https://sportengland-production-files.s3.eu-west-2.amazonaws.com/s3fs-public/spe003-active-design-published-october-2015-email-2.pdf.

Srnicek, N. (2017). *Platform Capitalism*. London: Polity.

Stajkovic, A.D. and Luthans, F. (2003). Behavioral management and task performance in organizations: conceptual backgrounds, meta-analysis, and test of alternative models. *Personnel Psychology*, 56(1), 155–94.

Stavrou, E. (2005). Flexible work bundles and organizational competitiveness: a cross national study of the European work context. *Journal of Organizational Behavior*, 26(8), 923–47.

Stevenson, D. and Farmer, P. (2017). *Thriving at Work: The Stevenson/Farmer Review of Mental Health and Employers*. London: Department for Work and Pensions.

Stier, H. (2015). The skill-divide in job quality: a cross-national analysis of 28 countries. *Social Science Research*, 49, 70–80.

Stiglitz, J., Sen, A. and Fitoussi, J.P. (2009). *Report by the Commission on the Measurement of Economic Performance and Social Progress* [online]. Available at: http://www.stiglitz-sen-fitoussi.fr/documents/rapport_anglais.pdf.

Sturges, J. and Guest, D. (2004). Working to live or living to work? Work/life balance early in the career. *Human Resource Management Journal*, 14(4), 5–13.

Stutzer, A. and Frey, B.S. (2010). Recent advances in the economics of individual subjective well-being. *Social Research*, 77(2), 679–714.

Suff, R. and Miller, J. (2016). *Growing the Health and Well-being Agenda: From First Steps to Full Potential. Policy Report*. Available at: https://www.cipd.co.uk/Images/health-well-being-agenda_2016-first-steps-full-potential_tcm18-10453.pdf.

Suggala, S., Thomas, S. and Kureshi, S. (2021). Impact of workplace bullying on employees' mental health and self-worth. In S. Dhiman (ed.), *The Palgrave Handbook of Workplace Well-being*. London: Palgrave Macmillan. https://doi.org/10.1007/978-3-030-02470-3_30-1.

Sullivan, C. (2003). What's in a name? Definitions and conceptualisations of teleworking and homeworking. *New Technology, Work and Employment*, 18(3), 158–65.

Sullivan, S., Forret, M., Carraher, S. and Mainiero, L. (2009). Using the kaleidoscope career model to examine generational differences in work attitudes. *Career Development International*, 14(3), 284–302.

Sundell, J., Levin, H., Nazaroff, W.W., Cain, W.S., Fisk, W.J., Grimsrud, D.T., Gyntelberg, F., Li, Y., Persily, A.K., Pickering, A.C., Samet, J.M., Spengler, J.D., Taylor, S.T. and Weschler, C.J. (2011). Ventilation rates and health: multidisciplinary review of the scientific literature. *Indoor Air*, 21(3), 191–204.

Sung, S.Y. and Choi, J.N. (2014). Do organizations spend wisely on employees? Effects of training and development investments on learning and innovation in organizations. *Journal of Organizational Behavior*, 35, 393–412.

Suzuki, Y. and Miah, M.D. (2015). Altruism, reciprocity and Islamic equity finance. *International Journal of Islamic and Middle Eastern Finance and Management*, 9(2), 205–21.

Sverke, M., Hellgren, J. and Näswall, K. (2002). No security: a meta-analysis and review of job insecurity and its consequences. *Journal of Occupational Health Psychology*, 7(3), 242–64.

Syrek, C.J., Apostel, E. and Antoni, C.H. (2013). Stress in highly demanding IT jobs: transformational leadership moderates the impact of time pressure on exhaustion and work–life balance. *Journal of Occupational Health Psychology*, 18(3), 252–61.

Tajfel, H., Billig, M.G. and Bundy, R.P. (1971). Social categorization and intergroup behaviour. *European Journal of Social Psychology*, 1(2), 149–78.

Takeuchi, R., Yun, S. and Wong, K.F.E. (2011). Social influence of a coworker: a test of the effect of employee and coworker exchange ideologies on employees' exchange qualities. *Organizational Behavior and Human Decision Processes*, 115(1), 226–37.

Tanabe, S.I., Haneda, M. and Nishihara, N. (2015). Workplace productivity and individual thermal satisfaction. *Building and Environment*, 91, 42–50.

Taylor, F. (1967). *The Principles of Scientific Management*. London: Norton.

Taylor, M., Marsh, G., Nicol, D. and Broadbent, P. (2017). *Good Work: The Taylor Review of Modern Working Practices*. London: Department for Business, Energy and Industrial Strategy.

Taylor, P., Davies, L., Wells, D., Gilbertson, J. and Tayleur, W. (2015). *CASE: A Review of the Social Impacts of Culture and Sport* [online]. Department for Culture, Media and Sport. Available at: https://www.gov.uk/government/uploads/system/uploads/attachment_data/file/416279/A_review_of_the_Social_Impacts_of_Culture_and_Sport.pdf.

Taylor, W.C., King, K.E., Shegog, R., Paxton, R.J., Evans-Hudnall, G.L., Rempel, D.M. and Yancey, A.K. (2013). Booster breaks in the workplace: participants' perspectives on health-promoting work breaks. *Health Education Research*, 28(3), 414–25.

Taylor, W.C., Paxton, R.J., Shegog, R., Coan, S.P., Dubin, A., Page, T.F. and Remple, D. (2016). Impact of booster breaks and computer prompts on physical activity and sedentary behavior among desk-based workers: a cluster-randomized controlled trial. *Preventing Chronic Disease*, 13. https://doi.org/10.5888/pcd13.160231.

Teasdale, N. (2013). Fragmented sisters? The implications of flexible working policies for professional women's workplace relationships. *Gender, Work and Organization*, 20(4), 397–412.

Tennant, R., Hiller, L., Fishwick, R., Platt, S., Joseph, S., Weich, S. and Stewart-Brown, S. (2007). The Warwick-Edinburgh mental well-being scale (WEMWBS): development and UK validation. *Health and Quality of Life Outcomes*, 5(1), 63. https://doi.org/10.1186/1477-7525-5-63.

Tesluk, P.E. and Mathieu, J.E. (1999). Overcoming roadblocks to effectiveness: incorporating management of performance barriers into models of work group effectiveness. *Journal of Applied Psychology*, 84(2), 200–17.

Tesser, A. and Collins, J. (1988). Emotion in social reflection and comparison situations: intuitive, systematic, and exploratory approaches. *Journal of Personality and Social Psychology*, 55(5), 695–709.

Tews, M., Michel, J., Xu, S. and Drost, A. (2015). Workplace fun matters ... but what else? *Employee Relations*, 37(2), 248–67.

The Economist (2010). Suicides at Foxconn: light and death [online]. Available at: http://www.economist.com/node/16231588.

Thomas, J. (2009). *Current Measures and the Challenges of Measuring Children's Wellbeing*. Newport: Office for National Statistics.

Thompson, C. and Prottas, D. (2006). Relationships among organizational family support, job autonomy, perceived control, and employee well-being. *Journal of Occupational Health Psychology*, 10(4), 100–18.

Thompson, D. (2019). *Resourcefulness @ University*. Student Wellbeing Series. Newark: Trigger Publishing.

Thompson, P. and Smith, C. (2010). *Working Life: Renewing Labour Process Analysis*. London: Palgrave Macmillan.

Thompson, S. and Marks, N. (2008). *Measuring Well-being in Policy: Issues and Applications*. London: New Economics Foundation. Available at: https://b.3cdn.net/nefoundation/575659b4f333001669_ohm6iiogp.pdf.

Tietze, S., Musson, G. and Scurry, T. (2009). Homebased work: a review of research into themes, directions and implications. *Personnel Review*, 38(6), 585–604.

Toepoel, V. (2013). Ageing, leisure, and social connectedness: how could leisure help reduce social isolation of older people? *Social Indicators Research*, 113(1), 355–72.

Toomingas, A., Hagberg, M., Heiden, M., Richter, H., Westergren, K.E. and Tornqvist, E. (2014). Risk factors, incidence and persistence of symptoms from the eyes among professional computer users. *Work*, 47(3), 291–301.

Topoel, V. (2013). Ageing, leisure, and social connectedness: how could leisure help reduce social isolation of older people? *Social Indicators Research*, 113(1), 355–72.

Torbeyns, T., Bailey, S., Bos, I. and Meeusen, R. (2014). Active workstations to fight sedentary behaviour. *Sports Medicine*, 44(9), 1261–73.

Torbeyns, T., de Geus, B., Bailey, S., Decroix, L. and Meeusen, R. (2017). The potential of bike desks to reduce sedentary time in the office: a mixed-method study. *Public Health*, 144, 16–22.

Tremblay, M.S., Aubert, S., Barnes, J.D., Saunders, T.J., Carson, V., Latimer-Cheung, A.E., Chastin, S.F.M., Altenburg, T.M., Chinapaw, M.J.M. and Project, S.T.C. (2017). Sedentary Behavior Research Network (SBRN) – terminology consensus project process and outcome. *International Journal of Behavioral Nutrition and Physical Activity*, 14(75). https://doi.org/10.1186/s12966-017-0525-8.

Trougakos, J.P., Hideg, I., Hayden Cheng, B. and Beal, D.J. (2014). Lunch breaks unpacked: the role of autonomy as a moderator of recovery during lunch. *Academy of Management Journal*, 57(2), 405–21.

Uehata, T. (1991). Long working hours and occupational stress-related cardiovascular attacks among middle aged workers in Japan. *Journal of Human Ergonomics*, 20(2), 147–53.

UK Department of Health (2011). *No Health Without Mental Health: A Cross-Government Mental Health Outcomes Strategy for People of all Ages* [online]. Crown Copyright. Available at: https://assets.publishing.service.gov.uk/government/uploads/system/uploads/attachment_data/file/213761/dh_124058.pdf.

UK Employment Tribunals (2016). *Judgement: Aslam, Farrar & Others v Uber BV* [online]. Available at: http://www.bailii.org/ew/cases/Misc/2016/B68.html.

Unite Union (2015). Working UK-style 2015. *Unite Works*, Spring 2015. Available at: https://unitelive.org/working-uk-style-2015/.

United Nations (2015). *Decent Work and Economic Growth: Why It Matters*. New York: United Nations.

van Bel, D.T., Smolders, K.C.H.J., Ijsselsteijn, W.A. and de Kort, Y. (2009). Social connectedness. Concept and measurement. Paper presented at the Proceedings of the 5th International Conference on Intelligent Environments.

van Doorn, N. and Badger, A. (2020). Platform capitalism's hidden abode: producing data assets in the gig economy. *Antipode*, 52(5), 1475–95.

van Miero, H., Rutte, C.G., Vermunt, J.K., Kompier, M.A.J. and Dooreward, J.A.M.C. (2006). Individual autonomy in work teams: the role of team autonomy, self-efficacy, and social support. *European Journal of Work and Organizational Psychology*, 15(3), 281–99.

van Praag, B.M., Frijters, P. and Ferrer-i-Carbonell, A. (2003). The anatomy of subjective well-being. *Journal of Economic Behavior & Organization*, 51(1), 29–49.

van Vegchel, N., de Jonge, J., Bosmab, H. and Schaufeli, W. (2005). Reviewing the effort–reward imbalance model: drawing up the balance of 45 empirical studies. *Social Science & Medicine*, 60(5), 1117–31.

van Wingerden, J., Derks, D. and Bakker, A.B. (2017). The impact of personal resources and job crafting interventions on work engagement and performance. *Human Resource Management*, 56(1), 51–67.

Vandenabeele, W. (2007). Toward a public administration theory of public service motivation: an institutional approach. *Public Management Review*, 9(4), 545–56.

Vartiainen, M. and Hyrkkänen, U. (2010). Changing requirements and mental workload factors in mobile multi-location working. *New Technology, Work and Employment*, 25(2), 117–35.

Vidal, M. (2013). Low-autonomy work and bad jobs in postfordist capitalism. *Human Relations*, 66(4), 587–612.

Virick, M., DaSilva, N. and Arrington, K. (2010). Moderators of the curvilinear relation between extent of telecommuting and life satisfaction: the role of performance outcome orientation and worker type. *Human Relations*, 63(1), 137–54.

Vischer, J.C. (2005). *Space Meets Status*. Abingdon: Routledge.

Vos, T., Barber, R.M., Bell, B., Bertozzi-Villa, A., Biruyukov, S., Bollinger, I. ... and Murray, C.J. (2013). Global, regional, and national incidence, prevalence, and years lived with disability for 301 acute and chronic diseases and injuries in 188 countries,

1990–2013: a systematic analysis for the Global Burden of Disease study. *The Lancet*, 386(9995), 743–800.

Waddington, J. (2015). Trade union membership retention in Europe: the challenge of difficult times. *European Journal of Industrial Relations*, 21(3), 205–21.

Walker, L.D. (2020). The Covid-19 office in transition: cost, efficiency and the social responsibility business case. *Accounting, Auditing and Accountability Journal*, 33(8), 1943–67.

Wallmann-Sperlich, B., Hoffmann, S., Salditt, A., Bipp, T. and Froboese, I. (2019). Moving to an 'active' biophilic designed office workplace: a pilot study about the effects on sitting time and sitting habits of office-based workers. *International Journal of Environmental Research and Public Health*, 16(9), 1559.

Wallop, H. (2015). How fair does Sports Direct play? [online]. *The Telegraph*. Available at: http://www.telegraph.co.uk/finance/11563435/How-fair-does-Sports-Direct-play.html.

Wanberg, C.R., Welsh, E.T. and Hezlett, S.A. (2003). Mentoring research: a review and dynamic process model. *Research in Personnel and Human Resources Management*, 22, 39–124.

Wang, P. and Walumbwa, F. (2007). Family-friendly programs, organizational commitment, and work withdrawal: the moderating role of transformational leadership. *Personnel Psychology*, 60(2), 397–427.

Wang, X., Cai, L., Qian, J. and Peng, J. (2014). Social support moderates stress effects on depression. *International Journal of Mental Health Systems*, 8(41). https://doi.org/10.1186/1752-4458-8-41.

Wargocki, P., Wyon, D., Baik, Y.K., Clausen, G. and Fanger, P.O. (1999). Perceived air quality, Sick Building Syndrome (SBS) symptoms and productivity in an office with two different pollution loads. *Indoor Air*, 9(3), 165–79.

Warhurst, C., Wright, S. and Lyonette, C. (2017). *Understanding and Measuring Job Quality: Part 1 – Thematic Literature Review*. London: Chartered Institute of Personnel and Development. Available at: http://www.cipd.co.uk/jobquality.

Warr, P. (2007). *Work, Happiness and Unhappiness*. Mahwah, NJ: Lawrence Erlbaum.

Warr, P. and Parker, S. (2016). *IWP Multi-affect Indicator* [online]. Sheffield: Institute of Work Psychology, University of Sheffield. Available at: https://www.sheffield.ac.uk/polopoly_fs/1.653515!/file/IWP_Multi-affect_Affect_Indicator_10.2016.pdf.

Weiß, E-E. and Süß, S. (2016). The relationship between transformational leadership and effort–reward imbalance. *Leadership and Organization Development Journal*, 37(4), 450–66.

Weiss, R. and Kahn, R. (1960). Definitions of work and occupation. *Social Problems*, 8(2), 142–51.

Western, M. and Tomaszewski, W. (2016). Subjective wellbeing, objective wellbeing and inequality in Australia. *PLoS One*, 11(10): e0163345.

What Works Well (2018). *Workplace Wellbeing Questionnaire: Methodology*. Available at: https://whatworkswellbeing.org/product/workplace-wellbeing-questionnaire-methodology/.

Wheatley, D. (2012a). Work–life balance, travel-to-work, and the dual career household. *Personnel Review*, 41(6), 813–31.

Wheatley, D. (2012b). Good to be home? Time-use and satisfaction levels among home-based teleworkers. *New Technology, Work and Employment*, 27(3), 224–41.

Wheatley, D. (2013). Location, vocation, location? Spatial entrapment among women in dual career households. *Gender, Work and Organization*, 20(6), 720–36.

Wheatley, D. (2014). Travel-to-work and subjective well-being: a study of UK dual career households. *Journal of Transport Geography*, 39, 187–96.

Wheatley, D. (2017a). Employee satisfaction and use of flexible working arrangements. *Work, Employment and Society*, 31(4), 567–85.

Wheatley, D. (2017b). Autonomy in paid work and employee subjective well-being. *Work and Occupations*, 44(3), 296–328.

Wheatley, D. (2017c). *Time Well Spent: Subjective Well-being and the Organization of Time*. London: Rowman and Littlefield International.

Wheatley, D. (2017d). How does flexible working impact on employee well-being? In *Insights 2017: Findings from the UK Household Longitudinal Study*, 28–9. Available at: https://issuu.com/usociety/docs/insights_202017_20a4_stg_206.

Wheatley, D. (2020). Changing places of work. In P. Holland and C. Brewster (eds), *Contemporary Work and the Future of Employment in Developed Societies*, chapter 8. London: Routledge.

Wheatley, D. (2021). Workplace location and the quality of work: the case of urban-based workers in the UK. *Urban Studies, Special Issue: New Spatialities of Work in the City*, 58(11), 2233–57. https://doi.org/10.1177/0042098020911887.

Wheatley, D. and Bickerton, C. (2016). Time-use and well-being impacts of travel-to-work and travel-for-work. *New Technology, Work and Employment*, 31(3), 238–54.

Wheatley, D. and Gifford, J. (2019). *UK Working Lives Survey Report 2019*. London: Chartered Institute of Personnel and Development (CIPD). Available at: https://www.cipd.co.uk/knowledge/work/trends/uk-working-lives.

Wheatley, D. Hardill, I. and Lawton, C. (2018). Gender differences in paid and unpaid work. In V. Caven and S. Nachmias (eds), *Hidden Inequalities in the Workplace*, 181–214. London: Palgrave Macmillan.

Wheatley, D., Hardill, I. and Philp, B. (2011). 'Managing' reductions in working hours: a study of work time and leisure preferences in UK industry. *Review of Political Economy*, 23(3), 409–20.

Wheatley, D. and Wu, Z (2014). Dual careers, time-use, and satisfaction levels: evidence from the British Household Panel Survey. *Industrial Relations Journal*, 45(5), 443–64.

White, M., Hill, S., McGovern, P., Mills, C. and Smeaton, D. (2003). High performance management practices, working hours and work–life balance. *British Journal of Industrial Relations*, 41(2), 175–95.

Wight, V. and Raley, S. (2009). When home becomes work: work and family time among workers at home. *Social Indicators Research*, 93(1), 197–202.

Wilensky, H. (1960). Work, careers and social integration. *International Social Science Journal*, 12(4), 543–60.

Wilkinson, A., Donaghey, J., Dundon, T. and Freeman, R.B. (eds) (2014). *Handbook of Research on Employee Voice*. Cheltenham, UK, and Northampton, MA, USA: Edward Elgar Publishing.

Wilkinson, A. and Fay, C. (2011). Guest editors' note: new times for employee voice? *Human Resource Management*, 50(1), 65–74.

Williams, C. (2003). Developing community participation in deprived neighbourhoods: a critical evaluation of the third sector approach. *Space and Polity*, 7(1), 65–73.

Williams, C. (2011). Socio-spatial variations in community self-help: a total organisation of labour perspective. *Social Policy and Society*, 10(3), 365–78

Wilson, J. (2000). Volunteering. *Annual Review of Sociology*, 26, 215–40.

Windle, M. (2002). Critical conceptual and measurement issues in the study of resilience. In M.D.E.J. Glantz and L. Jeannette (eds), *Resilience and Development: Positive Life Adaptations*, 161–76. Longitudinal Research in the Social and Behavioral Sciences: An Interdisciplinary Series. Boston, MA: Springer.

Wood, A.J. (2020). *Despotism on Demand: How Power Operates in the Flexible Workplace*. Ithaca, NY: Cornell University Press.

Wood, S. (2008). Job characteristics, employee voice and well-being in Britain. *Industrial Relations Journal*, 39(2), 153–68.

Woodcock, J., Edwards, P., Tonne, C., Armstrong, B.G., Ashiru, O., Banister, D. et al. (2009). Public health benefits of strategies to reduce greenhouse-gas emissions: urban land transport. *The Lancet*, 374(9705), 1930–43.

Woodcock, J. and Graham, M. (2019). *The Gig Economy: A Critical Introduction*. Cambridge: Polity.

Woolvin, M. and Hardill, I. (2013). Localism, voluntarism and devolution: experiences, opportunities and challenges in a changing policy context. *Local Economy*, 28(3), 273–88.

World Green Building Council (2016). *Building the Business Case: Health, Wellbeing and Productivity in Green Offices* [online]. Available at: https://www.worldgbc .org/news-media/building-business-case-health-wellbeing-and-productivity-green -offices.

World Health Organization (1997). *WHOQOL Measuring Quality of Life*. Geneva, Switzerland: World Health Organization.

Wright, S., Warhurst, C., Lyonette, C. and Sarkar, S. (2018). *Understanding and Measuring Job Quality: Part 2 – Indicators of Job Quality*. London: Chartered Institute of Personnel and Development. Available at http://www.cipd.co.uk/ jobquality.

Wright, T.A. and Huang, C.C. (2012). The many benefits of employee well-being in organizational research. *Journal of Organizational Behavior*, 33(8), 1188–92.

Wrzesniewski, A. and Dutton, J.E. (2001). Crafting a job: revisioning employees as active crafters of their work. *Academy of Management Review*, 26(2), 179–201.

Yam, K.C., Fehr, R. and Barnes, C.M. (2014). Morning employees are perceived as better employees: employees' start times influence supervisor performance ratings. *Journal of Applied Psychology*, 99(6), 1288–99.

Yamauchi, T., Yoshikawa, T., Takamoto, M., Sasaki, T., Matsumoto, S., Kayashima, K., Takeshima, T. and Takahashi, M. (2017). Overwork-related disorders in Japan: recent trends and development of a national policy to promote preventative measures. *Industrial Health*, 55(3), 293–302.

Yerkes, M. (2010). Diversity at work: the heterogeneity of women's employment patterns. *Gender, Work and Organization*, 17(6), 696–720.

Yeung, O. and Johnston, K. (2016). *Global Wellness Institute: The Future of Wellness at Work*. January 2016. Available at: https://globalwellnessinstitute.org/industry -research/the-future-of-wellness-at-work/.

Yu, Y., Hao, J.-X., Dong, X.-Y. and Khalifa, M. (2013). A multilevel model for effects of social capital and knowledge sharing in knowledge-intensive work teams. *International Journal of Information Management*, 33(5), 780–90.

Zappala, G. (2000). *How Many People Volunteer in Australia and Why Do They Do It?* Camperdown: The Smith Family.

Zheng, C., Molineux, J., Mirshekary, S. and Scarparo, S. (2015). Developing individual and organisational work–life balance strategies to improve employee health and wellbeing. *Employee Relations*, 37(3), 354–79.

Zhu, P. (2013). Telecommuting, household commute and location choice. *Urban Studies*, 50(12), 2441–59.

Zhu, X., Yoshikawa, A., Qiu, L., Lu, Z., Lee, C. and Ory, M. (2020). Healthy workplaces, active employees: a systematic literature review on impacts of workplace environments on employees' physical activity and sedentary behaviour. *Building and Environment*, 168, 106455.

Index

absenteeism 13, 43, 202, 241, 246, 260–63

active commuting *see* commuting

activity-based flexible offices *see* layout and design

activity-based working (ABW) 120–22

affect *see* subjective well-being

age
    and careers 146–9
    and diversity and inclusion 174–5
    and mentoring 205–10
    and volunteering 195–6

agency work *see* flexible labour

agile working 120–22
    and workplace layout and design 223–5

air quality *see* physical workplace characteristics

amenities 58–9, 137

Annual Survey of Hours and Earnings *see* survey

ASSET 46–8, 66, 94, 270

Australia 91, 104, 107, 165, 240, 276

autonomy
    definitions of 73–5
    and discretion 44–5, 60–61, 73, 78, 82, 90
    and job control 45–6, 73–7, 81, 102
    and schedule control 73–8, 81–2, 102–3, 113

benefits, employee 134–6, 171

bounded rationality 35

breaks *see* work recovery

British Household Panel Survey *see* survey

British Social Attitudes Survey *see* survey

burnout 45, 83–4, 132–3, 155, 165, 169–71
    and work engagement 265

business travel *see* travel-for-work

capabilities approach, Sen 22–4, 34

cardinal *see* methods

care 103–7, 125–6, 262
    and careers 147–9
    childcare 106–8, 115, 119, 134, 195
    and giving 188–90
    grandparenting 195
    for ill/elderly relative or friend 195, 197
    and work–life balance policies 103–6

career
    career success 149–53
    development and progression 145–7
    and effort–reward *see* effort–reward imbalance (ERI)
    and gender 147–9
    kaleidoscope career 147
    protean career 146

Carers (Equal Opportunities) Act 2004 105

case study *see* methods

causality 13–14

challenge *see* job properties

charitable giving 198–200
    philanthropy 191, 198

Chartered Institute of Personnel and Development (CIPD) 63–66, 74, 86–9, 172–3, 261, 277
    CIPD's Five Domains of Well-being 50–51
    CIPD's Model of Job Quality 60–61
    see also survey, UK Working Lives Survey

childcare *see* care

commitment 48, 57, 76–7, 131–3, 163
    and careers 148–9
    definitions of 76
    and giving 192, 194, 198–9

measurement of 265–7
and mentoring 208, 211
community 160, 191–6, 211–14
Community Life Survey *see* survey
commute 118, 226
active commuting 241–2, 244
complexity *see* job properties
compressed hours *see* flexible working
arrangements
conflict at work *see* relationships
connectedness *see* social connectedness
contingent work *see* flexible labour
contracts 107–8, 136, 139–42
and models of job quality 58–63
control *see* autonomy
Cooper, Sir Cary 46–8, 66, 270
corporate social responsibility 50, 191–4,
216, 226
Covid-19 *see* pandemic
culture
long hours culture 52, 58, 76–7,
108–10, 148, 211, 260–61
workplace culture 50–54, 63–4, 83,
133, 170–72, 204, 238, 273–5

decent work *see* job quality
demands *see* job properties
digital technology *see* technology
see also information and
communication technology
(ICT)
disability 38, 174–5
discretion *see* autonomy
display screen equipment (DSE) *see*
health and safety
domain satisfaction *see* well-being
domestic travel *see* travel-for-work

Easterlin paradox *see* income
economic crisis 5, 140, 145
education 23, 38, 142–5, 156, 174, 194–5
and physical activity, 237–8
effort–reward imbalance (ERI) 153–7,
270
emotion 30, 170, 177, 201–3, 225, 230,
262, 264–6
emotional labour 170
employee assistance programme (EAP)
263, 276–7

employee voice 50, 173, 181–3, 254, 269
trade unions 62, 126, 182
employer-supported volunteering *see*
volunteering
employment *see* paid work
engagement *see* work engagement
entrepreneur 123
social entrepreneurship *see* social
enterprise
environment 28–9, 35
natural 38, 118, 225–6, 231–2, 244
physical workplace 23, 51, 54, 64
see also physical workplace
characteristics
work 42, 45–6, 49–50, 63–5, 276–7
environmental clarity 49, 87, 94–6, 144,
175, 251, 268
ethnicity 174, 195
eudaimonia 1–2, 20–22, 28, 31, 96
European Social Survey *see* survey
European Union 2, 6, 108, 117, 213
European Working Time Directive 108
exercise 110, 135, 151, 237–40, 242–4
extensive work 83, 108
extrinsic
definitions of 131–4
hygiene factors 5, 72, 140, 274
motivators 137–8, 140, 153–4
reward 153–4, 187, 190–93, 196

finance
financial assistance benefits 135,
143, 276
financial pressure 128, 140
financial resources 161
financial status 136–9
financial well-being 38, 128, 140,
262
Finland 77, 105
Five Ways to Well-being 32–4, 66–7
flexibility
employee-led 57, 129, 252
employer-led 84, 107–8, 115, 252,
275
flexibilization *see* flexible labour
flexible labour 107–8
agency work 107
contingent work 107, 140, 145
gig economy 124–8, 140
temporary work 107, 116, 140

330   *Well-being and the quality of working lives*

zero hours contracts 84, 107, 113, 129, 140
flexible working arrangements 111–23
   compressed hours 111–15
   flexi-time 105, 111–14, 125
   home-based teleworking 112, 117, 234
   informal flexibility 113
   job share 111–12, 115–16, 121
   part-time work 84, 104–5, 107, 111–13, 115–16, 119–21, 140, 211, 214
   reduced hours 112, 115–16
   remote working 116–21, 129, 219, 232–3, 278
   term-time work 111–13, 115
Flexible Working Regulations 105, 107, 211
   allowance decisions 107
flexi-time *see* flexible working arrangements
flourishing *see* eudaimonia PERMA
Ford, Henry 218
France 80, 85, 93
friend *see* relationships
full-time *see* working hours
fun *see* workplace fun

gender 81, 113, 116, 147–9, 172, 174–5
   inequality 174–5
   pay gap 116
Germany 80, 104–5, 149
gig economy *see* flexible labour
giving
   altruism 188–91
   reciprocity 153, 161, 167, 189–90, 198, 201, 204–5
   self-interest 178, 188–91, 193
Global Wellness Institute 51–3
goals
   career goals 146, 205
   organizational goals 76, 131
   personal goals 107, 150, 163, 170, 191
   work goals 87, 158, 163, 178
good work *see* job quality
government 6, 22, 31–2, 38, 62, 104–6, 124, 213
grandparenting *see* care
green workplace 226

gross domestic product *see* well-being

happiness *see* well-being
health
   see mental health
   see physical health
health and safety 12, 49–51, 54, 57–60, 63–4, 67, 88, 123, 133, 217, 227, 232, 256
   display screen equipment (DSE) 227
   ergonomics 59, 227
hedonism 1, 20–22, 25
home-based teleworking *see* flexible working arrangements
household division of labour 102, 115–16, 148–9, 152, 195, 197
human capital 38, 143, 145–6, 148, 161, 163, 190, 193
hygiene factors *see* extrinsic

income 25, 134–9
   Easterlin paradox 47, 136
   see also pay
inequality *see* gender
informal flexibility *see* flexible working arrangements
information and communication technology (ICT) 6, 12, 101, 112, 117, 129, 218–19, 232
   see also internet
   see also technology
insecure *see* job security
intensive work 45, 52, 58, 82–7, 101, 116, 120, 123, 150–52, 234, 264
International Labour Organization (ILO) 61, 118–19
internet 78, 117, 124, 140, 219
   social media 170
interview *see* methods
intrinsic
   characteristics 5, 24, 56, 59, 60, 71–2, 91–2, 137, 274
   motivators 131–4
   rewards 59, 72, 76, 95, 216

job properties *see* Chapter 4
   autonomy *see* autonomy
   challenge 91–2, 131–2, 154, 175, 185

Index

complexity 57–8, 60, 91–4
demands 45–6, 60–62, 82, 84, 87,
　153, 175–6, 201, 233, 267
job crafting 73–4, 98, 251, 274
job-demands control (JD-C) 45–6,
　66, 270
job design 46, 49, 60, 71, 75, 96–8,
　132, 144, 251,
meaningfulness 30, 44–5, 58, 96,
　169, 194, 203, 263–4
purpose 44, 55, 94–6, 131, 134, 144,
　208, 251, 264, 267, 269
variety 44, 46, 57, 62, 91–4, 131–2,
　146, 251
job quality *see* Chapter 3
decent work 5, 61
definitions of 4–6, 56–8
good work 5, 56, 60, 62, 66, 143,
　154, 273
models of 58–63
job satisfaction *see* well-being
job security 66, 72, 77, 87, 124, 139–41,
　149–50, 153, 156
insecurity 6, 57, 82, 140–42, 154
measurement of 141–2
precarious 107, 124–5, 128, 140
job share *see* flexible working
arrangements

kaleidoscope career *see* career

Labour Force Survey *see* survey
labour market 5–6, 78, 104–6, 116, 134,
　140, 147–8, 155
layout and design 184, 223–6
active workplace design 239–40
activity-based flexible offices 225
open plan 121, 219, 223–5, 230, 233
private 52, 219, 220, 223, 225,
　232–4
workspace territoriality 218, 222,
　225, 239
leadership
destructive 177
laissez-faire 176–8
leader–member exchange *see* social
exchange theory
manager 6, 60, 119, 182

managerial and professional
occupations 78, 87, 109, 113
and relationships 174–9
Taylorist leadership *see* Taylorist
work organization
transactional 176, 178
transformational 176, 178
and trust 175–81
leisure
leisure time 101, 115, 120, 151, 194,
　236, 270
satisfaction with amount of leisure
see well-being
liberal 24, 106
life course 133, 147–8, 195
life satisfaction *see* well-being
lighting *see* physical workplace
characteristics
loneliness *see* relationships
long working hours *see* working hours

mainstream economics 24, 135, 161
manager *see* leadership
married 2, 23
maternity leave 103–6, 111–12
see also shared parental leave
meaning *see* job properties
mental health 3, 20, 22, 32, 43, 49–50,
　52–4, 262–3, 273, 276–7
impacts on 5, 153, 238, 241, 243
measurement of 271
mindfulness *see* mindfulness
resilience *see* resilience
self-efficacy 101, 154, 170–71, 176,
　181, 195, 205, 208, 214,
　276–7
self-esteem 31, 154, 170, 172, 277
Mental Health First Aid (MHFA) 187,
　275–6
mentoring
and career development 208–9
definitions of 205
forms of 208–11
mentor role instrument (MRI) 206–8
and relationships 30, 200, 206–8
methods
cardinal 36–7
case study 102, 104, 124–8, 133,
　150–53, 211–15, 242–6
interview 86, 126–7, 150–52

mixed methods 14
ordinal 36–7
primary data 37, 85
qualitative 13–14, 111, 141–2, 150, 202, 258
quantitative 13–14, 141–2, 150, 258
regression 37
secondary data 85
mindfulness 18, 30, 244, 250, 277–8
momentary measure *see* well-being
motivation
    extrinsic *see* extrinsic
    intrinsic *see* intrinsic
    Two Factor Theory, Hertzberg
musculo-skeletal *see* physical

National Health Service (NHS) 22, 53–4
National Institute for Occupational Safety and Health (NIOSH) 54–5, 67
network
    professional 30, 123, 151, 159, 220
    social 30, 46, 119, 122, 160–63, 167–9, 190
New Economics Foundation (NEF) 32–4, 49–50, 55, 66
noise *see* physical workplace characteristics
Norway 79, 92–3, 105

objective well-being 27, 34–7, 55, 62, 85, 107, 138, 227
    capabilities approach *see* capabilities approach
    definitions of 22–3, 34–5
    measures of 34–7, 109, 138–41, 165, 229, 236, 257–8, 262
    objective list 22–4
occupation 78, 81, 108, 145–6, 148, 159, 216, 231, 235–6, 251
    highly skilled 6, 79, 113, 119, 124, 150–52, 176–7, 219
    low skilled 81, 218
occupational health 18, 63, 249, 263, 273
open plan *see* layout and design
opt-out *see* European Working Time Directive
ordinal *see* methods
organizational

commitment *see* commitment
environment *see* environment, work
leadership *see* leadership
objectives 75, 176, 181
performance *see* performance
overtime 76, 107–9, 155–6
overwork 78, 83, 108–10, 128, 133, 147, 211
workaholism 83, 108

paid work
    and careers *see* career
    in context 5–7
    see also entrepreneur
    see also flexible labour
    second job 140, 158
    self-employment 6, 78–9, 95, 107, 119, 124–6, 140, 148, 220, 252
    terms of *see* contracts
    see also unemployment
pandemic 6, 16, 98, 116–18, 120, 125, 150, 242, 250, 278
part-time work *see* flexible working arrangements
paternity leave 106
    see also shared parental leave
pay 132, 134–9
    see also income
    objective pay 138–9
    performance-related 78, 84, 127, 133, 136–8
    subjective pay 138–9
pension 134–5, 138
perceived organizational support (POS) *see* social support
performance
    definitions of 257–8
    employee/worker 43–8, 72–9, 82, 90, 95, 101, 111, 115, 131–2, 144, 164, 169, 171–2, 176–8, 181–2, 194, 200–203, 208, 220–22, 228–35, 239, 273–4, 278–9
    key performance indicators (KPIs) 68, 133, 230, 258
    measures of 257–63, 266–7
    organizational 47, 56, 121, 136, 143, 146, 186, 278
    team 163, 171–4, 239

Index

PERMA 30–31, 55, 106, 276
philanthropy *see* charitable giving
physical
    activity 32–3, 49, 53, 67, 111,
        217–18, 235–46
    health 21, 27, 31–2, 47, 50, 83, 119,
        128, 168, 217–18, 230–32,
        235, 238–44, 260–63, 279
    musculoskeletal 43, 53, 227, 232,
        256, 263
    space 65–7, 121, 220–35, 242–6
physical workplace characteristics
    access to green space and nature
        226, 231–2, 240
    air quality 228, 231, 232
    government 104–6, 108, 140, 213
    lighting 51, 225–6, 228–9, 234, 240
    noise 184, 225, 229–30, 232, 234
    temperature 51, 225, 226, 228–32
policy
    workplace 30, 43, 50–51, 53–4,
        61, 63–4, 97, 106, 121, 171,
        224–5, 239, 250–51, 254,
        266, 275
positive illusion *see* subjective
    well-being
positive psychology 30–31, 106, 276
    see also PERMA
presenteeism 260–62, 273
    definitions of 260
primary data *see* methods
private *see* layout and design
private sector 213
productivity 13, 27, 56, 61–2, 79, 90–91,
    110, 115, 122, 131, 140–43, 165,
    171, 177, 184, 203, 208, 221,
    226–8, 230–31, 238–9, 246
    definitions of 257–8
    measures of 257–62
protean career *see* career
psychological safety 171–2, 185, 203–4,
    254, 263–4
psychological well-being (PWB) 28–9,
    33, 41, 46–8, 73, 94, 270
    see also Ryff, Carol
    see also subjective well-being
public sector 38, 151, 213, 225
purpose *see* job properties

qualitative *see* methods

quality of life 1–2, 8, 20–22, 34, 42, 132,
    134, 205, 241–2
quantitative *see* methods

reciprocity *see* giving
reduced hours *see* flexible working
    arrangements
reflexive measure *see* well-being
regression *see* methods
regulation, labour market
    see Carers (Equal Opportunities)
        Act 2004
    see European Working Time
        Directive
    see Flexible Working Regulations
relationships
    conflict at work 170–75
        relationship conflict 170–72,
            174, 186
        task conflict, 170
    and employee voice *see* employee
        voice
    family 30–32, 41, 52, 56, 58, 75–7,
        101–7, 125, 127, 147–52,
        163, 211–14, 232, 277
    friends 30, 32, 52, 127, 163, 166,
        195–6, 212, 225, 266, 269
    and leadership *see* leadership
    loneliness 21, 38, 225
    and mentoring *see* mentoring
    see also organizational commitment
    social comparison theory 169–70
    workplace fun 183–4
resilience 30–31, 33, 41, 50, 77, 115,
    166, 195, 238, 242–4, 276–7
resources
    job 46, 48, 60–61, 79, 87–91
    job-demands resources (JD-R) 45–6,
        60–61, 66, 84, 87, 233
retirement 115, 134, 195, 267
revealed preference *see* well-being
Ryff, Carol 28–9, 34, 36, 73
    see also psychological well-being
        (PWB)

school-age children *see* care
school run *see* commute
secondary data *see* methods
second job *see* paid work

self-determination theory 131, 269
self-efficacy *see* mental health
self-employment *see* paid work
self-esteem *see* mental health
self-interest *see* mainstream economics
Seligman, Martin 21, 30–31, 106, 276
Sen, Amartya *see* capabilities approach
Shared Parental Leave 105
sickness absence *see* absenteeism
skilled, highly *see* occupations
skilled, low *see* occupations
skills
    coping 277–8
    development 75, 91, 151, 163,
        176, 190, 192, 195, 207–8,
        210–12, 260, 269
    and education 23, 38
    see also education
    see also human capital
    skills–education match 49, 66, 91,
        142–5
sleep 39, 46, 151, 156, 171, 228, 235,
    243, 271
Smith, Adam 188
social capital 62, 160–63, 168, 180, 187,
    190, 205, 216, 240
    bonding 162, 217
    bridging 162
    definitions of 160–62
social comparison theory *see*
    relationships
social connectedness 32, 73, 164–6,
    168–9, 195, 220, 223, 240
    definition of 164–5
    measurement of 165–6
social enterprise 211–15
social exchange theory 153, 166–8, 176,
    189, 201–4
    co-worker exchanges 167–9
    leader–member exchange 167–9,
        209
    team–member exchanges 167–8
social media *see* internet
social support 200–203, 276
    measurement of 201
    perceived organizational support
        (POS) 200–201
    workplace helping 203–5
socio-economic 60, 148
spillover 77, 101, 103, 194, 220

sport 38, 214, 240
    see also physical activity
stated preference *see* well-being
statistical significance *see* methods
strategy 114, 116, 148, 182–3, 185, 194,
    212, 224
    well-being 15, 50, 68, 106, 234, 238,
        273–6, 278
stress
    see also ASSET
    see also burnout
    work-related 7, 10, 44, 52, 75–8,
        120, 123, 133, 137, 144, 169,
        171, 173, 177, 186, 203, 235,
        255, 270
structure *see* policy, workplace
subjective well-being 23, 31, 40, 48–9,
    81, 131, 136–7, 163, 267–70
    affect 25, 35–6, 40, 189
        negative affect 21, 25, 29, 35–6,
        171, 267, 271
        positive affect 25, 29, 35–6, 45,
        101, 184, 241
    definition of 21, 25–6
    domain satisfaction *see* well-being
    happiness set-point 26, 29, 37
    measurement of 35–40, 267–70
    positive illusion 27
survey
    British Household Panel Survey
        (BHPS) 109–10
    Community Life Survey (CLS)
        196–7
    European Social Survey (ESS)
        2, 38–9, 55, 79–82, 92–4,
        102–3, 143, 268
    European Working Conditions
        Survey (EWCS) 2, 87
    Skills and Employment Survey
        (SES) 87, 144
    UK Understanding Society Survey
        2, 36, 74, 81, 113–14, 139,
        141–2, 268, 270
    UK Working Lives Survey
        (UKWLS) 2–3, 74–5, 87–8,
        89–90, 95–6, 103, 109–10,
        134–5, 139, 172, 178–80,
        261, 267, 270
sustainability 215, 220, 226, 256

see also corporate social
responsibility
Sweden 79–80, 85, 105, 144, 149, 212,
225

Taylorist work organization 82, 90, 98,
109, 120, 176, 231
Taylor, Frederick 82, 90, 221
team 58, 77, 87, 119, 134, 136, 167–8,
171–2, 181–3, 192, 199, 221, 224,
242–4
see also performance, team
see also social exchange theory,
team–member exchange
technology 90, 117, 119, 122, 135, 140,
211, 219–20, 250, 256, 278
see also information and
communication technology
see also internet
temperature *see* physical workplace
characteristics
temporary work *see* flexible labour
term-time work *see* flexible working
arrangements
tools *see* resources
trade-off 12, 133, 150, 152, 195
trade unions *see* employee voice
training 30, 57–8, 60, 66, 89, 142–7, 150,
155–6, 166, 185, 198–9, 208–9,
224, 262, 277
see also education
see also skills
travel-for-work 66, 150–53
trust 38, 40, 48, 56, 120, 160, 162–8,
170–71, 174, 178–81, 192, 199,
207, 209
see also leadership
turnover
actual 18, 267, 273
intention, 18, 44, 84, 155, 167, 171,
177, 181, 202, 208, 211, 267
Two Factor Theory, Hertzberg *see*
motivation

uncertain 5–6, 12, 37, 57, 96, 123, 128,
140, 145, 150, 154, 200
see also flexible labour
see also job insecurity, precarious
understanding society *see* survey

unemployment 5, 6, 169
unpaid work
see care
see household division of labour
unpaid overtime *see* overtime
voluntary work *see* volunteering
USA 6, 54, 56, 75–6, 78, 106, 118, 123,
148, 165, 204, 230, 240
U-shape 136, 195

variety *see* job properties
voice *see* employee voice
volunteering
corporate volunteering
extrinsic rewards from
intrinsic rewards from

wage 56, 58, 116
see also pay
walking 33, 236–47
see also physical activity
welfare 23, 37, 125–6, 182, 189
well-being
and GDP 2, 43–4
at work *see* workplace well-being
definitions of 20–22
desire–satisfaction 24–5
domain satisfaction 2, 26, 36,
50–51, 270
eudaimonia *see* eudaimonia
evaluative 26, 31, 35, 38–40, 96,
267
Five Ways to Well-being *see* Five
Ways to Well-being
flourishing *see* flourishing
happiness 1–2, 9, 20–21, 24–6,
29–31, 35–8, 47, 84, 131,
146, 15–16, 213, 228, 268
hedonic *see* hedonism
job satisfaction 48, 62, 72, 75, 92,
131, 143, 149–51, 169, 171,
181, 184, 192, 200, 202, 211,
223, 231–5, 273
and autonomy 77–8, 82, 84, 95
and flexibility 119, 122, 129,
220
measurement of 38, 266–70
and work–life balance 113, 146,
150, 220

life satisfaction 21, 26, 29, 31, 36–8, 75, 82, 115, 267, 270
  models of *see* Chapter 2
  momentary measure 36
  objective well-being *see* objective well-being
  positive psychology *see* positive psychology
  quality of life *see* quality of life
  reflexive measure 36–7
  revealed preference 24–5, 34
  satisfaction with amount of leisure 194, 270
  stated preference 25, 35
  subjective well-being *see* subjective well-being
wellness 3, 42–3, 51–3, 64, 235
What Works Centre for Wellbeing 55, 64
workaholism *see* overwork
work engagement 30, 46, 74, 84, 111, 143, 150, 166, 181, 263–5
working hours 1, 13, 50, 59, 81, 108–9, 111, 113, 121, 123, 147–8, 151, 214, 222, 233, 262–3, 268
  see also extensive work
  see also overwork
work–life balance 30, 48–9, 57–61, 63, 66, 73, 88, 101–7, 111–18, 137, 149, 211, 242–4, 278
  definitions of 101–4
  improvements in 114–15, 129, 146, 176, 214

and work–life conflict 107, 119–20, 211, 214, 242
  work–life balance options/policies 104–6, 112
workload 46, 50, 53, 82–6, 89, 91–2, 116, 150, 156, 169, 173, 202, 234, 261–2
  see also burnout
  see also intensive work
  see also extensive work
  see also overwork
Workplace Employee Relations Survey *see* survey
workplace fun *see* relationships
workplace helping *see* social support
workplace well-being
  definitions of 3–5, 42–4
  framework for workplace well-being 63–8, 250–57
  models of *see* Chapter 3
work recovery 85, 88, 110–11, 194–5, 228
  breaks 52–3, 66, 110–12, 115–16, 126, 148, 235, 237, 239, 247, 261–2
work-related stress *see* stress
work-related travel
  travel-for-work *see* travel-for-work
  travel-to-work *see* commute
workspace territoriality *see* layout and design

zero hours contracts *see* flexible labour